GESELLSCHAFT
FÜR INFORMATIK

René Röpke und Ulrik Schroeder (Hrsg.)

21. Fachtagung Bildungstechnologien (DELFI)

11.-13. September 2023
Aachen, Deutschland

Gesellschaft für Informatik e.V. (GI)

Lecture Notes in Informatics (LNI) - Proceedings
Series of the Gesellschaft für Informatik (GI)

Volume P-338

ISBN 978-3-88579-732-6
ISSN 1617-5468

Volume Editors
Dr. rer. nat. René Röpke
Prof. Dr.-Ing. Ulrik Schroeder
   RWTH Aachen
   Ahornstraße 55, 52074 Aachen
   {roepke, schroeder}@informatik.rwth-aachen.de

Series Editorial Board
Andreas Oberweis, KIT Karlsruhe,
(Chairman, andreas.oberweis@kit.edu)
Torsten Brinda, Universität Duisburg-Essen, Germany
Dieter Fellner, Technische Universität Darmstadt, Germany
Ulrich Frank, Universität Duisburg-Essen, Germany
Barbara Hammer, Universität Bielefeld, Germany
Falk Schreiber, Universität Konstanz, Germany
Wolfgang Karl, KIT Karlsruhe, Germany
Michael Koch, Universität der Bundeswehr München, Germany
Heiko Roßnagel, Fraunhofer IAO Stuttgart, Germany
Kurt Schneider, Universität Hannover, Germany
Andreas Thor, HFT Leipzig, Germany
Ingo Timm, Universität Trier, Germany
Karin Vosseberg, Hochschule Bremerhaven, Germany
Maria Wimmer, Universität Koblenz-Landau, Germany

Dissertations
Rüdiger Reischuk, Universität Lübeck, Germany
Thematics
Agnes Koschmider, Universität Kiel, Germany
Seminars
Judith Michael, RWTH Aachen, Germany

© Gesellschaft für Informatik, Bonn 2023
printed by Köllen Druck+Verlag GmbH, Bonn

This book is licensed under a Creative Commons BY-SA 4.0 licence.

Vorwort

Die DELFI-Tagungsreihe der Gesellschaft für Informatik befasst sich mit Bildungstechnologien und lebt vom interdisziplinären Diskurs der Wissenschaftlerinnen und Wissenschaftler verschiedener Disziplinen und den Akteuren in unterschiedlichen Bildungskontexten. Die 21. Fachtagung Bildungstechnologien im Jahr 2023 beschäftigt sich mit einer großen Vielfalt von Informatikthemen im Kontext digital unterstützter Lehr- und Lernformen in Schule, Hochschule, beruflicher und privater Aus- und Weiterbildung. Die Forschungs- und Praxisarbeiten adressieren dabei insbesondere Technologien, Werkzeuge und Infrastrukturen, aber eben auch organisatorische, soziale und technische Rahmenbedingungen für die Gestaltung und den Einsatz unterschiedlicher Bildungstechnologien, unabhängig von Anwendungsfeldern und Lerninhalten.

Das Motto der 21. Fachtagung Bildungstechnologien lautet „Skalierbares digitales Lehren und Lernen" und legt den Fokus somit auf die wachsenden Herausforderungen und Anforderungen, welche es zu verstehen und zu meistern gilt; beides mit dem Ziel, die wachsenden Chancen und Möglichkeiten unter Einbezug von Bildungstechnologien zu gestalten und zu nutzen. Thematische Schwerpunkte bilden dabei:

- Künstliche Intelligenz in der Bildung, Adaptive Lehr- und Lernsysteme
- Conversational User Interfaces und Natural Language Processing
- Virtual, Augmented und Mixed Reality Learning
- Learning Analytics und Educational Data Mining
- Game-based Learning und Serious Games
- Digitale Prüfungen
- Digitale Bildung und Bildungstechnologien im Schulkontext
- Bildungstechnologien in der Hochschule oder der beruflichen Bildung
- Didaktik und Wirksamkeit von Bildungstechnologie

Die eingereichten wissenschaftlichen Beiträge wurden im Doppelblind-Verfahren von je mindestens drei Mitgliedern des Programmkomitees begutachtet. Bei einer Programmkomitee-Sitzung wurde dann über die Annahme und Ablehnung von Beiträgen entschieden. Eingereicht wurden 25 Langbeiträge, von denen 6 angenommen wurden (Annahmequote 24%) sowie 36 Kurzbeiträge, von denen 13 angenommen wurden (Annahmequote 36%). Zusammen mit umgewidmeten Langbeiträgen werden insgesamt 18 Kurzbeiträge präsentiert, ferner 3 Praxisbeiträge, 1 Positionspapier, 21 Demo-Sessions und 16 Poster. Die angenommenen Beiträge finden sich im vorliegenden Tagungsband, zusammen mit zwei Beiträgen zu den Keynotes. Zusammen mit dem Programmkomitee konnten wir so ein interessantes, abwechslungsreiches und qualitativ hochwertiges Programm zusammenstellen. Allen Autorinnen und Autoren sowie den Mitgliedern des Programmkomitees gilt unser herzlicher Dank.

Wir freuen uns darüber, Sie auf der 21. Fachtagung Bildungstechnologien in Aachen an der Rheinisch-Westfälischen Technischen Hochschule begrüßen zu dürfen!

Aachen, im Juli 2023

René Röpke und Ulrik Schroeder

Tagungsleitung

Gesamtleitung: Ulrik Schroeder, RWTH Aachen
    Malte Persike, RWTH Aachen
Leitung des Programmkomitees: Ulrik Schroeder, RWTH Aachen
    René Röpke, RWTH Aachen
Workshops: Thiemo Leonhardt, Technische Universität Dresden
Demos: Matthias Ehlenz, RWTH Aachen
Poster: Svenja Noichl, RWTH Aachen

Programmkomitee

Nadine Bergner
Technische Universität Dresden

Daniel Bodemer
Universität Duisburg-Essen

Andreas Breiter
Universität Bremen

Annabell Brocker
RWTH Aachen

Josef Buchner
Pädagogische Hochschule St. Gallen

Irene-Angelica Chounta
Universität Duisburg-Essen

Julian Dehne
Georg-August-Universität Göttingen

Ralf Doerner
Hochschule RheinMain

Hendrik Drachsler
DIPF | Leibniz-Institut für
Bildungsforschung und
Bildungsinformation

Martin Ebner
Technische Universität Graz

Albrecht Fortenbacher
HTW Berlin

Josef Guggemos
Universität St. Gallen

Joerg Haake
FernUniversität in Hagen

Christiane Hagedorn
Hasso-Plattner-Institut

Andreas Harrer
Fachhochschule Dortmund

Birte Heinemann
RWTH Aachen

Peter Henning
Hochschule Karlsruhe

Sebastian Hobert
Universität Göttingen

Dirk Ifenthaler
Universität Mannheim

Ioana Jivet
DIPF | Leibniz-Institut für
Bildungsforschung und
Bildungsinformation

Sven Judel
RWTH Aachen

Paul-Thomas Kandzia
DHBW Lörrach

Andrea Kienle
Fachhochschule Dortmund

Natalie Kiesler
DIPF | Leibniz-Institut für
Bildungsforschung und
Bildungsinformation

Ralph Koelle
Universität Hildesheim

Johannes Konert
Hochschule Fulda

Bastian Küppers
RWTH Aachen

Roland Küstermann
DHBW Karlsruhe

Carsten Lecon
Hochschule Aalen

Andreas Lingnau
Hochschule Ruhr West

Joern Loviscach
Fachhochschule Bielefeld

Ulrike Lucke
Universität Potsdam

Vlatko Lukarov
Allianz

Dana-Kristin Mah
Stifterverband

Martin Mandausch
Hochschule Karlsruhe

Christoph Meier
Universität St. Gallen

Agathe Merceron
Berliner Hochschule für Technik

Tobias Moebert
Universität Potsdam

Niels Pinkwart
Humboldt-Universität zu Berlin

Holger Rohland
Technische Universität Dresden

Guido Rößling
Technische Universität Darmstadt

Nikol Rummel
Ruhr-Universität Bochum

Daniel Schiffner
DIPF | Leibniz-Institut für
Bildungsforschung und
Bildungsinformation

Jan Schneider
DIPF | Leibniz-Institut für
Bildungsforschung und
Bildungsinformation

Mareike Schoop
Universität Hohenheim

Sandra Schulz
Universität Hamburg

Clara Schumacher
Universität Mannheim

Andreas Schwill
Universität Potsdam

Niels Seidel
FernUniversität in Hagen

Sabine Seufert
Universität St. Gallen

Heinrich Söbke
Bauhaus-Universität Weimar

Volodymyr Sokol
RWTH Aachen

Patrick Stalljohann
Fachhochschule Münster

Sven Strickroth
Ludwig-Maximilians-Universität München

Michael Striewe
Universität Duisburg-Essen

Alexander Tillmann
Goethe-Universität Frankfurt

Dimitra Tsovaltzi
DFKI Saarbrücken

Sarah Voß-Nakkour
Goethe-Universität Frankfurt

Joshua Weidlich
DIPF | Leibniz-Institut für Bildungsforschung und Bildungsinformation

Martin Wessner
Hochschule Darmstadt

Arno Wilhelm-Weidner
VDI/VDE-IT

Nadja Zaric
Logate Institute for Information Technologies

Raphael Zender
Humboldt-Universität zu Berlin

Organisationsteam

René Röpke	RWTH Aachen
Kevin Esser	RWTH Aachen
Kyra Thelen	RWTH Aachen

Inhaltsverzeichnis

Keynotes

Oleksandra Poquet
Learning analytics in the age of AI: Will we see the promised learning revolution? 21

Johan Jeuring
Automatic feedback and hints on steps students take when learning how to program 23

Best-Paper-Kandidaten

Anna Radtke, Meike Osinski, Maren Scheffel, Katja Serova, Nikol Rummel
Help me to help myself: Eine Feldstudie zur Wirksamkeit einer datenbasierten Unterstützung von Selbstregulationskompetenzen in digital gestützten Lernsettings 29

Frederik Baucks, Laurenz Wiskott
Mitigating Biases using an Additive Grade Point Model: Towards Trustworthy Curriculum Analytics Measures 41

Philipp Matter, Ninja Leikert-Böhm, Peter Heinrich
Depreciating the online experience: Relative evaluation of social presence in online, hybrid, and offline course environments 53

Sylvio Rüdian, Niels Pinkwart
Auto-generated language learning online courses using generative AI models like ChatGPT 65

E-Assessment und Feedback

Erik Buchmann, Andreas Thor
Online Exams in the Era of ChatGPT 79

Martin Petersohn, Konrad Schöbel, Andreas Thor
Kopplung von Jupyter Notebooks mit externen E-Assessment-Systemen am Beispiel des Data Management Testers 85

Martin Breuer, Annabell Brocker, Malte Persike, Ulrik Schroeder
AxEL - Eine modulare Softwarekomponente für ein dediziertes E-Prüfungssystem zur Generierung von xAPI Statements für Assessment Analytics 91

Erik Morawetz, Nadine Hahm, Andreas Thor
Automatisierte Bewertung und Feedback-Generierung für grafische Modellierungen und Diagramme mit FeeDI 97

Annabell Brocker, Ulrik Schroeder
Investigating Feedback Types in JupyterLab for Programming Novices 103

Kollaboration und Interaktion

Ninja Leikert-Boehm, Philipp Matter, Peter Heinrich
Now you (don't) see me – Camera use in online course settings 111

Niels Seidel, Robin Dürhager, Marcel Goldammer, Alexander Henze, Frank Langenbrink, Joachim Otto, Veronika Stirling
Shared listening experience for hyperaudio textbooks 123

Marwin Wiegard, Verena Schürmann, Tammy Brandenberg, Timo Kahl
Interaktive Kollaborationswerkzeuge und integrative Clouddienste: Erfahrungen zum Einsatz von Microsoft 365 in der Hochschullehre 129

Victor Jüttner, Erik Buchmann
Die Entwicklung eines digitalen Praktikums der Cybersicherheit im Bereich „Smart Home" 135

Infrastrukturen und Artefakte

Steffen Rörtgen, Ronald Brenner, Holger Zimmermann, Matthias Hupfer, Annett Zobel, Ulrike Lucke
Metadata Standards in National Education Infrastructure: Development of Evaluation Criteria and Their Exemplary Application 143

André Selmanagić, Katharina Simbeck
Breaking It Down: On the Presentation of Fine-Grained Learning Objects in Virtual Learning Environments 155

Thomas Hübsch, Elke Vogel-Adham, Susanne Ritzmann, Arno Wilhelm-Weidner
Zukunftsfähige Bildungsplattformen – Monitoring technischer Plattformdimensionen anhand einer multidimensionalen Analysematrix 161

Wabi Melkamu Jate, Michael Striewe
Umgang der DELFI-Community mit Forschungsdaten und Softwareartefakten 167

Conversational Systems und Virtual Reality

Chrysanthi Melanou, Andreas Bildstein, Bernd Dörr, Martin Lachmair, Blanche Schoch, Martin Kimmig
Einführungskriterien für Chatbots in der Kommunikation und der Lehre an Hochschulen 175

Bijan Khosrawi-Rad, Heidi Rinn, Dominik Augenstein, Daniel Markgraf, Susanne Robra-Bissantz
Designing Pedagogical Conversational Agents in Virtual Worlds 181

Peter Heinrich, Dagmar Hollerer, Christoph Karthaus, Mario Gellrich
"Don't drop the plane to fly the mic!" – Designing for Modern Radiotelephony Education in General Aviation 187

Thiemo Leonhardt, Lanea Lilienthal, David Baberowski, Nadine Bergner
The tension between abstract and realistic visualization in VR learning applications for the classroom 193

Johannes Tümler, Juan Enrique Erazo Sanchez, Christian Hänig
Virtual Reality, Eye Tracking and Machine Learning: Analysis of Learning Outcomes in Off-the-Shelve VR-Software 199

Learning Analytics und Künstliche Intelligenz

Anja Hawlitschek, Galina Rudolf, Sarah Berndt, Sebastian Zug
Automated alerts to avoid unfavourable interaction patterns in collaborative learning: Which design do students prefer? 207

Lars Quakulinski, Sven Judel, Miriam Wagner, Ulrik Schroeder
Anwendung von Process Mining zur kontinuierlichen Lernpfadidentifikation in Lernmanagementsystemen 213

Marlene Bültemann, Nathalie Rzepka, Dennis Junger, Katharina Simbeck, Hans-Georg Müller
Energy Consumption of AI in Education: A Case Study 219

Sven Judel, René Röpke, Maximilian Azendorf, Ulrik Schroeder
Supporting Individualized Study Paths Using an Interactive Study Planning Tool
.... 225

Swathi Krishnaraja, Thiemo Wambsganss, Paola Mejia, Niels Pinkwart
Towards a Creativity Support Tool for Facilitating Students' Creative Thinking on Writing Tasks 231

Positionspapiere

Marco Di Maria, David Walter, Paul-Ferdinand Steuck, Ralf Knackstedt
Mitigating Educational Challenges Through Unlearning 239

Demobeiträge

Malte Neugebauer, Jörg Frochte
Steigerung von Lernerfolg und Motivation durch gamifizierte Mathematik-Aufgaben in Lernmanagementsystemen 247

Joshua Martius, Sergej Görzen, Sven Judel, Ulrik Schroeder
Weiterentwicklung eines Dashboards zur digitalen Betreuung wissenschaftlicher Schreibprozesse 249

Antonia Dörringer, Marco Klopp, Lukas Schaab, Marvin Hochstetter, Daniel Glaab, Paula Bartel, Jörg Abke, Jens Elsebach, Raphael Rossmann, Georg Hagel
AdLer: 3D-Lernumgebung für Studierende 251

Marco Di Maria, David Walter, Fabian Segieth, Ralf Knackstedt
COREFLECTOR – Eine Webanwendung für Studierende zur Unterstützung von Reflexion und Verlernen beim analytischen Lesen 253

André Dietrich, Fessel Karl, Sebastian Zug
Modulare und konfigurierbare Remote Labore mit Edrys 255

Birte Heinemann, Sergej Görzen, Daniel Gotzen, Ulrik Schroeder
Ansätze um der Darstellungsflüchtigkeit in Virtual Reality entgegenzuwirken
.... 257

René Röpke, Maximilian Nell, Ulrik Schroeder
Semi-assisted Module Handbook Content Extraction for the Application of
Curriculum Analytics 259

Sven Judel, Paul Nitzke, Ulrik Schroeder
Ein Assistenzsystem zur Annotation von Learning Analytics Reports 261

Martin Petersohn, Konrad Schöbel, Andreas Thor
DMT-Magic: Interaktives E-Assessment in der Datenbank-Lehre mit Jupyter
Notebooks 263

Thiemo Leonhardt, Johanna Walther, Jens Podeyn, Anne Hamann
Code and Consequences - an Educational Game about Social Scoring 265

Karl Wenzel, David Baberowski, Thiemo Leonhardt
Inside the CPU - eine interaktive VR-Lernanwendung zur Van-Neumann-
Architektur 267

Anke Brocker, Simon Voelker
Flowboard: Visual Flow-Based Embedded Programming for Young Learners
.... 269

Natalie Kiesler, Daniel Schiffner, Axel Nieder-Vahrenholz
Adapting RDMO for the Efficient Management of Educational Research Data
.... 271

Michael Striewe
Strukturformeln für Moleküle zeichnen und differenziertes Feedback erhalten:
Eine integrierte Lösung im Rahmen des E-Assessment-Systems JACK 273

Erik Morawetz, Nadine Hahm, Andreas Thor
E-Assessment für Entity-Relationship-Diagramme mit FeeDI 275

Kensuke Akao
Multimodales kooperatives Lernen mit einem digitalen Stift im inklusiven
Unterricht 277

Julia Frohn, Frank Wehrmann, Dominik Bechinie
Getch: a Web App for Personalized and Cooperative Learning Path
Documentation 279

Andrea Linxen, Simone Opel, Stephanie Ebbing, Christian Beecks
Prototyping a virtual tutor with modular teaching styles for higher education
.... 281

Sam Sabah, Imran Hossain, David Weiss, Alexander Tillmann
A Fusion of XR Technology and Physical Objects to Increase Citizens Participation in Urban Planning 283

Ulrich Hofmann-von Kap-Herr
OnePageLayout für Lehrinhalte & -szenarien in ILIAS 285

Posterbeiträge

Nathalie Rzepka, Katharina Simbeck, Hans-Georg Müller, Marlene Bültemann, Niels Pinkwart
Show me the numbers! - Student-facing Interventions in Adaptive Learning Environments for German Spelling 289

Tobias Hirmer, Michaela Ochs, Andreas Henrich
Studierende und die Studienplanung: Untersuchung von Herausforderungen und Entwicklungsperspektiven eines digitalen Studienplanungsassistenten 291

Berit Blanc, Insa Reichow, Benjamin Paaßen
Was wirkt? Eine Literaturstudie zur Wirksamkeit von Systemeigenschaften in Mathematik-Lernumgebungen 293

Arno Wilhelm-Weidner, Annika Fünfhaus, Stefanie Brzoska, Marcel Dux, Andrea Vogt
Künstliche Intelligenz in der öffentlichen Bildungsförderung 295

David Walter, Marco Di Maria, Ralf Knackstedt
Tool-Support for Managing Technostress in Hybrid Learning Settings 297

Raphael Zender, Caterina Schaefer, Thiemo Leonhardt, Nadine Bergner, Josef Buchner, David Wiesche
Virtual Reality für den Schulunterricht?! 299

Frederic Maquet, Jean-Pierre Sterck-Degueldre, Matthias Ehlenz
Immersive und interaktive Lernerfahrungen in der schulischen Bildung mit 360°-Videos 301

Frank Wehrmann, Raphael Zender
Potenziale von Virtual Reality für inklusive Schulbildung 303

Svenja Noichl, Ulrik Schroeder
Interaktionsmöglichkeiten und Potenziale digitaler Gamebooks unter Berücksichtigung der CELG-Taxonomie 305

Caroline Schon, Olaf Ueberschär, Johannes Tümler
Virtual Reality im Grundschulkontext: Bienen-Lerninhalte im Sachunterricht 307

Janine Schledjewski, Alina Zumbruch, Sofia Schneider, Claudia Schrader
Navigationsgestaltung in Lernvideos 309

Sergej Görzen, Birte Heinemann, Ulrik Schroeder
Ein Konzept zur Evaluierung eines Ökosystems für die Integration von Learning Analytics in Virtual Reality 311

Teodora Dogaru, Nora Götze, Agathe Merceron, Daniela Rotelli, Petra Sauer, Yoel Berendsohn
Task Definition in Big Sets of Heterogeneously Structured Moodle LMS Courses 313

Tim Komorowski, Daniel König, Meike Weiland, Michael Heister, Thomai Svenja Gruber, Lilli Heimes
Motivationen von Schülerinnen und Schülern bei der Nutzung digitaler Technologien am Lernort Berufsschule 315

Marc Dannemann, Pia Bothe, Simon Adler, Sandy Grawe
Erkenntnisse über die Entwicklung einer VR-Lernumgebung im Rahmen der Hochschullehre 317

Stephen Tobin, Axel Wiepke, Ulrike Lucke
A VR Classroom with Digital Media for Foreign Language Teacher Training 319

Verzeichnis der Autorinnen und Autoren 321

Keynotes

Learning analytics in the age of AI:
Will we see the promised learning revolution?

Oleksandra Poquet [1]

Abstract: Current advances in generative AI represent a paradigm shift for educational technology. Affordances of generative AI change our perceptions of what can be possible, prompting to re-evaluate research questions, interventions, and applications in the field of educational technology. Against this backdrop, what should the focus on using data to inform teaching and learning look like? Learning analytics, an applied domain centred on data about learners, their processes, and learning artefacts, has gained traction over the last decade. The talk will take a historical perspective to position learning analytics within existing educational technology paradigms and discuss it within the context of AI, highlighting the adjacent possible for the future development.

Keywords: learner capabilities, learning analytics, AI, educational technology

1 Introduction

For those unfamiliar with the field of educational technology, the recent surge in generative AI might appear to be a ground-breaking advancement. However, experts and practitioners in educational technology have witnessed similar cycles of hype and promises of revolutionary transformations before. Additionally, the scholarship surrounding artificial intelligence in education (AIED) has been steadily evolving over the past few decades, providing well-researched recommendations for the design and implementation of AI systems in education. In this discussion, I will contextualize generative AI within the broader historical development of educational technology and the existing body of work in AIED. By doing so, I aim to assert that the changes brought about by generative AI are indeed significant and warrant attention, prompting us to reconsider our research questions and explore new applications of technology in the realm of teaching and learning.

2 Learning Analytics

The use of data collected by educational technologies during teaching and learning, known as learning analytics, is a relatively new development in educational technology. The implementation and potential innovation possible with learning analytics are closely tied

---

[1] Technical University of Munich, School of Social Sciences and Technology, Arcisstraße 21, Munich, 80333, sasha.poquet@gmail.com, https://orcid.org/0000-0001-9527-816X

to legal regulations about data usage. As a result, the adoption and use cases of learning analytics vary among instructors, learners, and administrators in terms of how they utilize the data for decision-making and activities. The fundamental idea behind learning analytics is that data streams capturing students' activities when studying with technology can be transformed into insights about learning, which can then be presented to students or instructors with the noble goal of improving educational practices.

To provide an overview of the current development of learning analytics, I will briefly discuss different types of use cases. These include predictive analytics, multimodal analytics, writing analytics, curriculum, and employability analytics, each aiming to address specific problems and advance learning outcomes. In addition to analyzing data, sensemaking plays a central role in learning analytics. It expands the concept of a feedback loop to encompass human activity, attitudes, and perceptions of data during the learning or teaching process. Upon providing examples of learning analytics, I will comment on its challenges such as adoption, reproducibility, and implications for equity. Despite the diverse implementation of learning analytics, my major assumption is that it complements and enhances teaching and learning by strengthening and supporting these processes.

3   The Intersection of Data and Generative AI in Education

Three decades ago, Gavriel Salomon identified three key reasons why educational technology often fails to meet its expectations. These reasons include trivializing the potential benefits by applying new technologies in trivial ways, adopting a technocentric perspective that places excessive faith in technology alone, and conducting research that is misguided by narrowly focusing on specific questions related to the use of technology in the classroom. I will discuss how current applications around generative AI often fall into the same pitfalls. Salomon also offered a vision for human-AI partnerships, emphasizing that intelligent technologies need to reach beyond the so-called 'effects with' tools – a reference to a simple optimization of joint tasks conducted by humans and technologies. This vision imagines that intelligent tools enhance human cognition in ways that persist after the use of technology. This view is also advocated in contemporary scholarship that shifts the focus to non-epistemic outcomes and supporting learners with domain-generic transferable skills. In the talk I will reflect on how learning analytics can contribute to this vision, while being transformed by generative AI into a new generation of approaches for data-informed teaching and learning.

Automatic feedback and hints on steps students take when learning how to program

Johan Jeuring [1]

Abstract: Every year, millions of students learn how to write programs. Learning activities for beginners almost always include programming tasks that require a student to write a program to solve a particular problem. When learning how to solve such a task, many students need feedback on their previous actions, and hints on how to proceed. For tasks such as programming, which are most often solved stepwise, the feedback should take the steps a student has taken towards implementing a solution into account, and the hints should help a student to complete or improve a possibly partial solution. In this talk I will give an overview of the approaches to automatic feedback and hints on programming steps and discuss our research on how to evaluate the quality of feedback and hints. I will also take the opportunity to involve the audience in some of the dilemmas we are facing.

Keywords: Programming education, feedback, automatic feedback and hints, stepwise solutions

Introduction

Every year, millions of students study some form of computing. In many countries, computer science is part of the obligatory part of the secondary school curriculum, many universities offer computing programs, and at quite a few universities it is one of the largest programs. A computer science program consists of many components, but every program includes at least one module on learning to program.

Learning to program can be done in many ways. It involves amongst others understanding and decomposing a problem, and planning, implementing, and evaluating a solution [RRR03]. When learning to program students may solve Parsons problems, trace code, complete a program with a hole, etc. At some stage in their learning, a student needs to write (part of) a program.

When learning, a student needs feedback [Ra05]. Feedback can be defined as information provided to a learner relating to their skills or understanding as demonstrated on a task or in the completion of a task; usually after instruction [HT07]. Hattie and Timperley propose that effective feedback answers three key questions: "Where am I going?" (Feed-up), "How am I going?" (Feed-back), and "Where to next?" (Feed-forward). Feed-up is about the reason why a student should complete a task and is related to the learning goals of the

---

[1] Utrecht University, department of Information and Computing Sciences, Utrecht, NL, j.t.jeuring@uu.nl, https://orcid.org/0000-0001-5645-7681

doi: 10.18420/delfi2023-02

task. Feed-back analyses and gives information about a learner's progress on a task. Feed-forward, finally, consists of help to move students from their current level of understanding towards task mastery.

The influence of feedback on student achievement is well established, with the potential to lead to significant learning gains [KD96]. The effects of feedback vary a lot, depending on the kind of feedback that is provided. Feedback can be on the level of self ("Well done!"), task ("The input-output behavior of your solution is not expected behavior"), process ("First write some test cases before you start on the implementation of the solution"), and self-regulation ("Did you watch the video about testing?"). These levels all vary in their influence on student outcomes, but there is some proof that the latter three categories lead to better results.

Computing education research has studied the potential of providing automatic grading and feedback [Al05,KJH18,Me23] to both realise the potential advantages of providing feedback, and address the large numbers of students taking programming courses and the lack of computer science teachers in many countries. There are many environments that (may) support beginners learning how to write a program, including intelligent tutoring systems [CLW18], online coding environments (Codecademy, Datacamp, Khan academy, Code.org, and many more), and educational games [GX20]. In addition, LLM-based tools such as ChatGPT and Github Copilot may also be helpful in providing feedback to beginners [He23]. Some of these learning environments give automatic feedback on (sometimes partially finished) student solutions, and hints on how to proceed.

Feedback and hints need to be of good quality to support learning. But when do students need feedback and hints when learning how to program, how should it be given, and how can it be automatically generated? How do the general principles for feedback described above translate to the situation in which a student is writing a program? Designers of learning environments make different choices here. How can we evaluate the quality of the feedback and hints provided by the different learning environments?

An ITiCSE Working Group tried to answer the above questions by collecting datasets of steps students take when solving programming problems and annotating these datasets with feedback [Je22]. It turned out that there was quite some disagreement among different experts on providing feedback on student programs. Together with several colleagues, I'm currently working on trying to gain more insight into why experts disagree on giving feedback.

In this talk I will give an overview of the approaches to automatic feedback and hints on programming steps and discuss our research on how to evaluate the quality of feedback and hints. I will also take the opportunity to involve the audience in some of the dilemmas we are facing.

Acknowledgements

This work builds upon the work of the 2022 ITiCSE working group on "Steps learners take when solving programming tasks, and how learning environments (should) respond to them". Together with Hieke Keuning, Nathalie Kiesler, and Dominic Lohr, I am looking further into how experts would give feedback on programming steps of students learning to program.

Bibliography

[Al05] Ala-Mutka, K. M.: A survey of automated assessment approaches for programming assignments. Computer science education, 15(2), 83-102, 2005.

[CLW18] Crow, T.; Luxton-Reilly, A.; Wuensche, B.: Intelligent tutoring systems for programming education: a systematic review. In Proceedings of the 20th Australasian Computing Education Conference (pp. 53-62), 2018.

[GX20] Giannakoulas, A.; Xinogalos, S.: A review of educational games for teaching programming to primary school students. In Handbook of Research on Tools for Teaching Computational Thinking in P-12 Education, 2020.

[HT07] Hattie, J.; Timperley, H.: The power of feedback. Review of educational research 77.1, 81-112, 2007.

[He23] Hellas, A.; Leinonen, J.; Sarsa, S.; Koutcheme, C.; Kujanpää, L.; Sorva, J.: Exploring the Responses of Large Language Models to Beginner Programmers' Help Requests. arXiv preprint arXiv:2306.05715, 2023. To appear in ICER 2023.

[Je22] Jeuring, J.; Keuning, H.; Marwan, S.; Bouvier, D.; Izu, C.; Kiesler, N.; Lehtinen, T.; Lohr, D.; Peterson, A.; Sarsa, S.: Towards Giving Timely Formative Feedback and Hints to Novice Programmers. In Proceedings of the 2022 Working Group Reports on Innovation and Technology in Computer Science Education, 95-115, 2022.

[KJH18] Keuning, H.; Jeuring, J.; Heeren, B.: A systematic literature review of automated feedback generation for programming exercises. ACM Transactions on Computing Education (TOCE), 19(1), 1-43, 2018.

[KD96] Kluger, A. N.; DeNisi, A.: The effects of feedback interventions on performance: a historical review, a meta-analysis, and a preliminary feedback intervention theory. Psychological bulletin, 119(2), 254, 1996.

[Me23] Messer, M.; Brown, N. C.; Kölling, M.; Shi, M.: Automated Grading and Feedback Tools for Programming Education: A Systematic Review. arXiv preprint arXiv:2306.11722, 2023.

[Ra05] Race, P.: Making learning happen – A guide for post-compulsory education. Sage, 2005.

[RRR03] Robins, A.; Rountree, J.; Rountree, N.: Learning and teaching programming: A review and discussion. Computer science education, 13(2), 137-172, 20

Best-Paper-Kandidaten

# Help me to help myself: Eine Feldstudie zur Wirksamkeit einer datenbasierten Unterstützung von Selbstregulationskompetenzen in digital gestützten Lernsettings

Anna Radtke [1], Meike Osinski [2], Maren Scheffel [3], Katja Serova[4] und Nikol Rummel [5]

Abstract: Lerndatenanalysen eröffnen in digital gestützten Settings weitreichende Möglichkeiten, Lernende individuell zu unterstützen. Eine datenbasierte Lernunterstützung erscheint insbesondere für die Förderung der Kompetenzen zum Selbstregulierten Lernen (SRL) relevant und zielführend. In diesem Bereich weisen Lernende häufig unterschiedliche Unterstützungsbedarfe auf, die es gezielt zu adressieren gilt. Im Rahmen einer Feldstudie erhielten Studierende ($N = 77$) während ihrer Teilnahme an einem Statistik-Modul, abhängig von der Ausprägung individueller Selbstregulationskompetenzen, eine Lernunterstützung auf metakognitiver oder motivationaler Ebene in Form von Prompts. Diese zielten primär auf die Entwicklung und Anwendung von Regulationsstrategien auf der jeweiligen SRL-Ebene ab und wurden als Selbstreflexionsfragen und Handlungsempfehlungen im Online-Kurs implementiert. Studierende, denen motivationale Prompts dargeboten wurden, verfügten am Ende ihrer Modulteilnahme über stärker ausgeprägte motivationale SRL-Kompetenzen als zum Modulbeginn. Ihre metakognitiven SRL-Kompetenzen blieben unverändert. Studierende, die metakognitive Prompts erhielten, verbesserten ihre metakognitiven SRL-Kompetenzen während der Modul-teilnehme nicht. Somit erwies sich die datenbasierte Unterstützung bezogen auf die SRL-Kompetenzentwicklung teilweise als wirksam.

Keywords: Selbstreguliertes Lernen, SRL-Kompetenzen, Lerndatenanalyse, motivationale Prompts, metakognitive Prompts

1 Einleitung

Selbstreguliert lernen zu können zählt zu den Schlüsselkompetenzen unserer Zeit. Dynamische Veränderungen in der Arbeits- und Lebenswelt erfordern eine stetige eigenverantwortliche Aktualisierung von Wissen und Kompetenzen. Die Relevanz der Fähigkeit, den eigenen Lernprozess gestalten und steuern zu können, spiegelt sich auch in den 21st Century Skills der OECD wider, s. [OECD19]. Nicht selten sind die

---

[1] Center for Advanced Internet Studies (CAIS), Bochum, 44799, anna.radtke@cais-research.de, https://orcid.org/0009-0006-6952-7531
[2] Ruhr-Universität Bochum, 44801, meike.osinski@rub.de, https://orcid.org/0009-0006-4854-3890
[3] Ruhr-Universität Bochum, 44801, maren.scheffel@rub.de, https://orcid.org/0000-0003-4395-4819
[4] Ruhr-Universität Bochum, 44801, katja.serova@rub.de
[5] Ruhr-Universität Bochum, 44801, nikol.rummel@rub.de, https://orcid.org/0000-0002-3187-5534

doi: 10.18420/delfi2023-11

Selbstregulationskompetenzen von Lernenden jedoch defizitär, z. B. [EB21]. Besonderes Interesse gilt daher der Entwicklung von Konzepten und Maßnahmen, mithilfe derer Lernende darin unterstützt werden können, Kompetenzen für das Selbstregulierte Lernen (SRL) nachhaltig zu entwickeln und anzuwenden. In besonderem Maße erfordert asynchrones Lernen in digital gestützten Settings selbstregulatorische Fähigkeiten, z. B. [BP15]: Lernende müssen hierfür in der Lage sein, ihr Lernverhalten eigenständig zu initiieren, auszurichten, aufrechtzuerhalten und bei Bedarf neu zu justieren. Es stellt demnach ein zentrales Moment im Lernprozess dar, sowohl auf *motivationaler* als auch auf *metakognitiver* Ebene, für bestimmte Lernsituationen und -aufgaben angemessene Strategien zur Regulation des eigenen Lernverhaltens auszuwählen und anzuwenden.

So anspruchsvoll das Lernen in digital gestützten Lehr-Lernsettings ist, so weitreichend sind die Möglichkeiten, die digitale Kontexte bieten, Lernende individuell zu unterstützen. Digital gestützte Settings ermöglichen es, lernbezogene Daten automatisiert zu sammeln und zu analysieren, um hieraus beispielsweise individualisierte Handlungsempfehlungen abzuleiten, z. B. [RW15]. Häufig rekurrieren Arbeiten in Forschung und Entwicklung im Feld von *Lerndatenanalysen* bzw. *Learning Analytics* (LA) auf Selbstreguliertes Lernen als theoretische Hintergrundfolie und erheben zugleich den Anspruch, mit entsprechenden Implementationen Selbstregulationskompetenzen von Lernenden zu fördern. Meist fehlt es jedoch an der empirischen Überprüfung dieses theoretischen Anspruchs, z. B. [Ji18]. Die vorliegende Arbeit trägt zur Schließung dieser Lücke bei, indem sie sich theoretisch wie empirisch der Frage widmet, ob und inwiefern eine in einem digital gestützten Setting implementierte datenbasierte Unterstützung die Entwicklung individueller SRL-Kompetenzen fördert.

2 Theoretischer Hintergrund

Beim Selbstregulierten Lernen stellen Lernende eigeninitiativ und eigenständig den Lernbedarf fest, setzen sich Lernziele und richten die eigenen Handlungen, Gedanken und Emotionen auf diese aus, z. B. [WH98]. Das sozio-kognitive Modell des Selbstregulierten Lernens nach [Zi02] beschreibt SRL als einen iterativ-zyklischen Prozess aus drei Phasen, im Zuge dessen die Lernenden zunächst die zu bewältigende Aufgabe analysieren sowie Lernziele und -pläne definieren (*forethought*). Anschließend werden diese mithilfe angemessener Lernstrategien umgesetzt, der eigene Lernprozess kontinuierlich überwacht, bei Bedarf neu justiert (*performance*) sowie letztlich reflektiert (*reflection*). Selbstregulationskompetenzen gelten als bedeutende Determinante erfolgreichen lebenslangen Lernens und haben sich speziell in Bezug auf akademische Leistung wiederholt als zentrale Voraussetzung erwiesen, u. a. [WH15]. Es zeigt sich allerdings, dass die Selbstregulationskompetenzen von Lernenden häufig mangelhaft sind und einer gezielten Förderung bedürfen, insbesondere in digital gestützten asynchronen Lehr- und Lernsettings z. B. [Wo19]. Prompts gelten als effektive Maßnahme zur Förderung von SRL in digital gestützten Settings, z. B. [DD19]. Dargeboten als Hinweise, Handlungsempfehlungen oder Fragen, ermöglichen es Prompts, die Aufmerksamkeit der

Lernenden auf bestimmte lernrelevante Aspekte zu lenken und auf diese Weise erwünschte bzw. produktive Lernaktivitäten anzuregen, u. a. [LHI14]. Zudem können Prompts gezielt einzelne Ebenen der Selbstregulation beim Lernen adressieren, wie z. B. Metakognition oder Motivation: *Metakognitive Selbstregulations-Prompts* sollen Lernende bspw. bei der Formulierung von Zielen sowie der Überwachung und Evaluation des eigenen Lernprozesses unterstützen. *Motivationale Selbstregulations-Prompts* zielen darauf ab, Lernende zu befähigen, Strategien zur Aufrechterhaltung bzw. Steigerung ihrer Lernmotivation anzuwenden, z. B. [Ba09]. Trotz zahlreicher Hinweise auf eine übergeordnete Rolle motivationaler Regulation beim SRL, u. a. [BM13], [DD19], liegen im Vergleich zu metakognitiven Prompts bislang kaum empirische Erkenntnisse zur Wirksamkeit motivationaler Selbstregulations-Prompts vor, z. B. [DD19], [SSS09].

Als besonders effektiv gelten Maßnahmen zur Unterstützung von SRL, wenn sie individuelle Voraussetzungen von Lernenden berücksichtigen, z. B. [Wo19]. Es gilt demnach zunächst, individuelle Bedarfe von Lernenden in Bezug auf SRL zu identifizieren. Hierfür bieten sich in digital gestützten Settings *Lerndatenanalysen* bzw. *Learning Analytics* (LA) an, z. B. [Yi14]. Unter LA wird das Sammeln, Analysieren und Berichten von Daten über Lernende und ihre Lernprozesse verstanden. Eine Möglichkeit der Unterstützung in Bezug auf SRL stellt die Visualisierung von Prozessdaten auf Dashboards für Lernende dar, mithilfe derer das Bewusstsein für das eigene Lernen angeregt und die Überwachung des eigenen Lernprozesses unterstützt werden soll, z. B. [Ji17]. Es zeigt sich jedoch, dass allein die Spiegelung von Lerndaten als Unterstützung von SRL meist zu kurz greift, da hierbei u. a. nicht sichergestellt werden kann, dass Lernende daraufhin eigenständig angemessene und produktive Handlungsstrategien auswählen und anwenden können. Hingegen versprechen auf Grundlage von LA generierte und auf den individuellen Unterstützungsbedarf zugeschnittene Prompts besonderes Potenzial zur Förderung von SRL, da sie für Lernende konkrete Empfehlungen für die Regulation ihres Lernverhaltens bereithalten.

Die übergeordnete Forschungsfrage dieser Arbeit lautet demnach: Kann eine auf LA beruhende Darbietung von metakognitiven oder motivationalen Prompts die Kompetenzen von Lernenden auf der jeweils adressierten, metakognitiven oder motivationalen, SRL-Ebene fördern? Zum einen wurde erwartet, dass die Darbietung *metakognitiver* Prompts bei Lernenden mit Unterstützungsbedarf auf metakognitiver SRL-Ebene zu einem Zuwachs an *metakognitiven* SRL-Kompetenzen führt (*H1*). Zum anderen wurde davon ausgegangen, dass die Darbietung *motivationaler* Prompts bei Lernenden mit defizitären Selbstregulationskompetenzen auf motivationaler Ebene zu einem Zuwachs an *motivationalen* SRL-Kompetenzen führt (*H2*). Zudem wird der Regulation auf motivationaler Ebene eine übergeordnete Rolle zugeschrieben, da nur wenn sie gelingt, der SRL-Prozess durch die Lernenden überhaupt erst in Gang gesetzt bzw. fortgeführt und die Anwendung metakognitiver Strategien angestoßen werden kann, z. B. [DD19], [PD90]. Demnach wurde angenommen, dass die Darbietung *motivationaler* Prompts bei Lernenden mit Unterstützungsbedarf auf motivationaler SRL-Ebene auch zu einem Zuwachs an *metakognitiven* SRL-Kompetenzen führt (*H3*).

3 Methode

3.1 Stichprobe und Vorgehen

Um die Hypothesen zu untersuchen, wurde eine Feldstudie im Rahmen eines Statistik-Moduls im Bachelorstudiengang Erziehungswissenschaft an einer großen deutschen Universität durchgeführt. Von 165 Kursteilnehmenden nahmen $N = 77$ Studierende die Empfehlung der bedarfsorientierten Lernunterstützung durch Prompts an und füllten zu beiden Messzeitpunkten den Fragebogen zur Erfassung der SRL-Kompetenzen aus (siehe 3.2). 90.9% der an der Studie teilnehmenden Studierenden waren weiblich, 7.8% männlich und 1.3% divers. Das Durchschnittsalter lag bei 21.40 Jahren ($SD = 1.69$). Die meisten Studierenden (89.5%) nahmen zum ersten Mal an dem Modul teil.

In der ersten Vorlesungswoche wurden die Kursteilnehmenden gebeten, einen Online-Fragebogen auszufüllen, der der Erfassung ihrer individuellen SRL-Kompetenzen auf motivationaler sowie metakognitiver Ebene diente. Auf Grundlage der ermittelten SRL-Kompetenzen auf beiden Ebenen wurde ein individueller Unterstützungsbedarf – entweder auf motivationaler *oder* auf metakognitiver Ebene – identifiziert (siehe 3.2). Entsprechend wurde den Studierenden in dem modulbegleitenden Moodle-Kurs eine Empfehlung für eine auf ihren Bedarf zugeschnittene Lernunterstützung mit Fokus auf Planung und Organisation (Metakognition) oder mit Fokus auf Motivation gegeben, die sie auf eigenem Wunsch annehmen oder ablehnen konnten. Schlussendlich erhielten im Rahmen dieser Studie $n = 58$ Studierende die motivationale und $n = 19$ Studierende die metakognitive Unterstützung. Im Laufe der Vorlesungszeit wurden den Kursteilnehmenden, die das Unterstützungsangebot angenommen haben, wöchentlich drei Prompts (angelehnt an die in 2. skizzierten SRL-Phasen) im Online-Kurs dargeboten (für Beispiele siehe Abb. 1).

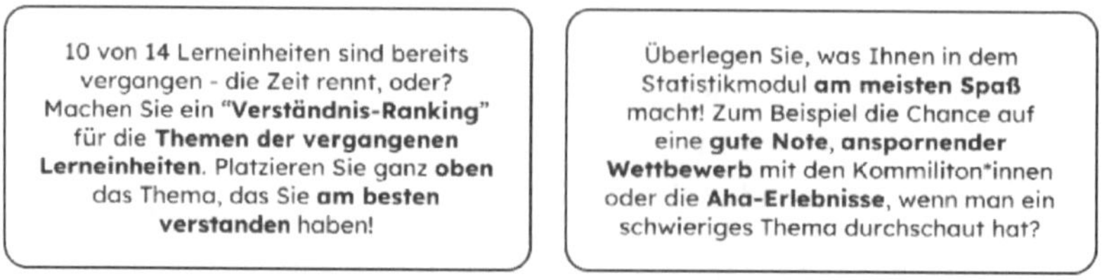

> 10 von 14 Lerneinheiten sind bereits vergangen - die Zeit rennt, oder? Machen Sie ein **"Verständnis-Ranking"** für die **Themen der vergangenen Lerneinheiten**. Platzieren Sie ganz **oben** das Thema, das Sie **am besten verstanden** haben!

> Überlegen Sie, was Ihnen in dem Statistikmodul **am meisten Spaß** macht! Zum Beispiel die Chance auf eine **gute Note, ansporndender Wettbewerb** mit den Kommiliton*innen oder die **Aha-Erlebnisse**, wenn man ein schwieriges Thema durchschaut hat?

Abb. 1: Beispiele für einen metakognitiven (links) und motivationalen (rechts) Prompt[6]

Die Prompts waren in Form von Selbstreflexionsfragen und/oder Handlungsempfehlungen für die Anwendung von Regulationsstrategien auf der jeweiligen SRL-Ebene formuliert. Um die Entwicklung der SRL-Kompetenzen überprüfen zu können, wurden die Studierenden am Ende der Vorlesungszeit erneut gebeten, den Fragebogen zur Erfassung der SRL-Kompetenzen sowie weitere Fragebögen (siehe 3.2) auszufüllen.

---

[6] Design der Prompts (Graphiken, Farbwahl) wurde an das Design des bestehenden Online-Kurses angepasst.

3.2 Erhebungsinstrumente

Unterstützungsbedarf auf metakognitiver und motivationaler SRL-Ebene und *Entwicklung der SRL-Kompetenzen*: Zur Erfassung der individuellen metakognitiven und motivationalen SRL-Kompetenzen am Anfang und am Ende des Semesters wurden einzelne Subskalen[7] aus dem *Motivated Strategies for Learning Questionnaire* (MSLQ, [PD90]) verwendet, die diese beiden Ebenen adressieren. Insgesamt bestand der Fragebogen aus 62 Items (jeweils 31 Items je SRL-Ebene). Die Antworten wurden auf einer Likert-Skala von 1 (*trifft überhaupt nicht zu*) bis 7 (*trifft voll und ganz zu*) erfasst. Die Analyse der internen Konsistenz zu beiden Messzeitpunkten zeigte für alle Subskalen akzeptable bis sehr gute Werte (.662 ≤ Cronbachs α ≤ .993), ausgenommen der Skala „Metakognition: Hilfesuche (*Help Seeking*)" (.479 ≤ Cronbachs α ≤ .457).[8] Der individuelle *Unterstützungsbedarf* wurde ermittelt, indem für jede Versuchsperson ein Summen-Score für *Metakognitive SRL-Kompetenzen* und ein Summen-Score für *Motivationale SRL-Kompetenzen* über die jeweils zugehörigen Subskalen berechnet (jeweils min. = 31, max. = 217) und anschließend gegenübergestellt wurden. Der geringere Score wurde als Indikator dafür genutzt, dass die Person auf der entsprechenden SRL-Ebene am ehesten Unterstützung bedarf. Die *Entwicklung der SRL-Kompetenzen* wurde durch den Vergleich der SRL-Kompetenzen je Ebene am Anfang und am Ende des Semesters bestimmt.

Nutzung der Prompts: Um Aufschluss über die Nutzung der Prompts zu erhalten, sollten die Kursteilnehmenden am Ende des Semesters auf einer Likert-Skala von 1 (*trifft überhaupt nicht zu*) bis 7 (*trifft voll und ganz zu*) bewerten, ob sie die jeweiligen Prompts wahrgenommen, gelesen und sich mit ihnen intensiv auseinandergesetzt haben.[9]

Statistik-bezogene Einstellungen: Am Ende des Semesters wurden Statistik-bezogene Einstellungen der Kursteilnehmenden (s. Tab. 1) erfasst.

---

[7] Subskalen *Intrinsic Goal Orientation*, *Extrinsic Goal Orientation*, *Task Value*, *Control Beliefs*, *Self-Efficacy for Learning and Performance* sowie *Test Anxiety* erfassten motivationale SRL-Kompetenzen.
Subskalen *Metacognitive Self-Regulation*, *Time and Study Environment*, *Effort Regulation*, *Peer Learning* sowie *Help Seeking* erfassten metakognitive SRL-Kompetenzen.
[8] Dabei ist anzumerken, dass die Subskala „Hilfesuche" bei der ursprünglichen Analyse der internen Konsistenz in [PD90] bereits einen niedrigen Cronbachs α-Wert von .52 aufwies.
[9] Items: (1) „Jedes Mal, wenn ich mich in den Moodle-Kurs eingeloggt habe, habe ich die Handlungsempfehlung wahrgenommen." (2) „Ich habe jede neue Handlungsempfehlung aufmerksam gelesen." (3) „Ich habe mich inhaltlich intensiv mit den Handlungsempfehlungen auseinandergesetzt."

Dimension	Skala	Quelle	N der Items	Cronbachs α
Fachinteresse an Statistik	Fachinteresse	[Fe14]	8**	.899
Wahrgenommene Nützlichkeit der Statistik	von der Modulleitung konstruiert und validiert		5***	.869
Statatistik-bezogene Selbstwirksamkeitserwartungen	Skala zur Allgemeinen Selbstwirksamkeitserwartung (Kurzform)	[SJ03]	10***	.937
Interesse bzw. Vergnügen*	Kurzskala intrinsischer Motivation (KIM)	[Wi09]	3***	.870
wahrgenommene Kompetenz*			3***	.884
wahrgenommene Wahlfreiheit*			3***	.903
Druck bzw. Anspannung*			3***	.760

Anmerkung. *am/im Statistik-Modul, **Antwortskala: 1 (stimmt wenig) – 5 (stimmt sehr), ***Antwortskala: 1 (trifft überhaupt nicht zu) – 7 (trifft voll und ganz zu)

Tab. 1: Erhebungsinstrumente für Statistik-bezogene Einstellungen[10]

4 Ergebnisse

4.1 Entwicklung der motivationalen SRL-Kompetenzen

In *H2* wurde die Annahme getroffen, dass die motivationale Prompt-basierte Unterstützung einen fördernden Effekt auf die motivationalen SRL-Kompetenzen der Kursteilnehmenden hat. Der durchschnittliche Wert für die motivationalen SRL-Kompetenzen der Kursteilnehmenden in der Bedingung mit motivationaler Unterstützung ($n = 58$) lag am Anfang des Semesters bei 133.88 ($SD = 22.73$) und am Ende des Semesters bei 145.66 ($SD = 25.02$). Die motivationalen SRL-Kompetenzen der Studierenden in der Bedingung mit metakognitiver Unterstützung ($n = 19$) stieg von 154.32 ($SD = 26.89$; am Anfang des Semesters) auf 154.84 ($SD = 25.73$; am Ende des Semesters; siehe Abb. 2).

Um die Unterschiede in der Entwicklung der motivationalen SRL-Kompetenzen zwischen der Studierenden in beiden Bedingungen statistisch zu prüfen, wurde eine zweifaktorielle Varianzanalyse mit Messwiederholung auf einem Faktor berechnet.[11] Das Signifikanzniveau für alle statistischen Analysen wurde auf 5 Prozent gesetzt, bei den Post-Hoc-Tests mit einer Bonferroni-Korrektur. Die Veränderung auf dem Hauptfaktor Messzeitpunkt (am Anfang und am Ende des Semesters) war signifikant ($p = .046$). Die Wahrscheinlichkeit, einen mittleren Effekt (partielles $\eta^2 = .052$) bei gleichen Konditionen zu finden, betrug 51.8% (beobachtete Trennschärfe). Der Haupteffekt des Faktors Bedingung (mit metakognitiver und mit motivationaler Unterstützung) war ebenfalls

---

[10] Items aus den Fragebögen wurden bei Bedarf sprachlich an den Statistik-bezogenen Lernkontext angepasst bzw. in die Vergangenheitsform umformuliert, um retrospektive Einschätzungen abzufragen.
[11] Voraussetzungen für diese und weitere Analysen waren erfüllt.

signifikant ($p = .012$, partielles $\eta^2 = .082$, beobachtete Trennschärfe = .724). Die Wechselwirkung zwischen dem Faktor Messzeitpunkt und der Bedingung war nicht signifikant ($p = .067$). Die beobachtete Trennschärfe der Effektstärke ($\eta^2 = .044$) von .450 war aufgrund niedriger Effektgröße nicht aussagekräftig. Anschließend wurde eine Post-Hoc-Analyse mithilfe des Tukey-Tests durchgeführt, um die Mittelwertsunterschiede zwischen und innerhalb der Bedingungen zu vergleichen (siehe Abb. 2). Da die Zuordnung zu den beiden Bedingungen auf Basis der Werte der SRL-Kompetenzen zu Beginn des Semesters stattfand, zeigte sich zum ersten Messzeitpunkt zwischen den Kursteilnehmenden in beiden Bedingungen erwartungskonform ein großer signifikanter Unterschied bezogen auf die motivationalen SRL-Kompetenzen ($p = .002$, *Cohens d* = .86). Dieser Unterschied war am Ende des Semesters nicht signifikant ($p = .172$, *Cohens d* = .37). Beim Vergleich der motivationalen SRL-Kompetenzen zu Anfang und zu Ende des Semesters zeigte sich entsprechend der *H1*, dass die mittlere Kompetenzsteigerung bei den Studierenden in der Bedingung mit motivationaler Unterstützung (um 11.78 Punkte) signifikant war ($p < .001$, *Cohens d* = .53). Die Kompetenzsteigerung bei den Kursteilnehmenden in der Bedingung mit metakognitiver Unterstützung (um 0.53 Punkte) war hingegen nicht signifikant ($p = .928$, *Cohens d* = .02).

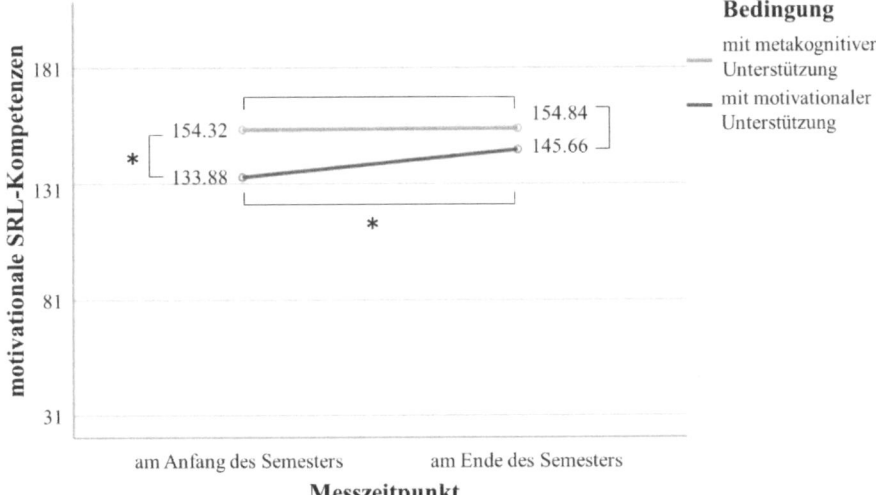

Anmerkung. Signifikante *p*-Werte aus der Post-Hoc-Analyse sind mit * markiert.
Abb. 2: Entwicklung der motivationalen SRL-Kompetenzen

4.2 Entwicklung der metakognitiven SRL-Kompetenzen

In *H1* und *H3* wurde die Annahme getroffen, dass sowohl die metakognitive als auch die motivationale Prompt-basierte Unterstützung einen fördernden Effekt auf die metakognitiven SRL-Kompetenzen der Kursteilnehmenden hat. Bei den Studierenden in der Bedingung mit motivationaler Unterstützung ($n = 58$) sank der durchschnittliche Wert für die metakognitiven SRL-Kompetenzen von 161.98 ($SD = 20.65$) zu Semesterbeginn auf 160.66 ($SD = 20.06$) zu Semesterende. Bei den Kursteilnehmenden in der Bedingung mit metakognitiver Unterstützung ($n = 19$) lag der Wert zu Beginn bei 144.84 ($SD = 26.81$) und am Ende der Unterstützungsphase bei 146.16 ($SD = 22.96$; siehe Abb. 3).

Um die Entwicklung der metakognitiven SRL-Kompetenzen bei den Studierenden in beiden Bedingungen zu beurteilen, wurde ebenfalls eine zweifaktorielle Varianzanalyse mit Messwiederholung auf einem Faktor durchgeführt. Der Effekt des Faktors Messzeitpunkt (am Anfang und am Ende des Semesters) war nicht signifikant ($p = .998$, partielles $\eta^2 = .000$, beobachtete Trennschärfe = .050). Der Haupteffekt des Faktors Bedingung war signifikant ($p = .004$, partielles $\eta^2 = .106$, beobachtete Trennschärfe = .836). Der Wechselwirkungseffekt zwischen dem Faktor Messzeitpunkt und der Bedingung war nicht signifikant ($p = .520$, partielles $\eta^2 = .006$, beobachtete Trennschärfe = .098). Die Post-Hoc-Analyse zum Vergleich der einzelnen Mittelwerte wurde mithilfe der Tukey-Tests durchgeführt (siehe Abb. 3). Es zeigte sich zwischen den Studierenden in beiden Bedingungen ein mittlerer signifikanter Unterschied in metakognitiven SRL-Kompetenzen zu Beginn des Semesters ($p = .005$, *Cohens d* = .77). Dieser Unterschied blieb ebenso am Ende der Unterstützungsphase bestehen ($p = .010$, *Cohens d* = .70). Die Steigerung der metakognitiven SRL-Kompetenzen war für Kursteilnehmende in beiden Bedingungen nicht signifikant ($p = .712$ in der Bedingung mit metakognitiver Unterstützung, $p = .515$ in der Bedingung mit motivationaler Unterstützung; jeweils *Cohens d* = .09). Die *H1* und *H3* konnten demnach nicht angenommen werden.

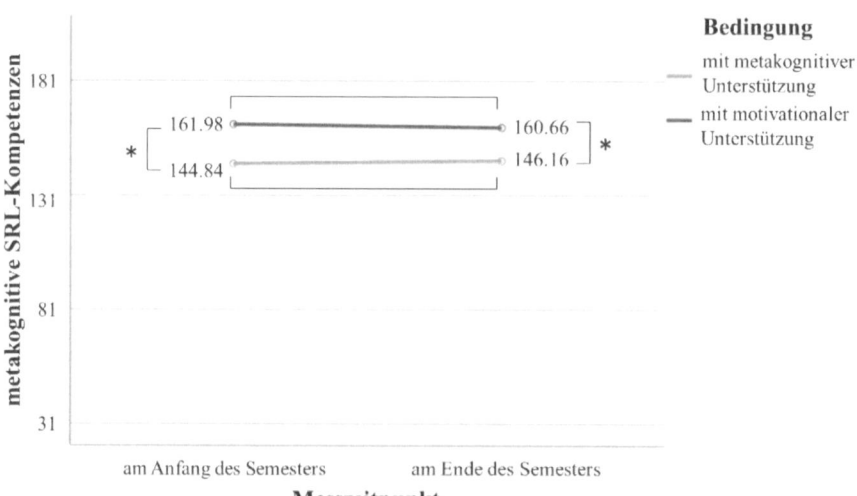

Anmerkung. Signifikante *p*-Werte aus der Post-Hoc-Analyse sind mit * markiert.
Abb. 3: Entwicklung der metakognitiven SRL-Kompetenzen

4.3 Explorative Datenanalyse: Nutzung der Prompts und Statistik-bezogene Einstellungen

Am Ende der Unterstützungsphase wurden die Kursteilnehmenden gebeten, ihre Nutzung der Prompts (siehe 3.2) zu beurteilen, d. h. anzugeben, inwiefern sie diese wahrgenommen, gelesen und sich mit ihnen intensiv auseinandergesetzt haben (siehe Tab. 2). Die resultierenden Werte lagen im eher niedrigen bis mittleren Bereich der vorgegebenen Skala. Laut den t-Tests für unabhängige Stichproben gab es zwischen beiden Bedingungen keine signifikanten Unterschiede in der Nutzung der Prompts ($p > .050$, $Cohens\ d < .40$).

Nutzungsaspekt	M^*	SD
Wahrnehmung der Prompts im Kurs	3.71	1.86
Lesen der Prompts	3.57	1.71
Intensität der Auseinandersetzung mit den Prompts	2.86	1.42

Anmerkung. *Die Items (jeweils eins pro Nutzungsaspekt) wurden auf einer Likert-Skala von 1 (*trifft überhaupt nicht zu*) bis 7 (*trifft voll und ganz zu*) gemessen; $N = 77$

Tab.2: Nutzung der Prompts

Anschließend wurden die Statistik-bezogenen Einstellungen der Studierenden in beiden Bedingungen (siehe Tab. 1) am Ende des Semesters verglichen. Laut dem t-Test für unabhängige Stichproben empfanden Studierende in der Bedingung mit motivationaler Unterstützung signifikant weniger Druck bzw. Anspannung im Statistik-Modul ($p = .010$, $Cohens\ d = .70$). Der t-Test für Variable Nützlichkeit der Statistik verfehlte die Signifikanzvoraussetzung knapp ($p = .054$; $Cohens\ d = .52$). Die Unterschiede in weiteren Statistik-bezogenen Einstellungen (siehe Tab. 1) zwischen den Bedingungen waren ebenfalls nicht signifikant ($p > .050$, $Cohens\ d < .50$).

5 Diskussion

Ziel der vorliegenden Feldstudie war es zu untersuchen, inwiefern die Selbstregulationskompetenzen durch eine datenbasierte Lernunterstützung in einem digital gestützten Setting gefördert werden können. Die implementierte Lernunterstützung in Form von metakognitiven oder motivationalen Prompts zeigte sich in Hinblick auf die SRL-Kompetenzentwicklung teilweise als wirksam. Konform zu *H2* konnte bei den Lernenden, die eine Unterstützung mit motivationalem Fokus erhielten, eine signifikante Steigerung motivationaler SRL-Kompetenzen mit mittlerer Effektstärke am Ende des Semesters nachgewiesen werden. Ihre metakognitiven SRL-Kompetenzen blieben hingegen im Laufe des Semesters unverändert, womit *H3* nicht angenommen werden konnte. Entgegen der Erwartungen gemäß *H1* konnten Studierende, die metakognitive Prompts erhielten, ihre metakognitiven SRL-Kompetenzen nicht signifikant verbessern. In Einklang mit Ergebnissen von [DD19], indizieren auch unsere Befunde eine wichtige Rolle der Aktivierung motivationaler Strategien beim SRL: Lernende, denen motivationale Prompts dargeboten wurden, empfanden im Vergleich zu Lernenden, die keine motivationalen Prompts erhielten, am Ende des Semesters signifikant weniger Druck im Statistik-Kurs. Ausgehend von diesen Ergebnissen sollten die Wirkmechanismen motivationaler Selbstregulations-Prompts in zukünftigen Forschungsarbeiten noch mehr als bisher in den Fokus gerückt werden. Auch wenn die vorliegende Arbeit, entgegen der Annahme von [DD19], keine Hinweise für einen übergreifenden Einfluss motivationaler auf metakognitive SRL-Kompetenzen liefert, deuten die Befunde auf eine positive Wirkung motivationaler Selbstregulations-Prompts auf für das Lernen zentrale affektive Aspekte hin.

Eine mögliche Erklärung für den nicht signifikanten Effekt metakognitiver Unterstützung auf metakognitive SRL-Kompetenzen ist, dass die metakognitiven Prompts von den Lernenden inhaltlich inkorrekt oder unzureichend umgesetzt wurden. Auf diese Problematik weisen bereits vorhandene Studien hin, z. B. [Fu09]. Auch die Ergebnisse der explorativen Datenanalyse hinsichtlich der Nutzung der Prompts (siehe 4.3) stützen diesen Erklärungsansatz. Um die Wirkung der datenbasierten Unterstützung durch Prompts und insbesondere die festgestellten Unterschiede in der Wirkung motivationaler und metakognitiver Prompts weiter zu ergründen, könnten in zukünftigen Forschungsvorhaben Selbstberichte mit Verhaltens- und Leistungsdaten kombiniert werden. Ein solches Vorgehen verspricht, Aufschluss über die tatsächliche Strategienutzung zu erhalten. In der hier dargestellten Studie wurde die Nutzung der Prompts per retrospektiver Selbstauskunft der Lernenden erhoben. Eine möglicherweise defizitäre Akkuratheit der Selbsteinschätzung (am Ende des Kurses bezogen auf das ganze Semester) könnte erklären, warum die Ergebnisse auf eine Nutzung der Prompts auf lediglich niedrigem bis mittlerem Niveau hindeuten. Dieser Problematik könnte durch eine andere Implementierung der Prompts entgegengewirkt werden. So könnte eine inhaltliche Auseinandersetzung und Anwendung der angesprochenen Strategien etwa durch die Möglichkeit der schriftlichen Eingabe von Gedanken zu Reflexionsfragen gefördert werden. Um Lernende in ihrer Kompetenzentwicklung noch individueller zu unterstützen, könnten darüber hinaus adaptive Prompts Anwendung finden, z. B. im Sinne einer sukzessiven Reduzierung der Unterstützung bei einem bestimmten Ausprägungsgrad von SRL-Kompetenzen, z. B. [GK19].

Zur Überprüfung der Generalisierbarkeit der Erkenntnisse erscheint es zudem notwendig, die Studie in einem anderen Lernsetting und mit einer anderen Zielgruppe zu replizieren. Da es sich um eine Feldstudie handelt, kann davon ausgegangen werden, dass die Ergebnisse reale Lernsituationen gut abbilden und somit eine höhere externe Validität im Vergleich zu Ergebnissen einer ähnlichen Laborstudie aufweisen. Allerdings wird die Generalisierbarkeit der Ergebnisse durch die Stichprobenauswahl beeinträchtigt. Hinsichtlich der internen Validität ist die Aussagekraft der Ergebnisse einer Studie im Feld im Vergleich zu einer Studie im Labor limitiert. Beispielsweise erfolgte keine Randomisierung der Versuchsgruppen, da die Unterstützung auf die Ausprägung individueller Selbstregulationskompetenzen der Lernenden zugeschnitten war. Ebenfalls wurde den Studierenden mit zu Semesterbeginn gleich ausgeprägten metakognitiven und motivationalen SRL-Kompetenzen freie Wahl überlassen, welches Unterstützungsangebot sie annehmen möchten, was die Zusammensetzung der ohnehin kleineren Gruppe mit metakognitiver Unterstützung stark beeinflusst hat. Zudem ließ das Setting (aus ethischen Gründen) nicht zu, eine Kontrollgruppe (ohne Unterstützung) zu bilden und die Kontextfaktoren (z. B. Merkmale der Lehrveranstaltung) sowie weitere Personenmerkmale (z. B. Vorwissen oder Studienleistungen) hinlänglich zu kontrollieren. Daran schließt sich jedoch die für zukünftige Forschungsvorhaben interessante Frage nach Variablen an, die die Wirkung der Prompts möglicherweise vermitteln.

6 Fazit

Zusammenfassend kann die implementierte Unterstützung als wirksam für die Förderung von motivationalen, nicht aber von metakognitiven SRL-Kompetenzen beurteilt werden. Über dieses Ergebnis hinaus liefert die Arbeit weitere relevante Erkenntnisse für die Forschung zu der Entwicklung von datenbasierten Lernunterstützungsmaßnahmen mit Fokus auf SRL. *Erstens* unterstreichen die Befunde die theoretische Annahme, z. B. [Ji18], dass mithilfe von LA SRL-Kompetenzen gefördert werden können, entsprechende Unterstützungsmaßnahmen jedoch bestimmte, zukünftig noch näher zu untersuchende Voraussetzungen erfüllen müssen. *Zweitens* liefert diese Studie wichtige Hinweise auf eine Wirkung motivationaler Prompts, die bislang in anderen Forschungsarbeiten kaum im Fokus standen. *Drittens* eröffnet die Arbeit mehrere Anknüpfungspunkte für zukünftige Forschung, sei es in Bezug auf eine Replikation der Studie in verschiedenen Settings, in Bezug auf die Weiterentwicklung des Unterstützungsangebots, bspw. hinsichtlich von Interaktivität und Adaptivität der dargebotenen Prompts, oder in Bezug auf eine einhergehende Forschung potenziell interagierender Personenmerkmalen und Kontextfaktoren.

Literaturverzeichnis

[Ba09]   Bannert, M.: Promoting self-regulated learning through prompts. Zeitschrift für Pädagogische Psychologie/Journal of Pedagogical Psychology 23, S. 139-145, 2009.

[BM13] Bannert, M.; Mengelkamp, C.: Scaffolding hypermedia learning through metacognitive prompts. In (Azevedo, R.; Aleven, V.): International handbook of metacognition and learning technologies. Springer, New York, S. 171-186, 2013.

[BP15]   Broadbent, J.; Poon, W. L.: Self-regulated learning strategies & academic achievement in online higher education learning environments: A systematic review. The Internet and Higher Education 27, S. 1-13, 2015.

[DD19] Daumiller, M.; Dresel, M.: Supporting self-regulated learning with digital media using motivational regulation and metacognitive prompts. J. Exp. Ed. 87/1, S. 161-176, 2019.

[EB21]   Engelmann, K.; Bannert, M.: Analyzing temporal data for understanding the learning process induced by metacognitive prompts. Learning and Instruction 72, 101205, 2021.

[Fe14]   Ferdinand, H.: Entwicklung von Fachinteresse. Längsschnittstudie zu Interessenverläufen und Determinanten positiver Entwicklung in der Schule. Waxmann, 2014.

[Fu09]   Furberg, A.: Socio-cultural aspects of prompting student reflection in web-based inquiry learning environments. Journal of Computer Assisted Learning 25/4, S. 397-409, 2009.

[GK19]   Gidalevich, S.; Kramarski, B.: The value of fixed versus faded self-regulatory scaffolds on fourth graders' mathematical problem solving. Instructional Science, S. 39-68, 2019.

[Ji17]   Jivet, I. et al.: Awareness is not enough. Pitfalls of learning analytics dashboards in the educational practice. In (Lavoué, É. et al.): Data Driven Approaches in Digital Education: ECTEL Conference, Tallinn, S. 12-15, 2017.

[Ji18]   Jivet, I. et al.: License to evaluate: Preparing learning analytics dashboards for educational practice. In Proceedings of LAK'18, S. 31-40, 2018.

[LHI14]   Lehmann, T.; Hähnlein, I.; Ifenthaler, D.: Cognitive, metacognitive and motivational perspectives on preflection in self-regulated online learning. Computers in Human Behavior 32, S. 313-323, 2014.

[OECD19]   OECD: Lernkompass 2030, 2019.

[PD90]   Pintrich, P. R.; De Groot, E. V.: Motivational and self-regulated learning components of classroom academic performance. J. Educ. Psychol. 82/1, S. 33-40, 1990.

[RW15]   Roll, I.; Winne, P. H..: Understanding, evaluating, and supporting self-regulated learning using learning analytics. Journal of Learning Analytics 2/1, S. 7-12, 2015.

[SJ03]   Schwarzer, R.; Jerusalem, M.: SWE. Skala zur Allgemeinen Selbstwirksamkeitserwartung. In (Leibniz-Institut für Psychologie, ZPID): Open Test Archive, 2003.

[SSS09]   Schwinger, M.; Steinmayr, R.; Spinath, B.: How do motivational regulation strategies affect achievement: Mediated by effort management and moderated by intelligence. Learning and Individual Differences 19/4, S. 621-627, 2009.

[WH98]   Winne, P. H.; Hadwin, A. F.: Studying as self-regulated learning. In (Hacker, D. J.; Dunlosky, J.; Graesser, A. C.): Metacognition in educational theory and practice. Lawrence Erlbaum Associates Publishers, Hillsdale, S. 171-186, 1998.

[WH15]   Wolters, C. A.; Hussain, M.: Investigating grit and its relations with college students' self-regulated learning and academic achievement. Metac. Learn. 10, S 293-311, 2015.

[Wi09]   Wilde, M. et al.: Überprüfung einer Kurzskala intrinsischer Motivation (KIM). Zeitschrift für Didaktik der Naturwissenschaften 15, S. 31-45, 2009.

[Wo19]   Wong, J. et al.: Supporting self-regulated learning in online learning environments and MOOCs: A systematic review. J. Exp. Educ. 35/4–5, S. 356-373, 2019.

[Yi14]   Yin, C. J. et al.: Smartphone based data collecting system for analyzing learning behaviors. In Proceedings of ICCE 2023, Nara, S. 575-577, 2014.

[Zi02]   Zimmerman, B. J.: Becoming a self-regulated learner: An overview. Theory into practice 41/2, S. 64-70, 2002.

Mitigating Biases using an Additive Grade Point Model: Towards Trustworthy Curriculum Analytics Measures

Frederik Baucks[1] and Laurenz Wiskott[1]

Abstract: Curriculum Analytics (CA) tries to improve degree program quality and learning experience by studying curriculum structure and student data. In particular, descriptive data measures (e.g., correlation-based curriculum graphs) are essential to monitor whether the learning process proceeds as intended. Therefore, identifying confounders and resulting biases and mitigating them should be critical to ensure reliable and fair results. Still, CA approaches often use raw student data without considering the influence of possible confounders such as student performance, course difficulty, workload, and time, which can lead to biased results. In this paper, we use an additive grade model to estimate these confounders and verify the validity and reliability of the estimates. Further, we mitigate the estimated confounders and investigate their impact on the CA measures course-to-course correlation and order benefit. Using data from 574 Computer Science Bachelor students, we show that these measures are significantly confounded and mislead to biased interpretations.

Keywords: curriculum analytics, confounding, bias, mitigation, fairness

1 Introduction

Trustworthy results of measures used to describe and understand student activity in degree programs are essential to ensure fair and appropriate decisions for improving degree quality. Therefore, identifying student-dependent and course-dependent confounders and bias is central to guaranteeing equal opportunities for all students.

Curriculum Analytics (CA), as a sub-field of Learning Analytics (LA), aims to assess degree program quality and course relations using student data and program structure. CA methods associated with process mining and prediction use descriptive measures such as the correlation between course grades [Ba18; Ra21] and order benefit (OB) [Gu21] to describe course relations and build graphical curriculum representations. In order to measure relations, e.g., the content overlap of courses, using course grades, confounders [HR20] need to be identified and mitigated [WGD22]. Existing descriptive CA measures try to mitigate confounders, like student performance, by, e.g., normalizing student grades but do not quantify student and course-specific confounding that may bias the interpretation of the measured outcome. In addition, the normalization of grades often leads to a loss of information, e.g., correcting grades using the grade point average (GPA)

---
[1] Ruhr-Universität Bochum, Institut für Neuroinformatik, Universitätsstr. 150, 44801 Bochum, frederik.baucks@ini.rub.de; laurenz.wiskott@ini.rub.de

doi: 10.18420/delfi2023-12

[Oc16], which is known to be confounded by itself [HSS19]. The resulting confounded or even biased graphical representations of the curriculum are further used in process mining and prediction methods, leading to concept drift issues [BCR18] or violations of the IID assumption, respectively.

This paper addresses the open problem of quantifying and mitigating possible confounders in descriptive CA measures. We adopt a matrix factorization (MF) approach [RRS10] to model statistically independent confounders accounting for student performance, course difficulty, workload, and time. This methodology can quantify confounding in widely used CA measures such as course-to-course correlation and OB and mitigate it. Using course point grades of a Computer Science bachelor's degree program, we reveal that measure interpretations can be significantly and misleadingly biased, if confounders are not mitigated. When employing CA analyses, we reveal that our additive model is a valuable preprocessing tool. Our key contributions are **1.) Additive modeling as a CA methodology:** We modify MF to additively model different student and course-dependent confounders as statistically independent random variables, namely student performance, course difficulty, workload, and time. Further, we test the estimated confounders for validity and reliability. Using the independence of the modeled estimates, we can quantify their impact using variance and also mitigate them. **2.) Case study application:** Using data from CS students over nine years, we quantify the confounding in the grade data and the effect of mitigation on the widely used course-to-course correlation and the OB between courses. We observe that student performance and course difficulty confounders had the most impact, accounting for 54.8% of the variance, while workload and time accounted for less than 2%.

2 Related Work

Curriculum Analytics (CA) is a recognized branch of Learning Analytics (LA) [Gr16] and examines the structure of curricula to understand degree programs and improve their quality [Hi22]. One central tool of using curriculum structure is a representation of the curriculum, usually graphical, called a curriculum graph [Ra21]. These rely on descriptive measures (e.g., correlation), prerequisites, or process mining techniques (e.g., Bayesian networks). When no prerequisites are available, typically, curriculum representations use course grades to catch relations between courses, e.g., a prerequisite structure [Ba18]. Although grades are known to suffer from confounders [Oc16], sometimes called confounding bias [WGD22], these confounders are usually not addressed in the representations if the data set is to small for causal modelling. This paper focuses on grades used to calculate descriptive measures for building curriculum graphs. We tackle the open problem of optimally identifying, quantifying, and mitigating confounders to address distribution shifts in hindsight applications such as visualization, process mining (concept drift [BCR18]), or next-term grade prediction (IID assumption [BSW23]). Only some approaches, not necessarily used in CA, already consider potential confounders in grades and their induced biases, namely normalization, item response theory (IRT), MF, and covariate adjustment (CAD).

Normalization tries to remove the effects course difficulty and student performance from student grades in different contexts. The standard approaches here are to subtract the GPA as a measure of student performance, model the course difficulty as the distance between students' GPA and course outcomes [Oc16], or normalize grades course-wide to account for course difficulty [Gu21]. A significant downside to this is that the GPA is confounded by itself [Jo97] and that, therefore, the subtraction and normalization may lead to a considerable loss of information. IRT addresses this problem by modeling students' grades using student and course-dependent latent traits in a logistic model [BSW23]. In degree-wide applications, IRT is used to model students' GPAs independently of the courses attended [Jo97] or to model course difficulties independently of students attending [BSW23]. One limitation is that the latent traits shift to zero mean and unit variance, so the latent traits are not easy to interpret.

Like IRT, MF approaches model grades using latent variables and low dimensional estimates of the interaction between students and courses. MF is commonly used for recommender systems and next-term grade prediction [BBR21]. Most MF approaches incorporate a so-called student bias and course bias. In contrast to IRT, these biases are modeled additively and not with unit variance. This additivity allows us to fit more so-called biases while staying within the original scale of the grades, leaving grades and biases comparable. This approach is comparable with CAD, in which variables (e.g., confounded GPA) are fitted in a multivariate regression model to address their influence on course grades [WGD22]. In our approach, we are fitting latent variables using MF as approximately statistically independent summands, eliminating the confoundedness of the fitted variables in CAD approaches (e.g., GPA).

The grade prediction MF approach by Barrollet et al. [BBR21] is closest to our work. They tried to capture static student and course information in degree program data. The resulting one-dimensional MF model yielded a good fit using student and course bias estimates. In contrast, our paper employs a reduced MF approach, setting the lower dimensional representation to zero, fitting only bias factors, which we call *confounders*. Further, we re-purpose MF to describe exclusively historical course grade data, fitting student performance, course difficulty, workload, and time confounders. Our work mitigates these confounders and enables a bias-reduced perspective on CA measures.

3 Methodology

We assume a prerequisite-free curriculum consisting of courses offered several times over *different* semesters. We define these offerings as *course offerings* (CO) and write the word *course* for the time-aggregated COs.

3.1 Confounding and Bias

To reduce possible bias in interpreting CA measure results, it is essential first to define confounding. Assume, we are given grades in two COs, C_1 and C_2, and a third random variable G, where the grades in C_1 and C_2 depend on G. Suppose we calculate the correlation between the grades of COs C_1 and C_2, then variable G confounds the correlation as a measure. For example, G could be the student performance measured by the grade point average (GPA). That is, GPA (G) affects the measure correlation through the statistical dependence, e.g., we expect high GPA students to perform well in both COs C_1 and C_2.

To describe bias in that context, suppose we do not want to calculate the correlation between CO's C_1 and C_2 but rather estimate the courses' content overlap (OV) based on the grades. For example, an estimator for OV could again be the correlation of the grades of the two COs C_1 and C_2. That is, we approximate OV by correlation and denote the correlation as the estimate of OV. Then our result is impacted because the confounder G shifts our estimate (correlation) systematically. Therefore, it is, in particular, shifted away from the concept OV that we expect it to estimate. This shift, then, is called bias or biased interpretation. Overall, confounders can lead to bias if they systematically shift our estimate away from what we want to measure. So, it is highly relevant what concept we want to measure, and which estimate we use to measure it to distinguish between confounding and bias. The first step to counteract bias is to determine and eliminate confounders. Because then we can reduce the confounding effect on the grades of C_1 and C_2 and thereby get a more bias-free OV estimate. Therefore, confounders (e.g., student performance) and, in this context, as a source of bias, should be identified and eliminated. In theory, we can write any grade $g_{s,c}$ of a student s in CO c, as the sum of the confounder $b_{s,c}$ and the deconfounded grade $\xi_{s,c}$:

$$g_{s,c} = \xi_{s,c} + b_{s,c}. \qquad (1)$$

To align with MF [RRS10], $\xi_{s,c}$ and $b_{s,c}$ are assumed to be statistically independent. If we know $g_{s,c}$, $b_{s,c}$, and $\xi_{s,c}$ for any student s and CO c, we can calculate the variances of each summand, which add up to the variance of $g_{s,c}$ due to the independence:

$$Var(g_{s,c}) = Var(\xi_{s,c}) + Var(b_{s,c}) \qquad (2)$$

Further, we quantify the confounding in the grade data $g_{s,c}$ as the variance of the confounder $b_{s,c}$ relative to the variance of the overall grade $\xi_{s,c} + b_{s,c}$:

$$\frac{Var(b_{s,c})}{Var(g_{s,c})} = \frac{Var(b_{s,c})}{Var(\xi_{s,c}) + Var(b_{s,c})} \qquad (3)$$

This equality becomes helpful in the following additive grade point model, where we approximate different confounders as independent summands, so that we can write the confounder $b_{s,c}$ as a sum of more specific confounders. Then, we can use the variances to quantify the confounding in the grades using Eq. 3.

3.2 Additive Grade Point Model

To model grades as the sum of independent summands, we use a *bias-only* approach motivated by MF, where we set the factorization to zero [KRB21]. The model approximates each grade $g_{s,c}$ as the sum of confounders, namely student performance b_s, CO difficulty b_c, workload b_w, and time b_t. Let Y be the set of tuples of students and CO grades that exist in our data and μ_Y the mean of all grades, and $\xi_{s,c}$ the model error, then we write:

$$g_{s,c} = \tilde{g}_{s,c} + \xi_{s,c} = (\mu_Y + b_s + b_c + b_w + b_t) + \xi_{s,c} \qquad (4)$$

CA measures, such as the correlation between course grades, are only applied to historical data. Especially for COs held in the past, we do not expect to gain more grades in the future. Therefore, we estimate the confounders only in-sample since we know the exact error $\xi_{s,c}$ for each grade here. We declare $\mu_Y + \xi_{s,c}$ as the *deconfounded grade*. We optimize the grade estimates $\tilde{g}_{s,c}$ for all $(s, c) \in Y$ using the optimization problem

$$\min \Sigma_{(s,c) \in Y} (g_{s,c} - \tilde{g}_{s,c})^2 + \lambda(|b_s| + |b_c| + |b_w| + |b_t|), \qquad (5)$$

and stochastic gradient descent for optimization with step size $\alpha = 0.005$ and regularization parameter $\lambda = 0.02$ since these led to convergence. Using the mean grade value μ_Y as a positioning summand and the regularization in the optimization, we can identify confounders on the same scale as the confounded grade $g_{s,c}$. Using this identification, we can mitigate the confounders from $g_{s,c}$ by subtraction while staying on the same grade scale, so that the deconfounded grade $\mu_Y + \xi_{s,c}$ stays comparable to $g_{s,c}$.

Model Assumption: The central model assumption is the time-invariance of the confounders. For courses, we address the invariance by using COs. For workload and time, we use categorical variables. However, whether an invariant student confounder b_s is sufficient must be verified [BBR21]. Therefore, we establish reliability in our student confounder by employing a time-dependent split-half test described in Section 3.3. Here, we compare estimates of models fitted to student's first- and second-half grades.

Model Fit and Independence: To test the model fit, we compare the variances of the confounded grades $Var(g_{s,c})$ against the variances of the model estimates $Var(\tilde{g}_{s,c}) + Var(\xi_{s,c})$. Due to the variance argument made in Eq. 3, these should be equal if we achieve optimal model fit. We expect the variance of the fitted confounder estimates to be higher if they correlate. In addition, we investigate the statistical independence of each summand using Pearson correlation, which is a necessary criterion. All confounders should be uncorrelated to the deconfounded grade $\mu_Y + \xi_{s,c}$ and to each other.

3.3 Validity and Reliability Assessment

Concurrent Validity: We study concurrent validity by considering correlations between b_s vs. GPA and b_c vs. mean CO grade. In line with IRT research [BSW23], we expect high positive correlations indicating that the student performance confounder measures student performance and CO difficulty confounder measures CO's difficulty.

Internal Consistency Reliability: To test the stability of our model, we employ two split-half reliability tests [BSW23]. First, we split the training data into two randomly assigned disjoint data sets of equal size and calculate the Pearson correlation between the estimates of the two fitted models. Second, we employ a time-dependent split-half test for the time-invariance assumption (Section 3.2). We separate each student's grades in the data set into the earlier and later half. Then we compare the fitted confounders of the earlier and later half of the student's history using Pearson correlation. We expect a high correlation indicating a stable time-invariant student performance confounder.

3.4 Curriculum Analytics Measures

To visualize the impact of the estimated confounders, we calculate two established CA measures for our curriculum twice, where we aggregate the COs over time into single courses as it is common in the literature. First, we calculate each measure for all course combinations similar to the literature, and second, using the deconfounded estimates $\mu_Y + \xi_{s,c}$ as grades, leading to bias-reduced CA measure estimates of course relation.

Correlation: CA methods use correlation to estimate course content overlap or other course relations, e.g. [Ba18; Ra21], to construct graphical representations of the curriculum. We calculate Pearson correlation using minimum p-value and sample size according to the existing literature on CA. We use the standard threshold of $p < 0.05$ and calculate the correlations between grades of courses with a minimum size $N = 20$ [Ba18].

Order Benefit: Order benefit (OB) assesses the influence of the order of a pair of courses on the corresponding grades [Gu21]. For two courses, A, B let $S_{A \to B}$ be the subset of students who first took course A and then B in some COs. Then for all students $s \in S_{A \to B}$ exist grades $g_{s,A}(t_1)$ and $g_{s,B}(t_2)$ with student-dependent times t_1 and t_2 for courses A and B with $t_1 < t_2$. We denote the set of grades of course A of the group $S_{A \to B}$ as $G_A(S_{A \to B})$ and the corresponding ordered mean grade as $\mu_A(A \to B) := \mu_{G_A(S_{A \to B})}$. Analogously for $\mu_B(A \to B)$, $\mu_A(A \to B)$, and $\mu_B(A \to B)$. Then, for two courses A, B, the order benefit $OB_{A \to B}$ from course A to course B is defined as:

$$OB_{A \to B} := \mu_A(A \to B) + \mu_B(A \to B) - \mu_A(B \to A) - \mu_B(B \to A). \tag{8}$$

This measure is only significant if there is sufficient data. We set two thresholds to guarantee that the two order groups $S_{A \to B}$ and $S_{B \to A}$ are sufficiently large and comparable in size [Gu21]: 1.) $S_{A \to B}, S_{B \to A} > 50$, 2.) $\frac{\min(S_{A \to B}, S_{B \to A})}{\max(S_{A \to B}, S_{B \to A})} > 0.30$.

4 Experiments

Data Set: For our research, we utilized a data set containing exam scores from a CS bachelor's program at Ruhr-University Bochum in Germany. The data set includes data from 1098 students who took 19 compulsory courses between 2013 and 2022, including still enrolled, graduated or drop-out students. The grading scale for each exam is from 0 to 100, with a passing score of at least 50. Each CO grade was determined via a single written examination taken at the end of the semester. Before the data was obtained, anonymization was performed, which involved removing all demographic information and adding a uniform stochastic noise between -5 to 5 to each grade. To ensure a more stable parameter fit, we filtered the data to include only students with at least 10 non-zero grades and COs with at least 20 students. Further, we limited the grades to first try-exams to strengthen student confounders reliability. The resulting data set comprises 574 students and 127 COs. In addition to exam data, we have the CO's corresponding workload and recommended semester in which a CO should be examined. We model both workload and time as categorical variables. For workload, we measure each students mean compulsory CO workload over all semesters. The resulting distribution of all students' mean workloads is split into three equal-sized parts, where each part consists of the same amount of students' mean workloads. Then we label each student with {0, 1, 2} corresponding to the subpart of the distribution. We model time, similarly, as a variable in {0, 1, 2}. We assign the label 0 if the semester the student takes a CO is before the recommended time, 1 if taken as recommended, and 2 if taken later.

$Var(g_{s,c})$	$Var(\tilde{g}_{s,c}+\xi_{s,c})$	$Var(\xi_{s,c})$	$Var(b_s)$	$Var(b_c)$	$Var(b_w)$	$Var(b_t)$
715.248	737.831	303.787	318.746	100.504	14.498	0.295

Tab. 1: Variance model fit showing an error of 22.583 between grade point variance and fitted Variance, indicating a sufficient decorrelated fit. Student and CO confounders b_s, b_c account for most of the variance, whereas workload and time confounders show small variances.

4.1 Model Fit

Additive Model Fit: To evaluate the quality of the model fit, we calculate the difference of the variances of the grades in the data set and the respective estimates in Table 1. The difference of 22.583 is relatively small and indicates the approximated independence of the summands in Eq. 4. The variance of the student performance and CO difficulty confounders is the highest, accounting for 54.8% of the total variance. The workload confounder {0: -6.715; 1: 1.721; 2: 0.948} indicate poorer performance among students with a low mean workload. Categories 1 and 2 do not seem to have an impact, and the time confounder categories have negligible effects on grades (<1.000).

Independence of Summands: A statistically significant low Pearson correlation of less than 0.06 provides the necessary criterion that our modeled confounders are approximately independent. In Fig. 1, we see the correlations of all confounder estimates on the left side, and the scatter plot of b_s and the deconfounded grade $\mu_Y + \xi_{s,c}$ on the right side, showing the most structure of all variable combinations, which remains very weak.

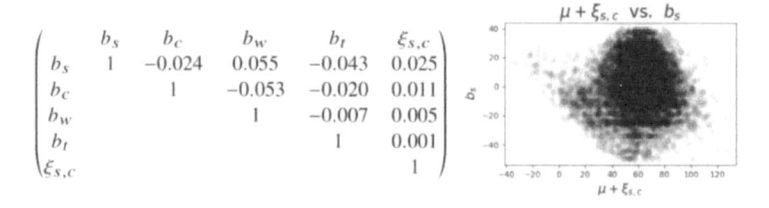

$$\begin{pmatrix} & b_s & b_c & b_w & b_t & \xi_{s,c} \\ b_s & 1 & -0.024 & 0.055 & -0.043 & 0.025 \\ b_c & & 1 & -0.053 & -0.020 & 0.011 \\ b_w & & & 1 & -0.007 & 0.005 \\ b_t & & & & 1 & 0.001 \\ \xi_{s,c} & & & & & 1 \end{pmatrix}$$

Fig. 1: [Left] Table showing Pearson correlations between the estimates of the additive model indicating very low correlations for all combinations. [Right] Scatter plot indicating statistically significant (p<0.001) absence of correlation between deconfounded grades $\mu_Y + \xi_{s,c}$ and student confounder estimate b_s as fitted by the additive model.

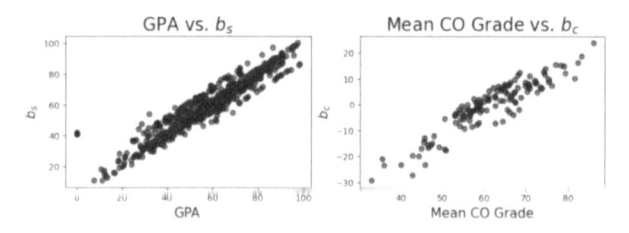

Fig. 2: [Left] Scatter plot indicating high correlation ($r = 0.966$, $p < 0.001$) between student's GPA and confounder b_s as fitted by the additive model. [Right] Scatter plot indicating high correlation ($r = 0.928$, $p < 0.001$) between mean CO grades and fitted CO confounder b_c.

4.2 Validity and Reliability Assessment

Concurrent Validity: In order to quantify the validity of the student performance and CO difficulty confounders, we show in Fig. 2 two scatter plots indicating very high statistically significant Pearson correlation ($r > 0.900$, $p < 0.001$) for both b_s vs. GPA and b_c vs. mean CO grades. These show us that the confounders we fitted do describe what we expect them to describe: student performance and CO difficulty.

Internal Consistency Reliability: Following the methodology, we first obtain Pearson correlations for the student performance and CO difficulty confounders using a random split-half test. The highly significant correlations ($p < 0.001$) for the student confounder b_s with 0.83 and the CO confounder b_c with 0.92 indicate a stable model fit. Second, the time-dependent split-half reliability test points to a similar correlation for b_s by 0.84, indicating that the student confounder estimates are stable for the first and second half of student grades. The high correlation suggests that a time-invariant student confounder is an adequate assumption in our setting.

4.3 Curriculum Analytics Measures

We calculate OBs and correlations for each course pair in the degree program. We visualize the pairs using graphs, where vertices represent courses and edges represent the value of a CA measure. The visualizations in Fig. 3 and Fig. 4 show graphs of the OBs and correlations, where the order of courses corresponds to the university's recommendation. We arrange the graph vertices from bottom to top in semester ascending order.

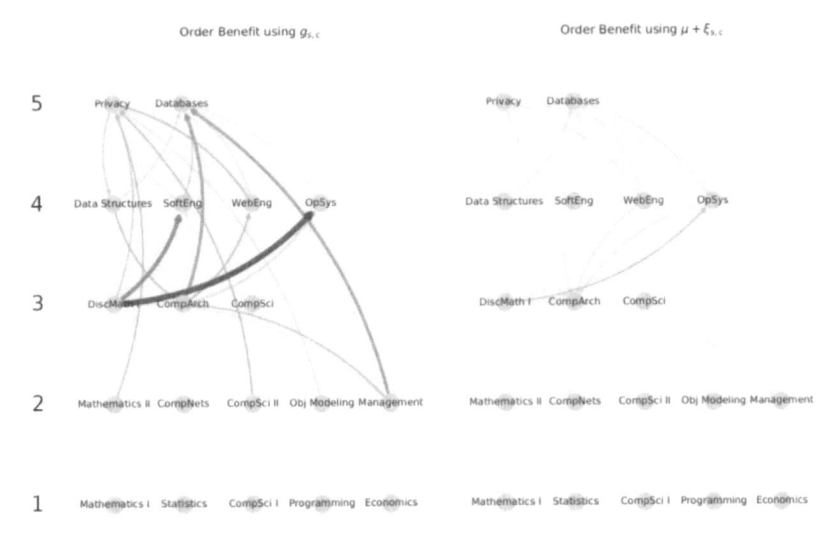

Fig 3: Curriculum graphs with colored OB edges indicating the beneficial direction of study. Color intensity and edge thickness corresponds to the value of the OB. [Left] We us the grades $g_{s,c}$. [Right] We use deconfounded grades $\mu_Y + \xi_{s,c}$.

Order Benefit: Since the OB is a directed and asymmetric measure, we visualize only positive edges in Fig. 3. The thickness and color intensity corresponds to the value of the OB, where the color scale is the same for both figures. The left side shows the OBs for the confounded grades $g_{s,c}$. Notably, there are no edges to first-semester courses, indicating that students violate the recommendation in first-semester courses not enough and, therefore, not meeting the thresholds. For existing edges, we observe that most point from bottom to top in the recommended direction of study. Compared to that on the right side, we can observe a different picture when using deconfounded grades. In general, edge weights appear less intense, and edges point far more often from top to bottom against the recommendation. The mitigation has an enormous impact on all edges of the graph, which often even change directions, indicating that the OB is largely confounded and biased as an estimate of beneficial course direction.

Correlation: Correlation is a symmetric undirected measure. Thus, we visualize undirected edges on the color scale $[0, 1]$ using the absolute r-value. The graph in Fig. 4 on the left side, showing the correlation of the confounded grades, is characterized by high density. Almost every edge holds the conditions for sample size and p-value. The graph of the deconfounded grades (right) is much sparser. Only single edges stand the conditions. Similar to OB, mitigation dramatically impacts the results of the measure. Therefore, correlation is biased as an estimate of, e.g., course overlap. Interestingly, the edges now show expected insights for courses related strongly content wise, e.g., (Mathematics I/Mathematics II) and (CompSci I/CompSci II).

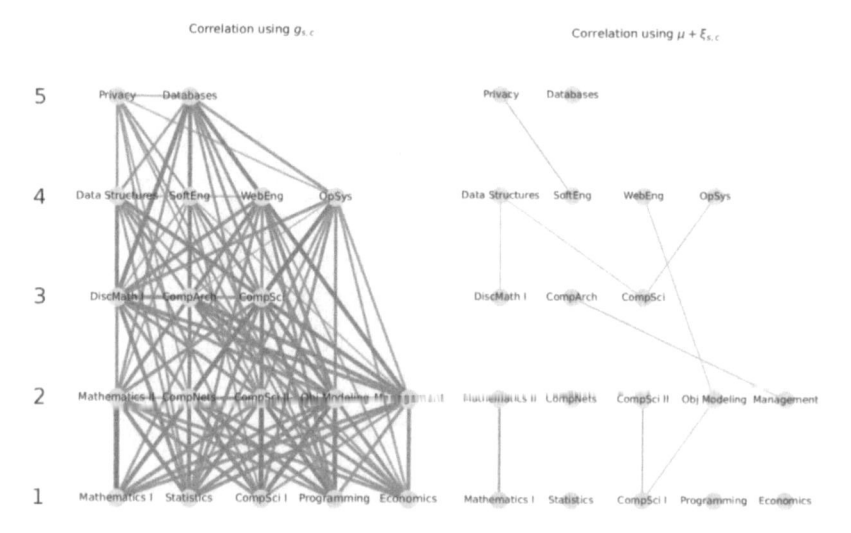

Fig. 4: Curriculum graphs with colored correlation edges indicating the correlation of grades pairs of courses. Color intensity and edge thickness corresponds to the absolute value of the correlation. [Left] We use the grades $g_{s,c}$. [Right] We use the deconfounded grades $\mu_Y + \xi_{s,c}$.

5 Discussion and Future Work

Our experiments show that the additive model in Eq. 4 can be used to estimate and mitigate course offering (CO) and student-specific confounders that induce bias in the context of graphical representations of the curriculum. We show that the amount to which Curriculum Analytics (CA) measures, such as the order benefit and correlation, are confounded can be substantially high. The confoundedness distorts the outcome completely and, ultimately, leads to severe bias.

We estimated reliable and valid confounder estimates relating to student performance, CO difficulty, workload, and time. Student and CO confounder estimates had the most impact, accounting for 54.8% of the variance, whereas categorical workload and time confounders account for less than 2%. Although the small variance of the workload confounder is in in line with research [PBY23], it should be interpreted carefully. Workload, in our setting, is limited to the compulsory courses of the degree program and given as a relative position to all students. The workload could be distorted by non-compulsory courses that are not included in the data, taken together with compulsory courses. Second, the workload assigned to courses by the university is not guaranteed to represent the courses well [MOC14]. Assessing non-compulsory course grades and the quality of workload assignments to courses will be important in future work.

CA-related process mining and prediction approaches use confounded graphical representations of the curriculum. They do not estimate confounders as statistically independent variables and even assume time-invariant COs as the concept drift issue in process mining [BCR18] or the IID assumption in prediction show. Our additive model can mitigate such limitations. However, one possible limitation of our model is the critical assumption of a time-invariant student confounder. We accounted for that in two ways. First, we limited the data set to first exam attempts. Second, we employed a time-dependent split-half reliability test that showed the stability of the student confounder. Future work can contain an extended model using a time-dependent student performance change factor. Then we can include the second exam tries on the student side.

This limitation does not occur for CO estimates. Similar to item response theory (IRT) [BSW23], an exciting line of future research is the investigation of model estimates for each CO to monitor CO difficulty independent of students attending. In contrast to IRT's unit variance transformation of confounders, our approach leaves them explainable. Compared to normalization and covariate adjustment approaches using student GPAs to mitigate confounders [Oc16], our approach yields optimized approximately statistically independent confounders. Conversely, mitigation using the possibly confounded GPA [Jo97] does not guarantee to catch confounders.

In conclusion, we hope that additive models for confounders and bias estimation become standard when employing CA measures, leading to reliable and fair measure results inducing bias-reduced interpretations.

Acknowledgements: This work is funded by the Ministry of Science (NRW, GER) via the project KI.edu:NRW.

Bibliography

[Ba18]   Backenköhler, M.; Scherzinger, F.; Singla, A.; Wolf, V.: Data-Driven Approach Towards a Personalized Curriculum. In Proc. (Boyer, K; Yudelson, M.) of the 11th Conf. of Educational Data Mining, Raleigh, NC, USA, 246-251, 2018.

[BBR21] Barollet, T.; Bouchez Tichadou, F.; Rastello, F.: Do Common Educational Datasets Contain Static Information? A Statistical Study. In Proc. (Hsiao, I.; Sahebi, S.; Bouchet,

	F.; Vie, J.) of the 14th Int. Conf. of Educational Data Mining, Int. Data Mining Soc., Paris, France, 310-316, 2021.
[BCR18]	Bogarın, A.; Cerezo, R.; Romero, C.: A survey on educational process mining. Wiley Interdisciplinary Reviews: Data Mining and Knowledge Discovery 8/1, 2018.
[BSW23]	Baucks, F.; Schmucker, R.; Wiskott, L.: Tracing Changes in University Course Difficulty Using Item Response Theory. AI4EDU Workshop at AAAI 2023.
[Gr16]	Greer, J.; Molinaro, M.; Ochoa, X.; McKay, T.: Learning analytics for curriculum and program quality improvement (PCLA 2016). In Proc. (Dawson, S.; Drachsler, H.; Penstein Rosé, C.) of the 6th Int. Conf. on Learning Analytics & Knowledge. Assoc. for Computing Machinery, New York, NY, USA, 494-495, 2016.
[Gu21]	Gutenbrunner, T.; Leeds, D. D.; Ross, S.; Riad-Zaky, M.; Weiss, G. M.: Measuring the academic impact of course sequencing using student grade data. In Proc. (Hsiao, I.; Sahebi, S.; Bouchet, F.; Vie, J.) of the 14th Int. Conf. of Educational Data Mining, Int. Data Mining Society, Paris, France, 799-803, 2021.
[Hi22]	Hilliger, I.; Aguirre, C.; Miranda, C.; Celis, S.; Pérez-Sanagustın, M.: Lessons learned from designing a curriculum analytics tool for improving student learning and program quality. Journal of computing in higher education, 633–657, 2022.
[HR20]	Hernán, M. A.; Robins, J. M.: Causal Inference: What If, Chapman & Hall, 2020.
[HSS19]	Hansen, J.; Sadler, P.; Sonnert, G.: Estimating high school GPA weighting parameters with a graded response model. Educational Measurement: Issues and Practice 38/1, 16–24, 2019.
[Jo97]	Johnson, V. E.: An alternative to traditional GPA for evaluating student performance. Statistical Science 12/4, 251–278, 1997.
[KRB21]	Koren, Y.; Rendle, S.; Bell, R.: Advances in collaborative filtering. Recommender systems handbook, 2021.
[MOC14]	Méndez, G.; Ochoa, X.; Chiluiza, K.: Techniques for data-driven curriculum analysis. In Proc. (Pardo, A.; Teasley, S.) of the 4th Int. Conf. on Learning Analytics and Knowledge, Association for Computing Machinery, 148-157, 2014.
[Oc16]	Ochoa, X.: Simple metrics for curricular analytics. In: CEUR Work. Proc., Bd. 1590, CEUR-WS, 20–26, 2016.
[PBY23]	Pardos, Z.; Borchers, C.; and Yu, R.: "Credit hours is not enough: Explaining undergraduate perceptions of course workload using LMS records." The Internet and Higher Education 56 (2023): 100882.
[Ra21]	Raji, M.; Duggan, J.; DeCotes, B.; Huang, J.; Zanden, B. V.: Modeling and Visualizing Student Flow. IEEE Transactions on Big Data 7/3, 510–523, 2021.
[RRS10]	Ricci, F.; Rokach, L.; Shapira, B.: Introduction to recommender systems handbook. In: Recommender systems handbook. Springer, 1–35, 2010.
[WGD22]	Weidlich, J.; Gašević, D.; Drachsler, H.: Causal Inference and Bias in Learning Analytics: A Primer on Pitfalls Using Directed Acyclic Graphs. Journal of Learning Analytics 9/3, 183–199, 2022.

Depreciating the online experience: Relative evaluation of social presence in online, hybrid, and offline course environments

Philipp Matter[1], Ninja Leikert-Boehm[1] and Peter Heinrich[1]

Abstract: COVID-19 accelerated the shift to online and hybrid instruction. While the literature shows that online courses can often perform as well as in-person classes, it is difficult to establish social presence, an important predictor of learning outcomes, at a distance. In this paper, we present exploratory observations of online, hybrid, and in-person environments of three courses at a Swiss university from 2021 to 2022. We were interested in our students' perceptions of social presence in and between courses. The results show significant differences in course ratings and suggest carry-over effects between different course modalities, such that students who attend a course in person systematically rate online courses lower than students who attend only online. These effects disappear when courses are delivered exclusively in person.

Keywords: Social presence, teaching modalities, online teaching, hybrid teaching, in-person teaching

1 Introduction

With the onset of the COVID-19 pandemic, classroom activities around the world quickly shifted to online settings. While this allowed instruction to continue, it radically changed the social environment of the classroom to a dispersed crowd of individuals rather than a collective learning community of students.

Research has shown that, in most cases, online instruction should perform as well as face-to-face (in-person) instruction, especially in terms of learning outcomes [e.g., DS21a, MM21]. Recently, Daigle and Stuvland [DS21b] compared learning outcomes between face-to-face and hybrid courses. They found that modality was not a significant predictor of learning performance. However, consistent with other research [Ho13], learning performance was significantly predicted by social presence. Since the characteristics of the learning environment ("sociability") can influence social presence [Kr07], modality may indirectly influence learning outcomes.

Thus, to equalize outcomes, addressing the potential gap between modalities is important. To investigate this gap, we launched an exploratory observational study to compare three

---

[1] Zurich University of Applied Sciences, School of Management and Law, Theaterstrasse 17, 8401 Winterthur, {philipp.matter, ninjairina.leikert-boehm, peter.heinrich}@zhaw.ch, https://orcid.org/0000-0002-8815-0198

courses in our master's degree program in Information Systems. During the pandemic, we were particularly interested in the differences between online and hybrid modalities, which allowed for in-person instruction despite contact restrictions, as some of the participants were able to attend online. Our school introduced this option in the fall semester of 2021/22. In the fall semester of 2022/23, all courses were again taught exclusively in person, so we could compare the evaluations of online and hybrid courses with their "offline" (i.e., in-person) counterparts.

Accordingly, the guiding research question of our study was as follows: *How do ratings of social presence of online or hybrid courses differ from those of in-person classes?*

Our findings suggest that perceptions of social presence may not only vary across course modality but may also be influenced by differences in modality, such that future course design should also consider the learning environments of other courses in the semester program.

2 Related work

Since the initial conception of the theory of social presence by Short et al. [SWC76, p. 65] as the "degree of salience of the other person in the interaction and the consequent salience of the interpersonal relationship", it has been extensively applied in the field of computer-mediated communication (CMC) with different definitions and conceptualizations [KXW22, Re03a]. More specifically, it has been characterized as "the degree to which a person is perceived as a 'real person' in mediated communication" [Gu95, p. 151] or the "sense of being with another" [BHB03, p. 456].

The concept of social presence is closely related to connectedness [Re03a], which is a fundamental factor of human motivation [BL95] and confers mental and physical health benefits [HSG08]. Furthermore, research suggests that feeling "connected with" (connectedness) or "being with" others (social presence) is more important for building empathy than "being there" (spatial presence) [Pi21].

Social presence has been studied extensively in the context of online learning. It has been shown that there are many strategies for creating social presence in online environments, such as participation and interaction, course design, delivery, feedback, and management by the instructor [Ar03, WB19, LD18]. Social presence has been found to be a strong predictor of student satisfaction [Bu12, Co09, GZ97] and perceived learning [RS03].

Positive effects have also been found for actual learning outcomes; Hostetter [Ho13] noticed a significant relationship between high social presence and higher performance ratings, and Daigle and Stuvland [DS21a] found that social presence was a significant predictor of knowledge gains. The latter also suggest that by increasing perceived social presence, the performance of students attending online can be matched to that of students attending in person. Daigle and Stuvland [DS21b] compared learning outcomes between face-to-face and distance-hybrid courses. While they found no evidence that modality predicted student performance, the perception of social presence was a significant predictor of academic performance. However, the positive relationship between social presence and learning outcomes is not undisputed [WB19].

The findings of Daigle and Stuvland [DS21b] also suggest that students are more satisfied in courses where they perceive a stronger sense of community. This is also reflected in Garrison et al.'s "community of inquiry" [GAA99]. In addition to social presence, it suggests two elements that are essential to the educational experience: cognitive and teaching presence.

Cognitive presence refers to a sequence of practical inquiry from a triggering event (leading to a state of dissonance or discomfort) to the exploration of information, its integration into an idea or concept, and the resolution of the problem [GAA99, pp. 98-99]. It was operationalized by Law et al. [LGL19] as the suitability of the learning environment to enable efficient knowledge acquisition, exploration of information with different means of learning (e.g., videos, discussions), linking of information learned from the course, and reflection and integration of ideas into solutions. Kang et al. [KKP08] found that cognitive presence predicted academic achievement, and Shea and Bidjerano [SB09] found that 70 percent of the variation in cognitive presence could be modeled based on the teacher's ability to facilitate teaching and social presence.

Teaching presence includes instructional management (e.g., curriculum), the building of understanding (i.e., productive and valid knowledge acquisition), and direct instruction (e.g., facilitating reflection and discourse with constructive feedback) [GAA99, pp. 101-102]. It was operationalized as participants' perceptions of clarity of guidelines, distribution of moderate tasks, degree of innovation in course structure, tools or technologies used to facilitate learning and interaction, and as satisfaction with information delivery channels [LGL19]. Kim et al. found that instructor teaching quality was a strong predictor of both social presence and learning satisfaction [KKC11].

Kreijns et al. investigated the role of computer-supported learning environments for social presence [Kr07]. They found that such environments can vary widely in their sociability, i.e., their ability to facilitate sound social spaces that are "characterized by affective work relationships, strong group cohesiveness, trust, respect and belonging, satisfaction, and a strong sense of community" [Kr07, p. 179]. Thus, they hypothesize that sociability affects social presence and social interaction: higher sociability leads to more social interaction, which in turn leads to sound social spaces. Such relationships are supported by several studies [Gö20, WB17].

Finally, and importantly, social presence is mostly hypothesized to lead to more positive social outcomes, which may not always be true [OBW18, p. 25]: individuals who are less socially oriented or who feel uncomfortable during social interactions may benefit less from increased social presence.

3 Study design and procedure

We explored our research question with three courses in our master's program in Information Systems in the fall semesters of 2021/22 (*Semester S1*) and 2022/23 (*Semester S2*).[2]

The courses were selected according to their modality: in general, in *S1*, the courses were offered online. We selected IT Security (*ITS*) because it was offered as a hybrid course, and two online courses (Enterprise Architecture *EPA*, Project and Change Management *PCM*) to be able to detect possible effects within the same modality. In *S2*, all courses were delivered only in person (i.e., on-site). All course features were the same in both semesters, with one exception: for organizational reasons, in *S2* EPA and PCM offered 7 double units instead of 14 single units (with no changes in other aspects). All courses in both semesters were rewarded with three credit points (ECTS). The course characteristics are summarized in Tab. 1.

Students were surveyed at the end of each semester using an online questionnaire distributed through the central learning management system. All students were invited to participate in the survey, resulting in a total of 97 (*S1*) and 59 (*S2*) participants. 30 students from *S1* completed the survey in full (30.93% response rate), and 17 students from *S2* (28.81% response rate).

The online questionnaire consisted of a general section to collect participant information (class affiliation, academic background, employment status). In addition, specific questions were asked per course (i.e., three times in total; one block of questions per course to avoid relative evaluations), including the number of course units attended and the use of video cameras during online classes.[3]

Reflecting the exploratory nature of our study and its aim to learn about students' perceptions in different course environments, the main questions were based on notions of social presence and related or influencing variables:

- We used the 18 items of the community of inquiry scale of Law et al. [LGL19] to measure the perceived *social presence, cognitive presence,* and *teaching presence* as well as students' subjective *performance*.
- To assess the perception of the different learning environments that affect social presence, we used the *sociability* scale of Kreijns et al. [Kr07], with 10 items.

The items of each scale variable were rated on 5-point Likert scales (1 = do not agree at all; 5 = fully agree). The results for each scale variable were aggregated as the average of the individual responses. We conducted the following analyses and tests.

---

[2] At our business school, students are divided into classes of about 50 people. As a result, the three courses were attended and evaluated by two classes per semester.
[3] Results on camera use (*Semester 1* only) are presented in [LMH23].

	Enterprise Architecture (EPA)	**IT Security (ITS)**	**Project and Change Management (PCM)**
Syllabus	Modeling of enterprise architectures	Technical foundations of IT security	Leadership, change, and multi-project management
Teaching concept	Flipped classroom	Synchronous lectures and exercises	Synchronous lectures and exercises
Teaching modality	*S1*: Online (MS Teams), *S2*: in-person	S1: Hybrid (online via Cisco Webex or in person), in-person (*S2*)	Online (*S1*, Zoom), in-person (*S2*)
Attendance	Voluntary, 14 units *(S1)*, 7 double units *(S2)*	Voluntary, 14 units	Voluntary, 14 units *(S1)*, 7 double units *(S2)*
Grading	Written final exam	Written final exam	Group assignments and online test
Recording	All units were video recorded (*S1* only)	All units were video recorded (*S1* only)	Units were not recorded

Tab. 1: Course characteristics

For *S1*, we divided the online questionnaire participants (n = 30) into an online group and an in-person group based on their modality of participation in *ITS*. Thus, the online group included all participants that attended *ITS* as well as *EPA* and *PCM* online (n = 12). The in-person group included all participants who attended *ITS* in person and the other courses online (n = 18). We tested the normality of our dependent variables using Shapiro-Wilk tests. All variables were normally distributed, except for *PCM sociability* in the online group ($W(12) = 0.844$, $p = 0.031$) as well as *EPA performance* ($W(18) = 0.858$, $p = 0.012$) and *ITS performance* ($W(18) = 0.895$, $p = 0.048$) in the in-person group.

To test for differences in course ratings *between* the groups, we used independent t-tests (two-sided) for the normally distributed variables and Mann-Whitney U tests (two-sided) for their non-normally distributed counterparts. Differences in ratings *within* groups were tested using ANOVAs with repeated measures for all normally distributed variables, and Friedman tests for non-normally distributed variables. For pairwise comparisons of non-normally distributed variables for significant group differences (according to Friedman tests), we first checked the symmetry of variable differences between courses using boxplots. Variables with symmetric differences were further analyzed using Wilcoxon signed-rank tests, and sign tests were used for all other variables.

For *S2*, we also tested the normality of our dependent variables using Shapiro-Wilk tests. Except for *PCM teaching presence* ($W(17) = 0.884$, $p = 0.037$), all dependent variables were normally distributed. Differences in ratings between the courses were tested using ANOVAs with repeated measures for all normally distributed variables, and a Friedman test for *teaching presence*.

All statistical analyses were conducted using SPSS version 28. Due to the exploratory nature of our study, we analyzed all data without multiplicity adjustments [BL01, p. 344]. All significant results should therefore be regarded as preliminary, i.e., the corresponding hypotheses need to be tested in further confirmatory studies.

Finally, some remarks about test power are warranted. Our study was observational rather than experimental, i.e., we could not control for many aspects of the courses, particularly enrollment and class size. Cohen [Co77] suggests aiming for a test power of 0.8, i.e., an 80% chance of achieving statistical significance. A sensitivity analysis[4] of our study using G*Power version 3.1.9.7 [Fa09], following Lakens [La22, pp. 14-15], shows that our study had 80% power to detect large effects. In *Semester 1*, the study was able to detect effect sizes of at least $d = 1.08$ and $d = 1.11$ for the independent t-tests and Mann-Whitney U tests, respectively. For our ANOVA tests of the online group and the in-person group, the smallest detectable effect sizes were $f = 0.47$ and $f = 0.37$, respectively. In *Semester 2*, our ANOVA test could detect effects of at least $f = 0.44$.

Consequently, all observed effect sizes (see results) were smaller than the smallest detectable effect sizes in our study. However, our statistical tests indicated statistically significant results with medium to large effect sizes. We argue that these are of considerable practical value, even in an exploratory setting. For *Semester 2*, we found no statistically significant differences for any measure, with observed effect sizes below the smallest detectable effect sizes. We acknowledge that it is possible that there were smaller effects in Semester 2 (as opposed to the large effects seen in Semester 1) that our study was unable to detect.

4   Results

4.1   Differences between online and hybrid courses (*first semester, S1*)

Almost half of the participants came from class A (n = 13) and half from class B (n = 17). Exactly half of the respondents reported a technical background and the other half reported none. The majority of participants reported working part-time (80%); few worked full-time (13.33%), and two participants did not provide any information.

Most of the participants attended classes regularly, except for *PCM_online*[5]. Unlike the other two courses, which had end-of-semester exams, *PCM_online* exams were administered during the semester, so students often attended only the classes that were relevant to them.

For our research question, we analyzed whether the course ratings of participants who

---

[4] The authors would like to thank an anonymous reviewer for suggesting that sensitivity analysis is preferable to post hoc power analysis.
[5] For the sake of clarity, we will indicate the modality of the course in addition to the abbreviation for *S1*.

attended mainly online differed from those of participants who attended mainly in person (based on their attendance in the *ITS_hybrid* course). The analysis was conducted from two perspectives:

(a) Differences between groups: We found no significant differences between the online and in-person groups, with two notable exceptions. First, the mean ratings for *sociability* were statistically significantly higher for *ITS_hybrid* in the in-person group than in the online group, with a large effect size ($t(28) = -3.291, p = 0.003, d = 0.84$), i.e., participants who attended *ITS_hybrid* primarily in person perceived higher sociability than participants who attended the same course online (Fig. 1 and Fig. 2).

Second, although the mean ratings for *cognitive presence* were higher for all courses in the online group than in the in-person group, only for *EPA_online* were these differences statistically significant with a medium effect size ($t(28) = 2.408, p = 0.023, d = 0.61$), meaning that participants who attended all courses online perceived higher cognitive presence in *EPA_online* than those who attended *ITS_hybrid* in person.

For *social presence*, we could not find any statistically significant differences between the two groups (Fig. 3 and Fig. 4).

(b) Differences within groups: Regarding our within-group analyses, we found significant differences for the in-person group but none for the online group, i.e., the participants who attended *ITS_hybrid* in person rated their experiences differently for each of the three courses, while online participants showed no significant differences.

For the in-person group, we found statistically significant differences in reported *sociability* ($\chi^2(2) = 23.444, p < 0.001$) (see Fig. 2). Post hoc analysis using Wilcoxon signed-rank tests revealed that sociability ratings were significantly higher for *ITS_hybrid* than for *EPA_online* with a large effect size ($Z = -3.727, p < 0.001, r = -0.88$) and also higher for *PCM_online* than for *EPA_online* with a large effect size ($Z = -3.078, p = 0.002, r = -0.73$). An exact sign test revealed that sociability ratings were significantly higher for *ITS_hybrid* than for *PCM_online* with a large effect size ($p = 0.008, r = 0.67$).

We also found differences in reported *social presence* for the in-person group (see Fig. 4). Using an ANOVA with repeated measures with a Greenhouse-Geisser correction, the mean scores for social presence in the in-person group were statistically significantly different ($F(1.715, 29.150) = 8.535, p = 0.002$) with a large effect size ($\eta^2_p = 0.334$). Post hoc analysis revealed that social presence was statistically significantly higher for *ITS_hybrid* compared to *EPA_online* (0.722 (95% CI, 0.39 to 1.05), $p < 0.001$) and for *ITS_hybrid* compared to *PCM_online* (0.478 (95% CI, 0.03 to 0.92), $p = 0.037$).

A statistically significant difference was also found for the reported *performance* of the in-person group ($\chi^2(2) = 13.875, p < 0.001$). Post hoc analysis using a Wilcoxon signed-rank test showed that ratings were significantly higher for *ITS_hybrid* than for *EPA_online* with a large effect size ($Z = -2.986, p = 0.003, r = -0.70$). An exact sign test revealed that performance ratings were also significantly higher for *ITS_hybrid* than for *PCM_online* with a large effect size ($p = 0.006$, $r = 0.56$). Due to the anonymity of the survey, we were not able to relate these self-assessments directly to course grades. Therefore, we cannot make any assertions about possible differences in objective performance.

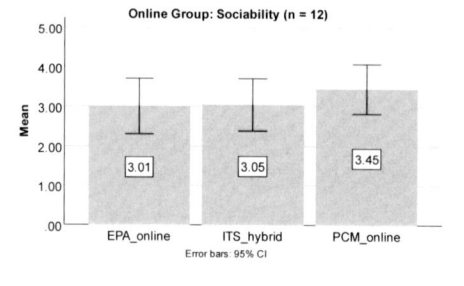

Fig. 1: Evaluation of sociability (online group)

Fig. 2: Evaluation of sociability (in-person group)

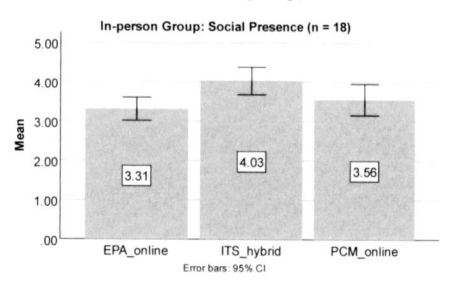

Fig. 3: Evaluation of social presence (online group)

Fig. 4: Evaluation of social presence (in-person group)

4.2 Differences between in-person courses (*second semester, S2*)

Almost half of the participants came from class A (n = 8) and half from class B (n = 9). The majority of the respondents reported having a technical background (76.5%) and working part-time (94.1%). Most of the participants attended classes regularly, except for PCM as in the first semester (*S1*).

Regarding our main dependent variables, we found no effects between the three in-person courses. The ANOVAs with repeated measures revealed no statistically significant differences for *sociability* ($F(1.366, 21.855) = 2.597$, $p = 0.112$; with Greenhouse-Geisser correction; $\eta^2_p = 0.140$), *social presence* ($F(1.411, 22.578) = 1.630$, $p = 0.219$; with Greenhouse-Geisser correction; $\eta^2_p = 0.092$), *cognitive presence* ($F(2, 32) = 0.049$, $p = 0.925$; $\eta^2_p = 0.003$) and *performance* ($F(2, 32) = 0.559$, $p = 0.572$; $\eta^2_p = 0.034$). The Friedman test for *teaching presence* also showed no statistically significant differences between the courses ($\chi^2(2) = 2.935$, $p = 0.23$, Kendall's $W = 0.086$).

5 Discussion

We found significant differences in our students' subjective course ratings in the first semester depending on whether they participated in the courses only online (online group) or in a mix of online and in-person (in-person group). These differences in ratings, however, disappeared when all courses were delivered in person in the second semester.

If there were systematically large differences between the better-rated course in the first semester (*ITS*) compared to the other courses (*EPA* and *PCM*), we should have detected these differences in the second semester as well. Since all relevant factors except the modality of the courses did not change, we suggest that the modality caused or moderated these differences.

In the first semester, ratings for the sociability of the *ITS_hybrid* course were significantly higher for in-person and online participants, and by a considerable margin. Sociability is defined as the extent to which students perceive the environment as conducive to sound social spaces [Kr07]; the in-person group rated this environment much more favorably for *ITS_hybrid* than for the other courses. Personal contact and interaction seem to play an important role here – this is also reflected within the group regarding the evaluation of the social presence, i.e., the participant's perceived ability to relate to and interact with their classmates [LGL19]. This aspect of interaction could also explain the significantly higher sociability of *PCM_online* compared to *EPA_online*: in the former, students had more opportunities to work together in groups than in the latter.

Such differences were also observed between the groups. Students of the in-person group rated the sociability of *ITS_hybrid* higher than online participants and rated the other courses lower, although the differences were not statistically significant. These results were similar for social presence.

We suspect that there may have been a (negative) carry-over effect between courses, such that the more "social" experience of in-person attendance was established as a benchmark for the online courses, which were therefore systematically depreciated. Of course, ratings of social presence were also quite positive for the online-only courses; however, possible influences between different modalities should be considered when designing blended model curricula.

Sociability is also considered influential for social interaction, which in turn is a dominant factor influencing learning performance [Kr07]. Indeed, the evaluation shows that students who attended *ITS_hybrid* in person rated their performance in this course much higher than in their other (online) courses.

Next, we would like to draw attention to those aspects that were *not* rated differently in the two semesters. Surprisingly, we generally found no significant differences in the ratings of cognitive presence (with one exception) and teaching presence. Cognitive presence refers to a student's ability to construct meaning, e.g., through discussion and reflection, and has been found to correlate strongly with social presence and teaching presence [SB09]. We found that cognitive presence was rated only slightly higher for all courses in the online group than in the in-person group (statistically significant only for *EPA_online*). In general, this could be related to a better match of social and learning preferences for the online group: in the online-only courses, less socially oriented individuals who preferred online to in-person interaction [OBW18, p. 25] or who generally sought less connectedness [Re03b] may have found a more appropriate setting for their learning, while the in-person group was constrained to participate online. This could also explain why the ratings for *ITS_hybrid* were very similar for both groups: each group was able to choose according to their preferences. Finally, the significant difference in *EPA_online* may also have been due to the flipped classroom design, which emphasized individual, self-directed work.

Teaching presence refers to the overall course design (content, learning activities, interaction) and facilitation by the lecturer; it is a strong predictor of perceived learning and student satisfaction [LGL19]. We found no differences in the ratings of this aspect, either within or between the groups. Given the differences in the content and structure of the courses and the fact that they were taught by different lecturers, we found this rather surprising. This was particularly true for *ITS*, which was focused primarily on in-person participation with an additional online option; again, we found no differences in the ratings. Overall, we suspect that cognitive presence and teaching presence depend more subtly or indirectly on social presence and the course setting (i.e., online or in-person).

6   Conclusion

The demand for flexible course modalities has increased in recent years and has been further accelerated by COVID-19. In our study, we examined how course modality affected participants' perceived social presence, which research has shown to be a strong predictor of learning outcomes.

While we found no differences in course ratings when all courses were delivered in person, we found significant differences for different modalities (online and hybrid). Students rated sociability and social presence differently depending on whether they had taken courses primarily online or one of the courses in person, such that the online experience was significantly depreciated. Such possible carry-over effects between modalities are particularly important to consider in mixed-modality curricula, which we expect to become increasingly important in the future.

Bibliography

[Ar03]   Aragon, S.: Creating social presence in online environments. In: New Directions for Adult and Continuing Education 100, pp. 57–68, 2003.

[BL95]   Baumeister, R.; Leary, M.: The need to belong: Desire for interpersonal attachments as a fundamental human motivation. In: Psychological Bulletin 117(3), pp. 497–529, 1995.

[BL01] Bender, R.; Lange, S.: Adjusting for multiple testing - when and how? In: Journal of Clinical Epidemiology 54(4), pp. 343–349, 2001.

[BHB03] Biocca, F.; Harms, C.; Burgoon, J.: Toward a More Robust Theory and Measure of Social Presence: Review and Suggested Criteria. In: Presence: Teleoperators and Virtual Environments 12(5), pp. 456–480, 2003.

[Bu12] Bulu, S.: Place presence, social presence, co-presence, and satisfaction in virtual worlds. In: Computers & Education 58(1), pp. 154–161, 2012.

[Co09] Cobb, S.: Social Presence and Online Learning: A Current View from a Research Perspective. In: Journal of Interactive Online Learning 8(3), pp. 241-254, 2009.

[Co77] Cohen, J.: Statistical Power Analysis for the Behavioral Sciences. New York : Academic Press, 1977.

[DS21a] Daigle, D.; Stuvland, A.: Social Presence as Best Practice: The Online Classroom Needs to Feel Real. In: PS: Political Science & Politics 54(1), pp. 182–183, 2021.

[DS21b] Daigle, D.; Stuvland, A.: Teaching Political Science Research Methods Across Delivery Modalities: Comparing Outcomes Between Face-to-Face and Distance-Hybrid Courses. In: Journal of Political Science Education 17(S1), pp. 380–402, 2021.

[Fa09] Faul, F. et al.: Statistical power analyses using G*Power 3.1: Tests for correlation and regression analyses. In: Behavior Research Methods 41(4), pp. 1149–1160, 2009.

[GAA99] Garrison, D.; Anderson, T.; Archer, W.: Critical Inquiry in a Text-Based Environment: Computer Conferencing in Higher Education. In: The Internet and Higher Education 2(2-3), pp. 87–105, 1999.

[Gö20] Göksün, D. O.: Predictors of Perceived Learning in a Distance Learning Environment from the Perspective of SIPS Model. In: International Journal of Human–Computer Interaction, 36(10), pp. 941–952, 2020.

[Gu95] Gunawardena, C.: Social Presence Theory and Implications for Interaction and Collaborative Learning in Computer Conferences. In: International Journal of Educational Telecommunications 1(2-3), pp. 147–166, 1995.

[GZ97] Gunawardena, C.; Zittle, F.: Social presence as a predictor of satisfaction within a computer-mediated conferencing environment. In: American Journal of Distance Education 11(3), pp. 8–26, 1997.

[Ho13] Hostetter, C.: Community matters: Social presence and learning outcomes. In: Journal of the Scholarship of Teaching and Learning 13(1), pp. 77-86, 2013.

[HSG08] Hutcherson, C.; Seppala, E.; Gross, J.: Loving-kindness meditation increases social connectedness. In: Emotion 8(5), pp. 720–724, 2008.

[KKP08] Kang, M.; Kim, J.; Park, M.: Investigating Presence as a Predictor of Learning Outcomes in E-learning Environment. In: Proceedings of ED-MEDIA 2008, Vienna, pp. 4175-4180, 2008.

[KKC11] Kim, J.; Kwon, Y.; Cho, D.: Investigating factors that influence social presence and learning outcomes in distance higher education. In: Computers & Education 57(2), pp. 1512–1520, 2011.

[Kr07]	Kreijns, K. et al.: Measuring perceived sociability of computer-supported collaborative learning environments. In: Computers & Education 49(2), pp. 176–192, 2007.
[KXW22]	Kreijns, K.; Xu, K.; Weidlich, J.: Social Presence: Conceptualization and Measurement. In: Educational Psychology Review 34, pp. 139–170, 2022.
[La22]	Lakens, D.: Sample Size Justification. In: Collabra: Psychology, 8(1), 33267, 2022.
[LD18]	Lowenthal, P. R.; Dunlap, J. C.: Investigating students' perceptions of instructional strategies to establish social presence. In: Distance Education, 39(3), 281–298, 2018.
[LGL19]	Law, K.; Geng, S.; Li, T.: Student enrollment, motivation and learning performance in a blended learning environment: The mediating effects of social, teaching, and cognitive presence. In: Computers & Education 136, pp. 1–12, 2019.
[LMH23]	Leikert-Boehm, N.; Matter, P.; Heinrich, P.: Now you (don't) see me – Camera use in online Course Settings. In: DELFI 2023, 21. Fachtagung Bildungstechnologien der Gesellschaft für Informatik e.V. Aachen, Germany, 2023.
[MM21]	Müller, C.; Mildenberger, T.: Facilitating flexible learning by replacing classroom time with an online learning environment: A systematic review of blended learning in higher education. In: Educational Research Review 34, 100394, 2021.
[OBW18]	Oh, C.; Bailenson, J.; Welch, G.: A Systematic Review of Social Presence: Definition, Antecedents, and Implications. In: Frontiers in Robotics and AI 5, 2018.
[Pi21]	Pimentel, D. et al.: Voices of the unsung: The role of social presence and interactivity in building empathy in 360 video. In: New Media & Society 23(8), pp. 2230–2254, 2021.
[Re03a]	Rettie, R.: Connectedness, Awareness and Social Presence. 2003. http://eprints.kingston.ac.uk/2106/1/Rettie.pdf
[Re03b]	Rettie, R.: A Comparison of Four New Communication Technologies. In: Proceedings of HCI International Conference on Human-Computer Interaction. Crete, Greece, 2003.
[RS03]	Richardson, J.; Swan, K.: Examining social presence in online courses in relation to students' perceived learning and satisfaction. In: Online Learning 7(1), pp. 68–88, 2003.
[SB09]	Shea, P.; Bidjerano, T.: Community of inquiry as a theoretical framework to foster "epistemic engagement" and "cognitive presence" in online education. In: Computers & Education 52(3), pp. 543–553, 2009.
[SWC76]	Short, J.; Williams, E.; Christie, B.: The social psychology of telecommunications. Wiley, Toronto, London, New York, 1976.
[WB17]	Weidlich, J.; Bastiaens, T. J.: Explaining social presence and the quality of online learning with the SIPS model. Computers in Human Behavior, 72, pp. 479–487, 2017.
[WB19]	Weidlich, J.; Bastiaens, T. J.: Designing sociable online learning environments and enhancing social presence: An affordance enrichment approach. In: Computers & Education 142, 103622, 2019.

Auto-generated language learning online courses using generative AI models like ChatGPT

Sylvio Rüdian [1] and Niels Pinkwart [2]

Abstract: Generating online courses is always a trade-off between possibilities, technical limitations, and quality. State-of-the-art generative models can assist teachers in the creation process. However, generating learning materials is highly complex. Hence, teachers mainly create them manually. In this paper, learning content for a concrete micro-learning template is generated focusing on the field of language teaching. It intends that learners can find correct responses by logical thinking. Teachers provide a topic as input. Then, the approach asks for the required information using GPT3.5 with instructional prompts and combines responses to form a language learning unit. The quality of the resulting learning content, focusing on correctness, and appropriateness, is evaluated and discussed to examine the practicability of the tool, and alternatives are given.

Keywords: Language learning, generative AI models, auto-generated course units.

1 Introduction

Language learning apps to learn foreign languages become popular within the last decades. Course suppliers operate worldwide to teach languages. Duolingo, Rosetta Stone, Babbel, Busuu, or Lingoda are just a few examples of well-known brands. The main success of such brands teaching languages is sourced in the scalability to create course materials and the desire to learn languages by a large target group. In language teaching, learning content is highly structured. It consists of vocabulary, translations, grammar, dialogs, and more. The core competencies are pre-defined as language proficiency levels [Co21]. For each level, certain skills are defined, including vocabulary sets. Based on that source, language learning courses can be designed by teachers.

Recently, generative AI models become prominent. Models like GPT3.5, better known as ChatGPT [Ko23], allow teachers to generate texts, word lists with semantic relations, or even tasks. From the first view, such generative models are a great base to create rich teaching content. At the current state, those outputs are text-only, but responses of such models can be used to create texts as a base for learning materials. Further, technologies to create online courses become highly flexible. Exemplarily, H5P allows teachers to

---

[1] Humboldt-Universität zu Berlin, Department of Computer Science, Berlin, Germany, ruediasy@informatik.hu-berlin.de, https://orcid.org/0000-0003-3943-4682
[2] German Research Center for Artificial Intelligence (DFKI), Educational Technology Lab, Berlin, Germany, niels.pinkwart@dfki.de, https://orcid.org/0000-0001-7076-9537

doi: 10.18420/delfi2023-14

create tasks without the need to code tools. Due to the integration into learning management systems, such tasks can easily be integrated into courses [Pe16]. A course generator, as introduced by Rüdian et al. [RP21], allows teachers to fill H5P items with content, but the approach requires coding skills to apply. In combination, the existing technology allows generating course materials covering reading, and writing skills.

Text-to-speech approaches allow the generation of speeches with high quality, in any language where trained models exist [Ren20]. Any text can be read out. Generated audio files allow the creation of listening tasks. Tasks that are used to enhance speaking skills can be created using pre-defined models like the H5P dictating tool [HH19]. Alternatively, speech-to-text approaches can be used to identify what learners have spoken and compare that with existing patterns to identify possible divergences [Zh20].

Altogether, many experimental solutions allow teachers to create language learning courses for any topic. However, there is still no solution that generates the baseline: vocabulary, and texts, based on a given topic. This paper aims to bridge that gap by focusing on the research question, of whether an auto-generated language learning course unit using GPT3.5 creates correct and appropriate vocabulary, sentences, and texts to form learning material. The examination in this paper focuses on:

1. Identifying vocabulary sets,
2. Combining vocabulary,
3. Generating sentences, and
4. Generating texts.

Being able to generate language learning online courses is of high interest due to different reasons. First, creating learning units requires expertise for the considered domain. Second, creating a variety of units depends on the creativity of the creator. Third, learners have different learning goals, and fourth, they differ in pre-knowledge. Hence, courses should be personalized to suit learner needs. Personalized course sequencing aims to "dynamically select the most appropriate resource at any moment, based on the current needs and goals of the learner" [Ul07]. Item sequences can be arranged in different ways to fit learner needs. Normally, courses are created while tutors have some assumptions, e. g. about learners' pre-knowledge, on that basis a course progression is designed. This pre-defined course sequence may not be optimum for all learners. One challenge is to design online courses in a way to be engaging and to hold an appropriate difficulty level. However, the one-size-fits-all solution is still often preferred as this is the solution with minimal effort. But if course sequences suit learner needs, they can be highly engaging [Co02]. Further, tutors' assumptions can be wrong, or learner needs change over time. Then, adjustments are required. Yu et al. highlight that "it may be advantageous to allow students more freedom to access the learning contents without strictly following the pre-defined sequence" [Yu17]. The basis to personalize item sequences is the existence of micro-learning units, containing fixed blocks of learning materials, which can be arranged differently due to their independence [Yu17]. If learning material, using state-of-the-art approaches can be generated, those contents are correct and useful, we have the basis to generate personalized language learning online courses.

2 Methodology

To examine, whether generated item sequences are useful, a pipeline is designed which allows teachers to provide textual input (like a topic), which is then processed to generate learning content. Therefore, appropriate prompts for the generative model GPT3.5 are explored that lead to the aimed outputs. Then, the resulting content is rearranged and combined to simulate suitable tasks of micro-learning units. In this paper, the idea of language immersion is used, intending that the learner is situated in a foreign-language environment. The learner learns the language through visual relationships, without the need for translations from one into another language. This is comparable to learning a language in childhood. In computer-based dynamic immersion language learning, typical daily-life situations are created, and learners must find connections between images and texts, or spoken voice. The supplier "Rosetta Stone" uses the approach in its application [Ro07].

Within an immersion-based course, a set of lexical categories L is used, like subjects S, or predicates P. More categories are existing, but for better readability, the paper focuses on those two. Subjects can be nouns, with $\{A, B, C, D\} \in S$, predicates can be verbs, with $\{a, b, c, d\} \in P$. For all items $x \in \{S, P\}$ of a task T, a set of corresponding images $I_{x1} \ldots I_{xn}$ with $n \in \mathbb{N}$ exists. Hence, for noun A, there is a set of related images $I_{A1} \ldots I_{An}$. Different combinations of $\{S, P\}$ are possible and they can be related to images as well. A micro-learning unit consists of a task's set following the conditions, 1) that in each task new vocabulary is taken from one lexical category only, which can be combined with another category if related words are not new, and 2) that for new words, there is a logical inference to find related images. Thus either new vocabulary for S, and/or P is introduced within single tasks. The introduction of new words is done by showing images with related words, or by single-choice tasks. The presentation of images with related ones is straightforward. Single-choice tasks follow the pattern, that a subset of words with related images is shown, e.g. $[A, I_{A1}]$ and $[B, I_{B1}]$. Then, X in $[X, I_{A2}]$ must be determined by selecting the correct answer, A or B. By definition, only $[A, I_{A2}]$ exists, thus $X = A$. In the following task, X in $[X, I_{B2}]$ must be determined, etc. More complex single-choice questions are possible. Exemplarily, A is presented by two images I_{A1}, I_{A2} first. Then, X in $[A, X]$ must be determined by selecting the correct image from $\{I_{A3}, I_{B2}, I_{C1}\}$, where I_{A3} is the correct answer for the word A. Next, B is presented by one image I_{B1}, and X in $[B, X]$ must be determined using the set $\{I_{A3}, I_{B2}, I_{C1}\}$. Here, I_{B2} is the only correct answer. Finally, C is represented by an image, and X in $[C, X]$ must be selected from the set $\{I_{A3}, I_{B2}, I_{C1}\}$. Due to the logical inference $X = I_{C1}$. If some words are known due to previous tasks, they can be used for more complex logical inferences. One example follows. Assuming nouns $\{A, B\}$ are already known and two verbs $\{a, b\}$ need to be introduced. Then, $[\{A, a\}, I_{Aa1}]$ and $[\{B, b\}, I_{Bb1}]$ are presented. X_1 in $[X_1, I_{Ab1}]$ and X_2 in $[X_2, I_{Ba1}]$ must be determined by selecting the correct answers from $\{\{A, b\}, \{B, a\}\}$. As the relation of an image to A or B is already known, hence $[A, I_{A1}]$ and $[B, I_{B1}]$ exist, the task can be solved without knowing the meaning of a and b, because for I_{A1}, only the answer that contains A can be the correct one, which is I_{Ab1} and vice versa.

For sure, highly complex combinations are possible. Based on the concept of immersion, templates can be defined, which have to be filled with learning content. For the concrete experiment, 8 nouns $\{A, B, C, D, E, F, G, H\} \in S$, and 4 verbs $\{a, b, c, d\} \in P$ are used for each micro-learning unit, assuming that related images $I_{x1} \ldots I_{xn}$ exist. The unit consists of 8 sub-tasks (Fig. 1). In tasks 1-4, $\{A, B, C, D\}$, and $\{a, b, c, d\}$ are introduced. Therefore, a subset of both sets is selected ($\{A, B, C\}$ and $\{a, b, c\}$), used to introduce the relations of words to images (like $\{A\}$ to $\{I_A\}$), which are presented to the learner (tasks (1), and (2)). Then, $\{D\}$ and $\{d\}$ can be found in tasks (3), and (4). Learners can identify them by logical thinking, as those are the new words, where only one new word and new image exist. To repeat a verb like $\{a\}$, it can be combined with all nouns in task (3), but it is not mandatory. Introducing $\{D\}$ only, is also sufficient (like in task (4)). In task (5), words are combined to form short sentences. Nouns' combinations are created. As all nouns are semantically related to verb $\{\alpha\}$, their combination is also related to $\{\alpha\}$. Further, verbs $\{b, c\}$ are combined with $\{b\} + \{AB\}$, and $\{c\} + \{CD\}$. Related images must be found by detecting combined nouns that are related to given verbs. In (6), four new nouns $\{E, F, G, H\}$ are introduced, while for $\{E, F, G\}$, images of $\{A, B, C, D\}$ are used as distractors, so that the learner must recognize previous images to detect new ones. $\{H\}$ can be found due to logical thinking similar to tasks (3), or (4), but limited to a noun. Tasks (7), and (8) contain a text/story consisting of 8 short sentences, which include a subset of $\{A, B, C, D, E, F, G, H\}$, $\{a, b, c, d\}$, and related images. The set of 8 tasks is used as the sequence model in the experiment. The challenge is to fill that template with content.

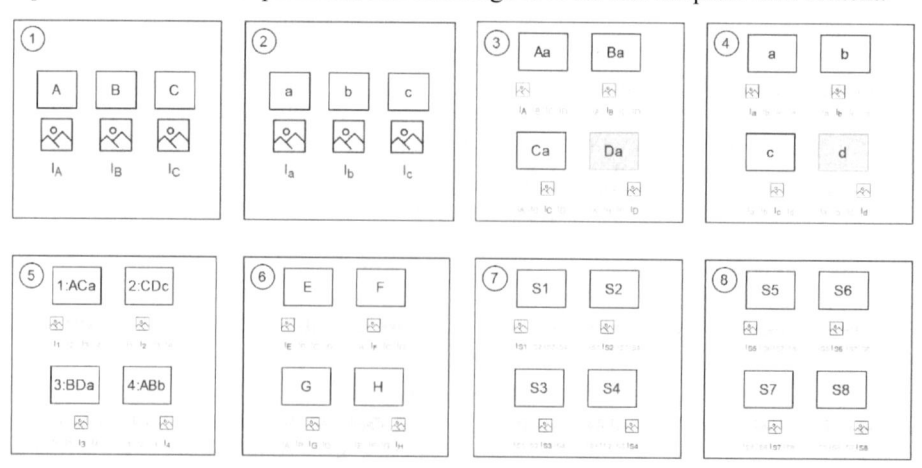

Fig. 1: Prepared template to generate 8 tasks based on language immersion

Micro-learning units are created based on this template. Contents are combined using rules as each task of the unit contains a fixed number of words, which must be identified, and combined. The approach allows generating tasks if required images exist. The order of images or answers within a task can be randomized. The investigation does not focus on personalization, which is not intended in this paper as the focus remains on generating texts for micro-learning units. Those units are then evaluated. As courses can be evaluated on different criteria, the most crucial: correctness and appropriateness are analyzed and evaluated by a teacher.

3 Architecture

Next, the architecture is described. The teacher or the learner provides a topic as input. Based on that, lists of related verbs, and nouns are asked for. Some of these nouns and verbs can be combined. Thus, a new list is generated by asking to merge both lists to create connections if there is a semantical relation. For the collected words, it must be determined whether all constraints are fulfilled so that the template can be filled with content. Therefore, the dataset is validated on the existence of words, with relations $\{A, B, C, D\}$ to $\{a\}$, $\{AB\}$ to $\{b\}$, and $\{CD\}$ to $\{c\}$. If that combination exists, the process continues. Otherwise, new word lists must be generated. Then, sentences are formulated based on combined word sets as defined in Fig. 1. Sentence lengths can be limited by word counts, and language level to avoid using words that might be unknown to the learner. Finally, a short text is generated based on the vocabulary used in the unit. To avoid a potential language mix, all prompts are formulated in German, intending to get responses in the same language. Principally, an instruction may contain the aimed target language, but trials have shown that this is not always the case. All used prompts are given in Tab. 1.

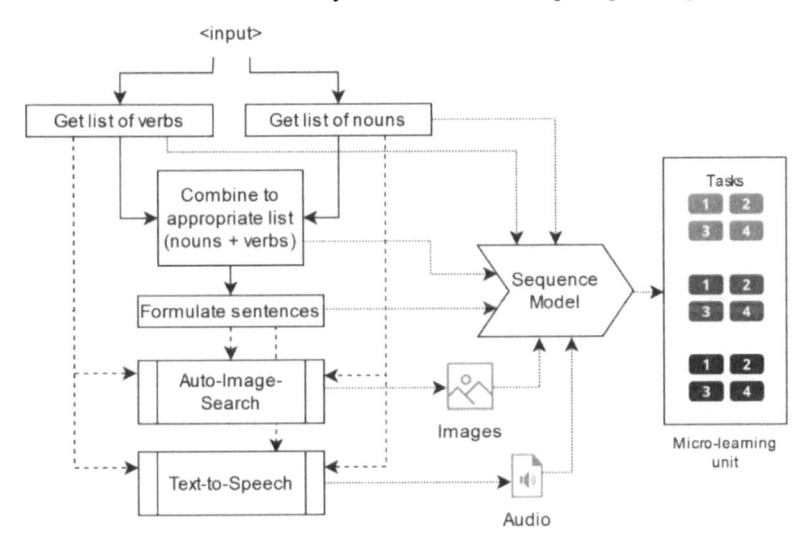

Fig. 2: Pipeline to auto-generate micro-learning units

For vocabulary (verbs, and nouns), and sentences, images can be generated using a generative model, which returns images based on textual inputs. All words, sentences, and files can be submitted to a sequence model, as visualized in Fig. 2. The same inputs can be used to derive sound files using a text-to-speech engine. As speech can already be generated easily with state-of-the-art tools, it is assumed that learning materials using appropriate textual contents are either appropriate combined with speech.

Types	Prompts
Nouns $\{A, B, C, D, E, F, G, H\}$	Erstelle eine Liste von 20 Substantiven zum Thema [#topic]. Sprachlevel A1. (*Make a list of 20 nouns related to the topic [#topic]. Language level A1.*)
Verbs $\{a, b, c, d\}$	Erstelle eine Liste von 20 Verben zum Thema [#topic]. Sprachlevel A1. (*Make a list of 20 verbs related to the topic [#topic]. Language level A1.*)
Relations $Nouns \Leftrightarrow Verbs$	Kombiniere Wörter [#nouns] mit [#verbs]. Die Liste soll nur das Substantiv und mindestens 4 Verben in einer Zeile enthalten. Verwende keine Nummern und keine Aufzählung. (*Combine words [#nouns] with [#verbs]. The list should contain only the noun and at least 4 verbs in one line. Do not use numbers or enumeration.*)
Sentence	Erstelle einen Satz, der die Wörter [#noun1,#noun2,#verb] enthält. Der Satz darf maximal 12 Wörter enthalten. Sprachlevel A1. (*Create a sentence that contains the words [#noun1,#noun2,#verb]. The sentence can contain a maximum of 12 words. Language level A1.*)
Text	Erstelle einen zusammenhängenden Text aus 10 Sätzen. Nutze folgende Wörter: [#words]. Jeder Satz darf maximal 7 Wörter enthalten. Sprachlevel A1. Jeder Satz in einer Zeile. Verwende keine Zahlen. (*Create a coherent text of 10 sentences. Use the following words: [#words]. Each sentence can contain a maximum of 7 words. Language level A1. Each sentence in one line. Do not use numbers.*)

Tab. 1: Prompts used to gather information

The approach generates a unit for a given topic. Then, the next topic must be provided. To automate that step, a "random surfer model" is used [CM08]. Hence, a random word is selected from $\{A, B, C, D, E, F, G, H\}$ of the current unit, which is used as topic to generate the next unit. The approach runs until 200 units are generated, which are then evaluated.

Principally, the evaluation of an online course (or its units) can cover a wide range of criteria, ranging from considering pre-knowledge [AMF03], quality of learning materials [XLZ20], to coherence [MJP15]. The evaluation in this study is limited to words, sentences, and texts, with a focus on the correctness, and appropriateness of the generated learning content using a generative GPT model (GPT-3.5-turbo). Appropriateness is an essential element when evaluating a course [AMF03]. For the study, words, sentences, or texts are appropriate, if they are coherent, with logical order, and sentence lengths as demanded that are suitable for a language level A1, without hallucinated contents [Ba23]. The latter is important to help learners to find the correct word meanings, and relations to contexts without confusing them. It must not be emphasized, that course material for language learners must be correct (at least spelling, and grammar in a language learning course) [XLZ20]. Incorrect learning materials are crucial as it is a knockout criterion to apply the approach in real-world scenarios. Hence, the two criteria are examined, appropriateness ("Is the output appropriate for the context?"), and correctness ("Is the output a correct response?"). Units are rated by an experienced language teacher on a binary scale (yes/no). To compare the resulting tasks within units, words, sentences, and texts are examined separately to uncover potential limitations.

4 Results

200 learning units are generated, limited to words (1, 2, 3, 4, 6 in Fig. 1), sentences (5 in Fig. 1), and texts (7, 8 in Fig. 1). A visualization of the evaluation is given in Fig. 3. Considering words, most of them are correct (.985), and appropriate (.97). If single sentences are formulated based on two, or three given words with maximum sentence length of 12 words, 4/5 are correct (.805), and appropriate (.835). Texts are mainly correct (.9), and most texts are appropriate (.935). In general, the evaluation shows that selected words and generated texts outperform in correctness, and appropriateness, while generated sentences have some weaknesses. Considering generated samples that are not erroneous at all, hence, words, sentences, and texts are correct, and appropriate within the unit, results in 56.5%. This subset can be directly processed without the need for further adjustments.

First, typical mistakes of selected, and combined words are examined. Exemplarily, "kaufne" (to buy), or "Kücken" (chicken) are misspelled. Such erroneous words are directly provided by the generative model. Also, semantical uncommon relations are found. The approach asks the generative model to create a list of related nouns with verbs. Exemplarily, words like "dip + cow" are used to form the sentence "The cow is dipped." (de: *Die Kuh wird portioniert.*), or "practice + bag" is combined to "I practice in the bag" (de: *Ich übe in der Schultasche.*). Those chunks must not be incorrect but can be unusual without further contextual embedding.

Second, generated sentences consisting of three given words are often grammatically incorrect or do not make sense. Tab. 2 shows some examples of uncommon sentences, that are not appropriate, or erroneous in German. Further, but rarely, a language switch can be found in the response. Exemplarily, for the word "fruit", the Finnish word

"Hedelmä" is used. Also, complete sentences are generated in another language, but with a given translation, exemplarily "Minä maistan banaania ja vadelmaa. (Ich schmecke Banane und Himbeere.)", which means "I taste banana and raspberry", but given in Finnish.

Correctness

Appropriateness

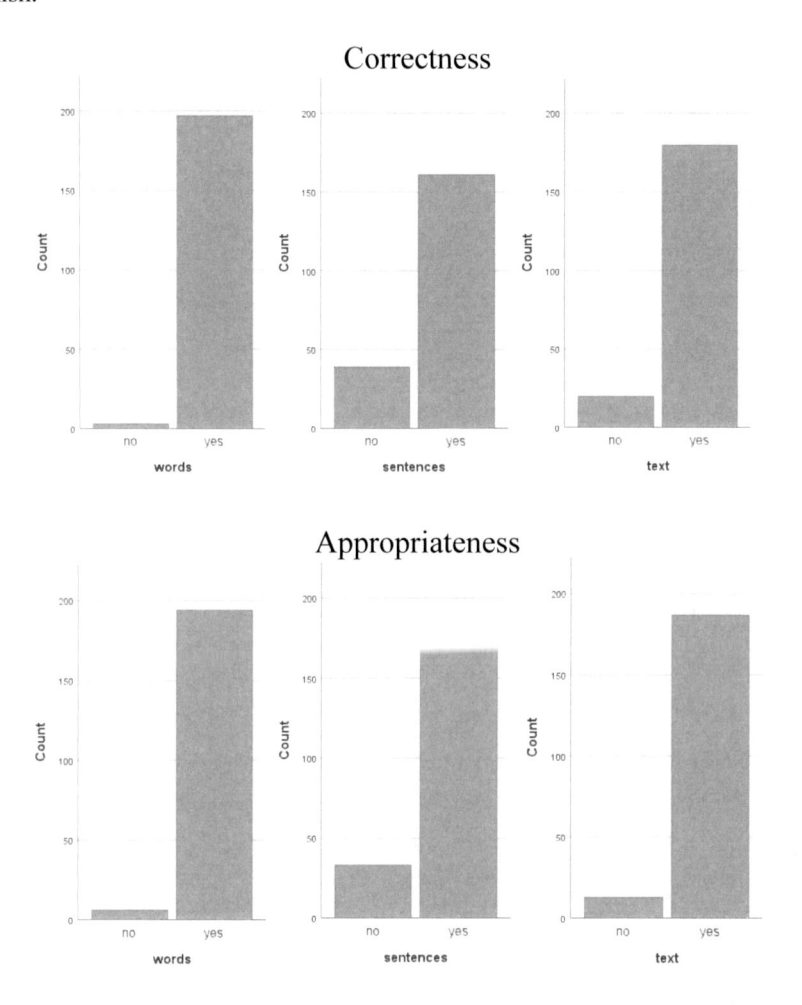

Fig. 3: Results of the evaluation (correctness and appropriateness)

If the model cannot generate an appropriate sentence with given conditions, the response looks like this: "I cannot create valid sentences that contain "[words]" and have language level A1", although the model previously claimed that there is a relation between those words. To give an example, words [chocolate, cheese, liquefy] cannot be combined by the model, but the model previously claimed that there is a relation between them. Further, responses are not deterministic. The response containing the information of not being able to create a sentence is manifold. Besides, generated sentences can directly be listed in the response, or a preamble is added like "I can create this sentence:", followed by quotes. Also, after some sentences, the number of words is given in brackets. Such information must be removed.

Types	Sentences
Uncommon	- Ich übe in der Schultasche. *(I practice in the school bag.)* - Ich bete im Taufbecken. *(I pray in the baptismal font.)* - Der schwüle Donner rollte heran. *(The sultry thunder rolled in.)* - Ich werde das Nest füttern. *(I will feed the nest.)* - Der Apfel ist voll. *(The apple is full.)* - Die Kuh servieren wir frisch. *(We serve the cow fresh.)* - Die Einbruchmeldeanlage beleuchten den Raum. *(The burglar alarm lights the room.)* - Ich kaufe eine Leseratte. *(I'll buy a bookworm.)* - Die Kuh wird portioniert. *(The cow is portioned.)* - Die Teppiche wachsen im Kaufhaus. *(The carpets grow in the department store.)* - Am Tag der Deutschen Einheit schmücken wir auch Heiligabend. *(On German Unity Day, we also decorate Christmas Eve.)* - Ich serviere Kaffeetrinkern in der Kaffeepause. *(I serve coffee drinkers during the coffee break.)* - Die Konservierungsmittel lagern in Zahnheilkunde. *(The preservatives are stored in dentistry.)*
Grammar mistakes (German-only)	- <u>Einen</u> Tischplatte abschrauben ist schwierig. - Ich suche den <u>Autorenname</u>. - Ich möchte <u>Kirsche</u> probieren. - Ich liebe es, Hühnchen <u>scharfzu</u> machen, indem ich es in Zitronensaft <u>marinieren</u>. - Ich muss <u>den</u> IBAN des Kontoinhabers prüfen. - Bitte <u>ausstecken Sie</u> das USB-Ladekabel vom USB-Netzteil.

Tab. 2: Common mistakes of generated sentences
with equivalent translation including erroneous parts

Next, generated texts are examined. They achieve the highest scores in the evaluation. Most of the texts are coherent, and they follow a logical order. Nevertheless, examples are found which are grammatically correct but do not make sense. Tab. 3 provides two examples in German. The first combines "heat" with "black ice". The second describes baking a "cake", but then, "paprika" is added – and at the end, everything must be "flavored", which is not typical when baking cakes.

Further, texts in responses can be formatted differently. Instead of creating one sentence per line as requested, sometimes no line breaks are included, or double line breaks are used. The last sentence of the generated text may contain: "these 20 nouns and verbs help with vocabulary training", which is not asked for. Again, such information must be removed to be useful in a learning unit. Nevertheless, texts perform remarkably better than generated single sentences.

Example 1	Example 2
Die **Hitze** drückt, ich brauche Abkühlung.	Ich koche gern.
Ein kühles Bad im See wäre super.	Heute backe ich einen **Kuchen**.
Aber das Wasser ist eiskalt, **Glatteis droht**.	Dafür brauche ich Backpulver, Mehl, Butter und Zucker.
Also doch zurück zur Klimaanlage im Büro.	Ich rühre alles zusammen.
Doch der Ventilator tut es auch.	Dann füge ich Eier hinzu.
Er sorgt für Luftbewegung und Ventilation.	Nach dem **Rühren** gebe ich **Paprika** hinzu.
Das Kühlen hilft bei der Konzentration.	Ich schneide die Zutaten klein und gebe Öl hinzu.
Entspannen und Relaxen ist einfach so möglich.	Alles vermische ich gut.
Chillen ist trotz der Hitze kein Problem.	Das Ganze kommt in den Ofen.
Hauptsache, ich bleibe kühl und entspannt.	Zum Schluss **abschmecken** und genießen.

Tab. 3: Semantical errors in generated texts

5 Limitations & Challenges

One challenge is the formatting of the response using generative large language models. An instruction-tuned GPT model is trained using existing prompts, and responses. More complex prompts are based on a variety of templates, which are filled with contents (responses from sub-queries). Such templates can be structured as proposed by Wang et al. [Wa22], exemplarily: "*Come up with a series of tasks· Task 1· {instruction for existing task 1}, Task 2: {instruction for existing task 2},....*". As long as those templates are not publicly known, there is the chance that a response does not meet the expected format, so it cannot be processed as expected. During the experiment, enumerations were given in responses, although the query explicitly includes not using numbers when generating texts. Further, instead of providing one sentence as requested, the model generates multiple sentences, or the response starts with "I will try three variants:". Such results are unexpected and must be handled separately, as we cannot be certain that the model will follow all instructions even if previous results were valid. Hence, even if instructions include that the response should contain one sentence per line, texts without line breaks are often seen. Despite the variety, most responses are formatted as expected to be useful.

Even if topics are selected from language level A1, resulting sentences, and texts can often be too complex for beginners. To name an example, for the topic "eye", the selected word list which fulfills all conditions, starts with words like "intraocular pressure, eye inflammation, or ophthalmology". From an educational perspective, those are not the words to begin with. If the random surfer model is applied, and one of the non-conventional words is selected, new units become unnecessarily complex. Hence, results should be filtered by language level afterward. The experiment is limited to A1 contents. Further research can examine other levels as well. Besides, generated units are evaluated by one teacher. Hence, the result may be biased due to his/her quality perception.

Generating course units using the proposed method leads to low costs. At the current state, using GPT-3.5, $0.002 per 1K tokens are charged [Op23]. Based on those costs, the final costs for the experiment focusing on words, sentences, and texts are 1.60$, resulting in 200 language learning units of different topics. However, an evaluation of whether generated images, or speech, are appropriate, is not part of the paper and is examined in further research.

For the experiments, GPT-3.5 is used, those responses are transferred into a structured format and processed to form a learning unit. Nevertheless, the GPT model is closed, and cannot further be controlled by researchers. From the privacy perspective, using such a model is acceptable as no personal data is used, or processed. Still, all prompts can be accessed by a company that provides the model, which may not be acceptable if prompts, and results are the base for further products. Alternative open models are required, which mimic the functionality of generating words, sentences, or coherent texts. Exemplarily, an open model like GPT-J [WK21] could be fine-tuned, using prompts, and responses from GPT-3.5. Then, the model can mimic responses for the concrete instructions, but with new contexts. Nevertheless, the resulting quality must be examined as the GPT-J model consists of 6B parameters, and GPT-3.5 covers 175B [Ko23]. Alternatively, collections like the "wordnet" [Fe12] can be used to get words with a semantical relation. Further research can examine, which approach leads to the best result.

6 Conclusion

In this paper, the generative language model GPT3.5 is used to create learning content for a concrete template. Results have shown that the model performs best in generating texts. Some weaknesses are found if sentences must be formulated using concrete words. All in all, fully auto-generated language learning online courses with high quality cannot be expected using the approach at the current state. A teacher-in-the-loop method must be favored. However, for teachers, auto-generation can be helpful, as they just need to select which result is acceptable and can generate new versions at low cost. For teachers, the procedure of creating course units with a given template is less time-consuming. They must not be that creative, as they can concentrate on providing topics, while the remaining part, including generating interactive H5P elements, can be done automatically. Further research will show whether open models achieve comparable results, which opens the door for generating highly varying adaptive language learning units that best suit learner needs.

Acknowledgments: This work was supported by the German Federal Ministry of Education and Research (BMBF), grant number 16DHBKI045 (IMPACT).

Bibliography

[AMF03] Achtemeier, S. D.; Morris, L. V.; Finnegan, C. L.: Considerations for developing

	evaluations of online courses. In Journal of Asynchronous Learning Networks 7.1, University of Georgia, pp. 1-13, 2003.
[Ba23]	Bang, Y. et al.: A multitask, multilingual, multimodal evaluation of chatgpt on reasoning, hallucination, and interactivity. arXiv preprint, 2023.
[CM08]	Chebolu, P.; Melsted, P.: PageRank and the random surfer model. In SODA (8), 2008.
[Co02]	Conrad, D. L.: Engagement, excitement, anxiety, and fear: Learners' experiences of starting an online course. In The American journal of distance education 16(4), pp. 205-226, 2002.
[Co21]	Council of Europe: A Common European Framework of Reference for Languages: Learning, Teaching, Assessment. In Council for Cultural Co-operation. Strasbourg: Cambridge University Press, 2001.
[Fe12]	Fellbaum, C: WordNet. In The Encyclopedia of Applied Linguistics, C. Chapelle, 2012.
[HH19]	Homanová, Z.; Havlásková, T.: H5P interactive didactic tools in education. In EDULEARN19. IATED, 2019.
[Ko23]	Koubaa, A.: GPT-4 vs. GPT-3.5: A Concise Showdown, 2023.
[MJP15]	McGahan, S. J.; Jackson, C. M.; Premer, K.: Online course quality assurance: Development of a quality checklist. In I. A. (10), 2015.
[Op23]	OpenAI: Pricing. Retrieved from https://web.archive.org/web/20230305235115/ https://openai.com/pricing, accessed: 2023 03 05.
[Pe16]	Petterson, F. et al.: Activities: Interactive Content – H5P. Retrieved from https://moodle.org/plugins/mod_hvp, accessed: 03 01 2023, 2016.
[Ren20]	Ren, Y. et al.: Fastspeech 2. Fast and high-quality end-to-end text to speech, 2020.
[Ro07]	Rosetta Stone Ltd.: Rosetta Stone User's Guide (2). US, 2007.
[RP21]	Rüdian, S.; Pinkwart, N.: Generating adaptive and personalized language learning online courses in Moodle with individual learning paths using templates. In International Conference on Advanced Learning Technologies (ICALT), pp. 53-55, 2021.
[Ul07]	Ullrich, C: Course Generation as a Hierarchical Task Network Planning Problem. In Dissertation. Saarbrücken, 2007.
[Wa22]	Wang, Y. et al.: Self-Instruct: Aligning Language Model with Self Generated Instructions. arXiv preprint, 2022.
[WK21]	Wang, B.; Komatsuzaki, A.: GPT-J-6B: A 6 billion parameter autoregressive language model, 2021.
[XLZ20]	Xu, D.; Li, Q.; Zhou, X.: Online course quality rubric: a tool box. In Online Learning Research Center, 2020.
[Yu17]	Yu, H. et al.: Towards AI-powered personalization in MOOC learning. In npj Science Learn 2 (15), pp. 1-5. Nature, 2017.
[Zh20]	Zhang, L. et al.: End-to-end automatic pronunciation error detection based on improved hybrid ctc/attention architecture. In Sensors, 20(7), p. 1809, 2020.

E-Assessment und Feedback

Online Exams in the Era of ChatGPT

Erik Buchmann[1,2] and Andreas Thor[3]

Abstract: Recent versions of ChatGPT demonstrate an amazing ability to answer difficult questions in natural languages on a wide range of topics. This puts homeworks or online exams at risk, where a student can simply forward a question to the chatbot and copy its answers. We have tested ChatGPT with three of our exams, to find out which kinds of exam questions are still difficult for a generative AI. Therefore, we categorized exam questions according to a knowledge taxonomy, and we analyze the wrong answers in each category. To our surprise, ChatGPT even performed well with procedural knowledge, and it earned a grade of 2.7 (B-) in the IT Security exam. However, we also observed five options to formulate questions that ChatGPT struggles with.

Keywords: Online Exams, ChatGPT

1 Introduction

In Nov. 2022, OpenAI rolled out ChatGPT[4], a chatbot based on Generative Pretrained Transformer Models. It answers question from simple ("How do i clean my cat?") to challenging ("What are the security properties of homomorphic encryption?"). It generates texts ("Write an invitation letter for a DAAD travel grant"), and it masters different writing styles. Alternatives such as ChatSonic[5] even access Google search. This puts exams in danger, where the student is without supervision, e.g., bachelor theses or online exams.

In this work, we let ChatGPT answer three exams, and we grade it as we grade our students. We analyze the way ChatGPT answers, particularly the questions ChatGPT was not able to answer correctly, in the four dimensions factual, conceptual, procedural and metacognitive knowledge. Furthermore, we let a plagiarism tool scan the answers. Finally, we compile five options to formulate questions that ChatGPT cannot answer easily. We were surprised to see ChatGPT earning a grade of 2.7 (B-) in our IT Security exam, one point short of a 2.3 (B). ChatGPT correctly spotted the pseudo-code that caused a buffer overflow, and generated firewall rules from a textual description, i.e., it applied procedural knowledge. On the other hand, ChatGPT just passed the other exams. For example, it gives broad answers to specific questions, and struggles with numbers and calculations. In Section 2, we describe our experiments with ChatGPT. In Section 3, we discuss our findings. In Section 4, we compare our findings with related work. Section 5 concludes.

---

[1] Dept. of Computer Science, Leipzig University, Germany. buchmann@informatik.uni-leipzig.de
[2] Center for Scalable Data Analytics and Artificial Intelligence (ScaDS.AI) Dresden/Leipzig, Germany
[3] Leipzig University of Applied Sciences, Germany. andreas.thor@htwk-leipzig.de
[4] https://chat.openai.com/chat
[5] https://writesonic.com

doi: 10.18420/delfi2023-15

2 Examining ChatGPT

We tested ChatGPT, release Jan 30, 2023, with three different exams that had to be answered in 90 minutes. The *IT Security* exam for international master students of computer science and business informatics consists of 18 questions in the topics "Access Control", "Encryption", "Secure Programming", "Network Security", and "IT-Grundschutz". Figure 1 shows a subset of the exam questions.

```
I1) Explain the difference between vulnerability and threat by using an example.
I2) Why is the private key of the RSA crypto system a prime number?
I3) Explain how the One-time Pad approach works.
I4) Is the One-time Pad approach more secure than a public-key crypto system?
I5) Describe the seven steps of the IT Security Process (BSI-Standard 200-2).
I6) Which line in the pseudo-code is vulnerable against a buffer overflow, and why?
         bool verifyWallet() {
              char wallet[512]; // declare buffer of 512 Bytes
              readFile(wallet, "C:\wallet.cry"); // read wallet file
              return (verify(wallet)); // validate the wallet
         }
```

Fig. 1: Questions from the IT Security exam

According to Bloom's revisited taxonomy [Kr02], the questions test factual (I3, I5), conceptual (I1, I2), procedural (I6) and, to some extent, metacognitive knowledge (I4). To exclude arbitrary answers, several questions build on each other (I3, I4). Figure 2 exemplarily shows the answer to question I2.

```
The private key in the RSA cryptography system is a prime number because of the
mathematical properties of prime numbers. The RSA encryption system is based on the
mathematical properties of prime factorization, where a large composite number can be
factored into two prime numbers. The security of RSA encryption is based on the
difficulty of finding the prime factors of a large composite number, which is used as
the private key. If someone were to obtain the private key, they would be able to
decode any message encrypted with that key, so it's important to keep the private key
secure.
```

Fig. 2: ChatGPT's answer to I2.

Table 1 shows the allocation of the points of the IT Security exam to the dimensions of knowledge. Numbers in brackets denote the points ChatGPT earned.

Exam	Factual Knowledge	Conceptual Knowledge	Procedural Knowledge	Metacognitive Knowledge
IT Security	12 (9)	51 (33)	24 (20)	3 (2)
Data Privacy	28 (11)	41 (19)	15 (11)	6 (5)
Foundations of CS	3 (0)	20 (9)	26 (17)	2 (0)

Tab. 1: Allocation of points to knowledge dimensions

The German *Data Privacy exam* has the same structure and target group as the IT Security exam. It tests the areas "Societal Foundations", "Anonymity Measures", "Internet Privacy", and "Internet of Things Privacy". As Table 1 shows, this exam emphasizes conceptual knowledge, and has a stronger focus on factual knowledge than the IT Security exam.

The exam *Foundations of Computer Science* targets at German Bachelor students of computer science in the first semester. This exam focuses on conceptual and procedural knowledge, as shown in Table 1: 46 of 51 points can be earned by answering questions like "What is the Hamming distance of the code words for A and D?" or "Transfer a pseudo-code into a flowchart". To avoid guessing, the students had to explain their answers. The exam addresses the areas "Data Structures", "Encoding Theory", "Computing Architectures", "Fundamentals of Programming" and "Logic". We omitted two image-based questions, because the version of ChatGPT we experimented with did not understand images.

Experiment Procedure: At first, we fed ChatGPT with our exam questions, one by one, for all three exams. If ChatGPT obviously did not understand, we rephrased the question as a student would do in an exam. We graded the answers with the same scheme as for the real exam. We also applied a commercial plagiarism tool[6]. We used a qualitative approach to analyze all answers that were not entirely correct, and we compiled hypotheses why ChatGPT might have given a wrong answer. We consolidated the hypotheses, and we tried to verify those hypotheses with different and rephrased questions. Finally, we derived common characteristics of questions that are challenging for ChatGPT (see Section 3).

Evaluation of the Answers: For each exam, Table 1 lists ChatGPT's score in brackets for each dimension of knowledge. In the *IT Security exam*, ChatGPT scored 64 from 90 points. This is sufficient for a 2.7 (B-), one point short of a 2.3 (B). As expected, a knowledge model is good with of factual knowledge. ChatGPT also demonstrated procedural knowledge in many cases, e.g., to assess pseudo-code (I6) and to generate firewall rules. However, it struggled to apply concepts to very specific cases, or to compare two concepts. For example, ChatGPT could answer I3, but it did not answer I4 correctly. Sometimes, ChatGPT answered inconsistently, e.g., Figure 2: The first sentence of the answer says that the private key is a prime number (wrong), followed by the explanation that the private key is the composite of two prime numbers (true). For I5, ChatGPT invented ("hallucinated") some steps.

In the Data Privacy exam, ChatGPT obtained 46 of 90 points, which means a grade of 4.0 (D). In this exam, ChatGPT missed many points for factual and conceptual knowledge. A closer inspection revealed, that this exam frequently asks for facts and concepts in relation to very specific use cases, e.g., "What are the differences between the interaction model of the Internet of Things and the interaction model of traditional PC applications?" We already know from the IT Security exam that this kind of question is difficult for ChatGPT. In the exam Foundations of Computer Science, ChatGPT earned 25 out of 51 points, which corresponds to a grade of 4.0 (D). Again, we observed that ChatGPT struggled with some calculations and questions that required a specific answer instead of a broad one.

---

[6] https://www.plagaware.com/

Identifying ChatGPT's Answers: For our *IT Security exam*, the plagiarism tool found that only 79 out of 2434 words in four sentences might have been paraphrased. The results for *Data Privacy* and *Foundations of Computer Science* were also not sufficient to prove plagiarism. Others tested AI tools [AJ23] for detecting AI-written text, with little success.

However, ChatGPT's answers have a unique pattern: At first, ChatGPT repeats the most important keyword(s) from the question. Then it relates the question to a generalized concept. ChatGPT always finishes with a summarizing sentence, even if it is repetitive or contradicting to the preceding text. ChatGPT often provides unnecessary details. For example, compare I2 with its answer (Figure 2). The answer starts by repeating the keywords "RSA cryptography" and "prime numbers". It describes the concept of RSA, and it concludes by saying that the private key must be kept secure, although this was not part of the question. It may indicate the use of ChatGPT, if this pattern can be found multiple times in an exam.

3 Exam Questions That are Difficult for ChatGPT

In this section, we list options for questions that are difficult for ChatGPT. We observed them in answers across all three exams, and we verified them with follow-up questions.

O1: Suggestive numbers of steps. ChatGPT tends to respond to suggestive numbers of steps, phases, cycles, stages, etc. Consider I5: ChatGPT invents any number of steps the questioner asks for, at least for reasonable numbers.

O2: Specific answers. Some question call for very specific cases. ChatGPT gives a perfect answer to I1, because this asks for a generic concept. However, ChatGPT still produces a generic answer, if I1 is turned into a specific question like "Explain the difference between vulnerability and threat for a UDP connection between a cloud server and an IoT device."

O3: Contradictions and repetitions. Control questions consider a subject from multiple perspectives, e.g., "(a) Does the code contain a buffer overflow?" and "(b) In which line is the buffer overflow?". If (a) is answered with "No", a consistent answer to (b) must be "There is no such line". We observed ChatGPT giving contradicting or repetitive answers, even within the same response (cf. Figure 2).

O4: Charts and figures. The version of ChatGPT we experimented with did not understand images. Thus, questions such as "If the certificate authority in a figure is exposed, which certificates are invalid?" could not be answered. However, in the meantime OpenAI offers a subscription model of GPT-v4 that also interprets images.

O5: Math beyond elementary school. The math knowledge of ChatGPT is limited. Questions like "Multiply two dual numbers 1101 and 101 in the dual system and explain your path to the solution." were answered incorrectly. For some math-related questions, ChatGPT produced an explanation that did not match the results it calculated.

4 Related Work

Related work for a *hot topic* like ChatGPT is practically always incomplete, as new field reports, analyses and handouts are published almost daily. Furthermore, since ChatGPT has only been available to the general public for a few months, there are hardly any peer-reviewed papers. The discussion on how ChatGPT can be used in university teaching, especially for exams, and whether this puts exam integrity in danger [Su22] is in full swing[7]. On one side are the "preventers" who want to ban and prevent the use of AI-based systems through rules, such as a return to pen and paper exams [Ca23], and software tools[8] to automatically detect whether text submitted by students has been auto-generated. On the other side are the "proponents" [Ru23; Sp23], who not only allow but also encourage the use of such tools. They emphasize good scientific practice (naming all tools and sources) and media literacy (assessing the possibilities and limitations of tools and sources).

Similar to our approach, other researchers have had ChatGPT answer exam questions from their fields of expertise, e.g., business administration [Te23] and law [Ch23]. Their experiences are similar to ours. In all cases ChatGPT would have passed the exam with grades between 2 (B) and 3 (C). ChatGPT is surprisingly good at describing facts and topics, which is especially evident in good performance on essay writing tasks. In contrast, the results for multiple choice questions were worse, but still significantly better than random guessing, as clueless students would do.

Regardless of the task format, ChatGPT surprisingly makes errors in simple mathematical calculations. ChatGPT's ability to change its answer through further hints allows ChatGPT to correct itself or to handle the task correctly.

Furthermore, ChatGPT can be effectively used in teaching and for the creation of exams [Mo23; Pr23]). For example, distractors for multiple choice questions or suggestions for exam questions in general can be auto-generated by ChatGPT. To avoid that such questions can be answered too easily by ChatGPT, teachers should (re-)formulate questions that challenge a computer more than a human [Su22]. These include multi-hop questions that combine multiple facts, and questions that require logical reasoning to answer.

This shows that students and teachers have to acquire the competence of *prompt engineering* [Wh23] in the long run, in order to be able to use ChatGPT efficiently for their studies also outside of exams. A prompt is a set of instructions provided to ChatGPT to customize the dialog. Examples for prompt engineering are question refinement, if ChatGPT apparently did not understand the question, or setting specific contexts.

---

[7] https://hochschulforumdigitalisierung.de/de/dossiers/generative-ki
[8] https://gptzero.me

5 Conclusion

Generative Pretrained Transformer Models such as ChatGPT have reached a degree of maturity, that puts any exam at risk, where a student is without supervision. The generated answers are seemingly convincing, and cannot be reliably identified by tools. To find out if there are questions an AI cannot easily answer, we tested ChatGPT with three different exams. ChatGPT demonstrated factual, conceptual and procedural knowledge, but it struggled with some calculations, questions aiming for specific (instead of broad) answers, and it invents procedure descriptions. Future approaches might overcome these issues.

Bibliography

[AJ23]   Alimardani, A.; Jane, E. A.: We pitted ChatGPT against tools for detecting AI-written text, and the results are troubling, https://theconversation.com/we-pitted-chatgpt-against-tools-for-detecting-ai-written-text-and-the-results-are-troubling-199774, retrieved: March 2023, 2023.

[Ca23]   Cassidy, C.: Australian universities to return to 'pen and paper' exams after students caught using AI to write essays. In: The Guardian. 2023.

[Ch23]   Choi, J. H.; Hickman, K. E.; Monahan, A.; Schwarcz, D. B.: ChatGPT Goes to Law School. In: Minnesota Legal Studies Research Paper No. 23-03. 2023.

[Kr02]   Krathwohl, D. R.: A Revision of Bloom's Taxonomy: An Overview. Theory Into Practice 41/4, pp. 212–218, 2002.

[Mo23]   Mohr, G. et al.: Übersicht zu ChatGPT im Kontext Hochschullehre, https://www.hul.uni-hamburg.de/selbstlernmaterialien/dokumente/hul-chatgpt im kontext-lehre-2023 01 20.pdf, retrieved: March 2023, 2023.

[Pr23]   ProLehre TUM: Einsatz von ChatGPT in der Lehre, https://www.prolehre.tum.de/fileadmin/w00btq/www/Angebote_Broschueren_Handreichungen/prolehre-handreichung-chatgpt-v2.2.pdf, retrieved: March 2023, 2023.

[Ru23]   Rudolph, J. et al.: ChatGPT: Bullshit spewer or the end of traditional assessments in higher education? Journal of Applied Learning & Teaching 6(1)/, 2023.

[Sp23]   Spannagel, C.: Rules for Tools, https://csp.uber.space/phhd/rulesfortools.pdf, retrieved: March 2023, 2023.

[Su22]   Susnjak, T.: ChatGPT: The End of Online Exam Integrity?, 2022, url: https://arxiv.org/abs/2212.09292.

[Te23]   Terwiesch, C.: Would Chat GPT3 Get a Wharton MBA? A Prediction Based on Its Performance in the Operations Management Course, Mack Institute for Innovation Management, University of Pennsylvania, 2023.

[Wh23]   White, J.; Fu, Q.; Hays, S.; Sandborn, M.; Olea, C.; Gilbert, H.; Elnashar, A.; Spencer-Smith, J.; Schmidt, D. C.: A Prompt Pattern Catalog to Enhance Prompt Engineering with ChatGPT, 2023, url: https://arxiv.org/abs/2302.11382.

Kopplung von Jupyter Notebooks mit externen E-Assessment-Systemen am Beispiel des Data Management Testers

Martin Petersohn[1], Konrad Schöbel[2] und Andreas Thor [3]

Abstract: Wir präsentieren einen generischen Ansatz für interaktives E-Assessment mit Jupyter Notebooks, bei dem ein externes E-Assessment-System in ein Notebook integriert wird. Im Unterschied zu bisherigen Arbeiten ist das Notebook nicht selbst das Artefakt, welches vom System prozessiert wird, sondern dient vielmehr als User Interface für das E-Assessment-System. Unsere Integration ermöglicht dadurch ein interaktives Assessment während des Bearbeitungszyklus des Notebooks, d.h. Lernende können während der Bearbeitung des Notebooks ohne Unterbrechung bzw. Systemwechsel ihre Lösungen live bewerten lassen. Wir stellen eine prototypische Implementation für die Anbindung des E-Assessment-Tools DMT (Data Management Tester) vor und zeigen dabei auf, welche Schnittstelle ein beliebiges E-Assessment-System implementieren muss, um durch unseren Ansatz in Jupyter Notebooks integriert werden zu können.

Keywords: Jupyter Notebook, E-Assessment, Data Management Tester

1 Einleitung

Jupyter Notebooks [Kl16] sind in den letzten Jahren zu einem populären Element der Hochschullehre in MINT-Fächern geworden und werden in verschiedenen Lernszenarien eingesetzt [Jo20]. Lehrende nutzen Jupyter Notebooks z. B. für interaktive Vorlesungen, bei denen sie (vorbereiteten) Quellcode inklusive Beschreibungen im Markdown-Format präsentieren, live entwickeln, verändern und ausführen können. Zusätzlich können vorbereitete Jupyter Notebooks auch an die Lernenden verteilt werden, um ihnen praktische Übungsmöglichkeiten zu ermöglichen.

Damit spielt auch das E-Assessment für Jupyter Notebooks zunehmend eine Rolle, da die von Lernenden innerhalb eines Notebooks erstellten digitalen Artefakte auch Grundlage einer manuellen oder automatischen Bewertung sein können. Werkzeuge wie z. B. nbgrader [Ju19] ermöglichen es Lernenden, Lösungen zu einzelnen Aufgaben in den Zellen entsprechend vorbereiteter Notebooks einzutragen und anschließend zur Bewertung einzureichen. Im Unterschied zu bisherigen Systemen, die Jupyter Notebooks mit E-Assessment-Systemen kombinieren, ist in unserem Ansatz das Notebook *nicht* das Artefakt, welches vom System prozessiert wird. Das Notebook dient vielmehr als *User Interface* für

---

[1] Hochschule für Technik, Wirtschaft und Kultur Leipzig, martin.petersohn@stud.htwk-leipzig.de
[2] Hochschule für Technik, Wirtschaft und Kultur Leipzig, konrad.schoebel@htwk-leipzig.de
[3] Hochschule für Technik, Wirtschaft und Kultur Leipzig, andreas.thor@htwk-leipzig.de

doi: 10.18420/delfi2023-16

das E-Assessment-System. Dabei nutzen wir die Möglichkeit, dass der Output von Notebook-Zellen auch typische User-Interface-Elemente wie Buttons oder Textboxen enthalten kann. Dies ermöglicht die Integration eines *interaktiven Assessments während des Bearbeitungszyklus*, d.h. Lernende können das Notebook bearbeiten, z. B. in einer Zelle Code entwickeln, und ohne Unterbrechung bzw. Systemwechsel ihre Lösung in einer anderen Zelle bewerten lassen. Diese Form ermöglicht es auch, E-Assessment in einer interaktiven Vorlesung direkt in der Lehrveranstaltung einzusetzen.

Wir illustrieren unseren Ansatz prototypisch mit dem E-Assessment-Tool DMT (Data Management Tester) [TK21], welches für typische Aufgaben in der Datenbank-Lehre eingesetzt werden kann. Dabei zeigen wir auf, dass unser Vorgehen generisch ist und beschreiben, welche Schnittstelle (API) ein *beliebiges* E-Assessment-System implementieren muss, um durch unseren Ansatz in Jupyter Notebooks integriert werden zu können. Der Rest des Beitrags ist wie folgt strukturiert: Wir fassen in Kapitel 2 verwandte Arbeiten kurz zusammen und stellen in Kapitel 3 zunächst das anzubindende E-Assessment-Tool DMT näher vor. Unseren Integrationsansatz beschreiben wir in Kapitel 4 und gehen dabei auch auf Details der Implementation ein.

2 Related Work

Bei der Kopplung von Jupyter Notebooks mit E-Assessment-Systemen gibt es grundsätzlich zwei Richtungen. Werkzeuge wie z. B. nbgrader [Ju19] führen das Jupyter Notebook als digitales Artefakt dem Bewertungssystem zu, das in der Regel sowohl automatische als auch manuelle Bewertungen zulässt. Hierbei wird auf die Struktur eines Notebooks inkl. Metadaten der Zellen zurückgegriffen, um eine zuverlässige und effiziente Bewertung zu ermöglichen. Die automatische Bewertung (Auto-Grading) kann dabei durch externe E-Assessment-Systeme erfolgen, wie z. B. UNCode [Go21] für die Bewertung von Programmcode, oder durch selbst definierte Testszenarien wie z. B. beim Unit Testing Framework [THS23]. Für einen Vergleich verschiedener Auto-Grader sei auf [Go21] verwiesen.

Die andere Richtung ist die Integration auf Ebene des User Interface. Während unser Ansatz das User Interface nativ als Output der Zelle generiert, nutzt der in [PGA21] vorgestellte Ansatz Webbrowser-Technologien wie IFrames. Damit lassen sich sowohl die Aufgabenstellung und etwaiges Feedback (vom E-Assessment-System) als auch das Jupyter Notebook, auf das dann dynamisch zur Bewertung zugegriffen wird, gleichzeitig ("nebeneinander") darstellen, obwohl sie auf getrennten Systemen liegen. Einen hybriden Ansatz präsentiert [Ma20]. Hier wird das E-Assessment-System Web-CAT, welches automatisch Code verschiedener Programmiersprachen bewerten kann, mittels einer Jupyter-Front-End-Erweiterung angeschlossen. Dabei können Lernende ihr speziell aufbereitetes Notebook direkt an das Web-CAT-System senden und erhalten Bewertung und Feedback als Popup-Fenster von Web-CAT. Im Gegensatz dazu integriert unser Ansatz das Feedback direkt in den Output der jeweiligen Notebook-Zelle.

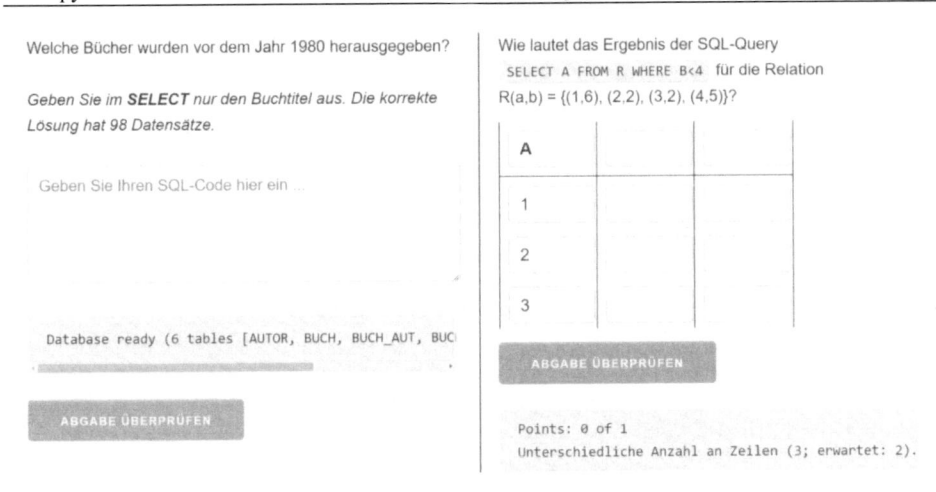

Abb. 1: Screenshot des Data Management Testers für zwei verschiedene Aufgaben vom Typ SELECT (links) und TABLE (rechts, mit eingetragener, falscher Lösung und Feedback)

3 Data Management Tester

Das E-Assessment-Tool DMT (Data Management Tester) [TK21] erlaubt die automatische Bewertung strukturierter Ergebnisse, die häufig als Lösung von Aufgaben in der Datenbank-Lehre entstehen. Die Ergebnisformate umfassen u.a. SQL-Anfragen, die Spezifikation von Schemata und Relationen sowie View- und Constraint-Definitionen. Abb. 1 zeigt zwei verschiedene Aufgabentypen, die im Folgenden kurz charakterisiert werden.

Bei Aufgaben des Typs SELECT geben Lernende als Lösung eine SQL-Anfrage an (siehe Abb. 1, links). Zur automatischen Bewertung spezifiziert die Lehrperson eine SQL-Anfrage als Musterlösung und gibt zusätzlich an, ob die Reihenfolge der Datensätze relevant ist. Beim Aufgabentyp TABLE geben Lernende die Attributnamen und Tupel einer Relation in Tabellenform an (Abb. 1, rechts). Zum Vergleich mit der korrekten Lösung gibt die Lehrperson entweder eine SQL-Query oder das tabellarische Ergebnis im CSV-Format an. Zusätzlich kann die Lehrperson auch hier spezifizieren, ob die Reihenfolge der Datensätze relevant ist, z. B. wenn das Ergebnis einer ORDER BY-Query gesucht ist.

Wesentlicher Bestandteil von DMT ist die automatische Bewertung sowie die automatische Generierung von Feedback bzgl. der eingereichten Lösung der Studierenden. Für Aufgaben der Formate SELECT und TABLE wird z. B. das Anfrage-Ergebnis bzw. die angegebene Tupel-Menge mit einer Musterlösung verglichen, die ggf. selbst durch eine SQL-Anfrage spezifiziert ist. DMT nimmt anhand der Prüfung nicht nur eine Bewertung vor, ob die Lösung *korrekt* oder *nicht korrekt* ist, sondern generiert auch hinweisgebendes Feedback bei fehlerhaften Lösungen. Dieses bezieht sich auf die Syntax der SQL-Anfrage,

Grad und Kardinalität der Tupel-Mengen (wie im rechten Beispiel von Abb. 1), die Korrektheit des Schemas (Attributnamen) sowie der Tupel und ggf. deren korrekte Reihenfolge. Gemäß der Klassifikation in [Na08] fällt DMTs Feedback in die Bereiche KM (Knowledge about mistakes) sowie AUC (Answer-until-correct). Für weitere Details zur automatischen Bewertung und Generierung von Feedback (auch für alle anderen Aufgabentypen) sei auf [TK21] verwiesen.

Die aktuelle DMT-Implementation ist eine Webservice-basierte Webanwendung unter Verwendung von Java-Servlets, HTML und Javascript. Die Funktionalität wird durch zwei REST-basierte Webservices realisiert: /getTaskInfo?taskid=... sowie /getTaskResult?taskid=...&answer=.... Die Task-Id ist dabei ein String, der eine Aufgabe innerhalb von DMT eindeutig referenziert. Die Lösung der Lernenden wird im Parameter answer als String übergeben. Dieser ist je nach Aufgabentyp speziell strukturiert, z. B. im CSV-Format für den Aufgabentyp TABLE.

4 Integration von DMT in Jupyter Notebooks

Abb. 2 zeigt die schematische Architektur und den Workflow zur Kopplung von Jupyter Notebooks mit einem externen E-Assessment-System am Beispiel von DMT. Mit dem vorgestellten Ansatz kann prinzipiell jedes System angebunden werden, welches Informationen zur Aufgabenstellung (getTaskInfo) sowie zur Bewertung (getTaskResult) programmatisch per API bereitstellt. Die Kopplung wird durch eine Jupyter Extension realisiert. Für die prototypische Integration von DMT erfolgt dies durch DMT-Magic, welches durch das Jupyter Magic Command dmt innerhalb des Notebooks nutzbar wird.

Der linke Teil von Abb. 2 zeigt einen Ausschnitt eines Jupyter Notebooks bestehend aus zwei Zellen. Zelle [1] initialisiert die Nutzung von DMT für das Notebook (Schritt ❶). Die geschieht durch das Laden der Extension DMT-Magic[4] und Konfigurieren der URL, unter der DMT erreichbar ist. Die Ausführung (Schritt ❷) von Zelle [2] generiert die zu bearbeitende Aufgabe in der darunter befindlichen Zellausgabe (beginnend mit „Welche Bücher wurden ..."). Die Zelleingabe besteht dabei – neben dem optionalen Kommentar – lediglich aus einem Magic Command (%dmt, siehe weiter unten für technische Details) und der Angabe einer Task-Id (bibliothek:5), die eine im E-Assessment-System hinterlegte Aufgabe referenziert[5]. Durch das Ausführen von Zelle [2] wird letztendlich die Zellausgabe produziert (Schritt ❸), die das eigentliche User Interface zur Eingabe der Lösung durch die Lernenden bereitstellt. Im Beispiel von Abb. 2 ist die Aufgabe vom Typ SELECT, so dass – analog zu Abb. 1 links – die Aufgabenstellung, eine Textbox, eine Statusleiste sowie ein Button zur Abgabe generiert werden.

---

[4] Die Extension muss vorher einmalig mittels pip install dmt-magic installiert werden, wobei auch abhängige Pakete, wie z. B. ipywidgets für Jupyter Widgets, automatisch bei Bedarf installiert werden.
[5] Die per Task-Id referenzierte Aufgabe kann sowohl statisch sein als auch dynamisch durch das E-Assessment-System zur Laufzeit generiert werden, z. B. mittels zufälliger Parameterwerte.

Jupyter Notebooks mit externem E-Assessment am Beispiel des Data Management Testers   89

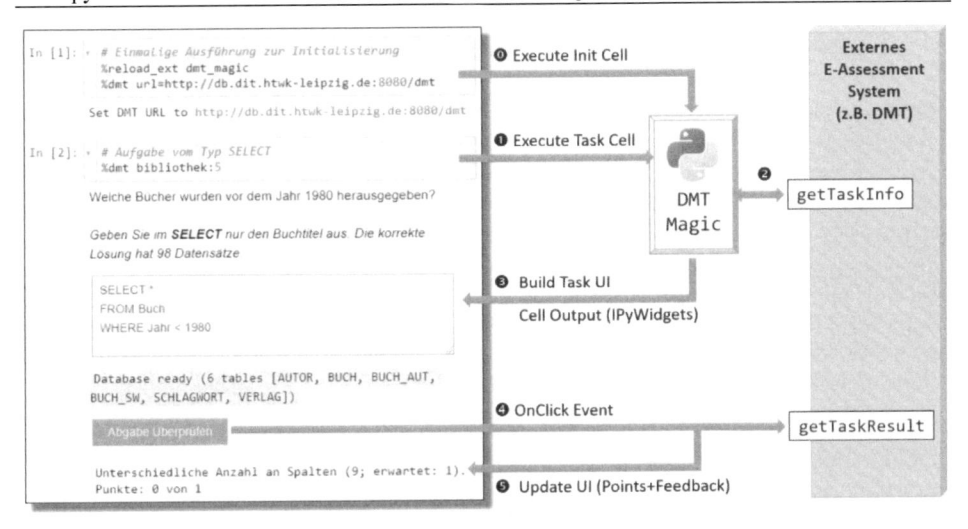

Abb. 2: Schematische Architektur und Workflow zur Kopplung eines Jupyter Notebooks (links) mit E-Assessment-System (rechts) am Beispiel von DMT mit Hilfe von DMT-Magic (mittig)

Zur dynamischen Generierung des User Interface sendet DMT-Magic einen `getTaskInfo`-Request an das E-Assessment-Tool DMT (Schritt ❷), welches mit der übergebenen Task-Id alle zum Anzeigen der Aufgabe notwendigen Informationen, u.a. Aufgabenstellung und -typ, zurückliefert. Daraufhin kann das User Interface unter Verwendung von Jupyter Widgets, einer Sammlung interaktiver Steuerelemente zur Erstellung grafischer Benutzeroberflächen, gerendert werden. Dabei wird insbesondere dem Button „Abgabe überprüfen" dynamisch eine `On-Click`-Methode zugewiesen, welche die eingegebene Lösung (im Beispiel die in der Textbox eingegebene SQL-Query) wiederum in einem `getTaskResult`-Request an DMT sendet (Schritt ❹), welches Bewertung und Feedback zurückliefert. Dieses wird dann unterhalb des Buttons angezeigt (Schritt ❺).

Wie in Abb. 2 ersichtlich, muss das externe E-Assessment-System – in unserem Beispiel der Data Management Tester – lediglich die zwei Funktionen `getTaskInfo` und `getTaskResult` bereitstellen, um in das Jupyter Notebook integriert werden zu können. Die Implementation der Anbindung an Jupyter Notebooks erfolgt mit Hilfe eines *Jupyter Magic Commands* oder kurz einer *Magic*. Solche Magics bieten eine einfache Möglichkeit, die Funktionalität des Notebook Kernels zu erweitern. Sie werden durch das Präfix `%` (siehe Zelle [2] in Abb. 2) bzw. `%%` gekennzeichnet und leiten den Inhalt der Zeile bzw. Zelle an die zugehörige Magic-Klasse weiter. Zur Implementation der DMT-Magic wurde eine Unterklasse von Magics gebildet, welche entsprechende Funktionen implementiert, u.a. zur Kommunikation mit DMT via HTTP-Rest-Requests, wobei die Daten im JSON-Format ausgetauscht werden. Um eine externe Magic innerhalb eines Notebooks zu verwenden, muss sie zunächst geladen werden (`%load_ext dmt_magic` bzw. `%reload_ext dmt_magic`). Darüber hinaus muss einmalig im Notebook die URL des DMT-Servers spezifiziert werden (`%dmt url=…`).

5 Zusammenfassung und Ausblick

Dieser Beitrag präsentierte einen generischen Ansatz für interaktives E-Assessment mit Jupyter Notebooks. Durch die Verwendung von Jupyter Magic Commands ist es möglich, externe E-Assessment-Systeme in das User Interface der Notebooks zu integrieren, sofern die Systeme entsprechende Schnittstellen bereitstellen. Die Integration ermöglicht ein interaktives E-Assessment während der Bearbeitung des Notebooks, so dass flexible Einsatzmöglichkeiten für Notebooks resultieren, u.a. für interaktive Vorlesungen oder als digitales Übungsblatt. Der vorgestellte Ansatz wurde prototypisch für das E-Assessment-System DMT implementiert. Zukünftige Arbeiten umfassen die Anbindung weiterer Systeme, auch unter Berücksichtigung von Sicherheitsaspekten durch Authentifizierungsverfahren, sowie die Evaluation des Ansatzes im Rahmen der Lehrveranstaltungen.

Literaturverzeichnis

[Go21] González-Carrillo, C. D.; Restrepo-Calle, F.; Ramírez-Echeverry, J. J.; González, F. A.: Automatic Grading Tool for Jupyter Notebooks in Artificial Intelligence Courses. Sustainability 13/21, 2021.

[Jo20] Johnson, J. W.: Benefits and Pitfalls of Jupyter Notebooks in the Classroom. In: Proceedings of the 21st Annual Conference on Information Technology Education. SIGITE '20, 2020.

[Ju19] Jupyter et al.: nbgrader: A Tool for Creating and Grading Assignments in the Jupyter Notebook. Journal of Open Source Education 2/16, 2019.

[Kl16] Kluyver, T, et al.: Jupyter Notebooks – a publishing format for reproducible computational workflows. In: Positioning and Power in Academic Publishing: Players, Agents and Agendas. 2016.

[Ma20] Manzoor, H.; Naik, A.; Shaffer, C. A.; North, C.; Edwards, S. H.: Auto-Grading Jupyter Notebooks. In: Proceedings of the 51st ACM Technical Symposium on Computer Science Education. SIGCSE '20, 2020.

[Na08] Narciss, S.: Feedback Strategies for Interactive Learning Tasks. In: Handbook of Research on Educational Communications and Technology, 2008.

[PGA21] Panyahuti; Ganefri; Ambiyar: Jupyter Notebook-Based Diagnostic E-Assessment Model for Novice Programmer. Turkish Journal of Computer and Mathematics Education 12/10, 2021.

[THS23] Tröbs, E.; Hagedorn, S.; Sattler, K.-U.: JPTest - Grading Data Science Exercises in Jupyter Made Short, Fast and Scalable. In: BTW. 2023.

[TK21] Thor, A.; Kirsten, T.: Das E-Assessment-Tool DMT. Datenbank-Spektrum 21/1, 2021.

AxEL - Eine modulare Softwarekomponente für ein dediziertes E-Prüfungssystem zur Generierung von xAPI-Statements für Assessment Analytics

Martin Breuer [1], Annabell Brocker [2], Malte Persike [1] und Ulrik Schroeder [2]

Abstract: Um Lehrende zukünftig bei der Qualitätssicherung digitaler Prüfungen sowie der Optimierung von prüfungsbezogenen Lehr- und Lerninhalten zu unterstützen, ist die Entwicklung von Assessment Analytics Tools für das E-Prüfungssystem Dynexite geplant. Dieser Beitrag stellt die Entwicklung einer modularen Softwarekomponente vor, die bestehende Interaktions- und Ergebnisdaten von Studierenden in xAPI Statements umwandelt und diese der zentral an der Hochschule bereitgestellten Learning Analytics Infrastruktur zugänglich macht. Die vorgestellte Softwarekomponente und die geplante Weiterverarbeitung der Daten werden in das Learning Analytics Referenzmodell nach Chatti et. al. eingeordnet, um den Datenbedarf zu ermitteln. Die Softwarekomponente ermöglicht Untersuchungen auf unterschiedlichen Detailebenen. Für die Qualitätssicherung der Prüfungen ist meist eine genaue Zuordnung von feingranularen Interaktionsdaten auf Eingabemöglichkeiten von Interesse. Bei der diagnostischen Untersuchung von Ergebnisdaten kann hingegen auf Detailstrukturen verzichtet werden.

Keywords: E-Prüfungssystem, Assessment Analytics, Learning Analytics, xAPI, Prüfungsdaten.

1 Einleitung

Die Durchführung digitaler Prüfungen bietet für akademisches Personal technische, didaktische, rechtliche sowie organisatorische Chancen und Herausforderungen [Pe21]. Um diese zu adressieren, bildet das dedizierte E-Prüfungssystem Dynexite[3] verschiedene Phasen der Prüfung in einem einheitlichen Prozess ab. Allerdings fehlt bisher eine Assessment Analytics (AA) Komponente zur Auswertung der Prüfungsdaten mit dem Ziel der Optimierung von Lehr-, Lern- und Prüfungsinhalten.

Zum Schließen der Lücke werden die benötigten Daten im E-Prüfungssystem in xAPI Statements[4] umgewandelt und an die zentrale Learning Analytics (LA) Infrastruktur basierend auf Excalibur LA [JS22] gesendet. Innerhalb dieser Infrastruktur werden in Dynexite generierte Daten zunächst in einem Learning Record Store (LRS) abgelegt,

---

[1] RWTH Aachen, Center für Lehr- und Lernservices, {breuer@medien, persike@cls}.rwth-aachen.de, https://orcid.org/{0009-0008-0749-5110, 0000-0002-7825-089X}
[2] RWTH Aachen, Lerntechnologien, {a.brocker, schroeder}@cs.rwth-aachen.de, https://orcid.org/{0009-0007-6708-0892, 0000-0002-5178-8497}
[3] Dynexite Dokumentation, https://docs.dynexite.rwth-aachen.de, Stand: 27.03.2023
[4] xAPI-Spec, https://github.com/adlnet/xAPI-Spec, Stand: 27.03.2023

doi: 10.18420/delfi2023-17

dann mithilfe so genannter Analytics Engines ausgewertet und in einem Result Store gespeichert. Individuelle Einwilligungen werden durch eine Rights Engine in der zentralen LA Infrastruktur verwaltet, geprüft und gesichert, sodass nur berechtigte Personen Zugriff auf die erhobenen und ausgewerteten Daten haben. [JS22]

Dieser Beitrag beleuchtet die Frage, wie ein dediziertes E-Prüfungssystem an eine LA Infrastruktur zur kontinuierlichen Datenübertragung angeschlossen werden kann und wie Daten aus dem E-Prüfungssystem umgewandelt werden sollten. Das Ziel besteht darin, eine modulare Softwarekomponente für ein dediziertes E-Prüfungssystem zu entwickeln, um plattformübergreifende Analysen mittels xAPI Statements für AA zu ermöglichen.

2 Assessment Analytics im Hochschulkontext

Ellis definiert den Begriff AA als LA im Kontext von Assessments [El13]. LA ist zunächst das Messen, Sammeln, Analysieren und Auswerten von Daten über Lernende und ihren Kontext mit dem Ziel, das Lernen und die Lernumgebung zu verstehen und zu optimieren [SL11]. AA fokussiert die Definition auf den Kontext von elektronischen Assessments. Um zu entscheiden, in welcher Form Daten für eine AA Komponente benötigt werden, erfolgt eine Einordnung des Vorhabens in das LA Referenzmodell nach [Ch12] anhand der vier Dimensionen: Daten und Umgebungen (what?), Stakeholder (who?), Ziele (why?) und Methoden (how?).

2.1 Daten und Umgebungen (what?)

Dynexite ist eine an der RWTH Aachen entwickelte Prüfungssoftware, die als verteilte Infrastruktur konzipiert ist (vgl. Dynexite-Aufbau[5]). Die zentrale Plattformkomponente namens *Orbit* adressiert zwei Zielgruppen. Zum einen können Dozierende in *Orbit* Prüfungen erstellen und den Prüfungsprozess verwalten. Zum anderen können Studierende mithilfe von *Orbit* an Klausureinsichten teilnehmen sowie formative Self-Assessments mit automatischer Auswertung sowie untersemestrige Prüfungsleistungen (Hausübungen) absolvieren.

Der wesentliche von *Orbit* nicht abgedeckte Bereich sind die summativen Abschlussprüfungen. Für deren Durchführung dienen die *Satelliten* – speziell für die Durchführung von Abschlussprüfungen konzipierte Prüfungsserver. Sie werden in lokalen Netzwerken betrieben, in denen lediglich die Prüfungssoftware genutzt oder auf Anfrage von Dozierenden um weitere Tools erweitert werden kann. Auf externe Abhängigkeiten wird verzichtet, um Verzögerungen zu vermeiden. Vor der Durchführung einer Prüfung mit einem Satelliten müssen Prüfungen deshalb von *Orbit* übertragen werden. Dabei werden für die Durchführung der Prüfung notwendige Informationen migriert – für die nachfolgende Bewertung relevante Informationen

---

[5] Dynexite Aufbau, https://docs.dynexite.rwth-aachen.de/administration/structure, Stand: 26.03.2023

befinden sich ausschließlich im *Orbit*. Zur rechtssicheren Durchführung der Prüfungen werden Interaktionsdaten in Form von Events aufgezeichnet. Seit 2018 existiert ein Event-Log Datensatz mit über 53.000 Studierenden und 270 mio. Events (Stand 06/23).

2.2 Stakeholder (who?)

Die beiden primären Stakeholdergruppen für eine AA Anwendung sind Dozierende sowie Studierende. Statistische Auswertungskenntnisse seitens der Dozierenden können aufgrund der Heterogenität nicht vorausgesetzt werden. Sowohl Dozierende als auch Studierende könnten gleichermaßen von einer AA Anwendung profitieren, die auf mögliche Probleme bei Prüfungsaufgaben oder bei der Abstimmung von Prüfungs- auf Kursangebote hindeuten. Dabei liegt die Verhinderung von Datenmissbrauch im Interesse der Studierenden, da persönliche Daten nicht nur zur formativen Evaluation, sondern auch zur Prüfung und Bewertung verwendet werden könnten [Ch12].

2.3 Ziele (why?)

Gründe und Potenziale für den Einsatz einer AA Anwendung sind vielfältig. Schwierigkeitswerte können zur Optimierung des Aufgabenpools und als Basis für die Erstellung neuer Prüfungen dienen. Weitere Gütekriterien können herangezogen werden, um qualitativ unzureichende oder problematische Aufgaben zu identifizieren [SS22]. Neben der Erstellung der Prüfungen kann ein weiteres Ziel die Optimierung des prüfungsvorbereitenden Kontextes sein, indem erfolgskritische Übungsaufgaben fokussiert werden [SS22]. Ein weiteres Ziel ist die Weiterentwicklung bestehender Autorentools für Prüfungsaufgaben. Hier könnte die Aufgabenformulierung durch die Vorhersage von Gütekriterien anhand der Prüfungsdaten ähnlicher Aufgaben unterstützt werden. Über AA Ziele hinausgehend könnte akademisches Personal bei der Korrektur der Klausuren entlastet werden; eine Stakeholder Befragung diesbezüglich ist geplant.

2.4 Methoden (how?)

Zum aktuellen Zeitpunkt des Projekts, lässt sich eine Antwort auf die Frage „how?" nur übergreifend skizzieren. Eine Übersicht von Auswertungs- und Anwendungsmöglichkeiten im Rahmen von AA sowie möglicher Integrationen in LMS ist in [SS22] zu finden. Die Methoden zur Erreichung der vorgenannten Ziele sind vielfältig. Für die geplante AA Anwendung liegt der Fokus auf Auswertungs- und Darstellungsmethoden, die Dozierende auf aufgabenbezogene Probleme mit dem Ziel der weiteren Untersuchung hinweisen. Erste Limitierungen und Möglichkeiten bei der Anwendung der Methoden lassen sich durch die Datenberücksichtigung unterschiedlicher Granularitäten ableiten. Die inhaltlichen Auswertungen der Prüfungsaufgaben erfordert keine Verarbeitung personenbezogener Studierendendaten, sodass ein anonymes Logging möglich ist. Bei zunehmender Granularität der Daten sind tiefergehende

Untersuchungen möglich, die Anforderungen an den Schutz der Daten hingegen wachsen, sodass je nach universitärem Kontext eine Konfiguration des Datenlogging wünschenswert oder notwendig ist.

3 Anforderung an eine Logging-Erweiterung

Bei der Entwicklung einer Logging-Erweiterung für das Prüfungssystem dienten bereits bestehende Logging-Systeme anderer Plattformen wie JupyterLab [Br22] und Moodle [JSS22] als Grundlage. Die ersten Herausforderungen ergeben sich beim Transfer von Daten aus dem Quellsystem Dynexite. Zwar wird die Laufzeit der Eventverarbeitung in anderen Systemen bereits durch einen Statement Puffer reduziert, die Datenumwandlung erfolgt jedoch direkt nach Eintreten des Ereignisses [JSS22]. Die verteilte Dynexite Architektur mit gegebenenfalls eingeschränkten Internetverbindungen, verbietet ein direktes Übertragen der Daten während der Prüfung. Zusätzlich werden kontextuelle Informationen, die nicht notwendig für die Bearbeitung einer Prüfung sind, wie z. B. Musterlösungen, Kurszuordnung usw., nicht auf die Prüfungsserver *Satellite* migriert. Ein vollständiges generieren der xAPI Statements (vgl. Abb. 1) mit Kontext und Erweiterungen ist somit während einer Prüfung nicht ohne weiteres möglich.

Ein einheitliches Übertragen der Daten kann ohne große Änderungen am Prüfungssystem nur über die zentrale SQL-Datenbank des *Orbits* im Backend erfolgen (vgl. Abb. 1). Insgesamt birgt ein vollständig asynchroner Ablauf der Verarbeitung und Übertragung der Daten am wenigsten Risiken. Die Versionierung der Daten in Dynexite erfolgt per so genanntem *Upcasting* beim Laden der Daten aus der Datenbank. Dies muss analog beim Logging erfolgen, um Kompatibilität mit historischen und zukünftigen Daten zu sichern. Hieraus ergibt sich Verwendung des gleichen Technologie-Stack mit Golang[6] als Programmiersprache und Docker[7] zum Deployment.

Zur Ermöglichung von Untersuchungen auf unterschiedlichen Detailebenen und zur Schnürung von Paketen für die Studierendenzustimmung, werden Statements auf drei Ebenen definiert. Diese ermöglichen eine flexible und detaillierte Erfassung von Prüfungsdaten. Auf der höchsten Ebene werden übergeordnete Prüfungsvorgänge erfasst, wie z. B. der Start oder das Ende einer Prüfung. Auf der zweiten Ebene werden Aktionen erfasst, die sich auf Fragen innerhalb der Prüfung beziehen, wie zum Beispiel das Öffnen, Beantworten oder Überspringen einer Frage. Diese Ebene erlaubt Analysen auf Basis der Zeitstempel zur Ermittlung der Bearbeitungsdauer einer Aufgabe und zur Abschätzung, wie viel Zeit künftig für die Bearbeitung eingeräumt werden sollte [SS22]. Auf der niedrigsten Ebene kann zusätzlich erfasst werden, auf welche Aufgabenteile sich die Statements beziehen. Ein Statement, das die Auswahl einer Antwortoption repräsentiert, kann zur Distraktoranalyse (vgl. [SS22]) verwendet werden. Zeitstempel erlauben auf dieser Ebene Untersuchungen des Rateverhaltens [SS22].

---

[6] Go, https://go.dev/, Stand: 27.03.2023
[7] Docker, https://www.docker.com/, Stand: 27.03.2023

4 AxEL: Asynchronous xAPI Event Logger

Die Herausforderungen bei der Umwandlung von Prüfungsdaten aus Dynexite in xAPI Statements werden durch die Implementierung eines sogenannten asynchronen xAPI Event Logger (AxEL) adressiert. AxEL besteht aus einem zentralen Service (*AxEL (Core)*) und drei modularen Komponenten (vgl. Abb. 1). Der *AttemptFinder* verwaltet, welche Events bereits umgewandelt wurden und bei welchem Versuch neue Events zur Umwandlung verfügbar sind. Die Events dieses Versuches werden vom *StatementGenerator* in xAPI Statements überführt. Der interne Zustand von Prüfungen und Versuchen ändert sich im Laufe der Zeit. Für die Umwandlung eines Events in ein xAPI Statement müssen daher alle vorherigen Events des Versuches berücksichtigt und in den Gesamtzustand integriert werden, sodass die Reproduzierbarkeit der Statement-Generierung möglich ist. Die Authentifizierung beim LRS und die Übertragung der Statements über die API des LRS übernimmt der *XAPIAdapter*. Diese Services werden in AxEL geladen und können flexibel je nach Kontext (z. B. Produktion oder Testumgebung) ausgetauscht werden. AxEL übernimmt zudem die Fehlerbehandlung, Queueing und Batching des Statement-Versandes sowie zu welchem Zeitpunkt ein Logging stattfinden soll, z. B. immer um drei Uhr morgens.

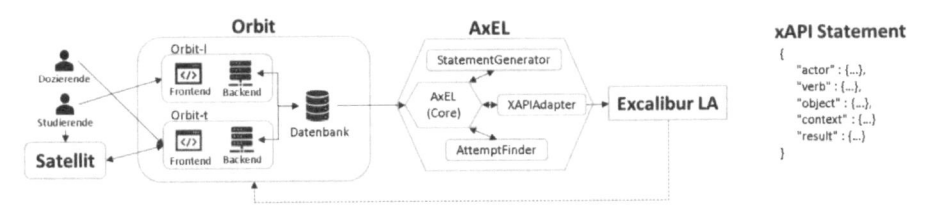

Abb. 1: Softwarearchitektur. Excalibur LA siehe [JS22]. xAPI Statement-Struktur (rechts).

In einem xAPI Statement sind bestimmte Angaben verpflichtend, wie zum Beispiel der *Aktor*, der die Aktion ausführt, das *Verb*, das die Aktion beschreibt, und das *Objekt*, das die Aktivität beschreibt. Darüber hinaus können optionale Felder hinzugefügt werden, die den *Kontext* und das *Ergebnis* beschreiben. Auf der obersten Ebene beziehen sich die Statements jeweils auf ein Assessment, sodass das Objekt eindeutig eine Prüfung (Blueprint) referenziert und mithilfe von *Erweiterungen* Basisinformationen zum Typ des Assessments (überwachte Prüfung, Hausübung oder Übung), Bearbeitungszeitraum, mögliche Bearbeitungszeit sowie bei Prüfungen Informationen zur Kohorte beinhaltet. Im Kontext befinden sich Informationen zum Prüfungssystem, Kurs sowie Organisationseinheit. Die Verben *started, stopped* und *graded* geben Aufschluss über Start und Ende einer Prüfung sowie im Falle eines *graded*-Statements, wie viele Punkte erreicht wurden. Durch weitere, über AxEL hinausgehende Maßnahmen, wird der Schutz der Dozierenden gewährleistet. Analog werden auf den tieferen Ebenen jeweils Aufgabenteile referenziert.

5 Fazit und Ausblick

In diesem Beitrag wurde eine Erweiterung für das Prüfungssystem Dynexite vorgestellt, die interne Event-Daten in xAPI Statements überführt und in die zentrale Learning Analytics Infrastruktur basierend auf [JS22] überträgt. Die Definition der xAPI Statements auf unterschiedlichen Detailebenen ermöglicht die Zusammenstellung von Paketen für die Zustimmung der Studierenden, so können Studierende beispielsweise nur generellen Statistiken oder auch detaillierteren Auswertungen des Antwortverhaltens zustimmen. Sowohl ein reines Berücksichtigen von Ergebnisdaten, als auch ein kleinschrittiges Verfolgen der Prüfungsbearbeitung ist möglich. Durch die vollständig asynchrone Strategie der Erweiterung, wird der Prüfungsprozess nicht beeinflusst.

In zukünftigen Versionen des Prüfungssystems wird eine Zuordnung von Aufgabenteilen erleichtert. Dies vereinfacht die hier vorgestellte Datenübertragung und ermöglicht die Entwicklung konkreter AA Komponenten, wie einer Distraktoranalyse, die genaue Referenzierung der Detailstrukturen benötigt [SS22]. Im Rahmen des Projektes NOVA:ea, gefördert durch die Stiftung Innovation in der Hochschullehre, wird ein Prüfungscockpits zur iterativen Verbesserung der E-Prüfungen entwickelt.

Literaturverzeichnis

[Br22] Brocker, A. et.al.: Juxl: JupyterLab xAPI Logging Interface. In: 2022 International Conference on Advanced Learning Technologies (ICALT), S. 158–160, 2022.

[Ch12] Chatti, M.A. et.al.: A Reference Model for Learning Analytics. In: International Journal of Technology Enhanced Learning (IJTEL) – Special Issue on "State-of-the-Art in TEL", 3. 318–331, 2012.

[El13] Ellis, C.: Broadening the scope and increasing the usefulness of learning analytics: The case for assessment analytics. In: British Journal of Educational Technology, S. 662-664, 2013.

[JSS22] Judel, S.; Schnell, E.; Schroeder, U.: Performantes xAPI Logging in Moodle. In: 20. Fachtagung Bildungstechnologien (DELFI), S. 159–164, 2022.

[JS22] Judel, S.; Schroeder, U.: EXCALIBUR LA - An Extendable and Scalable Infrastructure Build for Learning Analytics. In: 2022 International Conference on Advanced Learning Technologies (ICALT), S. 155–157, 2022.

[Pe21] Persike, M. et.al.: Digitale Prüfungspraxis: Szenarien, Perspektiven, Empfehlungen. In: Whitepaper - Digitale Prüfungen in der Hochschule, 2021.

[SS22] Scheidig, F.; Schweinberger, K.: Assessment Analytics - Daten digitaler Prüfungen auswerten. In: Neues Handbuch Hochschullehre (NHHL), Ausgabe 108, 2022.

[SL11] Siemens, G.; Long, P.: Penetrating the fog: Analytics in learning and education. In: EDUCAUSE review 46(5), S. 31-40, 2011.

Automatisierte Bewertung und Feedback-Generierung für grafische Modellierungen und Diagramme mit FEEDI

Erik Morawetz [1], Nadine Hahm [1] und Andreas Thor [1]

Abstract: Dieser Beitrag präsentiert FEEDI (Feedback im Diagramm-Assessment), ein Web-basiertes System zur automatischen Bewertung und Feedback-Generierung für grafische Modellierungen und Diagramme. FEEDI verfolgt dabei einen generischen Ansatz, in dem es sowohl unterschiedliche Eingabeformate als auch Diagrammtypen prozessiert und Lehrenden die Möglichkeit gibt, Elemente ihrer Musterlösung einfach zu annotieren. Damit ermöglicht FEEDI ein effizientes E-Assessment insbesondere im MINT-Bereich, bei dem Diagramme wichtiger Bestandteil der Hochschullehre sind. Der Beitrag beschreibt die Graph-basierte Repräsentation der Diagramme sowie die Bewertung und Feedback-Generierung unter Verwendung von Graph-Matching. Darüber hinaus skizziert er die prototypische Entwicklung am Beispiel von Entity-Relationship-Diagrammen.

Keywords: E-Assessment, Feedback, Diagramm, Grafische Modellierung

1 Motivation

Grafische Modellierungen und die Erstellung von Diagrammen, wie z.B. UML-Diagramme, Schaltpläne oder Signaldiagramme, spielen eine wichtige Rolle in der Hochschullehre in MINT-Fächern. Sie sind oft Bestandteil von Übungs- und Prüfungsaufgaben, bei denen Studierende insbesondere anwendungsbezogene Kompetenzen nachweisen können. Für das Thema E-Assessment stellen solche Aufgabentypen jedoch eine Herausforderung dar, da die ihre automatisierte Bewertung sehr anspruchsvoll ist. Diagramme visualisieren in der Regel komplexe Zusammenhänge und es existieren meist verschiedene Varianten korrekter Lösungen. Darüber hinaus können Studierende an vielen Stellen kleinere Fehler machen, was eine aufwändige Bewertung mit Teilpunkten notwendig macht.

Es existieren bereits E-Assessment-Lösungen für spezifische Diagrammtypen, wie z.B. für Entity-Relationship- oder UML-Diagramme (u.a. [SG14; SM02]), die dann in der Regel auch mit einer eigenen Anwendung bzw. User Interface für die Erstellung und Bewertung der Diagramme einhergehen. Diese Ansätze können die Spezifika des Diagrammtyps effektiv abbilden und bieten eine sehr gute Unterstützung für die Lernenden, obwohl viele publizierte Arbeiten die technischen Details in den Vordergrund rücken und didaktische Aspekte vermissen lassen [Ul23]. Leider schränken Diagrammtyp-spezifische Ansätze auch die breite Nutzbarkeit ein. Lehrende und Studierende müssen mit einem speziellen

---

[1] Hochschule für Technik, Wirtschaft und Kultur Leipzig, {erik.morawetz, nadine.hahm, andreas.thor}@htwk-leipzig.de

doi: 10.18420/delfi2023-18

Werkzeug arbeiten und können gewohnte Anwendungen, wie z.B. PowerPoint, nicht nutzen. Darüber hinaus erfordert die Einführung eines neuen Diagrammtyps meist die Entwicklung einer neuen Anwendung *from scratch* und damit einen hohen Aufwand.

Dieser Beitrag präsentiert daher mit FEEDI (Feedback im Diagramm-Assessment) einen generischen Ansatz für ein flexibles E-Assessment von Diagrammen, bei dem sowohl unterschiedliche Eingabeformate als auch Diagrammtypen unterstützt werden. FEEDI kann für E-Assessment-Aufgaben eingesetzt werden, bei denen Studierende ein Diagramm als Lösung einreichen, und gibt automatisiert eine Bewertung sowie Feedback. Dazu transformiert es sowohl die Musterlösung (ML) als auch studentische Lösungen (SL) in eine generische Graphstruktur, aus der dann mittels Graph-Matching ein Mapping berechnet wird. Darüber hinaus können Lehrende ihre ML noch annotieren, um den konkreten Bewertungsmaßstab (Punkte für einzelne Elemente), etwaige alternative Lösungen (Varianten) sowie Feedbacktexte für Elemente zu hinterlegen, die z.B. angezeigt werden können, wenn diese Elemente in der SL nicht oder fehlerhaft vorkommen.

Durch FEEDI soll es Lehrenden möglichst einfach gemacht werden, Diagramme als ML zu erstellen, da sie auch bereits existierende Diagramme (z.B. in PowerPoint-Folien ihrer Lehrmaterialien) direkt nutzen können. Auch unterstützt die Architektur von FEEDI die zügige Integration neuer Diagrammtypen, um eine große Verbreitung in unterschiedlichen Fachdisziplinen zu erreichen.

2 FEEDI-Architektur

Abb. 1 illustriert die erweiterbare Architektur von FEEDI. Diagramme können in einem ersten Schritt in unterschiedlichen Formaten eingegeben werden. Dazu bietet FEEDI eine Reihe von **Format-Konvertern**, die jeweils ein bestimmtes Eingabeformat in ein generisches, JSON-basiertes Bildbeschreibungsformat transformieren. Der derzeitige Prototyp unterstützt mit PowerPoint und Diagrams.net zwei häufig zur Erstellung von Diagrammen genutzte Werkzeuge. Damit können insbesondere Lehrende z.B. in PowerPoint gezeichnete Diagramme sowohl in ihren Lehrmaterialien als auch ohne zusätzlichen Aufwand für das E-Assessment mit FEEDI verwenden. Der Format-Konverter für PNG-Bilder, z.B. als eingescannte Stiftzeichnung, ist derzeit noch in Entwicklung.

Alle Format-Konverter erzeugen eine **JSON-basierte Bildbeschreibung**, welche die relevanten Bildelemente, wie z.B. Rechtecke, Pfeile oder Text, in entsprechenden JSON-Objekten repräsentiert. Dazu werden die wesentlichen geometrischen Eigenschaften, u.a. Größe, Position und Rotation, als Attribute gespeichert. Für das E-Assessment irrelevante Information, wie z.B. die Schriftart, werden in diesem Schritt bereits herausgefiltert. Der zentrale Vorteil dieser *generischen* Bildbeschreibung liegt in der Unabhängigkeit sowohl vom Eingabeformat als auch vom Diagrammtyp, wie z.B. Entity-Relationship-Modell oder Signaldiagramm. Es ermöglicht dabei als Austauschformat eine flexible Erweiterbarkeit von FEEDI hinsichtlich neuer Eingabeformate sowie Diagrammtypen. Darüber hinaus können Musterlösungen später einfach im JSON-Format annotiert werden.

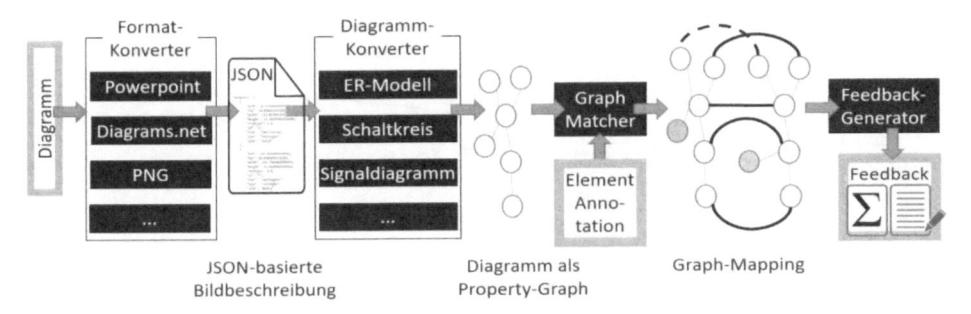

Abb. 1: Architektur und schematischer Workflow von FEEDI.

Im nächsten Schritt wird die generische Bildbeschreibung des Diagramms in einen **Property-Graphen** überführt, d.h. die Bildelemente werden in Knoten sowie Kanten inkl. Attribute (Properties) transformiert. Diese Transformation ist *spezifisch* für jeden Diagramm-Typ und wird von einem **Diagramm-Konverter** realisiert. Für den Diagrammtyp ER-Modell werden z.B. Rechtecke zu Knoten vom Typ Entität und erhalten ein entsprechendes Label – entsprechend dem Text innerhalb des Rechtecks. Abb. 2 zeigt die Transformation für ein Beispiel, das in Kapitel 3 näher diskutiert wird. Die generische Property-Graph-Struktur erlaubt es, die weiteren Verarbeitungsschritte (Graph-Matching sowie Feedback-Generierung) zu vereinheitlichen.

Die bisher skizzierten Verarbeitungsschritte, d.h. die sukzessive Konvertierung von Diagrammen in einen Property-Graphen, werden im Rahmen des E-Assessments sowohl für die von Lehrenden spezifizierte Musterlösung (ML) als auch für eingereichte studentische Lösung (SL) durchgeführt. Beide Graphen sind im Folgenden Eingabe für das **Graph-Matching**, bei dem eine bestmögliche Abbildung zwischen den beiden Graphen gesucht wird. Das Matching wird dabei durch hinzugefügte Kanten zwischen den Knoten aus ML und SL repräsentiert, so dass ein zusammenhängender Graph resultiert. Zusätzliche Eingabe für den Graph-Matcher ist auch eine **Element-Annotation**, mit der Lehrende etwaige Varianten der Lösung spezifizieren, sowie die Bepunktung und Feedback-Texte für die Elemente angeben. Letzteres wird vom **Feedback-Generator** verwendet, um sowohl eine Bewertung (Punktzahl) als auch ein Feedback bzgl. Fehler in der SL zu geben.

3 Automatische Bewertung und Feedback-Generierung

Nachdem alle Diagramme, d.h. sowohl die Musterlösung (ML) als auch die studentische Lösung (SL), jeweils in einen Property-Graphen transformiert wurden, wird der automatische Abgleich auf ein Graph-Matching-Problem reduziert. Abb. 2 zeigt ein einfaches

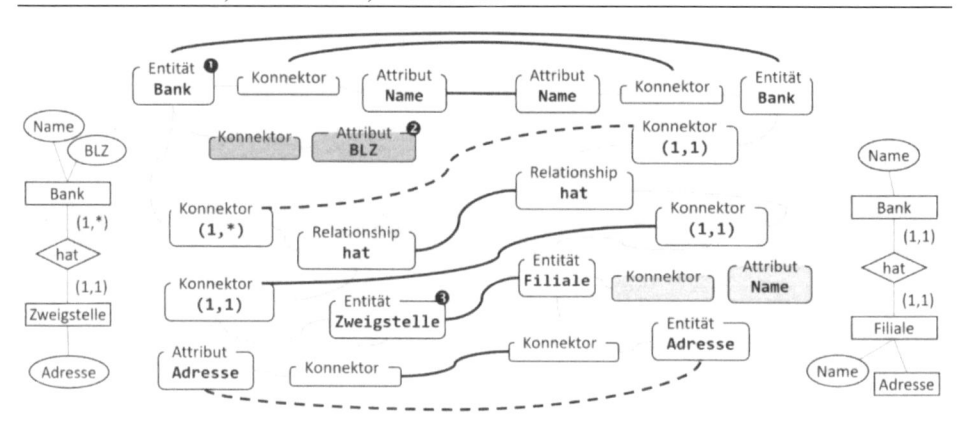

❶ 2 Punkte, "Es gibt mehrere Banken und sie sind eindeutig identifizierbar, daher eine Entität."
❷ 1 Punkt, "Das Attribut BLZ ist relevant zur Beschreibung einer Bank.", changeValue (Label, [Bankleitzahl])
❸ 2 Punkte, "Zweigstelle hat eigene Attribute, daher eine Entität.", changeValue (Label, [Filiale, Niederlassung, Standort])

Abb. 2: Beispiel für eine Musterlösung (links) und eine zugehörige studentische Lösung (rechts), jeweils dargestellt als ER-Diagramm (außen) und Property-Graph (innen). Zusätzlich ist das Mapping zwischen den Graphen dargestellt sowie die Annotation (Punktzahl, Feedbacktext, Variation) für drei ausgewählte Elemente der Musterlösung. Die farblich hinterlegten Graph-Knoten haben keinen Mapping-Partner.

Beispiel. Auf der linken Seite ist ein vereinfachtes[2] Entity-Relationship-Diagramm als ML dargestellt, daneben die interne Repräsentation als Property-Graph. Wie in Kapitel 2 ausgeführt, ist die Konvertierung spezifisch für den Diagrammtyp. Für ER-Diagramme werden u.a. Rechtecke (Entitäten), Rauten (Beziehungen), Ellipsen (Attribute) und die verbindenden Striche (Konnektoren) als relevante Bildelemente in Knoten überführt und mit Kanten verbunden. Informationen zur bildlichen Position werden ignoriert, da sie für die Modellierung keine Rolle spielen – im Gegensatz etwa zu Signaldiagrammen, wo die Positionierung z.B. von Datenpunkten einen Informationsgehalt hat. Für jeden Graph-Knoten (abgerundetes Rechteck) sind in Abb. 2 als Properties der type (oben) sowie – sofern vorhanden – das label im Rechteck notiert. Weitere Properties, z.B. ob es sich bei einem Attribut um ein Primärattribut handelt, können entsprechend ergänzt werden. Auf der rechten Seite sind Diagramm und Graph einer SL dargestellt.

Das **Graph-Matching** erhält nun als Input die zwei Property-Graphen ML und SL und liefert Korrespondenzen (Zuordnungen) zwischen den Knoten der beiden Graphen. Korrespondierende Knoten sind dabei im einfachsten Fall äquivalent, d.h. besitzen die gleichen Werte für alle Properties. Häufig gibt es *ähnliche* Knotenpaare, bei denen Abweichungen in den Property-Werten und benachbarten Knoten auftreten. Zur Quantifizierung wird eine Ähnlichkeitsfunktion verwendet, welche die Knoten bzgl. der Property-Werte

---

[2] Aus Gründen der besseren Lesbarkeit wurde auf die Angabe der Primärschlüssel und Datentypen verzichtet.

und ggf. der benachbarten Knoten miteinander vergleicht und einen Ähnlichkeitswert zwischen 0 (maximale Unähnlichkeit) und 1 (Gleichheit) ermittelt. Für die Entität Bank würde sich z.B. ein Ähnlichkeitswert von 1 ergeben; für den Konnektor zwischen Bank und hat z.B. ein Wert von 0.7, weil es eine kleine Abweichung im label gibt ((1,*) vs. (1,1)).

Das Ergebnis eines Graph-Matching wird als **Mapping** M dargestellt, das alle Knotenpaare (a, b) mit $a \in$ ML und $b \in$ SL enthält, für die eine Korrespondenz mit einer Mindestähnlichkeit $sim \geq sim_{min}$ existiert. Das Mapping kann als bipartiter Graph interpretiert werden, d.h. Knoten von ML und SL werden durch gewichtete Kanten (Gewicht=Ähnlichkeit) verbunden. In Abb. 2 sind die Mapping-Kanten den beiden Graphen ML und SL hinzugefügt worden, so dass ein gemeinsamer (zusammenhängender) Graph entsteht. Zur vereinfachten Darstellung entsprechen durchgezogene Kanten einem Gewicht von 1, die gestrichelten einem Gewicht kleiner als 1. Darüber hinaus bezeichnet $N_{ML} = \{a | \nexists b : (a, b) \in M\}$ alle Knoten, die keinen Match-Partner in SL gefunden haben, d.h. diese Diagrammelemente der ML konnten der SL nicht zugeordnet werden (gelb hinterlegt in Abb. 2). Analog ist N_{SL} die Menge der Knoten, die keine Korrespondenz zu ML haben, d.h. Elemente der SL, die nicht in der ML auftreten (hellblau).

Aus den so erhaltenen Mengen M, N_{SL} und N_{ML} lassen sich nun gemeinsam mit den Annotationen der ML (siehe unten) eine Punktzahl und spezifisches Feedback ableiten. Für die **Punktzahl** werden nur diejenigen Knoten der ML, die in M enthalten sind, d.h. $\{a | \exists b : (a, b) \in M\}$, betrachtet und die annotierte Punktzahl jeweils mit der Ähnlichkeit sim multipliziert und aufsummiert. Abweichungen bzw. Ungenauigkeiten, die sich in einem Ähnlichkeitswert kleiner als 1 widerspiegeln, entspricht das einer Teilpunktbewertung. **Textuelles Feedback** kann zunächst für alle Knoten aus N_{ML} produziert werden, da diese Elemente in der SL erwartet, aber nicht gefunden wurden. Der Annotationstext dieser Elemente kann als allgemeines Feedback à la „Folgende Elemente fehlen" ausgegeben werden. Darüber hinaus kann für die zugeordneten Knoten in SL, die allerdings einen Ähnlichkeitswert $sim < 1$ haben, ein spezifisches Feedback gegeben werden. Der Feedbacktext des zugehörigen Elements in der ML kann als Hinweis für eine Korrektur an die SL ergänzt werden. Für Knoten aus N_{SL} kann es kein textuelles Feedback geben, da die Annotationen nur für die ML vorliegen. Hier bietet FEEDI ein **grafisches Feedback**, d.h. diese Elemente werden in der SL farblich hinterlegt, um anzuzeigen, dass sie in keinem Bezug zur ML stehen. Auch die ML selbst kann als Feedback angezeigt werden.

Wie bereits erwähnt, können Lehrende durch die Annotation ihrer ML Einfluss auf die Bewertung und Feedback-Generierung nehmen (siehe auch Abb. 1). Über ein einfaches GUI können Lehrende die Graph-Darstellung ihrer ML erweitern, in dem sie den Elementen zusätzliche Feedack-Properties geben. In Abb. 2 sind dazu Punktzahl und Feedbacktext exemplarisch für die Entitäten Bank und Zweigstelle sowie für das Attribut BLZ dargestellt. Sollten mehrere Elemente des Diagramms in der Feedbackgenerierung als geschlossene Komponente betrachtet werden, so können diese in Feedbackgruppen zusammengefasst werden. Darüber hinaus besteht die Möglichkeit, **Variationen der Musterlösung** zu spezifizieren, da häufig nicht nur eine Lösung als korrekt angesehen wird. Auch hier nutzt FEEDI die generische Graph-Repräsentation und stellt Variationen als Graph-

Transformationen dar. Ausgehend von der ML können Transformationen wie das Hinzufügen von Knoten (addNode, z.B. für optionale Inhalte) oder das Verändern von Werten (changeValue, z.B. für synonyme Begriffe) auf den Graphen angewendet werden. Im Beispiel von Abb. 2 gibt es für BLZ und Zweigstelle die Möglichkeit, synonyme Begriffe zu verwenden. Synonyme können in der ML angegeben werden, während kleine Schreibfehler durch Ähnlichkeitsschwellenwerte abgefangen werden. Beim Graph-Matching ermittelt FEEDI dann alle möglichen Variationen mit Hilfe der Graph-Transformationen auf der ML und bestimmt das *beste Mapping*, d.h. dasjenige Mapping, welche die höchste Punktzahl liefert. Sollten mehrere unterschiedliche Lösungen existieren, so können mehrere ML hinterlegt werden. FEEDI wählt dann die Option mit der höchsten Ähnlichkeit.

Die prototypische Implementation von FEEDI beinhaltet derzeit mehrere Format- und Diagramm-Konverter sowie einen Graph-Matching-Algorithmus. Für die Annotation der ML können Punkte, Feedbacktext und einfache Variationen spezifiziert werden. Der Einsatz komplexerer Graph-Transformationen ist gerade in Entwicklung. Die einzelnen Komponenten der FEEDI-Architektur sind in Python implementiert und werden als REST-Webservice publiziert, so dass sie flexibel kombiniert werden können.

4 Zusammenfassung und Ausblick

Dieser Beitrag präsentierte mit FEEDI ein E-Assessment-System zur automatischen Bewertung und Feedback-Generierung für grafische Modellierungen und Diagramme. Es soll insbesondere Studierende in MINT-Fächern unterstützen, da die Erstellung solcher Diagramme eine wichtige zu erlernende Kompetenz darstellt. Durch eine generische Architektur unterstützt FEEDI sowohl unterschiedliche Eingabeformate als auch Diagrammtypen. Zentrale Idee von FEEDI ist dabei die Überführung der Diagramme in eine einheitliche Graph-Struktur, auf der ein Graph-Matching angewendet wird, um Gemeinsamkeiten und Unterschiede zwischen Musterlösung und studentischen Lösungen zu identifizieren. Zukünftige Arbeiten umfassen die Fertigstellung der Implementation sowie den praktischen Einsatz von FEEDI in der Lehre.

Literaturverzeichnis

[SG14]   Striewe, M.; Goedicke, M.: Automated Assessment of UML Activity Diagrams. In: Proceedings of the 2014 Conference on Innovation & Technology in Computer Science Education. 2014.

[SM02]   Suraweera, P.; Mitrovic, A.: KERMIT: A Constraint-Based Tutor for Database Modeling. In: Intelligent Tutoring Systems. 2002.

[Ul23]   Ullrich, M. et al.: Automated Assessment of Conceptual Models in Education. Enterprise Modelling and Information Systems Architectures (EMISAJ) 18/2, 2023.

Investigating Feedback Types in JupyterLab for Programming Novices

Annabell Brocker [1] and Ulrik Schroeder [1]

Abstract: Providing valuable, actionable feedback, such as small-step hints and explanations of errors and misconceptions, is essential for guiding novice programmers towards solutions while fostering their code development. This paper presents a comprehensive review of feedback types, available within the interactive programming environment JupyterLab. We distinguish between lower-level, immediate feedback during programming and higher-level, follow-up feedback for reoccurring misconceptions and problems over time. We further discuss potential extensions to provide even more feedback in JupyterLab, such as valuation and recognition of correct activities.

Keywords: Jupyter, Feedback, Programming, Novices

1 Introduction

Despite available technical resources, novices encounter challenges in programming that require substantial cognitive effort [Ka21]. In this context feedback is essential in providing learners with relevant information about their learning progress [HT07, Na08]. This paper therefore examines the feedback capabilities of JupyterLab, an interactive programming environment, and its extensions, exploring the potential for integrating new or revised extensions to enhance and introduce feedback types based on user interactions and learning steps. Due to limited scientific literature on JupyterLab at the time writing this article, a conventional literature review could not be conducted. Instead, both the official JupyterLab repository[2] and various private repositories for JupyterLab extensions were analysed, considering feedback types from [Na08, KJH18] including its complexity and time frame. We categorized feedback into lower-level, immediate feedback, focusing on the current situation without additional context, and higher-level, follow-up feedback, which leverages data and provides information over a longer period.

2 Background and Related Work

JupyterLab[2] is an open source interactive programming environment and can be used as a learning environment. Its main function is to view, edit, and execute Jupyter Notebook

---

[1] RWTH Aachen University, Learning Technologies, {a.brocker, schroeder}@cs.rwth-aachen.de, https://orcid.org/{0009-0007-6708-0892, 0000-0002-5178-8497}
[2] JupyterLab GitHub Repository, https://github.com/jupyterlab/jupyterlab, last accessed: 18.06.2023

doi: 10.18420/delfi2023-19

documents[3] containing cells presenting programming content in easily digestible steps with code, text, images, and/or videos. JupyterLab's modular design supports extensions and pre-configured developments via JupyterHub[4], eliminating the need for OS-specific development environments. This makes it particularly suitable for novices. Additionally, JupyterLab can track learners' interactions using the Juxl extension [Br22a].

Feedback is a fundamental component of effective learning and teaching and aims to increase learners' awareness of their progress and bridge the gap between their current level and desired learning outcomes [HT07, Na08]. For interactive learning environments such as JupyterLab, [Na08] has summarised various feedback types that have been extended to programming education by [KJH18], as illustrated in Figure 1. Elaborative feedback (EF) has been proven to be highly supportive for learning in general as well as in the field of programming [Ha21]. A comprehensive study by [KJH18] examined the use of EF in 101 different programming learning environments and tools, revealing that Knowledge about Mistakes (KM) was integrated into nearly all tools (96%). While existing learning environments offer code feedback through automated testing like unit tests [KJH18], [Je22] highlights the need to provide feedback for achievements as well to motivate learners [MAG18]. Moreover, [Je22] developed intervention guidelines for programming novices based on extended feedback types by [KJH18]. Deciding when to intervene relies on granularity, with seven levels of data collection: (1) keystroke, (2) token, (3) line, (4) file-save, (5) compile, (6) execute and (7) submit. Tokens are often identified by whitespaces or delimiters [Ih15, Je22]. Individual feedback can be provided by monitoring learners' code development interactions at various granularity levels.

Abbreviation			Full Form	Description
KP			Knowledge of Performance	Summative information about achieved performance
KR			Knowledge of Result/Response	Information about correctness
KCR			Knowledge of the Correct Response	Provision of a sample solution
EF			Elaborated Feedback	Additional information other than KR/KCR
	KTC		Knowledge about Task Constraints	Information about task itself / how to deal with the task
		TR	Hints on Task Requirements	Information about task itself
		TPR	Hints on Task-Processing Rules	Information about how to deal with the task
	KC		Knowledge about Concepts	Information on conceptual knowledge for the task
		EXP	Explanations on Subject Matter	Information about task relevant concepts when working on a task
		EXA	Examples Illustrating Concepts	Provision of examples for the relevant concept
	KM		Knowledge about Mistakes	Information on errors / mistakes
		TF	Test Failures	Information from automatic testing
		CE	Compiler Errors	Information about syntactic / semantic errors provided by a compiler
		SE	Solution Errors	Information about runtime / logic errors
		SI	Style Issues	Information about "incorrect" code style
		PI	Performance Issues	Information about code performance
	KH		Knowledge about How to Proceed	Information about how to fix "errors" / mistakes
		EC	Bug-related hints for Error Correction	Concrete information about fixing an error
		TPS	Task-Processing Steps	Information about single steps of task
		IM	Improvements	Information how to make a correct solution more efficient
	KMC		Knowledge about Metacognition	Information for reflecting own learning process

Figure 1: Feedback types for interactive learning environments according to [Na08, KJH18].

---

[3] Jupyter Notebook, https://jupyter-notebook.readthedocs.io/en/stable/notebook.html, last accessed: 18.06.2023
[4] JupyterHub, https://jupyterhub.readthedocs.io/en/stable/, last accessed: 18.06.2023

3 Classification of JupyterLab into Feedback Types

JupyterLab is a constantly developed software with version-dependent extensions and features. The subsequent analyses are based on various versions of JupyterLab 3. All findings are summarized in Figure 2.

JupyterLab's base version incorporates various feedback types. As it is primarily a development environment with an integrated kernel, feedback is provided to learners by the compiler itself. At the compile and execute granularity level, simple feedback informs learners if their code is compilable / executable (KR). However, in cases where code cells have no output, identifying successfully compiled / executed cells can be challenging, often relying on numbering on the left side of the cell. This issue is particularly evident with code cells that lacks output. If a code cell fails to compile / execute, the compiler provides EF in the form of an error message containing details like the exception type and message (EF KM-CE). These error messages sometimes provide specific information about the issue (EF KH-EC). At the execution level, learners receive additional feedback indicating runtime errors (e.g., overflows) or logical errors (EF KM-SE). In cases of code cells ending in infinite loops, an asterisk is displayed in the square brackets on the left side of the cell (EF KM-PI). This feedback does not provide detailed information about the problem but simply signifies the presence of performance issues. JupyterLab 3 introduced an *integrated debugger*, which can be activated and deactivated as needed if the kernel supports debugging, such as ipykernel. The debugger mode includes a variable assignment table and a call stack, offering visualizations of the current state to users (EF KC-EXA). Additionally, JupyterLab provides an *auto-completion mode* pressing the tab key while writing code. However, auto-completion suggestions are limited to instances known to the kernel, potentially providing feedback on available methods for an object (EF KC-EXA). Moreover, JupyterLab allows learners to *view documentation* for already known objects by clicking shift + tab on an instance. Depending on the documentation of the instance, learners receive information about the instance (EF KC-EXP) as well as how to use those (EF KC-EXA). Furthermore, JupyterLab offers to *hide cells*, enabling learners to selectively reveal the solution of tasks in a notebook (KCR). However, it is not entirely reliable, as the inadvertent insertion of hidden cells can occur, limiting its didactic value.

JupyterLab extensions allow the programming environment to be customised to individual needs. [KJH18] highlights automatic code evaluation as an effective feedback mechanism, which can be seamlessly incorporated into JupyterLab using the *nbgrader*[5] extension. nbgrader simplifies the creation of exercise notebooks and enables automatic grading through unit testing [Ju19]. Exercise notebooks can include public tests, allowing learners to execute them and receive feedback as compiler messages (EF KM-TF, EF KM-CE, and EF KM-SE). Lecturers can provide instructions on error rectification (EF KH-EC) or task progression (EF KH-TPS) through the feedback message. Upon submission, lecturers can automatically grade the exercise notebooks and generate HTML feedback

---
[5] nbgrader, https://github.com/jupyter/nbgrader/, last accessed: 18.06.2023

files. These files provide a comprehensive overview of the task requirements, the student's solution, and the test cells, along with their respective compiler messages. The feedback file serves to indicate, at granularity level of submission, whether the submitted code is correct or if there are issues with it (KR) and includes error messages from the tests written by the instructor (EF KM-TF, EF KM-CE, and EF KM-SE). Overall, this feature-rich extension streamlines the grading process and enables students to receive timely feedback on their coding exercises. The *JupyterLab LSP*[6] extension integrates a language server protocol for multiple programming languages into JupyterLab. The extension provides learners with feedback regarding errors and warnings, as well as hints on how to utilize specific instances (EF KC-EXP and EF KC-EXA). However, the feedback may be overwhelming for novices as it assumes a basic understanding of programming. *Juxl Cell Test*[7] incorporates test cells directly into a notebook. These tests are hidden by default from the learner, but can be executed through a "run test" button and the content of the tests itself can only be displayed by navigating via a "View" tab, thus reducing the chance of accidental visibility. If all tests pass, the learner is given visible feedback via a green box labelled "Tests succeeded" (KR). If any of the tests fail, it will be marked with a red box labelled "Tests failed", along with feedback written in test cells by the instructor (KR, EF KM-TF, EF KM-CE, EF KM-SE). Similar to public tests from nbgrader, learners may receive information about how to fix errors (EF KM-EC) or how to process (EF KH-TPS).

Component	Action / Feature	Granularity	Context	KP	KR	KCR	EF KTC TR	EF KC TPR	EF KC EXP	EF KC EXA	EF KM TF	EF KM CE	EF KM SE	EF KM PI	EF KH EC	EF KH TPS	EF KH IM	KMC
JupyterLab	Executing a cell	5 / 6	↓		✓							✓	✓		☑	✓		
	Debugging Modus	5 / 6	↓						✓										
	Code Completion (Tab)	1	↓						✓										
	Tooltip (Shift+Tab)	1	↓					✓	☑										
	Hidden Cells with Sample Solution	1	↓			✓													
nbgrader	Executing public tests	5 / 6	↓/↑		✓		☑				✓	✓	✓		☑	☑		
	HTML Feedback File	7	↓/↑	✓	✓						✓	✓	✓					
JupyterLab LSP	Diagnostic (Panel)	1 / 2 / 3	↓									✓							
	Code Completion & Suggestion	1	↓						✓										
	Jump to Definitions and References	1	↓																
	Hover (Alt)	1	↓					✓	☑										
JupyterLab System Monitor	Display memory and cpu usage of the system	time dependent	↓												☑				
Juxl Cell Test	Run Tests	6 / 7	↓/↑		✓		☑				✓	✓	✓		☑	☑		

Granularity: 1: keystroke   2: token   3: line   4: file-save   5: compile   6: execute   7: submit
Context: ↓: lower-level, immediate   ↑: higher-level, follow-up
Symbols: ✓: fulfilled   ☑: partially fulfilled

Figure 2: Feedback types for JupyterLab and extensions according to [Na08, KJH18].

4 Discussion

JupyterLab and its extensions already provide different types of feedback visualized in Figure 2. Similar to the findings of previous research [KJH18], EF is mostly provided by

---

[6] Language Server Protocol integration for Jupyter(Lab), https://github.com/krassowski/jupyterlab-lsp, last accessed: 18.06.2023
[7] Juxl Cell Test, https://www.npmjs.com/package/@juxl/cut, last accessed: 18.06.2023

KM, particularly KM-CE and KM-SE. The feedback types identified in this review correspond primarily to the category of lower-level, immediate feedback, as they are provided without additional background information, such as an analysis over an extended period or the task context. Only nbgrader provides feedback related to the context, as test cases are adapted to a task. However, the feedback messages mainly depend on the lecturer and can thus be more or less related to the task. To generate higher-level, follow-up feedback, interactions in the environment must be logged and analysed. The Juxl extension provides a basis for this by logging the interactions in the environment, such as editing or executing a code cell, allowing for monitoring and generating feedback on the development of the learner's programming code. For example, it could be used to identify the errors that the compiler throws during code development and thus provide the learner with more detailed feedback on mixing programming concepts (EF KM-EXP). Individual feedback on learners' code could be given by comparing their code with others' code to give hints on how to solve the given problem (EF KH-TPS) or how to improve their code (EF KH-IM), as suggested in previous work by [Co17]. However, appropriate analyses or JupyterLab extensions to generate higher-level, follow-up feedback from the interaction data are currently missing. In addition, JupyterLab currently lacks a centralized location for learners to access their feedback. A possible solution could be the implementation of a dashboard, as proposed in a previous study [Br22b]. Most of the feedback currently available in JupyterLab is designed for programmers with a basic understanding of the domain, making it unsuitable for programmering novices who may find themselves overwhelmed by compiler messages [WLG12]. Adapting feedback to the level of understanding of novices is necessary to enhance accessibility. For example, providing error messages in natural language (EF KM-CE) or offering hints on error resolution (EF KH-EC) can be beneficial. When encountering exceptions like *"NameError: name 'd' is not defined"*, learners may require specific instructions such as checking the spelling or executing the cell where 'd' is defined. To streamline the feedback process for instructors, it is crucial to define feedback in a universally applicable manner rather than addressing each cell individually. Research indicates that visual feedback directly tied to successful activities has positive effects on motivation and frustration reduction for novice learners [MAG18, Je22]. However, in JupyterLab, such feedback is primarily limited to error detection. To address this, a possible solution is to visually highlight code cells once they have been successfully executed, particularly when there is no visible output. Additionally, incorporating simple messages like "good to have you back" or "continue the good practice" when learners access JupyterLab or open specific notebooks can contribute to fostering a positive learning experience, drawing inspiration from the use of game elements [Br22b].

5 Summary and Outlook

This paper reviews the feedback types provided by JupyterLab and its extensions to support learners in their programming tasks. The analysis shows that JupyterLab currently provides several feedback types, but mainly focused on mistakes (KM) based on compiler messages and automatic code evaluation. However, the effectiveness of such feedback for novice learners is limited and requires either adaptation or the creation of new extensions. Additionally, the system's logging capabilities can be leveraged to generate feedback over time and support data-driven approaches. Hence, new extensions should be developed to facilitate the generation of more effective feedback and enhance the learners' experience.

Bibliography

[Br22a]   Brocker, A. et al.: Juxl: JupyterLab xAPI Logging Interface. In: 2022 Int. Conf. on Advanced Learning Technologies, pp. 158-160, 2022.

[Br22b]   Brocker, A et al.: Gamifying JupyterLab to Encourage Continuous Interaction in Programming Education. In: Int. Conf. Games and Learning All., pp. 316-322, 2022.

[Co17]   Chow, S et al: Automated Data-Driven Hints for Computer Programming Students. In: Adjunct Publication of the 25th Conf. on User Modeling, Adaptation and Personalization, pp. 5-10, 2017.

[Ha21]   Hao, Q. et al.: Towards understanding the effective design of automated formative feedback for programming assignment. In: Comput. Sci. Educ, 32, pp. 105-127, 2021.

[HT07]   Hattie, J.A.; Timperley, H.S.: The Power of Feedback. In: Review of Educational Research, 77(1), pp. 81-112, 2007.

[Ih15]   Ihantola, P. et al: Educational Data Mining and Learning Analytics in Programming: Literature Review and Case Studies. In: Proc. of the 2015 ITiCSE on Working Group Reports, pp. 41-63, 2015.

[Je22]   Jeuring, J. et al: Towards Giving Timely Formative Feedback and Hints to Novice Programmers. In: Proc. of the 2022 ITiCSE Working Group Reports, pp. 9-115, 2022.

[Ju19]   Jupyter et al.: nbgrader: A Tool for Creating and Grading Assignments in the Jupyter Notebook. In: Journal of Open Source Education, 2019.

[Ka21]   Kadar, R. et al.: A Study of Difficulties in Teaching and Learning Programming: A Systematic Literature Review. In: Int. Journal of Academic Research in Progressive Education and Development, 10(3), pp. 591-605, 2021.

[KJH18]   Keuning, H.; Jeuring, J.; Heeren, B.: A Systematic Literature Review of Automated Feedback Generation for Programming Exercises. In: ACM Transactions on Computing Education, 19, pp. 1-43, 2018.

[MAG18]   Mattheiss, S.R.; Alexander, E.J.; Graves, W.W.: Elaborative feedback: Engaging reward and task-relevant brain regions promotes learning in pseudoword reading aloud. In: Cognitive, Affective, & Behavioral Neuroscience, 18, pp. 68-87, 2018.

[Na08]   Narciss, S.: Feedback Strategies for Interactive Learning Tasks. In: Handbook of Research on Educational Communications and Technology (3rd ed.), pp. 125-144, 2008.

[WLG12]   Watson, C.; Li, F.W.; Godwin, J.L.: BlueFix: Using Crowd-Sourced Feedback to Support Programming Students in Error Diagnosis and Repair. In: Int. Conf. on Advances in Web-Based Learning, pp. 228-239, 2012.

Kollaboration und Interaktion

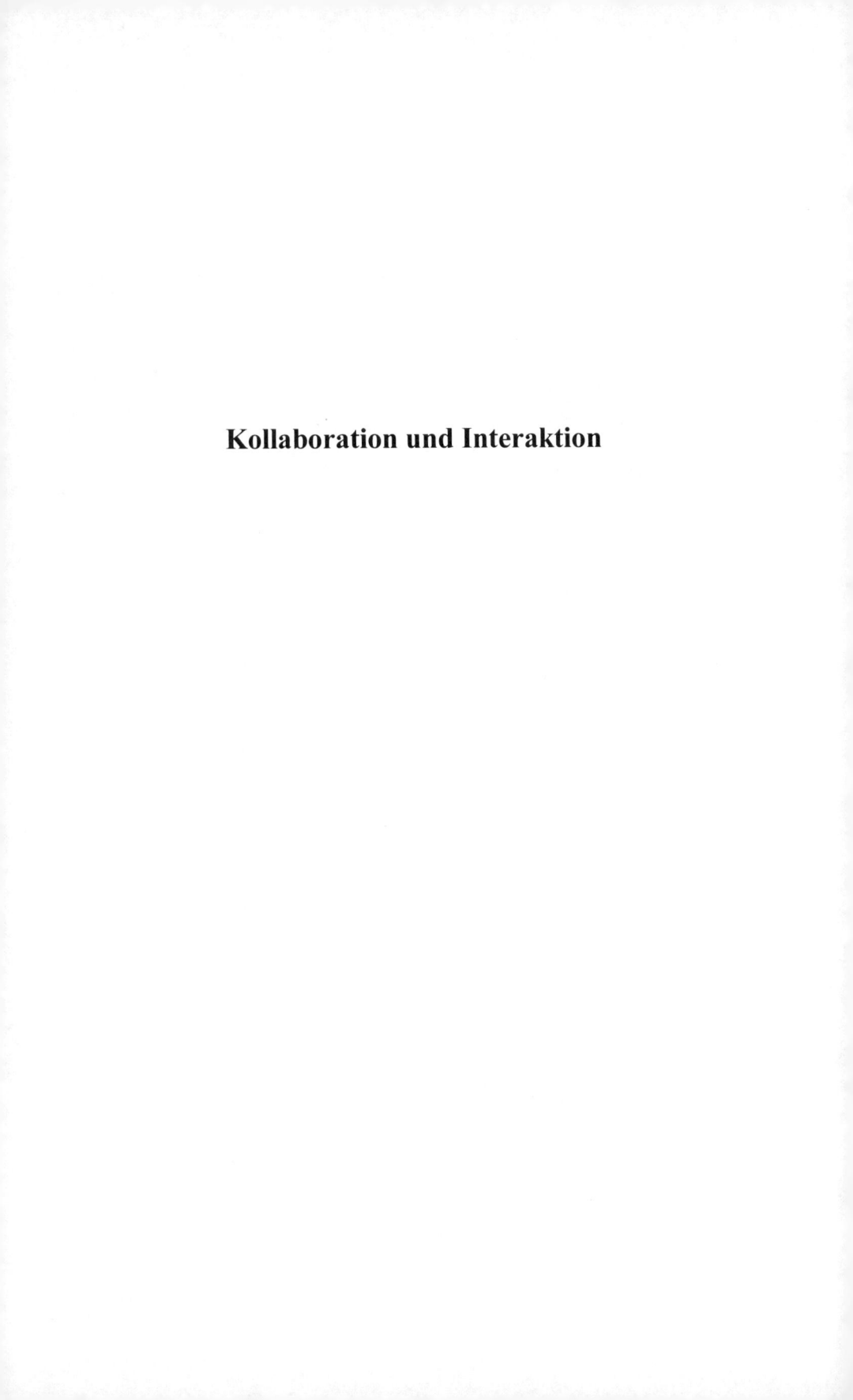

Now you (don't) see me – Camera use in online course settings

Ninja Leikert-Boehm [1], Philipp Matter[1] and Peter Heinrich[1]

Abstract: The COVID-19 pandemic has accelerated the transformation towards online and hybrid teaching. While these modalities have been shown to have many beneficial aspects, they can also limit the social presence and collective engagement in learning activities. In this paper, we present exploratory observations on the role of video features in online and hybrid course settings during the pandemic. By analyzing survey data from three university courses in 2021/2022, we identify different explanations for students' behavior in regulating their social presence by turning their cameras on (or rather off). We suggest that the benefits of cameras are highly contextual and may conflict with students' specific goals and expectations, as well as their territorial habits, which should be taken into account when designing course content and didactic methods.

Keywords: Camera use, online teaching, computer-mediated communication, social presence

1 Introduction

With the advent of the COVID-19 pandemic, teaching activities quickly transitioned to online settings worldwide. While this allowed instruction to continue, it radically changed the social environment of the classroom into a dispersed crowd of individuals rather than a collective learning community of students.

Beginning in the fall semester of 2021/2022, our business school allowed and (technically) enabled us to teach courses in hybrid classrooms, with some students on campus and others online. This allowed us to conduct an explorative study to investigate students' behavior in online settings compared to hybrid courses regarding social presence and camera use.

In terms of learning outcomes, recent literature suggests that online instruction should perform as well as face-to-face instruction in most cases [DS21a, MM21]. When comparing learning outcomes in face-to-face and hybrid distance courses, Daigle and Stuvland [DS21b] found that perceptions of social presence significantly predicted learning performance, far more so than modality.

Building on these observations, we were interested in comparing student ratings between hybrid (in-person or online attendance) and online-only courses, i.e., whether students who participated in in-person classes in one of the courses would evaluate their experience

---

[1] Zurich University of Applied Sciences, School of Management and Law, Theaterstrasse 17, 8401 Winterthur, {ninjairina.leikert-boehm, philipp.matter, peter.heinrich}@zhaw.ch, https://orcid.org/0000-0002-8815-0198

doi: 10.18420/delfi2023-20

differently than students who attended online only. Anecdotal evidence from our early COVID-19 emergency online classes indicated that students were passive participants and were reluctant to activate their video cameras, even when asked to do so. Because such behavior is likely to affect perceptions of collective social presence, we asked the students to provide reasons for using or not using the camera.

Against this background, in this paper, we present our findings on the following explorative research question: *How do participants use their video cameras in online courses and why?*

The results of this work are relevant to the design of future high-quality courses that not only impart knowledge but also embed students in a community of practice. The demand for flexible course formats has grown steadily over the last decade and has been further accelerated by COVID-19. We, therefore, do not expect it to slow down any time soon.

2 Related work

To address our research question, we focused on social presence, an important construct in computer-mediated communication, and its implications for online teaching, as well as the associations of social presence with technological support, especially the role of visual representations such as video.

Research on camera use suggests the benefits of video activation in terms of social presence [Ba20, CS21, SVA22]. However, negative aspects, such as invasion of privacy or technical problems that jeopardize the proper use of the video function, have also been discussed as justifications for not using a camera [CS21, SVA22]. The negative impact of perceived privacy on social presence is a well-known phenomenon and challenge in distance learning situations [TM02].

Computer-mediated communication technologies have long been studied in terms of how, to what extent, and with what effects they can convey social information. Media richness theory [DL86] attempts to compare communication media according to their "richness" and their ability to convey social cues, hypothesizing that richer media (e.g., video conferencing) should be more effective when communicating ambiguous information.

In their theory of media synchronicity, Dennis and Valacich [DV08] suggest that it is not the richness of a medium that is important, but its synchronicity, i.e., the extent to which communication participants are working together on the same tasks. They propose that lower synchronicity is required for conveyance processes (i.e., less need to transmit and process information simultaneously) than for convergence processes (i.e., the greater need to transmit and process information quickly to develop a common understanding). Suitable media for low synchronicity would be documents or email and for high synchronicity face-to-face meetings or video conferences [DV08, p. 589].

The common assumption of the above research is that certain characteristics of a medium can increase or decrease social presence, with most finding that face-to-face conversations are the "gold standard" for achieving social presence. Other research suggests that individuals can adapt to different communication media to achieve their goals, such that environments with fewer communication cues can produce the same social presence, although it may take longer to establish [OBW18, p. 3]. Rettie [Re03] suggests that, while media richness and social presence are important, individuals choose communication channels primarily according to the degree of desired connection.

From a more practical perspective, research has identified various antecedents of social presence and how to address them through technology, such as visual representation, interactivity, audio quality, and haptic feedback [OBW18]. For online learning environments, the role of video seems particularly interesting. While the visual representation of participants (e.g., avatars, profile pictures) has consistently been found to improve social presence, Oh et al. [OBW18] report that less than half of the studies reviewed found that adding video to audio improved social presence. This indicates that increasing immersion does not necessarily increase social presence, suggesting a threshold of diminishing returns [OBW18, p. 20].

Depending on the social orientation of the participants, visual interaction via video may or may not be preferable for online interaction [OBW18, p. 25]. Regarding the benefits of video on social presence, Yoo and Alavi [YA01] found that the media condition (audio vs. video conferencing) had a significantly smaller effect on social presence than group cohesion in established groups. Also, in cooperative digital games, Gajadhar [Ga12] found that communicating with other players via audio works better than via video because the player's visual channel is already heavily taxed by the game.

Finally, it should be mentioned that social presence is not only influenced by technology, but is also highly dependent on other factors, such as course design, participation, and instructors [Ar03].

3 Study design and procedure

We explored the research question by observing three courses in our MSc program in Information Systems in the fall semester of 2021/2022 for all classes.[2] All courses were rewarded with three credit points (ECTS) and spanned over 14 weeks (with a corresponding number of attendance units, 90 min each). Attendance was voluntary for all courses. The detailed course characteristics are shown in Tab. 1.

---

[2] Our business school groups students into classes of about 50, so the courses were evaluated by two classes.

	Enterprise Architecture (***EPA_online***)	**IT Security** (***ITS_hybrid***)	**Project and Change Management** (***PCM_online***)
Syllabus	Practical modeling of enterprise architectures.	Technical foundations of IT security with hands-on lab experience.	Basic Leadership, business transformation, and multi-project management.
Teaching concept	Flipped classroom: self-learning with videos and literature, discussion of exercises in units.	Synchronous lectures and hands-on lab homework.	Synchronous lectures, case analysis, and exercises (including group exercises).
Teaching mode	Online only (Microsoft Teams).	Hybrid: students were free to participate online (Cisco Webex) or in person.	Online only (Zoom).
Course assessment	Written final exam.	Written final exam.	Two graded group assignments and three online tests (pass/fail).
Recording	All attendance units were video recorded.	All attendance units were video recorded.	No attendance units were video recorded (with one exception for organizational reasons).

Tab. 1: Course characteristics

Students were surveyed at the end of the semester using an online questionnaire distributed through the central learning management system.

The online questionnaire consisted of a general section to collect participant information (class affiliation, academic background, employment status). In addition, specific questions per course were asked (i.e., three times total; one block of questions per course to avoid relative ratings of the courses).[3]

For our research question regarding camera usage, we collected the following information from the participants:

- *Number of synchronous units* attended (in steps of two from zero to 14)

---

[3] Quantitative results of the course evaluation regarding social presence are presented in [MLH23].

- *Usage of a video camera* when participating online ("mostly yes" or "mostly no")
- *Rationale* for video camera use (free text)

We analyzed participants' responses descriptively as to whether they activated their cameras during their online participation. Survey participants were able to give multiple reasons and to give different reasons for different courses. All students in the two classes of the semester (97 participants in total) were invited to participate in the survey. 30 students completed the survey (30.93% response rate), of which 25 students responded to the open-ended question (25.77% response rate).

Following Saldaña [Sa15], the first cycle of analysis focused on participants' rationales for using the camera, employing attribute coding (i.e., extracting meta-information for data management) and initial descriptive coding (i.e., coding the free text responses with their dominant themes). We inductively defined codes for and against camera use, resulting in an initial exploratory set of categories. We then applied code mapping [Sa15] to further categorize the emerging codes and categories (see Tab. 2). The coding process was performed sequentially by the first and second authors, and disagreements were resolved. All authors reviewed the results.

4 Results

Almost half of the participants came from class A (n = 13) and half from class B (n = 17). Exactly half of the respondents indicated a technical background and the other half reported none. Most participants reported working part-time (80%, n = 24), few worked full-time (13.33%, n = 4), and two participants did not provide any information.

Most of the participants attended classes regularly, apart from *PCM_online*. Unlike the other two courses, where end-of-semester exams had to be taken, *PCM_online* grading was administered during the semester – students were thus often present only at those units that were relevant to them.

Across all courses, participants consistently reported that they had not activated their cameras most of the time when participating online (Fig. 1). Participants gave various reasons why they did (not) activate the camera. In general, fewer reasons were given for the *ITS_hybrid* course, as only online participants answered the questions about camera usage for this course.

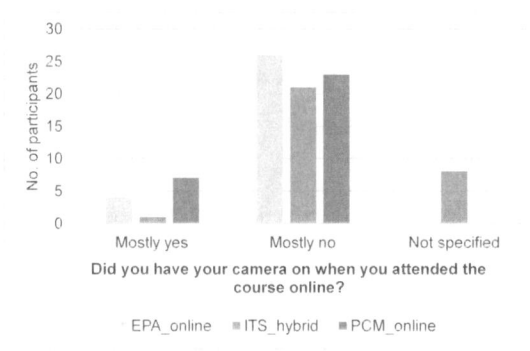

Fig. 1: Camera usage in online classes

Tab. 2 provides an overview of the reasons and the total number of participants who indicated these for at least one of the courses. Some reasons could be assigned to more than one category.

Category/reason	Camera	#
Learning		19
Group dynamics: "no one else turned on the camera", undesired focus on the visible few	OFF	9
Better concentration without camera, less biased, more active listening	OFF	2
Better social interaction, more dynamics, and more engagement with activated camera	ON	3
Using the camera when actively involved, e.g., speaking or presenting	ON/OFF	3
Using the camera when collaborating in smaller working groups	ON/OFF	2
Privacy		14
Wish not to be seen or observed (also during unrelated activities like housework or eating)	OFF	8
Wish not to be recorded on video	OFF	4
Better concentration without camera, less biased, more active listening	OFF	2
Lecturer		12
Better social interaction, more dynamics, and more engagement with activated camera	ON	3
Out of respect for the lecturer	ON	3
Actively addressed, asked, or wished for and/or requested by the lecturer	ON	3
Lecturer did not care; annoyed by lecturer's wish to turn the camera on	OFF	3
Technology		5
No camera, issues with internet connection, camera orientation, lighting	OFF	5

Tab. 2: Reasons for (not) using the camera

The most frequently mentioned reasons for not turning on the camera were related to the learning situation (19). The most common reason in this category was group dynamics (9). Participants mentioned that only a few other students turned on their cameras, making them the center of attention – students who found this uncomfortable thus refrained from using the camera. Another reason for turning off the camera was concentration, with participants finding that it allowed them to focus better on the content of the course or to listen with less distraction from appearances (2). Reasons for participating with an activated camera included better social interaction and dynamics, and that students were more engaged and involved (3).

Other participants indicated that they used the camera selectively or contextually, seeking a better interaction experience in certain situations. They activated the camera only when they were actively participating in class, such as speaking or presenting (3), or when they were working in small group exercises (2).

The second most common reasons were related to privacy (14). Some participants indicated that they did not want to be seen or observed, especially during activities unrelated to the course, such as housework or eating (8). Others specifically did not want to be recorded on video (4). To some extent, these privacy concerns overlap with reasons for better concentration and more active listening when the camera is turned off (2), as concerns about being observed are removed.

A comparison of the results between the courses shows that more participants mentioned privacy aspects in the *EPA_online* course. Although all attendance units were recorded in *ITS_hybrid* as well, in *EPA_online* the recordings invariably concerned all (online) participants, whereas in *ITS_hybrid* the in-person participants were not recorded.

Another category of frequently cited reasons for (not) using the camera concerns the lecturer (12). This is the only category that mainly provides reasons in favor of activating the camera. Reasons cited include better interaction, more dynamic and engaged participation (3), respect for the lecturer (3), and the lecturer actively asking to turn on the camera (3). Reasons for not using the camera included the impression that the lecturer was not interested or, on the contrary, was too demanding (3).

This last point is the biggest difference between the courses. The lecturer's active (and repeated) request in *PCM_online* to turn on the camera in class resulted in more cameras being turned on overall (as compared to the other courses). However, some students indicated that they felt compelled to do so. In one case, a student activated the camera despite feeling uncomfortable. In another case, a student felt the request was presumptuous, so he or she did not activate the camera at all.

Technical reasons for not using the camera were the least common (5). Some of the reasons were purely technical, such as no camera available or problems with the Internet connection. Others were related to unfavorable camera orientations and poor lighting conditions.

We did not find any significant effects of camera use on social presence in our study results. However, the test power was not sufficient to detect such effects with sufficient probability.[4]

5 Discussion

After three semesters of online instruction, we had ample evidence, albeit anecdotal, that students generally activated their cameras only when they needed to. Against this backdrop, the results of our survey were not surprising: as none of the courses had a requirement to activate the camera (mainly due to the recommendations from the school's legal department), the majority of participants reported not activating their cameras in online classes – but for very different reasons.

We found that camera use had little to do with technological conditions – very few participants reported that they did not have a camera, for example, or that the quality of their camera or Internet connection was inadequate. On the contrary, the motivation for and against camera use seemed to be strongly influenced by the learning context.

First and foremost, group dynamics seem to play an important role: students will not turn on their cameras if the others do not either. This can be explained from several perspectives: On the one hand, the principle of reciprocity may apply [WA99], i.e., participants will only show themselves if others do the same. On the other hand, and at the same time, network effects [SV99] may contribute to this behavior, i.e., activating the camera will only be helpful (e.g., to create increased social presence and interaction) if a certain minimum number of participants do so. Otherwise, there may even be negative effects of unwanted "more attention", as one participant pointed out.

Furthermore, the activation of the camera seems to be very task-dependent. In lectures, the focus of the participants is typically on the lecturer and his or her slides, so transmitting one's image or seeing other participants provides little additional benefit – thus, participants actively "filter out" the respective social cues [WP02]. This task dependency mirrors findings in cooperative digital games: video communication can increase the cognitive load of users who are already visually engaged with primary information [Ga12, p. 145]. In contrast, collaboration and discussion in groups seem to strongly promote camera activation: here, participants prefer increased interactivity, for which sharing facial expressions and gestures is seen as beneficial.

We suggest that the observed camera usage behavior could also be related to territorial habits known from environmental psychology [MU03, p. 9]: it is assumed that individuals exhibit different perceptions, attitudes, and behaviors depending on their social or physical context, e.g., private spaces, semi-public environments, and public environments. Coincidentally, cameras seem to contradict these habits by directly and immediately

---

[4] Quantitative results regarding social presence are presented in [MLH23].

linking private and (semi-) public environments. Since private spaces allow one to isolate or protect oneself from the intrusion of others [MU03, p. 9], it seems reasonable that participants would be wary of being seen or recorded in their private spaces; turning off the camera could be a coping strategy to regain control and overcome uncomfortable feelings.

Currently, online collaboration tools offer few options for limiting the association of private and public environments (e.g., selecting an image or blurring the video background). Future research could address this issue by providing better (technical) control over what is revealed from the private space, and in what context.

The observation that some students do not activate their cameras during online classes for fear of being seen doing household chores or eating raises the possibility that the phenomenon of fear of missing out (FOMO) may extend to class participation. While previous research has primarily examined FOMO in the context of social media use [GS21] and its effects on student performance [QA19], little attention has been paid to its relevance to online course participation. Some students who participate in an online course may do so in search of a sense of connection with others rather than learning, leading them to engage in parallel activities while turning off their cameras. Further investigation of the intersection of FOMO, camera use, and student engagement in online courses is warranted to gain a deeper understanding of these dynamics.

Finally, while students may have good reasons to be "invisible," there appear to be legitimate reasons for lecturers to activate cameras. For example, there is a basic need for them to be aware of their audience and to acknowledge their reactions (e.g., frowning, laughing), preferably in real-time. Future research should explore ways to obtain such feedback during lectures without the need for cameras (e.g., through digital "mood boards" that display feelings and feedback in an abstract form).

6 Conclusion

After several semesters of educational change forced by COVID-19, universities are struggling to establish a new "normal". The literature suggests that online environments can lead to similar learning outcomes as in-person classes, but that they also affect social presence.

In this exploratory study, we contribute to the understanding of the role of video in moderating social presence in the online classroom. The one-size-fits-all approach of current collaboration tools only partially meets the diverse needs of students and instructors. Particularly in lectures, this often leads to students turning off their cameras, suggesting interesting research opportunities for a more nuanced design of such tools, e.g., in terms of territorial habits.

As with any study, there are limitations to this research. Further research, such as the use of multiple case studies and interview techniques, could be considered to provide better validation. In addition, further quantitative research approaches may be helpful. It is important to acknowledge that our study was conducted during a period heavily influenced by the COVID-19 pandemic. Thus, our findings may have been subject to the unique circumstances associated with distance learning during the pandemic. It would be useful to gain further insight from future studies to understand the complex factors influencing camera use in online and hybrid courses in a post-pandemic context.

Bibliography

[Ar03] Aragon, S.: Creating social presence in online environments. In: New Directions for Adult and Continuing Education 100, pp. 57–68, 2003.

[Ba20] Basch, J. et.al.: Smile for the camera! The role of social presence and impression management in perceptions of technology-mediated interviews. In: Journal of Managerial Psychology 35, pp. 285–299, 2020.

[CS21] Castelli, F.; Sarvary, M.: Why students do not turn on their video cameras during online classes and an equitable and inclusive plan to encourage them to do so. In: Ecology and Evolution 11(8), pp. 3565–3576, 2021.

[DL86] Daft, R.; Lengel, R.: Organizational information requirements, media richness and structural design. In: Management Science 32(5), pp. 554–571, 1986.

[DS21a] Daigle, D.; Stuvland, A.: Social Presence as Best Practice: The Online Classroom Needs to Feel Real. In: PS: Political Science & Politics 54(1), pp. 182–183, 2021.

[DS21b] Daigle, D.; Stuvland, A.: Teaching Political Science Research Methods Across Delivery Modalities: Comparing Outcomes Between Face-to-Face and Distance-Hybrid Courses. In: Journal of Political Science Education 17(S1), pp. 380–402, 2021.

[DV08] Dennis, A.; Valacich, J.: Media, tasks, and communication processes: A theory of media synchronicity. In: MIS Quarterly 32(3), pp. 575-600, 2008.

[Ga12] Gajadhar, B.: Understanding player experience in social digital games: the role of social presence. Doctoral thesis, Technische Universiteit Eindhoven, 2012.

[GS21] Gupta, M.; Sharma, A.: Fear of missing out: A brief overview of origin, theoretical underpinnings and relationship with mental health. In: World Journal of Clinical Cases, 9(19), pp. 4881–4889, 2021.

[MLH23] Matter, P.; Leikert-Boehm, N.; Heinrich, P.: Depreciating the online experience: Relative evaluation of social presence in online, hybrid, and offline course environments. In: DELFI 2023, 21. Fachtagung Bildungstechnologien der Gesellschaft für Informatik e.V. Aachen, Germany, 2023.

[MU03] Moser, G.; Uzzell, D.: Environmental Psychology. In: Millon, T.; Lerner, M. (Eds.): Comprehensive Handbook of Psychology, Volume 5: Personality and Social Psychology. John Wiley & Sons, New York, pp. 419–445, 2003.

[MM21] Müller, C.; Mildenberger, T.: Facilitating flexible learning by replacing classroom time with an online learning environment: A systematic review of blended learning in higher education. In: Educational Research Review 34, 100394, 2021.

[OBW18] Oh, C.; Bailenson, J.; Welch, G.: A Systematic Review of Social Presence: Definition, Antecedents, and Implications. In: Frontiers in Robotics and AI 5, 114, 2018.

[QA19] Qutishat, M.; Abu Sharour, L.: Relationship Between Fear of Missing Out and Academic Performance Among Omani University Students: A Descriptive Correlation Study. In: Oman Medical Journal, 34(5), pp. 404–411, 2019.

[Re03] Rettie, R.: A Comparison of Four New Communication Technologies. In: Proceedings of HCI International Conference on Human-Computer Interaction. Crete, Greece, 2003.

[Sa15] Saldaña, J.: The coding manual for qualitative researchers. Sage, 2015.

[SVA22] Sederevičiūtė-Pačiauskienė, Ž.; Valantinaitė, I.; Asakavičiūtė, V.: 'Should I Turn on My Video Camera?' The Students' Perceptions of the use of Video Cameras in Synchronous Distant Learning. In: Electronics 11(5), 2022.

[SV99] Shapiro, C.; Varian, H.: Information rules: a strategic guide to the network economy. Harvard Business School Press, Boston, 1999.

[TM02] Tu, C.; McIsaac, M.: The Relationship of Social Presence and Interaction in Online Classes. In: American Journal of Distance Education 16(3), pp. 131–150, 2002.

[WP02] Walther, J.; Parks, M.: Cues Filtered Out, Cues Filtered in: Computer Mediated Communication and Relationships. In: Miller, G. R. (Ed.): The Handbook of Interpersonal Communication. Sage, Thousand Oaks, pp. 529–563, 2002.

[Wa99] Whatley, M.: The Effect of a Favor on Public and Private Compliance: How Internalized is the Norm of Reciprocity? In: Basic and Applied Social Psychology 21(3), pp. 251–259, 1999.

[YA01] Yoo, Y.; Alavi, M.: Media and Group Cohesion: Relative Influences on Social Presence, Task Participation, and Group Consensus. In: MIS Quarterly 25(3), pp. 371–390, 2001.

Shared listening experience for hyperaudio textbooks

Niels Seidel [1], Robin Dürhager[2], Marcel Goldammer[2], Alexander Henze[2], Frank Langenbrink[2], Joachim Otto[2] and Veronika Stirling[2]

Abstract: The integration of multimedia elements into educational materials has the potential to improve students' engagement and understanding. In this paper, we present the development of an hyperaudio player that represents textbook information in auditory format, providing a joint playback experience for groups of users. Additionally, the Moodle-based hyperaudio player includes a voice chat feature, allowing for real-time discussions among users when the audio is paused. We aim to investigate the appropriateness of hyperaudio as a new online learning format.

Keywords: Hyperaudio, Multimedia Learning, Collaborative Learning

1 Introduction

Informal knowledge transfer through podcasts, audiobooks, and radio documentaries enjoys great popularity. However, in formal learning settings at schools or universities, auditory learning resources are rarely used. Compared to text, audio productions are more expensive and have a less distinct academic tradition. Furthermore, audio-based learning is perceived as an individual learning activity. In this paper, we are contrasting common online textbooks with a well-designed interactive auditory complement summarized as hyperaudio. Furthermore, we propose hyperaudio as a format for collaborative learning. The combination of hyperaudio and collaborative learning shall provide a mobile learning experience comparable with a telephone conference among peers where the textbook is read aloud on request.

As a follow-up to our previous research [Se22] about the conversion pipeline and mapping from course text to a single hyperaudio document in Moodle, we present the design and development of an hyperaudio player that represents a textbook alongside its corresponding auditory representation, providing a joint playback experience for collaborative learning for groups of users.

---

[1] Forschungszentrum CATALPA, FernUniversität in Hagen, Universitätsstrasse 27, 58097 Hagen, niels.seidel@fernuni-hagen.de, https://orcid.org/0000-0003-1209-5038
This research was supported by the Center of Advanced Technology for Assisted Learning and Predictive Analytics (CATALPA) of the FernUniversität in Hagen, Germany.

[2] Fakultät für Mathematik und Informatik, Lehrgebiet Kooperative Systeme, Universitätsstrasse 27, 58097 Hagen, {vorname.nachname}@studium.fernuni-hagen.de

doi: 10.18420/delfi2023-21

2 Related Works

This section summarizes related work regarding hyperaudio learning environments as well as technical approaches to create audio from text-based resources. In contrast to other instructional formats such as hypertext, there is only little research on learning with hyperaudio yet [ZS14,ZM20,DB07]. Donker and Blenn laid a foundation for the use of audio in hypermedia applications with the Hyperaudio Encyclopedia [DB07]. In that project, unlike the use of screen readers, articles in the encyclopedia were not just recorded and read to the listener. The users were able to interact with the audio document. For instance, links, headings, and other salient test passages were highlighted by auditory markers and recognizably presented to the listener. In terms of learning, [Re09] encouraged receptive processes for listening rather than equating them with passivity. Receptive processes, such as listening to podcasts, must be contrasted with productive learning processes. Reinmann suggested improving the quality of storytelling and listening through modern technologies. In her doctoral dissertation [Ha18] revealed that the implementation of books that are read aloud using a human voice (audiobooks) can positively impact the reading experience, at least for elementary students. In a study, [ZS14] compared textually and auditorily represented information in linear and non-linear forms. The non-linear representation increased cognitive load compared to linear representations. In more recent research, [ZM20] investigated the design of mobile hyperaudio learning environments. Referring to these results, hyperaudio should be designed in a linear rather than non-linearity manner. Non-linearity increases cognitive load and is less conducive to learning.

In terms of hyperaudio technology, existing frameworks such as popcorn.js, wavsurfer.js, or timesheet.js [CQR11] can be used for implementation. Also, several commercial services like Soundcloud or YouTube offer the possibility to markup continuous audio documents similar to hyperaudio players. Capable text-to-speech systems for the German language are mainly provided by big players like Amazon Web Services (Polly), Google (text-to-speech), and Microsoft Azure. Open source systems like Thorstem Voice[3] are promising but cannot create customized time markers and features like pitch and pauses. For manual audiobook production, among others, the open source tool Obi[4] supports standards like DAISY 3[5], W3C Audio Books and Accessible EPUB 3.

To the best of our knowledge, no hyperaudio player is yet available that is capable to convert text to audio, presenting rich audible content, and facilitating collaborative learning.

---

[3] See https://www.thorsten-voice.de/ (accessed 2023/04/02).
[4] See https://daisy.org/activities/ (accessed 2023/04/02).
[5] See https://daisy.org/activities/standards/daisy/daisy-3/ (accessed 2023/04/02).

3 Design and Implementation

Since hyperaudio is an interplay of hypermedia and audio, neither ordinary audio players nor ordinary hypermedia systems can accurately represent such content. For this reason, a new hyperaudio player was conceived as a blend of audio player and hypermedia application dedicated to collaborative learning. The hyperaudio player was developed as an activity plugin for the learning management system Moodle. The source code is provided under GPLv3 license at https://github.com/nise/mod_hypercast.

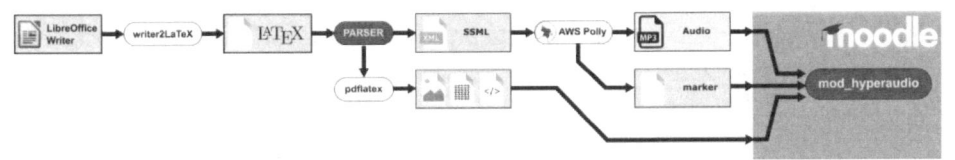

Fig. 1: Workflow of hyperaudio creation form course texts as proposed in Seidel [Se22].

Fig. 2: Hyperaudio player design with the (1) vertical progress bar, (2) personal marker, (3) group members' markers, (4) live session start option, (5) comment pop-over and a (6) comment highlighted in the text.

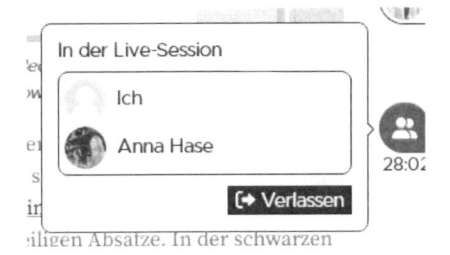

Fig. 3: Live session marker displaying the users who are in the current live session.

The hyperaudio player is based on a hypertext representation of a textbook chapter. For our intended use case a chapter may consist of 40 to 60 standard text pages including all kinds of content representations including images, tables, code, formulas as well interactive controls (e.g. links) and even videos or other audio. Referring to our previous work [Se22] we were able to map text-based design elements of typical course texts to an auditory hyperaudio representation using Amazon Polly as text-to-speech systems (TTS) as well as audio effects (e.g. panning for bulletin lists) and audio cues (e.g. acoustic indication of non-audio contents like images) during the playback. As shown in Fig. 1, we intended to provide teachers with a way to convert existing course text into ready-to-use hyperaudio documents to be implemented in Moodle courses. Thus, the course text remains a nicely readable text rather than a text-only transcript of the audio. In contrast to audiobooks or podcasts effects and audio cues are included at runtime considering recent interactions with other users (e.g. comments).

Other than common audio players we've turned the timeline of the audio player from horizontal to vertical to be in line with the scrollbar used for navigating the text (Fig. 2). Concerning a mobile-first design, the playback controls are arranged at the bottom of the screen. The text scrolls synchronously to the audio playback progress. While the vertical timeline indicated the current playback position with a personal marker, the current text passage gets visually highlighted. Navigation within the text and audio can be achieved through a click on the timeline or a text passage. The graphical user interface is currently optimized for right-handed users. For instance, the timeline is placed on the right to be controlled using the right thumb. The same accounts for the playback controls. The users are encouraged to take their eyes off the screen while listening to the audio. Due to the audio cues, they get notified about non-audio content visible on the screen. Collaboration is facilitated on a group level. Large student cohorts can self-organize collaborative activities by creating, managing, and joining one or multiple groups. These groups are persistent across all existing hyperaudio instances within a Moodle course. However, it is advisable to limit group size not to congest the collaboration space with the user's virtual representation (e.g. playback positions, avatars) and traces (e.g. comments). Group members share equal privileges except for the creator of a group is allowed to change group settings (e.g. maximal group size, group name). All group members are represented on their last playback position on the timeline. Their representation consists of a profile image, name, and current online status. This means the hyperaudio player provides support for workspace awareness.

The player supports asynchronous and synchronous communication facilities. Content-related communication is mainly supported through comments that are anchored to text passages that are linked to precise playback positions in the audio. Comments are visually highlighted in the text and audibly emphasized in the audio. A comment can be classified as a question, remark, or note to invoke direct replies from other group members. As a result, text and audio can be augmented with multiple threaded discussions. Synchronous communication is achieved through so-called *live sessions*. In contrast to listening to the audio individually, the live session is shared by multiple group members who are currently online. Group members joining a live session synchronously listen to the audio. Group members can join and leave the live session whenever they want. Each participant in the live session is in control of the audio playback affecting all participants. As long as a group member stays in the live session the audio plays or pauses for all participants at the same temporal position. Concurrency control is ensured by a social protocol and group awareness instruments indicating the current status of the live session and a list of participants (Fig. 3). In case one is changing the playback status (e.g. from play to pause, changing playback speed, seeking on the timeline) other participants of the live session are notified by a toast notification. When the audio is paused the participants can talk to each other using voice chat if they enable their microphones. The voice chat terminates as soon as the audio playback continues. Online group members who did not join the live session also see on the timeline who has joined the live session and where they are currently located in the text and audio.

4 Evaluation

Due to the novelty of the collaborative use of hyperaudio, usability and user experience was the main scope of the evaluation efforts presented in this paper. The evaluations aimed at getting insights on how to improve the design of the application and to increase the acceptance of individual and collaborative use in online learning. Ensuring high acceptance rates regarding the usability of the application and the audible representation of text learning is a requirement for future evaluations of learning success and implementation in teaching. As part of the design-based research process, expert reviews have been conducted at the end of each of the seven development iterations. To evaluate the usability of the final hyperaudio player we applied the think-aloud principle as follows.
Participants and design: Seven participants joined the think-aloud test remotely, 4 female and 3 male. The live session was performed in a wizard of oz mode.
Material: A course unit was prepared as a hyperaudio document and delivered through an online Moodle environment using the plugin presented in the previous section. The course unit entitled "Group Awareness" was part of a current course thought in a Computer Science Master's program at a German university. The participants were provided with a list of 15 instructions that covered the range of provided features. These instructions covered group management, audio player, live sessions, settings, and comments.
Procedure: The participants have been invited to participate online using a video conferencing software. In the respective online meeting, they have been introduced to the think-aloud method and provided with a list of instructions including the credentials to access the Moodle course.

Analysis and measures: During the study with the individual participants the screen and audio conversation were captured. Furthermore, the interactions on screen have been observed by the examiner. Clickstream data was collected in the standard Moodle logstore. After the think-aloud test, the participants were asked to express their opinion about the application.

Results: The evaluation revealed a couple of usability problems and user experience pitfalls. Regarding the group awareness support, the participants struggled to recognize their representation on the timeline. For seeking the timeline the participants were expected to click on an arbitrary position on the timeline rather than dragging their marker to the desired position. Also, the menu provided to switch between textbook chapters was not recognized and thus was not used properly. Finally, Moodle controls distracted from activities within the player. All the mentioned usability problems have been addressed in the latest revision of the Moodle plugin.

5 Conclusions and Outlook

In this paper, we presented a hyperaudio player for collaborative learning. Considering related works we discussed design considerations regarding the hyperaudio player, group management, and synchronous and asynchronous communication. The resulting Moodle plugin was evaluated to improve the usability of the novel learning format. The following contributions to the research about technology-enhanced learning have been made: We presented a new online learning format as a blend of hypertext and hyperaudio to be used for individual and collaborative learning. Our implementation of a Moodle plugin enables a joint listing experience for audio-based learning resources incorporating synchronous live sessions with voice chat and anchored threaded discussions of text/audio passages. We achieved an integrated presentation of rich-media course text (e.g. textbook chapters) with its corresponding audio document by mapping text-based design elements to audible representations. The Moodle hyperaudio plugin lays the foundation to further research about the effectiveness of hyperaudio learning. To further improve the audio quality we aim at tweaking the pronunciation and speech variety using up-to-date text-to-speech systems. In the next winter semester, we are planning to implement the hyperaudio player in a university course with about 80 participants. Using the implemented logging capabilities we'll be able to track click behaviour, reading behaviour, and audio usage on a fine-grained level.

Bibliography

[CQR11] Cazenave, F.; Quint, V.; Roisin, C.: Timesheets.js: When SMIL Meets HTML5 and CSS3. In: Proceedings of the 11th ACM Symposium on Document Engineering. ACM, New York, NY, USA, pp. 43–52, 2011.

[DB07] Donker, H.; Blenn, N.: Gestaltung von Hyperlinks in einer Hyperaudio- Enzyklopädie. In Gross, T. (ed.): Mensch & Computer 2007: Konferenz für interaktive und kooperative Medien. Vol. 7, Oldenbourg Verlag, München, pp. 139–148, 2007.

[Ha18] Hartell, A. W.: Audio Books' Impact On Students' Reading Experiences, Doctoral dissertation, University of South Carolina, 2018.

[Re09] Reinmann, G.: iTunes statt Hörsaal? Gedanken zur mündlichen Weitergabe von wissenschaftlichem Wissen Mündliche Weitergabe wissenschaftlichen Wissens. E-Learning – Lernen im digitalen Zeitalter 51, pp. 256–267, 2009.

[Se22] Seidel, N.: Mapping course text to hyperaudio. In (Henning, P. A.; Striewe, M.; Wölfel, M., eds.): DELFI'22. Gesellschaft für Informatik e.V., Bonn, pp. 69–74, 2022.

[ZM20] Zumbach, J.; Moser, S.: Examining the Effectiveness of Hyperaudio Learning Environments. In: Mobile Devices in Education: Breakthroughs in Research and Practice. IGI Global, pp. 421–437, 2020.

[ZS14] Zumbach, J.; Schwartz, N.: Hyperaudio learning for non-linear auditory knowledge acquisition. Computers in Human Behavior 41/1, pp. 365–373, 2014.

Interaktive Kollaborationswerkzeuge und integrative Clouddienste: Erfahrungen zum Einsatz von Microsoft 365 in der Hochschullehre

Marwin Wiegard[1], Verena Schürmann[2], Tammy Brandenberg[3] und Timo Kahl[4]

Abstract: Der Einsatz digitaler Werkzeuge und Plattformen in der Hochschullehre hat in den letzten Jahren stark zugenommen. Auch in der betrieblichen Praxis in Industrie und Verwaltung werden digitale Kollaborationstools vermehrt zur Unterstützung in der Projektarbeit eingesetzt. Der Fokus liegt hier auf der Schaffung einer Arbeitsumgebung ohne Medienbrüche, in der verschiedene Funktionalitäten wie digitale Werkzeuge für Teammeetings und kollaboratives Bearbeiten von Dokumenten integriert sind. Die hier vorgestellte Fallstudie untersucht, inwiefern eine verstärkt projektbasierte, medienbruchfreie und vollständig digital unterstützte Arbeitsmethodik mit Microsoft 365 in eine Lehrveranstaltung eingebunden werden kann und die Zusammenarbeit von studentischen Teams unterstützt. Dabei wurde eine quantitative Untersuchung im Ein-Gruppen Prä-Post-Design durchgeführt, welche die Arbeitsweise, die wahrgenommene Lehrqualität, die Systembenutzbarkeit und die Zusammenarbeit evaluierte. Die Ergebnisse bekräftigen den Einsatz von digitalen Kollaborationswerkzeugen und lassen eine positive Entwicklung verschiedener Teamprozesse erkennen. Dies, sowie die organisatorischen Herausforderungen in der Umsetzung solcher Konzepte werden im folgenden Beitrag vorgestellt.

Keywords: Kollaboration, digitale Tools, Microsoft 365, Hochschullehre

1 Einleitung

In den letzten Jahren hat der Einsatz digitaler Werkzeuge und Plattformen in der Hochschullehre stark zugenommen und wurde zuletzt durch den schnellen Umstieg auf digitale Lehrformate aufgrund staatlich angeordneter Schließungen in der Corona-Pandemie weiter verstärkt [Wa22]. Mit den eingesetzten Tools rückt die Schaffung einer möglichst medienbruchfreien Arbeitsumgebung in den Fokus, in der unterschiedliche Funktionalitäten der Tools (z. B. digitale Teammeetings, das synchrone Bearbeiten von Dokumenten etc.) gebündelt und zur kollaborativen Zusammenarbeit tiefgehender ausgeschöpft werden

---

[1] Hochschule Rhein-Waal, Fakultät Kommunikation und Umwelt, Friedrich-Heinrich-Allee 25, 47475 Kamp-Lintfort, marwin.wiegard@hochschule-rhein-waal.de
[2] Hochschule Rhein-Waal, Fakultät Kommunikation und Umwelt, Friedrich-Heinrich-Allee 25, 47475 Kamp-Lintfort, verena.schuermann@hochschule-rhein-waal.de
[3] Hochschule Rhein-Waal, Fakultät Kommunikation und Umwelt, Friedrich-Heinrich-Allee 25, 47475 Kamp-Lintfort, tammy.brandenberg@hochschule-rhein-waal.de
[4] Hochschule Rhein-Waal, Fakultät Kommunikation und Umwelt, Friedrich-Heinrich-Allee 25, 47475 Kamp-Lintfort, timo.kahl@hochschule-rhein-waal.de

doi: 10.18420/delfi2023-22

[Gu22; Mi20]. Dies ist insbesondere mit Blick auf die 21st Century Skills von hoher Relevanz. Unter den 21st Century Skills werden Wissen, Fähig- und Fertigkeiten verstanden, die in einer komplexen und durch Wandel geprägten Welt von besonderer Bedeutung sind. Dazu zählen neben digitalen Kompetenzen auch Fähigkeiten wie kritisches Denken, Problemlösen, Kreativität sowie Kommunikation und Kollaboration [z. B. Ri20]. Stellenanzeigenanalysen wie die von Rios et al. [Ri20] legen nahe, dass auf dem Arbeitsmarkt insbesondere Kommunikations- und Kollaborationsfähigkeiten gefragt sind. Personen aus Forschung und Praxis weisen jedoch auf eine Diskrepanz zwischen den organisationalen Anforderungen und den Kompetenzen von Graduierten hin (den sog. Soft Skills Gap) [AAB18]. Studierende berichten wiederum, dass die Entwicklung von Kollaborationsfähigkeiten in ihren Studienprogrammen kaum gefördert wird [Wi18]. Darüber hinaus ist eine projektbasierte und praxisorientierte Lehre insbesondere für Hochschulen für angewandte Wissenschaften essenziell [Ho19]. Die Studierenden sollen nicht nur Fachwissen erwerben, sondern auch anwendungsbezogene Problemlösungen erarbeiten und interpersonale Kompetenzen entwickeln. Dabei ist die kollaborative Zusammenarbeit in studentischen Teams ein Schlüsselfaktor für den Lernerfolg und die Vorbereitung auf spätere Arbeitssituationen [Wi18]. Die vorliegende Fallstudie untersucht daher, inwiefern eine medienbruchfreie und vollständig digital unterstützte Arbeitsmethodik mit Microsoft 365 gewinnbringend in eine Lehrveranstaltung eingebunden werden kann, um vor allem die kollaborative Zusammenarbeit von studentischen Teams zu fördern.

2 State of the Art

Die Zusammenarbeit in studentischen Teams stellt in hybriden oder digitalen Settings eine besondere Herausforderung dar, da diese nicht automatisch erfolgt, sondern zielgerichtet gefördert und fokussiert werden muss. Als Team wird der Zusammenschluss von mehreren Studierenden verstanden, die organisatorisch relevante Aufgaben mit Fokus auf gemeinsame Ziele erfüllen [MAB00]. Aus didaktischer Perspektive soll die Nutzung von Teamarbeiten darüber hinaus Kommunikations- und Kollaborationsfähigkeiten der Studierenden fördern und verbessern. Dabei gilt es jedoch zu berücksichtigen, dass nicht jede Zusammenarbeit kollaborativ ist. Häufig teilen Studierende die Aufgaben in Pakete ein, die dann einzeln bearbeitet und wieder zusammengefügt werden. Dies entspricht einer kooperativen Arbeitsteilung. Kollaboration, definiert als "a coordinated, synchronous activity that is the result of a continued attempt to construct and maintain a shared conception of a problem" [RT95:70], fokussiert hingegen nicht die Aufteilung des Arbeitsumfangs, sondern das geteilte Verständnis über ein Problem. Wenn Studierende kollaborativ Lernen finden meta-kognitive (z. B. das Überwachen der Zusammenarbeit), sozio-kognitive (z. B. das Teilen von Wissen und Informationen), sozio-affektive (z. B. die Aufrechterhaltung einer positiven Stimmung) und behaviorale Prozesse (z. B. die gleichmäßige Beteiligung der Gruppenmitglieder) statt [SMB22]. Die Regulation dieser Prozesse ist herausfordernd, aber für eine effektive und zufriedenstellende Zusammenarbeit von zentraler Bedeutung [JH13]. Digitale Technologien bergen hier Unterstützungspotential, z. B., indem Dokumente flexibel geteilt und besprochen werden können.

Aktuelle Studien und Praxisbeiträge im Bereich der digitalen Hochschullehre untermauern die zentrale Bedeutung digital gestützter Förderung von Kollaboration. Der Fokus liegt dabei insbesondere auf dem Einsatz von Microsoft Teams als Teil der Microsoft 365 Anwendungssuite. Als digitale Plattform und Netzwerk bietet sie einen virtuellen Raum, der die Kommunikation und das kollaborative Zusammenarbeiten vereinfacht. Guggenberger [Gu22] beschreibt Blended Learning Erfahrungen, die durch die beschleunigte Implementierung von Microsoft Teams und OneNote während des ersten Corona-Lockdowns gemacht wurden. Statt gedruckter Vorlesungsskripte wurden ausschließlich digitale Formate bereitgestellt und die Studierenden nutzten vermehrt Geräte mit Stift-Unterstützung und Apps für digitale Notizen. Gemäß Guggenberger [Gu22] setzten die Studierenden im digitalisierten Vorlesungsskript die geteilte Bearbeitung von Inhalten intensiv ein und erwarben so gleichzeitig wichtige interpersonale Kompetenzen. Eine umfängliche Betrachtung von Microsoft Teams als kollaboratives Lerninstrument nehmen Linke und Mertens [LM20] in ihrem Beitrag vor. Das dort gesammelte Feedback der Studierenden fiel im Vergleich zu Tools wie Adobe Connect und ILIAS sehr positiv aus. Insbesondere die zentrale Datenhaltung inkl. synchroner Bearbeitungsmöglichkeiten wurde wertgeschätzt.

Insgesamt scheint die synchrone Bearbeitung von Dokumenten eine stark kollaborativ geprägte Zusammenarbeit zu ermöglichen. Microsoft Teams nahm auch eine integrative Funktion wahr, indem es die Kommunikation und Inhalte in der Cloud medienbruchfrei bündelte. Die bisherigen Studien und Praxisbeiträge nutzten allerdings vor allem unstrukturierte Befragungen und Beobachtungen zum Technikeinsatz, um die Aneignung und Akzeptanz von digitalen Tools zu evaluieren. Der Einsatz von fundierten Skalen und einem strukturierten Studiendesign kann verlässliche Aussagen zum Einfluss von digitalen Tools auf die Arbeitsdynamik und kollaborative Arbeitsweise unterstützen. Die vorliegende Studie untersucht daher Zusammenhänge zwischen dem Einsatz von Microsoft 365 und der Kollaboration von Studierenden, deren Einschätzung zur Systembenutzbarkeit und zukünftigen Nutzungsintentionen in einem Ein-Gruppen-Prä-Post-Design.

3 Methode

Die vorliegende Studie wurde im Wintersemesters 2022/23 in einem betriebswirtschaftlichen Grundlagenmodul (1. Semester) zweier Informatikstudiengänge über einen Zeitraum von 9 Wochen durchgeführt. Zu Beginn der Präsenzlehre konnten die Studierenden eine der fünf zeitversetzten Übungsgruppen wählen und sich dort in kleineren Teams organisierten, um die Übungsaufgaben zu bearbeiten. Die Bearbeitung erfolgte in den 6 Wochen bis zum ersten Messzeitpunkt (t1) vornehmlich analog bzw. mit selbstgewählten Tools. Vor der Einführung von Microsoft 365 wurden im Sinne eines Ein-Gruppen-Prä-Post-Designs Teamzugehörigkeiten und -größen, sowie Kollaboration und Zufriedenheitswerte zur Organisation und den Inhalten der Lehrveranstaltung erfasst. Die studentische Kollaboration wurde mit Hilfe einer selbstentwickelten Skala mit 10 Items, welche die jeweiligen Teilbereiche (z. B. sozio-kognitiv, sozio-affektiv) von Kollaboration abdeckt [basierend auf SMB22], erhoben. Die Items umfassen je eine kurze Beschreibung (z. B. Facette

132   Marwin Wiegard et al.

Teilen und Sammeln von Informationen), wobei die Zustimmung bzw. Passung dieser Beschreibung auf das eigene Team anhand einer siebenstufigen Skala eingeschätzt werden soll. Die Zufriedenheit der Studierenden mit der Lehrveranstaltung wurde über 16 entwickelte Items mit einer überwiegend fünfstufigen Skala von *1 - stimme gar nicht zu* bis *5 - stimme völlig zu* abgefragt. Beispielhaft: „Die Gruppenübungen stellen gegenüber dem Selbststudium einen Mehrwert für mich dar".

Der Einsatz von Microsoft 365 (als Intervention) erfolgte nach t1 und dauerte 3 Wochen. Die Studierenden erhielten zuvor ein kurzes Onboarding, dass der Vorbereitung auf die kollaborativ umgestalteten Übungsaufgaben und Microsoft 365 diente. Je nach Übungsthema wurden die Aufgaben als Microsoft Whiteboard oder Excel-Datei in den digitalen Teamräumen bereitgestellt, über die auch der Arbeitsfortschritt der Teams kontinuierlich verfolgt und Zwischenergebnisse besprochen werden konnten. Die Vorlesungen wurden innerhalb des Zeitraums erstmalig hybrid über Microsoft Teams gestreamt (ohne Aufzeichnung). Teilweise hatten sich Studierende auch zu ihrer Übungszeit über Microsoft Teams hybrid hinzugeschaltet. Zudem stand den Studierenden vor Ort ein Microsoft Surface Hub 55" (interaktives Bildschirmgerät optimiert für Microsoft 365) zur freien Verfügung und wurde mit Beginn der Intervention aktiv von der Lehrperson einbezogen.

Nach der Intervention wurde noch einmal Kollaboration (siehe t1), die Zufriedenheit der Studierenden mit der Lehrveranstaltung in Bezug zur angepassten, digitalen Unterstützung, sowie zusätzlich die Skala zur Systembenutzbarkeit (10 Items, 5-stufig skaliert, bspw.: "Ich denke, dass ich Microsoft 365 (inkl. Microsoft Teams) häufig im Studium benutzen möchte." [Br96] und die Nutzungsintention (2 Items, 5-stufig skaliert, bspw. "Angenommen ich hätte dauerhaft Zugriff auf Microsoft 365 (inkl. Microsoft Teams) über die Hochschule, würde ich beabsichtigen, es zu benutzen.") [Da86] erfasst.

Die studentische Stichprobe bestand zu t1 aus 65 Personen in 16 Teams (mit 2-7 Personen) und zu t2 aus 38 Personen in 9 Teams. Die Studierenden waren zwischen 18 und 38 Jahren alt ($M^{t1} = 23.79$, SD^{t1} 5.07 / $M^{t2} = 24.19$ und $SD^{t2} = 5.48$). Die Stichprobe bestand zu beiden Zeitpunkten zu einem sehr großen Teil aus männlichen Teilnehmenden (81 %).

4   Ergebnisse

Bis zum ersten Zeitpunkt nutzten die Studierenden überwiegend Microsoft Office (79 %) und Google Docs (33,9 %) – 56 % griffen zur Bearbeitung der Übungsaufgaben auch klassisch auf Stift und Papier zurück. Insgesamt bewerteten ca. 80 % der Studierenden die Bearbeitung mit ihren selbst gewählten Tools als einfach. Jedoch wurde das Fehlen einer einheitlichen technischen Plattform angemerkt. Die Auswertung zur Zufriedenheit mit der Organisation der Lehrveranstaltung ergab zwischen beiden Messzeitpunkten eine Steigerung von etwa 6,3 %. Die Studierenden waren insgesamt zufriedener mit der Strukturierung und Durchführung der Veranstaltung – allerdings nur geringfügig zufriedener mit den Inhalten selbst. Die Zustimmung der Studierenden zum Mehrwert von Gruppenübungen gegenüber dem Selbststudium stieg um 12,75 % (0,5 Punkte) auf 4,42 (5 = höchste Zustimmung) und zeigt, dass die Gruppenübungen als wertvoll und hilfreich empfunden wurden. Im weiteren Vergleich konnten mit dem Toolset aus Microsoft 365 die Übungsergebnisse um etwa 20 % einfacher mit der Lehrperson besprochen werden. Der Austausch digitaler Mitschriften innerhalb der Teams verbesserte sich ähnlich stark.

Auf globaler Ebene zeigen die Ergebnisse der selbsteingeschätzten Kollaboration der Studierenden keinen merklichen Unterschied zwischen Messzeitpunkt 1 und 2. Bei Betrachtung der einzelnen Facetten von Kollaboration ist jedoch ein Anstieg der Mittelwerte bei den sozio-kognitiven Facetten und eine leichte Abnahme bei den sozio-affektiven Facetten zu erkennen. So legen die Ergebnisse nahe, dass die studentischen Teams es zum zweiten Messzeitpunkt einfacher fanden zu diskutieren und einen Konsens zu erreichen (t1 = 4,67; t2 = 5,08) sowie auf ihrem Weg dahin auf verschiedene Ressourcen und Tools zurückzugreifen (t1 = 4,64; t2 = 5,68). Die Aufrechterhaltung einer positiven Atmosphäre innerhalb der Teams hat im Mittel jedoch abgenommen (t1 = 6,08; t2 = 5,63).

Die Systembenutzbarkeit von Microsoft 365 inkl. Teams wird seitens der Studierenden als gut eingeschätzt (mittlerer Summenwert: 79,72 von 100). Auch die Nutzungsintention gegenüber dem System fällt mit 4,31 (5 = höchste Zustimmung) insgesamt hoch aus. Mehr als die Hälfte der Studierenden gaben zum Zeitpunkt 2 an, dass sie gerne häufiger ein digitales Whiteboard im Studium nutzen würden. Zudem fand sowohl eine kabellose Bildschirmübertragung zur einfachen Vorstellung und Besprechung von Inhalten in der Lehre als auch der Wunsch nach aufgezeichneten Livestreams der Vorlesung bei rund 75 % der Studierenden Zustimmung. Livestreams ohne Aufzeichnung waren kaum gefragt.

5 Zusammenfassung und Ausblick

Zusammenfassend bekräftigen die Ergebnisse den unterstützenden Einsatz von kollaborativen Plattformen wie Microsoft 365 in der Lehre. Die Werkzeuge ermöglichten den studentischen Teams die digitale Kollaboration einfach und medienbruchfrei zu gestalten und hatten eine positive Auswirkung auf die Zusammenarbeit in diesem hybriden Setting. Allerdings sind der limitierende Einfluss einzelner Faktoren des Studiendesigns zu berücksichtigen. So war die Stichprobe zum Zeitpunkt 2 deutlich geringer, da sich die Teams zum Teil neuformierten oder ihre Teilnahme aussetzten. Dies ist im Semesterverlauf nicht ungewöhnlich, wirkt sich jedoch auf die Repräsentativität der Ergebnisse aus. Das Design lässt darüber hinaus keine kausalen Schlüsse zu, da Alternativerklärungen (z. B. Einfluss der Zeit) möglich sind. Organisatorisch betrachtet fiel das Onboarding zu kurz aus. Die in Microsoft Teams abgebildete Struktur (Dateien, Übungsgruppen, Teams) haben einige Studierende nicht gänzlich verstanden oder falsch angewendet, so dass weitere Unterstützung notwendig war. Auf technischer Ebene gab es bei der Integration von den Endgeräten der Studierenden teils Probleme. Für einen weitergehenden Einsatz wäre zusätzlich eine zeitlich (über die gesamte Laufzeit der Lehrveranstaltung) und organisatorisch ausgeweitete Nutzung wünschenswert.

Literaturverzeichnis

[AAB18] Abbasi, F. K., Ali, A., & Bibi, N.: Analysis of skill gap for business graduates: managerial perspective from banking industry. Education and Training, 60(4), 354-367, 2018.

[Br96] Brooke, J.: SUS-A quick and dirty usability scale. Usability evaluation in industry, 189(194), 4-7, 1996.

[Da86] Davis, F. D.: A technology acceptance model for empirically testing new end-user information systems: Theory and results. MIT Sloan School of Management, Cambridge, 1986.

[Gu22] Guggenberger, M.: Using Microsoft Teams and OneNote as Key Technologies for Implementing Twenty-first Century Skills. In D. Paier (Hrsg.), Hochschule, Digitalisierung, Innovation: Forschungsergebnisse und Good Practices zur Weiterentwicklung der Hochschullehre. Springer Fachmedien, 73-94, 2022.

[Ho19] Hochschulen NRW – Landesrektorenkonferenz der Hochschulen für Angewandte Wissenschaften e.V. Die Stärken der Hochschulen für Angewandte Wissenschaften. https://haw-nrw.de/hochschulen, Zugriff am: 15.03.2023.

[JH13] Järvelä, S., & Hadwin, A. F.: New Frontiers: Regulating Learning in CSCL. Educational Psychologist, 48(1), 25-39, 2013.

[MAB00] McGrath, J. E., Arrow, H., & Berdahl, J. L.: The study of groups: Past, present, and future. Personality and Social Psychology Review, 4(1), 95-105, 2000.

[LM20] Linke, K., & Mertens, R.: Digitaler Präsenzunterricht: Erfahrungen aus der Corona-Krise 2020 für die Gestaltung von E-Learning, 9-34, 2020.

[Ri20] Rios, J. A., Ling, G., Pugh, R., Becker, D., & Bacall, A.: Identifying critical 21st-century skills for workplace success: A content analysis of job advertisements. Educational Researcher, 49(2), 80-89, 2020.

[RT95] Roschelle, J., & Teasley, S. D.: The Construction of Shared Knowledge in Collaborative Problem Solving. In C. E. O'Malley (Hrsg.), Computer Supported Collaborative Learning. Springer, 69-97, 1995.

[SMB22] Schürmann, V., Marquardt, N., & Bodemer, D.: Measuring peer collaboration in higher education and beyond: An integrative framework [Paper presentation]. EARLI SIG 27, Online Measures at the Crossroad of Ethical and Methodological Challenges, Southampton, Great Britain, 2022.

[Wa22] Wannemacher, K., Lübcke, M., Seyfeli-Özhizalan, F., & Graceva, V.: Reimagining the Future of Higher Education Teaching. In M. E. Auer, A. Pester, & D. May (Hrsg.), Learning with Technologies and Technologies in Learning: Experience, Trends and Challenges in Higher Education. Springer International Publishing, 7-30, 2022.

[Wi18] Wilson, L., Ho, S., & Brookes, R. H.: Student perceptions of teamwork within assessment tasks in undergraduate science degrees. Assessment and Evaluation in Higher Education, 43(5), 786–799, 2018.

Die Entwicklung eines digitalen Praktikums der Cybersicherheit im Bereich „Smart Home"

Victor Jüttner[1,2] und Erik Buchmann[2,3]

Abstract: Die Cybersicherheit ist ein Querschnittsthema, das alle Bereiche der Informatik berührt. Entsprechend wichtig ist es, Studierenden praktische Erfahrungen zu aktuellen Themen in diesem Gebiet zu vermitteln. Dies wird schwierig, wenn die Studierendenzahlen größer werden. Wünschenswert ist darum ein Praktikum der Cybersicherheit, das einen aktuellen Themenquerschnitt für Studierende niederschwellig abbildet, einen digitalen Zugang zu Experimenten bietet, und ohne viel Lehrpersonal oder Tutoren auskommt. Dieser Praxisbeitrag beschreibt unsere Erfahrungen aus einem Praktikum der Cybersicherheit, das eine Experimentierplattform für so ein digitales Praktikum entwickelt hat.

1 Einführung

Aufgrund seiner Komplexität existieren für die Cybersicherheit nur wenige praktische digitale Lehrangebote, z. B. der OWASP Juice Shop[4], Hack the Box[5] oder GRFICSv2[6]. Diese sind eher hochschwellig nutzbar, setzen eine intensive Betreuung und erhebliche Fachkenntnisse voraus, und zielen auf inhaltlich „tiefe" Kenntnisse.

Für die Vermittlung von „breit" angelegten, praktischen Grundlagen der Cybersicherheit [SF14] an größere Studierendengruppen sind jedoch andere Anforderungen zu setzen, insbesondere wenn nur Kenntnisse aus einem Informatik- oder Informatik-nahen Bachelorabschluss vorausgesetzt werden können. Hier ist ein Praktikum der Cybersicherheit gefragt, dass ein aktuelles Einsatzszenario in der Breite abdeckt, anstelle sich beispielsweise auf Penetrationstests zu fokussieren. Das Praktikum sollte niederschwellig angelegt sein, d. h., einen digitalen oder hybriden Zugang zu einer Experimentierplattform und weiteren Materialien wie Lehrvideos oder Hintergrundmaterialien bieten. Insbesondere sollte es auch möglich sein, auf diese Weise größere Zahlen von Studierenden zu betreuen.

In diesem Praxisbeitrag geht es um ein Präsenz-Praktikum, das eine Smart Home-Experimentierplattform für ein digitales Praktikum der Cybersicherheit entwickelt hat. Smart Home-Geräte sind z. B. über das Smartphone schaltbare Steckdosen, Türsensoren oder

---

[1] Dept. of Computer Science, Leipzig University, Germany. juettner@informatik.uni-leipzig.de
[2] Center for Scalable Data Analytics and Artificial Intelligence (ScaDS.AI) Dresden/Leipzig, Germany.
[3] Dept. of Computer Science, Leipzig University, Germany. buchmann@informatik.uni-leipzig.de
[4] https://pwning.owasp-juice.shop
[5] https://www.hackthebox.com/universities
[6] https://github.com/Fortiphyd/GRFICSv2

doi: 10.18420/delfi2023-23

Lampen. Wir haben die Aufgabe gestellt, eine intuitive Experimentierplattform mit typischen Smart Home-Geräten aufzubauen, die digital fernsteuerbar ist. Diese Plattform unterstützt Experimente im Bereich Cybersicherheit, die von der Integration und sicheren Konfiguration der Geräte über deren Absicherung bis hin zur Angriffserkennung reichen.

2 Abgrenzung und Verwandte Arbeiten

Die **Cybersicherheit** betrachtet defensive Methoden zur Absicherung von IT-Komponenten gegen Angreifer [Cr14], die auch vollautomatisch mit Viren oder Bot-Netzen Schäden verursachen können. Dabei ist wichtig, dass Cybersicherheit als ein Querschnittsthema vermittelt wird. Das heißt, es geht um Planung, Entwicklung, Einsatz und Erfolgskontrolle von Maßnahmen in einem komplexen IT-Ökosystem, und zwar über Abteilungs-, Prozess-, Netzwerk- und Rechnergrenzen hinweg [SF14].

Das **Smart Home** ist ein Konzept, um Alltagsgeräte wie Lampen, Waschmaschinen oder Garagentoröffner mit IT-Komponenten auszustatten und zu vernetzen, sodass sie beispielsweise mittels Sprachassistenten oder dem Smartphone kontrolliert werden können. Komplexere Funktionalität wie das Erkennen von Sprachbefehlen oder die Analyse von Sensordaten wird dabei an einen Cloud-Dienstleister ausgelagert. Für das Vermitteln von Themen der Cybersicherheit sind Smart Home-Szenarien [Ro10] besonders vielversprechend, weil sie eine hinreichend komplexe Infrastruktur aus Smartphones, Endgeräten, Internet- Gateway und Cloud-Dienstleistern benötigen, mit denen die Studierenden als „Digital Natives" aber bereits vertraut sind. Mit dem Internet-Gateway gibt es einen zentralen Punkt, über den alle Geräte und Angreifer kommunizieren müssen. Die Auswertung von am Gateway aufgezeichneten Netzwerkpaketen mittels Machine Learning und künstlicher Intelligenz ist ein aktuelles Forschungsthema [Ch18]. Existierende Experimentierumgebungen sind jedoch nicht frei zugänglich [Da22], simulieren eine künstliches Smart Home [Ku22] oder generieren künstliche Testdaten aus einer realen Umgebung [Da22].

E-Learning-Ansätze für Cybersicherheit simulieren eine komplexe, vernetzte Umgebung, in der Studierende Techniken zur Angriffserkennung und/oder Absicherung üben können. Ein typisches Beispiel ist der absichtlich unsichere OWASP Juice Shop. Das ist ein Onlineshop, bei dem Betriebssystem, Datenbank-Backend, Webserver und Web-Frontend Schwachstellen enthalten. Der Juice Shop kann als digitales Lehrangebot zur Verfügung gestellt werden, um Penetrationstests zu üben. Ein anderes Beispiel ist Hack the Box (HtB). Dabei handelt es sich um eine Online-Schulungsumgebung, um spielerisch offensive und defensive Sicherheitsfähigkeiten zu erlernen. HtB bietet verschiedene virtuelle Umgebungen wie „Hacking Labs", „Capture the Flag" oder „Hacking Battlegrounds" in denen Studierende in Teams oder allein praktisch lernen können. Ein drittes Beispiel ist das Graphical Realism Framework for Industrial Control Simulation (GRFICSv2). Dieser Simulator für eine Anlagensteuerung besteht aus verschiedenen industriellen IoT-Geräten und einer Firewall. GRFICSv2 legt einen Fokus auf eine grafische Darstellung der Geräte, um einen intuitiveren Zugang zu vermitteln. Überwiegend adressieren solche Ansätze klassische Client-

Server-Systeme, müssen den Studierenden sorgfältig erklärt werden bzw. setzen viel bereits vorhandenes Fachwissen voraus, und zielen auf eng fokussierte Themen wie Penetrationstests oder Firewall-Konfigurationen.

3 Konzeption des Cybersicherheits-Praktikums

Die **inhaltliche Ausrichtung** unseres Präsenz-Praktikums bestand darin, eine Experimentierplattform für ein zukünftiges digitales Praktikum der Cybersicherheit im Smart Home aufzubauen und prototypisch zu testen. Zu diesem Zweck haben wir 20 Smart Home-Geräte angeboten. Die Experimentierplattform sollte angeschlossene Geräte über das Netzwerk fernsteuerbar machen, und sie mittels Sensoren und Kameras überwachen. Mit typischen Werkzeugen der Cybersicherheit, z. B. nmap oder Metasploit, sollten Angriffe auf die Geräte gestartet werden. Am Gateway sollte aller Datenverkehr von und zu den Geräten aufgezeichnet werden. Zuletzt sollten die aufgezeichneten Netzwerkpakete mit Hilfe der Sensoren mit Labeln „Nutzeraktion", „Angriff" und „Unbekannt" annotiert und mit Machine-Learning-Verfahren ausgewertet werden. Diese Ausrichtung deckt ein breites Themenspektrum der Cybersicherheit ab.

Mit diesen Themen sollten vier **Qualifikationsziele** erreicht werden: Ein (I) fundamentales Verständnis von Angriffen auf aktuelle IT-Systeme, (II) selbständiges Identifizieren von Sicherheitslücken, (III) Planung und Umsetzung von Sicherheitstechniken, sowie (IV) selbständige und zielführende Arbeit im Team.

Formal war das Praktikum für 5 LP = 150 Arbeitsstunden ausgelegt, davon 15 · 2 Stunden in Präsenz. Es richtete sich an Studierende des M. Sc. Data Science und M. Sc. Informatik. Als Teilnahmevoraussetzungen wurden vertiefte Kenntnisse im Bereich Programmierung, Netzwerkprotokolle und Rechnernetze sowie Kenntnisse in Machine Learning und Cybersicherheit genannt. Eine zeitgleiche Belegung des Moduls „Grundlagen der IT-Sicherheit" wurde empfohlen. Die **Prüfungsleistung** sollte als Gruppenleistung erbracht werden. Jede Gruppe sollte ein 20-minütiges Videotutorial und eine schriftliche Dokumentation erstellen, wobei das Video zu 75%, die Dokumentation zu 25% in die Note einging. Den Teilnehmern wurde vorab erläutert, dass das Tutorial nach den Kriterien „sinnvoller Aufbau", „verständlicher Inhalt", „geeignete Mediennutzung" und „technische Durchführung" (Zeitvorgaben, Lautstärke, etc.) bewertet wird, die Dokumentation nach „fachlicher Tiefe" und „übersichtlicher Darstellung". Video und Dokumentation waren als Basis für ein zukünftiges digitales oder zumindest hybrides Praktikum der Cybersicherheit gedacht. Die **zeitliche Planung** des Praktikums hat 15 Wochen Bearbeitungszeit vorgesehen, mit einer **qualitative Lehrevaluation** nach dem ersten Drittel. Wir haben 8 Meilensteine vorgegeben, die die Selbstorganisation der Gruppen, den Aufbau der Geräte, die Inbetriebnahme der Sensorik zur Überwachung der Geräte, die Datenaufzeichnung, die Aufbereitung der Daten sowie die prototypische Angriffserkennung und die Prüfungsleistung umfassen. Das Praktikum enthielt einen hohen Forschungsanteil. Es war vorab nicht absehbar, inwiefern die Aufgabenstellung in der gegebenen Zeit vollständig lösbar war. Deshalb haben wir anstelle detaillierter inhaltlicher und organisatorischer Vorgaben eine **intensive Betreuung** vorgesehen: Ein Professor, ein Postdoc und eine studentische Hilfskraft für den Betrieb der technischen Infrastruktur haben 12 Praktikumsteilnehmer betreut.

4 Durchführung des Cybersicherheits-Praktikums

In einer **Beschaffungsphase** haben wir für die Experimentierplattform 20 typische Smart Home-Geräte, zwei stationäre Rechner als Internet-Gateway und Angreifer, zwei Tablets mit Android-Betriebssystem für die Steuerung, zwei Webcams sowie WLAN-fähige Mikrocontroller mit NodeMCU-Betriebssystem und Sensoren bestellt. Unsere Universität hat das Praktikum mit Mitteln aus einer Initiative für digitale Lehre unterstützt.

In der **Auftaktveranstaltung** wurden Aufgabenstellung und Zielsetzung des Praktikums, Meilensteine, Geräte, sowie Prüfungsleistung und Bewertungskriterien vorgestellt. Die 12 Teilnehmer haben sich in 4 Gruppen aufgeteilt. Eine Gruppe wollte sich auf das Gateway, eine andere auf Angriffe und zwei weitere auf die Smart Home-Geräte konzentrieren.

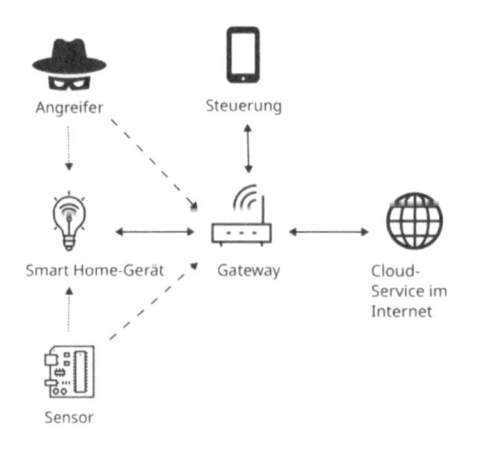

Abb. 1: Schematischer Aufbau   Abb. 2: Schematischer Aufbau

Im **weiteren Ablauf** hat die erste Gruppe das Gateway als Schnittstelle zwischen Geräten und Internet realisiert. Sie hat Aufzeichnung von Netzwerkpaketen implementiert, Schnittstellen für die Annotation der Pakete mit Labeln entwickelt und Filter für das Reduzieren der Datenmenge nach Attributen (IP-Adresse und Port, Protokoll, Zeitstempel, ...) programmiert. Die Infrastruktur ist in Abbildung 1 dargestellt. Die zweite Gruppe hat Smart Home-typische Angriffe recherchiert und automatisiert. Zu den Angriffen zählen Vorbereitungshandlungen (Geräteerkennung, Portscans), generische Angriffe (Denial-of-Service) und spezifischen Angriffe (Exploits aus dem Metasploit-Framework). Für das Label „Angriff" wurde bei jedem Angriff automatisch ein spezielles START/STOP-Datenpaket an das

Gateway versandt.

Die anderen beiden Gruppen haben festgestellt, dass Geräte schwer aufzuzeichnen sind, wenn sie nicht mittels WLAN oder Zigbee, sondern mittels Z-Wave-Protokoll kommunizieren. Dasselbe gilt für Geräte, deren Zustand nicht über Sensoren für Helligkeit, Bewegung oder Schalterposition prüfbar ist. Intelligente Lautsprecher, Türschlösser, Wasserstandsmelder o. Ä. wurden darum nicht verwendet. In die Plattform integriert wurden zwei Lampen, zwei Steckdosen, zwei Relais, ein Öffnungsmelder und ein Garagentoröffner. Die Studierenden haben dabei für den Öffnungsmelder eine kleine hölzerne Tür gebaut,

für den Garagentoröffner ein ferngesteuertes Garagentor aus Modellbau-Teilen. Für das Label „Nutzeraktion" haben die Sensoren spezielle ACTIVITY-Datenpakete an das Gateway geschickt. Abbildung 2 zeigt einen Ausschnitt der Plattform. Die qualitativen Lehrevaluation ergab, dass die Studierenden nach der Inbetriebnahme der Geräte die Meilensteine und den Zweck des Praktikums aus den Augen verloren hatten, und Schwierigkeiten mit der Selbstorganisation hatten. Darum haben wir zusätzlich Vortragstermine anberaumt, bei denen jede Gruppe den Stand der Arbeiten, aktuelle Probleme und Wünsche an andere Gruppen in 10 Minuten vorzutragen hatte. Am Ende haben alle Gruppen den Machbarkeitsnachweis für die Angriffserkennung mit Machine Learning erbracht und die Videos und Ausarbeitungen fristgerecht abgeliefert.

5 Auswertung

Wir verfolgten zwei Ziele: Beiträge für ein zukünftiges digitales Praktikum der Cybersicherheit (vgl. Abschnitte 1, 2) sowie den Lehrerfolg dieses Praktikums (vgl. Abschnitt 3).

Lehrerfolg dieses Praktikums Wir sahen 4 Qualifikationsziele vor, die mit den Prüfungsleistungen „Videotutorial" und „Dokumentation" nachzuweisen waren. Die Bewertungskriterien haben wir vorab bekannt gegeben. Informell hatten wir in zahlreichen Gesprächen in den Gruppen den Lehrerfolg überwacht. Dabei beobachteten wir, dass sich das Wissen der Teilnehmer hinsichtlich der Qualifikationsziele I-III (Angriffe, Schwachstellen, Gegenmaßnahmen) kontinuierlich gesteigert hat. Die Prüfungsleistungen haben dies bestätigt. Für das Qualifikationsziel IV (Teamarbeit) mussten wir intervenieren. Die qualitative Lehrevaluation nach dem ersten Drittel des Praktikums hat gezeigt, dass die Kommunikation zwischen den Gruppen nicht ausreichte, und das gemeinsame Praktikumsziel unklar war. Wir führen dies auf die Breite des Themas „Cybersicherheit" zurück, und haben mit Vorträgen und einer von uns vorgenommenen Strukturierung der Präsenztermine gegengesteuert.

Beiträge für ein digitales Praktikum der Cybersicherheit Aus Zeitgründen wurde nur einen Teil der angebotenen Geräte in Betrieb genommen, und nur einzelne Ansätze umgesetzt, z. B. Portscan- und Passwort-Angriffe, und „Gradient Boosting" als Machine Learning-Verfahren zur Angriffserkennung. Die Studierenden haben selbst den Wunsch geäußert, weitere Geräte in Betrieb zu nehmen, einen umfangreicheren Datensatz zu erstellen und mit zusätzlichen Verfahren zu evaluieren. Das Praktikum hat damit nachgewiesen, dass mit der

Plattform Themen der Cybersicherheit von der Inbetriebnahme der Geräte über Angriffe bis hin zur Analyse von Netzwerkdaten vermittelt, werden können. Die erstellten Videos und Dokumentationen bieten einen niederschwelligen Zugang zu Experimenten. Für ein zukünftiges digitales Praktikum der Cybersicherheit erfordern die Videos und Dokumente noch didaktische Aufbereitung. Damit die bislang überwiegend in Präsenz genutzte Plattform sicher betrieben werden kann, ist sie über einen VPN-Zugang ans Internet anzubinden, und über die noch nicht angeschlossenen Webcams zu überwachen.

6 Zusammenfassung

In diesem Praxisbeitrag haben wir ein Praktikum beschrieben, in dem wir mit einer überschaubaren Teilnehmerzahl Konzepte für ein zukünftiges digitales Praktikum der Cybersicherheit entwickeln und austesten wollten. Dabei haben wir folgende Erkenntnisse gewonnen: Thematisch sind unsere Erfahrungen durchweg positiv. Smart Homes sind für die Studierenden ein spannendes Thema, zu dem sie durch den täglichen Umgang mit Smartphones und intelligenten Geräten leicht Zugang finden. Das Thema ist sehr gut geeignet, um Anliegen der Cybersicherheit in der Breite zu vermitteln, vom sicheren Hardware-Einsatz bis zur Angriffserkennung durch künstliche Intelligenz. Organisatorisch war eine zu flexible Gestaltung des Praktikums problematisch. Unsere Teilnehmer haben den technischen Aufbau priorisiert, und wenig Zeit für Teamkommunikation, Wissenskonsolidierung, Datensammlung und Angriffserkennung aufgewendet. Dabei haben die Teilnehmer über den technischen Fragestellungen das Praktikumsziel aus den Augen verloren. Für ein digitales Format ist zu überlegen, wie Abgaben präziser definiert und Kommunikationsstrukturen vorgegeben werden können, ohne die Experimentiermöglichkeiten eines Praktikums einzuschränken. Eine Möglichkeit wären Prüfungsleistungen, bei deren Erwerb sich die Teilnehmer gegenseitig helfen können, aber nicht müssen.

Literaturverzeichnis

[CH18] Chernyshev, M. et al.: Internet of Things (IoT): Research, Simulators, and Testbeds. IEEE Internet of Things Journal 5/3, S. 1637–1647, 2018.

[Cr14] Craigen, D. et al.: Defining Cybersecurity. Technology Innovation Management Review 4/10, 2014.

[Da22] Dadkhah, S. et al.: Towards the Development of a Realistic Multidimensional IoT Profiling Dataset. In: Conference on Privacy, Security and Trust. 2022.

[Ku22] Kumar, P. et al.: Sad-IoT: Security Analysis of DDOS Attacks in IoT Networks. Wireless Personal Communications 122/1, S. 87–108, 2022.

[Ro10] Robles, R. J.; Kim, T. - h.; Cook, D.; Das, S.: A Review on Security in Smart Home Development. Journal of Advanced Science and Technology 15/, 2010.

[SF14] Singer, P. W.; Friedman, A.: Cybersecurity and Cyberwar: What Everyone Needs to Know. Oxford University Press, USA, 2014.

Infrastrukturen und Artefakte

Metadata Standards in National Education Infrastructure: Development of Evaluation Criteria and their Exemplary Application

Steffen Rörtgen [1], Ronald Brenner [2], Holger Zimmermann [2], Matthias Hupfer [3], Annett Zobel [4] and Ulrike Lucke [5]

Abstract: Many difficulties can arise during the implementation of a metadata standard. One reason may be the lack of prior examination of existing standards. These sometimes painful experiences led to the need for a catalogue of criteria to be used in infrastructure projects to assess suitability to the requirements. Against the National Education Infrastructure background, the paper presents an initial approach. For this purpose, criteria are developed, whose application enables a well-founded pre-selection of standards. These are discussed and tested exemplary in three use cases - educational offerings, educational resources, and digital credentials. An overview of current developments in the area accompanies this. Overall, the paper aims to provide a basis for further discussions on the selection and handling of standards in educational infrastructures. However, so far there is little literature on this highly relevant topic. Therefore, a discussion process in the community should be stimulated as a supplement.

Keywords: metadata standards, evaluation criteria, education infrastructure, educational offers, educational resources, digital credentials

1 The Role of Standards in the National Education Infrastructure

The necessity of standards[6] and interfaces was recognized as a crucial topic in the research and development of educational technology for decades [TK12]. However, there is little overview of the field, and many initiatives attempt to structure the field by setting their

---

[1] Hochschulbibliothekszentrum des Landes NRW, Offene Infrastruktur, Jülicher Str. 6, 50647 Köln, steffen.roertgen@hbz-nrw.de, https://orcid.org/0000-0001-6378-2618

[2] snoopmedia GmbH, Hohe Straße 93, 53119 Bonn, h.zimmermann|r.brenner@snoopmedia.com, https://orcid.org/0009-0001-2743-6547, https://orcid.org/0009-0003-2886-9138

[3] metaVentis GmbH, IT, Am Horn 21a, 99425 Weimar, hupfer@edu-sharing.net, https://orcid.org/0009-0001-4951-1608

[4] edu-sharing NETWORK Association, board of directors, Am Horn 21a, 99425 Weimar, zobel@edu-sharing.net, https://orcid.org/0009-0006-9917-460X

[5] Universität Potsdam, Institut für Informatik und Computational Science, An der Bahn 2, 14476 Potsdam, ulrike.lucke@uni-potsdam.de, https://orcid.org/0000-0003-4049-8088

[6] This paper focuses on the area of metadata standards. Even where the term "standard" is used in general, it always refers to the field of metadata standards.

own competing standards. At the same time, educational technologies are increasingly networked, data is exchanged within individual initiatives and in many educational areas. Projects such as a National Educational Infrastructure strive to map and easily connect the entire learning journey of its users. To network educational actors e.g. within a construct as the previously mentioned National Education Infrastructure (NEI) or EU-wide educational network, the use of standards and interfaces becomes a knock-out criterion for success [Kn22]. Education stakeholders face the challenge of choosing the right data exchange standard to build interoperable services.

In this field, metadata in particular has a long tradition as an important mechanism for interoperability. Starting in the library sector, metadata standards have been driven by the emergence of multimedia learning and education technologies, and not least spurred by recent OER initiatives, like WirLernenOnline[7] or the Open Educational Resource Search Index[8]. For most types of educational content metadata standards exist. They are usually developed and disseminated by standardisation bodies with the involvement of key actors in the respective field. At the same time, stakeholders have to choose between several existing standards for one type of content. In addition, data exchange systems are implemented differently in practice; sometimes they are based on standards, and sometimes big players define proprietary formats and try to establish them as standards.

Standards describe the sequence of repetitive tasks and established processes, guidelines and definitions for handling them. The development can take place both top down and bottom up and usually involves the expertise of specialists. The form usually corresponds to a formalised document that describes the correct implementation of the respective standard as completely as possible [DI23]. There are various reasons for using standards, but most of them relate to their cooperative, relieving and sustainable effects. The need of different players to exchange objects and to define the characteristics of these objects in a general way in advance leads to the formation of standards. Standardisation itself can occur in three ways [Ge97]:

- *De-Facto standardisation* takes place through the selection or elaboration of a standard by market participants.
- In *institutional standardisation*, committees (e.g. W3C, 1EdTech, DCMI/DublinCore/asist.org , DINI-AG-KIM), standardisation organisations (CEN, ISO) or nationally recognized normalisation institutes (e.g. DIN) organise the development of standards.
- *Legislative standardisation* is achieved through the enactment of laws or regulations.

It should be noted here that the types often merge into one another. Standards are always needed when several actors cooperate and agree in advance on the shape of the objects they want to exchange. For large educational infrastructures, these objects can be any information in the form of data. If the implementation is correct, i.e. compliant with

---

[7] https://wirlernenonline.de

[8] https://oersi.org

standards, the players can interconnect and exchange their data without additional implementation effort per additional participating partner. For institutions and projects that are publicly funded, another aspect regarding the use of standards is to be respected. In order to meet the "Public Money, Public Code" requirement of the campaign of the same name, it is recommended that established and open standards be used in publicly financed projects as far as possible [Pu23]. This enables subsequent use of the data and interfaces used as well as sustainable connectivity beyond the financed project period. But how is an informed decision made to use a particular standard in the first place? There is a lack of criteria, which help actors choose the right standard from all the available options.

In this paper, we derive criteria from the evaluation of Open Source Software to the evaluation of metadata standards. These criteria are then used to evaluate standards for three exemplary content types: Educational Offers, Educational Resources, and Digital Credentials. We hope to initiate a discussion on the evaluation criteria to establish this relevant topic in research and practice, and to make it easier for future stakeholders to make informed decisions on the selection of metadata standards.

2   Criteria and Evaluation Process of Metadata Standards

Before presenting and discussing exemplary use cases of metadata standards in a NEI [Kn22], it should be clarified which criteria can be used to verify whether a standard covers the use case. As [RHG21] note, there is little prior work in the literature on the topic. In order to be able to set up founded criteria nevertheless, the criteria from the evaluation of open source software (OSS) [Wi06, Ga10] as well as generally formulated principles to the topic metadata standards [Du02] are to be combined with the criteria outlined by [RHG21] for the selection of educational standards. This results in a criteria catalogue that is generally applicable to standards in the educational environment.

[Ga10] recommends that a distinction be made between informal and formal techniques in the evaluation of software, each of which brings with it its own criteria. With the informal criteria [Me04] is referred to, whose criteria overlap partly with [Wi06]. [Ga10] recommends the use of informal criteria to pre-select options that can then be formally reviewed. Informal criteria have the property that they are difficult to measure independently, whereas formal criteria can be verified in a clearly reproducible way. This basic distinction is to be related to the criteria presented in [RHG21] for the education area, in order to verify their applicability to educational infrastructures in general.

The use and implementation of a metadata standard entails additional effort. If an exchange of data with external partners is not necessary and planned, it may be that an in-house data model developed to meet individual needs can be implemented more quickly and with less effort. The first step is therefore to *clarify the objective* of the project [RHG, p. 66]. Only with the goal of exchanging data *sustainably* beyond one's own system or the duration of one's own project does the evaluation and finally the use of an appropriate standard become necessary. In the following two sections, the criteria proposed by [RHG21] are divided into informal and formal criteria. Where possible, it is referenced if a criterion is also found in the evaluation of OSS or generally formulated principles to the topic of metadata standards. Without reference, the criterion was developed by the authors.

2.1 Informal Criteria

For a standard to have a relieving effect, it requires *dissemination and acceptance* of the standard [Me04, RHG21, p. 65]. Acceptance usually correlates with *implementation effort and utility* [RHG21, p. 66]. Requirements for a standard are strongly *context-dependent*. A review of reference projects or exchange with partners who use the standard is useful to check the practical applicability.[9] *Relevance and community* around a standard should also be considered [Me04]. Current developments in the respective standard should be taken into account. Standards may be revised and come out in new versions soon. The implementation of a standard is not trivial, therefore it is desirable if there is an active community around the respective standard. This can serve the exchange or also the further development of a standard. For the correct implementation, *documentation and support* [Me04, RHG21, p. 66, Wi06] are important. Ideally, examples and schemas are provided to validate the data and its implementation.

2.2 Formal Criteria

Meeting didactic and technical requirements in equal measure is a challenge that is taken into account when testing *practicality* [RHG21, p. 65]. It must be checked whether the standard covers the necessary attributes and can be supplemented with missing ones. The existence of legal or other requirements should also be checked at this point. If a standard is based on specific protocols or has further dependencies, the question of *technical debt* should be examined so as not to inadvertently burden oneself with dependencies. Formats and data models should be designed to be *interoperable* to ensure convertibility and sustainability [Me04]. If validation schemes are not provided, it may make sense to have one's own implementation *certified*. Certification can be seen as a sign of quality [RHG21, p. 65]. Not all standard documents are freely available. Obtaining them may involve *costs* [RHG21, p. 67]. It must be clarified whether financial resources are available for acquisition and use. In order to be allowed to adapt them, it is necessary that they have been published under a *free licence* [Du02, RHG21, p. 65].

Finally, other than stated by [RHG21, p.67] we consider the criterion of openness must also be taken into account, especially in the public sector in order to avoid lock-in effects. This criterion combines formal and informal criteria, which primarily concern the opportunities for collaboration and further development. In addition to the costs and

---

[9] E.g. There are DIN-Specifications, e.g. DIN PAS 1032-2, DIN PAS 1068, which solved problems on a theoretical level, but did not grasp adoption.

licensing of the standard and access to the developing community, due process, compliance with the consensus principle, transparent development, fairness and opportunities for participation in the standardisation process must also be taken into account.10 A detailed elaboration is outside the scope of discussion, but will be similar to the structure of the Software Sustainability Maturity Model (SSMM) of [Ga10]. The Wiki of the Open Education Community11 provides a first overview of use cases and standards to support the evaluation process of the mentioned criteria.

3 Application Fields of Metadata Standards in the NEI

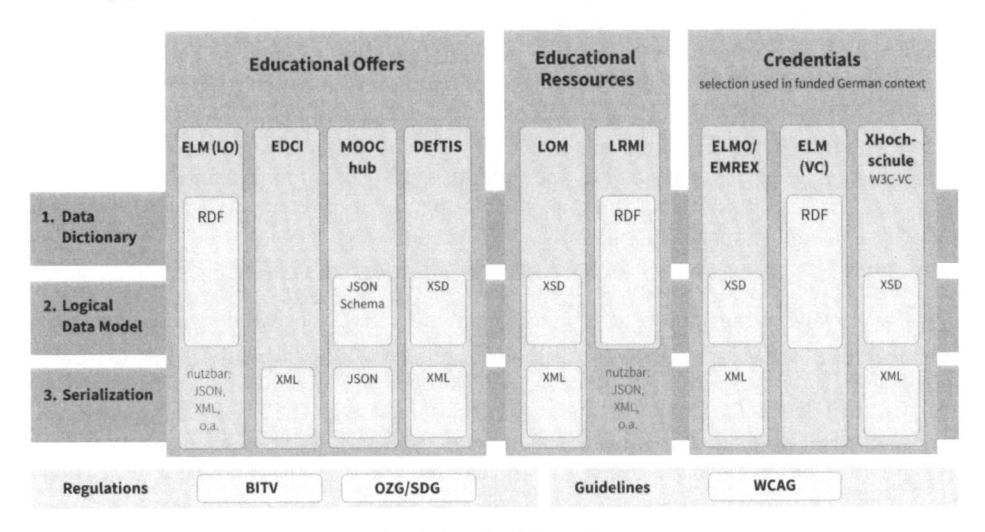

	Educational Offers				Educational Ressources		Credentials (selection used in funded German context)		
	ELM (LO)	EDCI	MOOC hub	DEfTIS	LOM	LRMI	ELMO/ EMREX	ELM (VC)	XHochschule W3C-VC
1. Data Dictionary	RDF					RDF		RDF	
2. Logical Data Model			JSON Schema	XSD	XSD		XSD		XSD
3. Serialization	nutzbar: JSON, XML, o.ä.	XML	JSON	XML	XML	nutzbar: JSON, XML, o.ä.	XML		XML
Regulations	BITV		OZG/SDG		Guidelines		WCAG		

Fig. 1: Standard Overview

Metadata plays an essential role if offers, credentials, resources or contents are to be bundled or exchanged in national, European or other networks. For this purpose different data models and serialisation formats can be used. The graphic gives an impression of the variety of standards that can be used and their underlying technologies. In the following, the listed criteria will be discussed and applied to three use cases - educational offerings, educational resources, and credentials.

---

[10] Overall, many aspects of the Software Sustainability Maturity Model [Ga10] can be transferred to the standardisation process.

[11] https://confluence.edu-sharing.net/confluence/x/K4ApBg

3.1 Educational Offers

Educational offers are time and place-bound learning opportunities. They can be found at central locations, e.g. in Germany in KURSNET of the Federal Employment Agency.[12] At a European level the Europass portal is an appropriate example.[13] In order to present educational offers on these kinds of platforms, individual providers must make metadata of the offers available to be collected from aggregators. In addition, a platform must be able to handle this data and be able to filter and select by user specific parameters.

The use case specific *requirements* for a standard are strongly context dependent. On one hand there are "didactical" requirements for the standard to represent the contents of an educational offer. Stakeholders see the need to not falsely advertise an offer and simultaneously make an offer as appealing as possible. On the other hand, there is a need for highly structured data to optimise the discoverability of individual offers. Automated processes must be able to correctly match the offer's data to the parameters of a given implementation. One challenge in this context will be a standardised breakdown of subjects into subject groups, which are defined differently in separate educational domains. The definition of cross-domain standards is a key to a standard's success in the context of an educational infrastructure.

EDCI[14] data model, MOOChub[15] Schema and ELM[16] were evaluated for this use case.[17] EDCI was tested as part of a prototype implementation. It is developed by the European Commission to provide a secure and sustainable infrastructure for the exchange of digital certificates. The given infrastructure also enables the representation of educational offers and was included in the prototype due to its widespread use. The MOOChub Schema is used to exchange course data (MOOCs[18]) in the MOOChub. A JSON schema is provided to share information about the courses, the providing organisations and other information. The amount of mandatory attributes has been kept low to easily onboard new partners. The specification only allows information in one language. ELM (also based on XML) is a further development of the EDCI standard and can be used for Educational Offers.

Two of these standards (EDCI, MOOChub Schema) have been tested in an experimental context. Both meet some of our defined informal criteria. In regards to *dissemination* the two standards differ quite a bit. EDCI being developed on the European level has a bigger reach than the MOOChub Schema which is only used in Germany and Austria. In terms

---

[12] https://www.arbeitsagentur.de/kursnet
[13] https://europa.eu/europass/de
[14] https://europa.eu/europass/en/europass-digital-credentials
[15] https://moochub.org/
[16] https://github.com/european-commission-empl/European-Learning-Model
[17] DEfTIS (http://projekt.iwwb-files.de/PAS/DEfTIS_zu_PAS1045_Ver_5_07.pdf) is widely used within the professional education sector. It is not further examined here, because we focus here on standards applicable across all education sectors. A comparison with similar standards would nonetheless be interesting.
[18] Massive Open Online Courses

of *acceptance* MOOChub is easier to implement since it is based on a simple JSON format. EDCI on the other hand is complex hence Reichow et al. [RHG21] explicitly call it not a standard but an infrastructure. Both EDCI as well as MOOChub Schema are being *developed further* as EDCI did bring forth another standard in the form of ELM. The MOOChub standard is being *further developed* and, for example, a multilingual option is currently being worked on. Both standards are *well documented and there are validation schemas* made available to support integration. Although both these standards fulfil some of the mentioned criteria both have proven to be suboptimal for this use case. The current iteration of the MOOChub Schema did not match the required attributes to communicate all data needed. Future versions can of course correct this issue. EDCI, on the other hand, is too flexible and thus difficult to evaluate. Restrictions of the EDCI template are necessary to allow a uniform presentation of the offers, which is close to an own standard. In contrast ELM has a well defined, but broader set of attributes within a class with a focus on the use case of educational offers.[19] These attributes are documented in the corresponding Github repository.[20]

3.2 Educational Resources

In this context, educational resources are physical or digital resources whose metadata can be retrieved digitally and are associated with a learning activity or experience. They differ from educational offerings in that they are not tied to place and time. In a networked infrastructure, providers of educational content want to share these resources and publish them, for example, in an overarching educational search engine.

To process that use case, the resources of the service providers must be made accessible. To keep the implementation effort of the aggregators low, it is desirable if many service providers agree on the use of a standard. When considering applicable standards, special requirements arise. Unlike library standards, such as MARC21[21], standards for educational resources must provide a set of pedagogical attributes (e.g. audience, educational level, competency references) to provide data for faceted searching. Two standards have been established in this area, *Learning Object Metadata* (LOM)[22] and *Learning Resource Metadata Innovation* (LRMI)[23]. Application profiles of LOM as well as LRMI are widely used in German-speaking countries. LOM-CH[24] is a profile from Switzerland, HS-OER-LOM[25] is used by various German OER repository operators. The "Allgemeine Metadatenprofil für Bildungsressourcen (AMB)"[26] (General Metadata Profile for

---

[19] In ELM educational offers are called "Learning Opportunities"
[20] https://github.com/european-commission-empl/European-Learning-Model/
[21] https://www.loc.gov/marc/
[22] https://standards.ieee.org/ieee/1484.12.1/7699/
[23] https://www.dublincore.org/specifications/lrmi/
[24] https://www.educa.ch/de/taetigkeiten/online-dienste/lom-ch
[25] https://dini-ag-kim.github.io/hs-oer-lom-profil/latest/
[26] https://dini-ag-kim.github.io/amb/draft/

Educational Resources) is a widely used LRMI-based profile. In addition, there are DIN and ISO standards that could potentially be used, but to the authors' knowledge have not found widespread use. Since the beginning of 2020, there is an initiative at IEEE, which deals with the further development of LOM, since the used attributes and value lists are partly outdated according to their own statement. Also other metadata concepts have been established in the meantime, which are to be incorporated into the new development "Learning Metadata (LMeta)"[27].

In terms of *acceptance and dissemination*, the LOM and LRMI standards are considered more closely, as they are *up-to-date and have a strong community*, which can be seen in the publication dates of the application profiles (LOM-CH 2020, HS-OER-LOM 2021, AMB 2023). For the HS-OER-LOM and AMB profiles, there is an active community within DINI-AG-KIM, which meets monthly, answers questions and takes care of further developments.[28] All mentioned standards and application profiles are *well documented*. *Practicality* is guaranteed, as the mentioned standards are used by many actors in the (O)ER environment. HS-OER-LOM is limited to the university sector, LOM-CH to the school sector. The application profiles can be obtained *free of charge* and are *openly licensed*, so that an adaptation to further needs is possible. According to their own statement, LOM-CH will not be further developed.[29] For the German-language profiles HS-OER-LOM and AMB suggestions can be submitted to the above-mentioned group. LRMI as the basis of AMB is also being developed openly. The developments of LRMI as well as AMB and HS-OER-LOM are thus very open, participation in IEEE Working Groups is also possible. The biggest difference is with regard to their *technologies used*. While LRMI does not specify anything about serialisation because it builds on RDF, AMB specifies the use of JSON-LD[30], SKOS[31] as well as general web standards. LOM-CH does not specify an interchange format at all. More commonly, LOM data is serialised in XML, as is the case with HS-OER-LOM. These, in turn, are mostly exchanged via OAI-PMH interfaces in the education sector.[32] Overall, the popularity of *purely* XML-based standards in the education sector tends to decline, which can also be seen in the further development of the "Europass Learning Model" (previously XML, now RDF) or the "Learning Metadata" standard (also RDF).[33] This supports the thesis set up by [Du02] already 2002 that syntax and semantics of metadata elements should be independent. LOM and LRMI *certifications* are not offered. However, schema files for both standards are available in some profiles. It can be concluded that both compared standards and their application

---

[27] https://development.standards.ieee.org/myproject-web/public/view.html#pardetail/8290

[28] https://wiki.dnb.de/display/DINIAGKIM/OER-Metadatengruppe

[29] https://www.educa.ch/sites/default/files/2020-11/applikationsprofil-lom-ch-v2.1-de.pdf, p. 6

[30] https://www.w3.org/TR/json-ld11/

[31] https://www.w3.org/TR/skos-reference/

[32] The use of OAI-PMH is much more widespread in the library sector, from where it was presumably transferred to the OER repositories.

[33] RDF can be serialised in various formats, e.g. XML, JSON, Turtle. XHochschule (see discussion below) uses XML, but also uses RDF components [X23, p. 16].

profiles are applicable for the mentioned use case. Overall, a slight trend towards RDF-based data models can be observed on a German, European and international level.

3.3 Digital Credentials

A digital credential is a digital machine-readable record that contains statements about an individual and is issued by an educational institution after a learning experience. A credential describes an activity, assessment, achievement of a learning goal, authorization, or qualification [Eu23]. In a joined educational infrastructure, service providers want to issue credentials to users and process previously acquired credentials in order to offer user-specific services. The Online Access Act at the national level and the Single Digital Gateway Regulation at the European level show that administrative services will take place digitally in the future [Di23]. Therefore, connectivity and compatibility with existing initiatives such as EMREX[34] or Erasmus Without Paper (EWP)[35] are important.

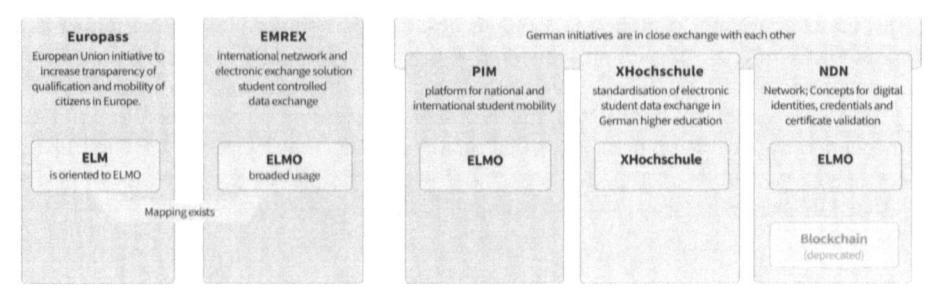

Fig. 2: Standards for Digital Credentials

Developments in this field are diverse and there are currently eleven different projects or standards in Germany [Re21]. The three largest projects are Platform for Inter*national Student Mobility (PIM)[36], XHochschule[37], and Netzwerk Digitale Nachweise (NDN)[38]. NDN changed its original blockchain-based approach after public criticism and a hack[39] and now uses ELMO (also used in EMREX) as its basic exchange format. On a European level, the European Learning Model (ELM) is also addressing this issue. XHochschule is developing a national standard in close coordination with EMREX and ELM.

At this point, the three standards ELMO (EMREX), ELM and XHochschule are examined with regard to the evaluation criteria. All three standards are developed in close coordination and are suitable for *achieving the objective* of the use case. There is a close

---

[34] https://emrex.eu/
[35] https://erasmus-plus.ec.europa.eu/european-student-card-initiative/ewp
[36] https://pim-plattform.de/
[37] https://www.xhochschule.de/
[38] http://netzwerkdigitalenachweise.de/
[39] The use of blockchain technology in that field was already marked as urgently to be cleared by [Re21, S. 18]

cooperation between PIM and XHochschule [Re21, S.11]. At the same time, ELM explicitly emphasises being aligned with ELMO.[40] In terms of *acceptance and dissemination*, ELMO's use in PIM makes it the most widely used standard with, according to its own data, 1674 connected institutions and more than 68,000 data transfers between partners. ELM is used on Europass platform as part of the European Commission's Europass Digital Credentials Infrastructure and is based on W3C-VC.[41] XHochschule also uses this standard, but is still in pilot operation. All three standards are characterised by a *high degree of relevance and an active community*. This is evident from the open development on GitHub. The same applies to *documentation and comprehensibility*. Documentation and validation schemes can be found for all standards. Only in the case of ELM, which can also be used for the presentation of educational offerings and is correspondingly complex, the presentation as a pure Markdown document can certainly be made clearer. ELM and ELMO have already been *tested in practice*, XHochschule is in the test phase. All three standards are openly licensed. The three projects are characterised by exemplary cooperation. This is probably since there is a strong political will in the background to make the topic successful and compatible. XHochschule as a national OZG project will certainly become authoritative in Germany; moreover, it will be compatible with ELM at the European level through the common denominator W3C-VC. The close contact with ELMO and ELM to ensure mapping and convertibility is defined as a design decision in the specification of XHochschule [XH23, p.15]. For further research and evaluation, "mapping" criteria should be added to the formal criteria list developed in section 2.2 as it ensures sustainability and future development.

4 Outlook to Further Development

The selection and application of standards is a complex task for which there is little literature to date that provides support in terms of applicable criteria. This lack sometimes even leads to the statements made by Stemmer and Goldacker that an assessment would often be made by the subjective assessment of an expert person. Just in certain cases, the decision on which the assessment is based could be traceable to objective criteria [SG14]. This will be countered at this point by the approach of this paper, which derives and develops criteria to place them on an objective basis that leads to a reasoned decision in a selection process. The criteria and their brief discussion on three use cases are intended to create a first impression with regard to their practicability and applicability and to stimulate further discussion and development. Further development would be helpful, for example offering a point system as desired by Stemmer and Goldacker. Overall, it should be noted that the topic is highly complex and initiatives such as the OEde Confluence within the NEI are welcome as they provide a common knowledge base and forum for exchange on the topic.[42] This makes it easier for other stakeholders to get started and make

---

[40] https://github.com/european-commission-empl/European-Learning-Model
[41] https://www.w3.org/TR/vc-data-model/
[42] https://confluence.edu-sharing.net/confluence/x/4wGhB

choices. At the same time, it can also make it clear which actors are familiar with which standards, in order to be able to gather experience and take it into account in the evaluation.

5 Recommendations on Using and Developing Metadata Standards

Metadata standards are critical for organising, describing, and managing objects of all kinds in an educational infrastructure. As such, there are recommendations that can guide the use and development of metadata standards. It is essential to adopt widely recognized metadata standards that are interoperable across different systems. Especially for a national platform, European and international developments have to be considered. Furthermore it is important to involve stakeholders from different areas of education in the development and implementation of metadata standards from the beginning on. These stakeholders can include educators, librarians, technologists, developers, and instructional designers, among others. The involvement of these stakeholders help ensure that metadata standards are chosen and developed to meet the needs of the education sector and are practical to implement as well. Lastly, it is recommended to join metadata groups and communities early on, especially if one's use case seems to require modifying existing standards. A lot of expertise is present in the groups around IEEE, LRMI or DINI-AG-KIM, which might be of help regarding practical experiences and best practices. If there is no standard present meeting the requirements, exchange with other partners having the same use case might lead to a new specification, which might then be transformed to a standard. To guarantee maintenance and sustainability of the developed specification it should be early on developed in a standardisation community.

6 Conclusion and Outlook

The paper collected and listed criteria that can be used to evaluate suitable metadata standards for a use case. For this purpose, criteria from the evaluation of open source software were used and transferred to evaluation of metadata standards. The criteria were then applied to three actual use cases of a NEI as examples and briefly discussed. This discussion can only be exemplary in this brevity, but show how the criteria can help with evaluation. In the context of BIRD, the prototype of the National Education Platform, it has been shown that such catalogues of criteria are lacking. Especially in a project that is standard agnostic and that cannot and should not prescribe the use of standards in advance, an appropriate criteria catalogue is necessary in order to be able to select standards for corresponding use cases in a well-founded way, both by oneself and with the partners involved. This paper makes an initial proposal for criteria and their application and opens up a further discussion in the evaluation of metadata standards.

Acknowledgements: This work was partially funded by the German Federal Ministry for Education and Research under grant no. 16NB001 (project "Bildungsraum Digital").

Bibliography

[Di23]   Die Single Digital Gateway-Verordnung (SDG), https://www.onlinezugangsgesetz.de/Webs/OZG/DE/grundlagen/info-sdg/info-sdg-node.html , accessed: 07/03/2023.

[Dl23]   DIN, https://www.din.de/en/about-standards/a-brief-introduction-to-standards, accessed: 07/03/2023.

[Du02]   Duval, E. et.al.: Metadata Principles and Practicalities. D Lib Mag 8/2002, 2002.

[Eu23]   Europass: What are Digital Credentials, https://europa.eu/europass/en/what-are-digital-credentials, accessed: 07/03/2023.

[Ga10]   Gardler, R.: Software Sustainability Model, http://oss-watch.ac.uk/resources/ssmm, accessed: 07/03/2023.

[Ge97]   Genschel, P., Standards in der Informationstechnik - Institutioneller Wandel in der internationalen Standardisierung. TATuP - Zeitschrift für Technikfolgenabschätzung in Theorie Und Praxis, 6(2)/1997, pp. 58–61, 1997.

[Kn22]   Knoth, A.; Blum, F.; Soldo, E.; Lucke, U.: Structural Challenges in the Educational System meet a Federated IT-Infrastructure for Education – Insights into a Real Lab. In: Proc. Int. Conf. on Computer Supported Education (CSEDU), pp. 369–375, 2022.

[Me04]   Metcalfe, R. Top Tips For Selecting Open Source Software, accessed 07/03/2023.

[Pu23]   Public Money, Public Code, https://publiccode.eu/en/, accessed: 07/03/2023.

[Re21]   Rentzsch, R.: Digitale Bildungsnachweise - Der Stand 2020 in Deutschland und Europa. Institut für Innovation und Technik, Berlin, 2021.

[RHG21] Reichow, I., Hochbauer, M., Goertz, L.: Standards und Empfehlungen zur Umsetzung digitaler Weiterbildungsplattformen in der beruflichen Bildung. Bundesinstitut für Berufsbildung, Bonn, 2021.

[SG14]   Stemmer, M., Goldackter, G.: Standardisierung für die öffentliche IT. Kompetenzzentrum Öffentliche IT, Frauenhofer-Institut für Offene Kommunikationssysteme, Berlin, 2014.

[TK12]   Trahasch, S., Kandzia, P.: E-Learning an Hochschulen - Vom Projekt zum Prozessmanagement. i-com 01/12, pp. 34-37, 2012.

[Wi06]   Wilson, J.: Open Source Maturity Model, http://oss-watch.ac.uk/resources/archived/osmm, accessed: 07/03/2023.

[XH23]   XHochschule, Spezifikation Version 0.94, BMBF u. Land Sachsen-Anhalt, https://xhochschule.de/def/xhochschule/0.94/spec/spezifikation_0.94.pdf, accessed: 07/03/2023.

[GI09]   GI, Gesellschaft für Informatik e.V., www.gi.de, Stand: 24.12.2016.

[Gl06]   Glück, H.I.: Formatierung leicht gemacht. Formatierungsjournal 11/09, S. 23-27, 2009.

Breaking It Down: On the Presentation of Fine-Grained Learning Objects in Virtual Learning Environments

André Selmanagić [1] and Katharina Simbeck [2]

Abstract: Current research on personalized learning environments has a strong focus on the individualized sequencing of learning objects and the creation of adaptive feedback within them. Little emphasis has been placed on designing virtual learning environments (VLEs) that retrieve the necessary learning objects from online repositories and utilize semantic metadata to present them dynamically. Thus, this paper presents an approach for transforming a semantic web of fine-grained learning objects into a functional VLE that delivers these objects to learners.

Keywords: Learning Objects, Virtual Learning Environments, Personalized Learning, Linked Data, Semantic Web

1 Introduction

The potential to personalize instruction using digital technologies was recognized more than half a century ago [GNR02]. This pursuit might culminate in the utilization of machines that possess human-like abilities for educational purposes [La23]. Such systems are envisioned to "automatically find appropriate learning objects that support an individual learner at some diagnosed stage of learning" [Pa04]. To accomplish these tasks, machines must make meaning of the world [Us03] and understand the educational content they present and adapt. This meaning is often conveyed from human to machine through semantic information [Us03]. While the automatic educational decision-making processes operate behind the scenes, their outcomes, such as how learning content and adaptive feedback is presented to the learner, must manifest in the user interface of the personalized learning environment. To illustrate this aspect of personalization, we present preliminary results of *adlete-vle*[3] – a prototypical virtual learning environment (VLE) that leverages semantic information for the presentation of fine-grained learning objects to the learner.

---

[1] HTW Berlin, Fachbereich 4, Ostendstr. 25, Berlin, 12459, andre.selmanagic@htw-berlin.de, https://orcid.org/0000-0002-6457-2791
[2] HTW Berlin, Fachbereich 4, Ostendstr. 25, Berlin, 12459, katharina.simbeck@htw-berlin.de, https://orcid.org/0000-0001-6792-461X
[3] https://gitlab.com/adaptive-learning-engine/vle

2 Related Works

The fundamental idea of learning objects (LOs) is to "make online instructional materials broadly accessible, searchable, and reusable" [Pa04]. Digital learning objects play a pivotal role in achieving the goals of computerized education by creating instruction that is "(1) adaptive to the individual, (2) generative rather than pre-composed, and (3) scalable to industrial production levels without proportional increases in cost" [GNR02]. Reusable LOs are thus an important facilitator for advanced forms of computerized education such as the use of intelligent machines to personalize learning [GNR02]. By adopting an "authoring-by-aggregation" approach [DH03], smaller LOs can be reused by composing them into larger LOs or assembling them into learning sequences [Ve08]. As such, the granularity of LOs – their "size" [YKS20] – can range from a snippet of text (e.g. a definition) to a whole course [Ve08]. In order to reuse existing LOs, they must first be discoverable and accessible [Pa04], e.g. via Learning Object Repositories [YKS20]. Metadata about LOs is crucial for enabling this discoverability [Pa04] as well as ensuring interoperability between LOs and infrastructure such as learning management systems (LMS). In order to embed and assemble LOs, the infrastructure has to process both the metadata of the LO as well as the content (e.g. file format, encoding, etc.) [DH03]. Multiple metadata standards exist to describe the attributes of LOs (e.g. LOM, Dublin Core, AMB [Ko22]), types of LOs and their granularity (e.g. SCORM), the sequencing of LOs as well as their packaging for LMS [Ve08]. AMB ("Allgemeines Metadatenprofil für Bildungsressourcen") is a cross-educational metadata profile for the description of LOs, which is heavily based on the online vocabulary schema.org and its educational extensions by the Learning Resource Metadata Initiative [Ko22]. The JSON-based metadata format combines various properties for general information (e.g. *name*, *language*), pedagogical information (e.g. *learningResourcType*), technical information (e.g. *encoding*) and links to other sources, e.g. the competencies taught, assessed, or required by the LO [Ko22]. The metadata document itself is an independent web resource [Ko22].

Research on the presentation of fine-grained learning objects in VLEs using semantic technologies is rare. Yoosooka & Wuwongse demonstrate an approach for dynamically creating personalized learning packages in the SCORM format based on linked data techniques. However, the student must manually import the package in a SCORM-compliant LMS (e.g. Moodle) [YW12]. Based on semantic annotations, Henning et. al. deliver open educational resources to learners by embedding them in an LMS [He14]. In contrast, Milutinović et al. created a mobile application that retrieves fine-grained LOs and their linked resources from an LO repository and presents them within custom interactive learning activities [Mi15]. However, none of these publications provide in-depth information about the presentation of LOs from a technological perspective.

3 Design & Development

Undoubtedly, the presentation of learning objects plays a crucial role in facilitating meaningful learning experiences for learners. This publication puts a special focus on the presentation of fine-grained LOs, which may not be bigger than snippets of information. Our fundamental assumption is that future intelligent algorithms, accountable for generating personalized learning sequences and assembling composite LOs, will employ an authoring-by-aggregation approach, harnessing the potential of reusable, fine-grained LOs. From a technological perspective, the delivery of such aggregated LOs and their constituent components requires the retrieval and subsequent presentation of these snippets to the learner. Subsequently, we will describe how this presentation of LOs within a prototypical VLE is informed by the semantic information associated with the LOs. However, the discussion of personalization algorithms falls beyond the scope of this paper.

In order to decouple the core logic of the VLE from the contents presented, *adlete-vle* requires LOs to be semantic web resources possessing unique identifiers (URLs). They must additionally be accompanied by metadata in the form of AMB. The VLE is given a learning object sequence, which contains the links to the LO web resources that are to be presented to the learner. Leveraging this information, the VLE gathers the LOs and their metadata from the web. The LOs of the prototype's exemplary domain reside in a self-hosted LO repository that is a combination of OERSI (a search engine for LOs that uses and serves AMB metadata [Ho23]) and a simple web server (for LO content data).

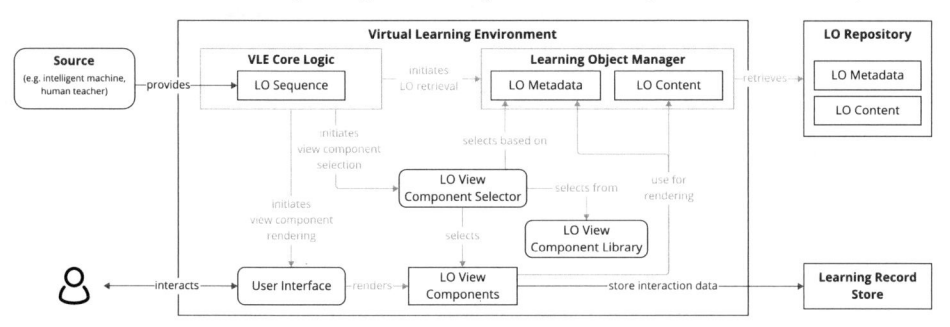

Figure 1: Process logic within the VLE (LO retrieval in blue, presentation in green)

adlete-vle provides an integrated course experience, where learners stay in the VLE and are not redirected to external resources. As such these external resources need to be visually embedded. A wide variety of digital LO types exist, from simple textual LOs (e.g. definitions, examples, and hints) to multi-media content (e.g. videos, interactive simulations). To optimize their instructional value, it is crucial to present them in a way that reflects their specific type. To this end, the frontend of the VLE was developed in the form of a web-based application built with the React framework, and uses the model-view-controller and factory design patterns [Wa02]. Consequently, the models (LO content, e.g. textual definitions, images) are displayed by views (React components, e.g. text blocks, image galleries), which are dynamically created using the factory design pattern (see Figure 1). The semantic information about the LOs stored in the metadata plays a crucial role in this process. Metadata fields like *learningResourceType* (e.g. *definition*, *example*, *assessment*) and *encoding* (media types, e.g. *text/markdown*) are used for automatically selecting the appropriate view component factory for a specific LO. A set of reusable view components was created for common learning resource types, e.g. *Definition*, *Example*, *Equation* and *Video*. Besides the LO content that is displayed, some of these components make direct use of the associated semantic data. The *Definition* component, for example, uses the concept referenced in the *about* field, when displaying the title. The *Example* component adds an illustrative image by utilizing the *thumbnail* field.

adlete-vle also supports the display of interactive LOs, either in the form of embedded websites or custom view components. Unlike static LOs that primarily consist of raw data, the latter LOs are self-contained React components associated with the particular media type *application/x.react-component*. These components have access to the underlying system, thereby enabling the retrieval and nested display of other LOs. This may, for instance, be used for the adaptive display of scaffolded information (e.g. hints, or links to LOs containing prerequisite knowledge). In certain domains, for example math, this can also be used to dynamically load additional datasets from external sources, allowing the learner to explore the learning content in the light of different contexts (e.g. sports vs. music).

As fine-grained LOs, such as definitions and examples, are usually not displayed independently, the VLE currently presents the LOs in a sequential order as collapsible blocks with titles, similar to popular LMS, such as Moodle (as shown in Figure 2).

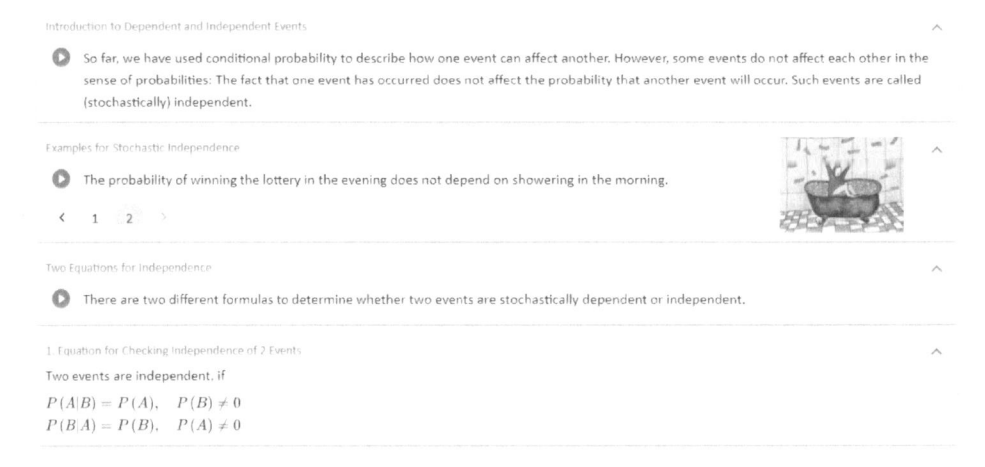

Introduction to Dependent and Independent Events

So far, we have used conditional probability to describe how one event can affect another. However, some events do not affect each other in the sense of probabilities: The fact that one event has occurred does not affect the probability that another event will occur. Such events are called (stochastically) independent.

Examples for Stochastic Independence

The probability of winning the lottery in the evening does not depend on showering in the morning.

< 1 2 >

Two Equations for Independence

There are two different formulas to determine whether two events are stochastically dependent or independent.

1. Equation for Checking Independence of 2 Events

Two events are independent, if

$P(A|B) = P(A), \quad P(B) \neq 0$
$P(B|A) = P(B), \quad P(A) \neq 0$

Figure 2: Screenshot of the VLE showing the block-based layout of multiple LOs

4 Discussion & Outlook

The current prototype of the VLE is limited in various aspects. While new view components can be added easily to the component library, the VLE currently only supports the rendering of the types of LOs that were necessary for learning in the exemplary domain of the prototype. The rendering of LOs makes strong use of their metadata. In line with one of the main criticisms of LOs, we can confirm that creating the necessary metadata is a time-consuming process [Pa04], especially at this level of granularity. Prior research has explored areas such as automatic metadata generation and metadata editors [Ve08], which have the potential to support this process. In this regard, exploring the potential of AI technologies such as large language models (e.g., ChatGPT) for metadata generation appears as a promising avenue for future research.

A user study of the VLE revealed a generally positive attitude concerning the block-based presentation of LOs (see Figure 2), though a non-negligible number of learners felt that the user interface appears cluttered and the information seems disconnected because of this structure. One potential approach to address this issue could involve merging multiple smaller LOs by generating text bridges, aiming to create a more natural text flow while minimizing visual clutter. In this context as well, large language models emerge as a viable tool.

To deliver personalized learning experiences, the prototypical VLE will soon integrate with an adaptive learning engine that is currently under active research [Gn23]. While the semantic information linking LOs to their associated competencies is valuable for these intelligent adaptive algorithms, such competency relations can also be manifested in the user interface, e.g. as part of a learner-centric approach to learning analytics [SP13]. For example, a learner-centric VLE could enable learners to directly navigate from the current LO to the subset of competencies influenced by that particular LO within an open learner model. This would empower learners with an understanding of how their learning experiences correspond to the system's decisions regarding their learning.

5 Conclusion

While the development of personalized learning environments presents various challenges in terms of automated educational decision-making (such as individualized learning sequences and adaptive feedback), this paper puts a special emphasis on the retrieval and presentation of learning objects within personalized learning environments. We introduced a prototypical VLE that extensively utilizes semantic information in the form of learning object metadata to embed external (composite) learning objects from the web. Moving forward, this VLE will serve as an experimental sandbox for investigating the diverse aspects of learning object presentation in personalized learning environments.

Bibliography

[DH03]   Duval, E.; Hodgins, W.: A LOM Research Agenda: WWW (Alternate Paper Tracks), 2003.

[Gn23]   Gnadlinger, F. et al.: Adapting Is Difficult! Introducing a Generic Adaptive Learning Framework for Learner Modeling and Task Recommendation Based on Dynamic

Bayesian Networks. In (Jovanovic, J. et al. ed.): Proceedings of the 15th International Conference on Computer Supported Education. SCITEPRESS, pp.272–280, 2023.

[GNR02] Gibbons, A. S.; Nelson, J.; Richards, R.: The nature and origin of instructional objects. In (Wiley, D. A. ed.): The instructional use of learning objects. Agency for Instructional Technology and Association for Educational Communications & Technology, Bloomington, Ind., pp.25–58, 2002.

[He14] Henning, P. A. et al.: Personalized web learning by joining OER. In (Trahasch, S. et al. ed.): DeLFI 2014. Die 12. e-Learning Fachtagung Informatik der Gesellschaft für Informatik e.V., pp.127–132, 2014.

[Ho23] Hochschulbibliothekszentrum NRW (hbz): About OERSI. https://oersi.org/resources/pages/en/about/, accessed: 31.03.2023.

[Ko22] Kompetenzzentrum Interoperable Metadaten: Allgemeines Metadatenprofil für Bildungsressourcen (AMB). https://dini-ag-kim.github.io/amb/draft/, accessed: 29.09.2022.

[La23] Latif, E. et al.: Artificial General Intelligence (AGI) for Education. arXiv, 2023.

[Mi15] Milutinović, M. et al.: Designing a mobile language learning system based on lightweight learning objects. Multimedia Tools and Applications 3/74, 2015.

[Pa04] Parrish, P. E.: The trouble with learning objects. Educational Technology Research and Development 1/52, pp.49–67, 2004.

[SP13] Slade, S.; Prinsloo, P.: Learning Analytics: Ethical Issues and Dilemmas. American Behavioral Scientist 10/57, pp.1510–1529, 2013.

[Us03] Uschold, M.: Where are the semantics in the semantic web? Ai Magazine 3/24, pp.25, 2003.

[Ve08] Verbert, K.: An architecture and framework for flexible reuse of learning object components, 2008.

[Wa02] Warford, J. S.: The MVC Design Pattern. In (Warford, J. S.; Hug, K. ed.): Computing Fundamentals. Vieweg+Teubner Verlag, Wiesbaden, pp.175–199, 2002.

[YKS20] Yassine, S.; Kadry, S.; Sicilia, M. A.: Learning Analytics and Learning Objects Repositories: Overview and Future Directions. In (Spector, M. J.; Lockee, B. B.; Childress, M. D. ed.): Learning, Design, and Technology. Springer International Publishing; Imprint: Springer, Cham, pp.1–30, 2020.

[YW12] Yoosooka, B.; Wuwongse, V.: Linked open data for learning object discovery in adaptive e-learning systems. International Journal of Knowledge and Learning 3/4/8, pp.188, 2012.

Zukunftsfähige Bildungsplattformen – Monitoring technischer Plattformdimensionen anhand einer multidimensionalen Analysematrix

Thomas Hübsch[1], Elke Vogel-Adham[2], Susanne Ritzmann[3] und Arno Wilhelm-Weidner[4]

Abstract: Das Paper gibt einen Überblick über den Einsatz einer multidimensionalen Analysematrix, Radarboard genannt, die im Rahmen der technologischen Begleitung des Innovationswettbewerbs INVITE entwickelt und eingesetzt wurde. Diese Methode ermöglicht einen Blick auf Plattformprojekte aus einem technologisch geprägten Blickwinkel, der sich im Wettbewerb bereits als hilfreich erwiesen hat. Neben einer Darstellung der Genese der Matrix und ihrer bisherigen Verwendung werden Erkenntnisse aus dem Einsatz und zukünftige Einsatzmöglichkeiten darüber hinaus im Bildungsbereich diskutiert.

Keywords: Bildungsplattformen, Analysematrix, Berufliche Bildung

1 Einleitung

Veränderungen der Arbeitswelt durch neue Arbeitsabläufe, digitale Transformation und Weiterentwicklung technologischer Möglichkeiten schreiten mit steigendem Tempo voran. Gleichzeitig verändern sich auch die Bedarfe der Arbeitenden, beispielsweise durch mobiles Arbeiten, dem Wunsch nach einer Work-Life-Balance und persönlicher beruflicher Weiterentwicklung (vgl. hierzu bspw. die Ausführung in [GK19]).

Für beide Seiten dieser Medaille spielt lebenslanges Lernen in der beruflichen Weiterbildung eine große Rolle, um veränderten Anforderungen gerecht zu werden und persönliche Bedarfe umsetzen zu können. Um Bildungsplattformen in der beruflichen Weiterbildung zu stärken, hat das BMBF 2020 den Innovationswettbewerb INVITE zur Förderung von Vernetzung und Weiterentwicklung von Bildungsplattformen ins Leben gerufen. Das Bundesinstitut für Berufsbildung (BIBB) wurde mit der fachlichen und

---

[1] VDI/VDE-IT, Innovation und Kooperation, Steinplatz 1, 10623 Berlin, thomas.huebsch@vdivde-it.de, https://orcid.org/0009-0001-0741-2951
[2] VDI/VDE-IT, Bildung und Wissenschaft, Steinplatz 1, 10623 Berlin, elke.vogel-adham@vdivde-it.de, https://orcid.org/0009-0004-5202-4212
[3] Kunsthochschule Kassel, Menzelstraße 13-15, 34121 Kassel, susanne.ritzmann@uni-kassel.de, https://orcid.org/0000-0003-1707-6039
[4] VDI/VDE-IT, Bildung und Wissenschaft, Steinplatz 1, 10623 Berlin, arno.wilhelm-weidner@vdivde-it.de, https://orcid.org/0000-0003-2604-3327

doi: 10.18420/delfi2023-26

administrativen Begleitung des Wettbewerbs beauftragt, unterstützt durch VDI/VDE-IT als Digitalbegleitung [Bi23]. Im Rahmen der Begleitung wurde eine eingehende Analyse unterschiedlicher Bildungsplattformen durchgeführt. Auf Basis dieser Erkenntnisse gehen wir in diesem Papier der Leitfrage nach: "Wie können technologische Aspekte von Bildungsplattformen multidimensional evaluiert werden?" Dazu stellen wir eine Analysematrix und ihre Genese vor und beschreiben zentrale Erkenntnisse, Defizite und Potenziale. Die Analyse kann als Grundlage für technologische Gelingensbedingungen dienen und durch ihre grafische Aufarbeitung einen Überblick über multidimensionale Einschätzungen von Plattformen geben.

2 Aufbau der Matrix

Im Rahmen der Digitalbegleitung des Innovationswettbewerbs INVITE werden die geförderten Plattformprojekte zu zentralen technologischen Themen in regelmäßigen Abständen systematisch analysiert. Zu diesem Zweck wurden sogenannte Radarboards als multidimensionale Analysematrizen in einem Netzdiagramm entwickelt.

2.1 Genese der multidimensionalen Analysematrix

Bereits zum Auswahlprozess der zu fördernden Projekte wurde die erste Fassung der Matrix eingesetzt. Sie sollte die Einschätzung des technologischen Innovationsgrads der jeweiligen Projekte in unterschiedlichen Bereichen systematisieren und erleichtern. Das Bewertungsraster der in den Vorhaben geplanten Entwicklungen basierte dabei auf der Analyse einschlägiger technischer State-of-the-Art-Lösungen, Normen und Standards.

Im Verlauf des wettbewerblichen Auswahlverfahrens stellte sich heraus, dass die technologische Matrix nicht deckungsgleich mit dem Spektrum der eingereichten Vorhaben war. In vielen Aspekten waren die Angaben in den Skizzen nicht detailliert genug. Auf der anderen Seite waren spezifisch technologische Aspekte zur Ausgestaltung des Lernerlebnisses auf Plattformen nicht eindeutig in der Matrix zu verorten. Aus diesem Grund wurde das Raster überarbeitet und auf Basis der technologischen Beschreibungen der ausgewählten Skizzen und folgenden Anträge zu einem multidimensionalen Radarboard mit fünf Hauptdimensionen und jeweiligen Unterdimensionen weiterentwickelt (siehe Abb. 1):

- **Interoperabilität durch offene Bildungsstandards:** Kompetenzstandards, Bildungsnachweise, Standards für Lerninhalte, Wissensrepräsentation
- **Algorithmen zur Unterstützung der Lernenden:** Intelligente Suchfunktionen, Learning Analytics, Adaptive Lerninhalte, Recommendersysteme
- **Mitgestaltung, Zugänglichkeit und Zusammenarbeit:** Kollaboration, Peer-Support, Partizipation, Accessibility

Zukunftsfähige Bildungsplattformen – Monitoring technischer Plattformdimensionen 163

- **Nachnutzbarkeit durch Dritte:** Open Source Software & KI-Modelle, Open Source LMS & Plugins, API Zugriff, Open Educational Resources
- **Informationssicherheit & Datensouveränität:** IT-Sicherheit, Datenschutz, Datenethik, Digitale Identitäten

Neben der Schärfung der Dimensionen durch die Definition eines Begriffsverständnisses jeder Unterdimension (im Anhang zum Paper unter [Hu23] zu finden), wurde auch das Raster mit dem Fokus auf eine qualitative Einschätzung angepasst. Die verwendete Skala reicht von 0 (Kreismitte: Die Unterdimension wird im Projekt nicht thematisiert.) bis 3 (Kreisäußeres: Die Unterdimension ist ein Schwerpunkt des Vorhabens).

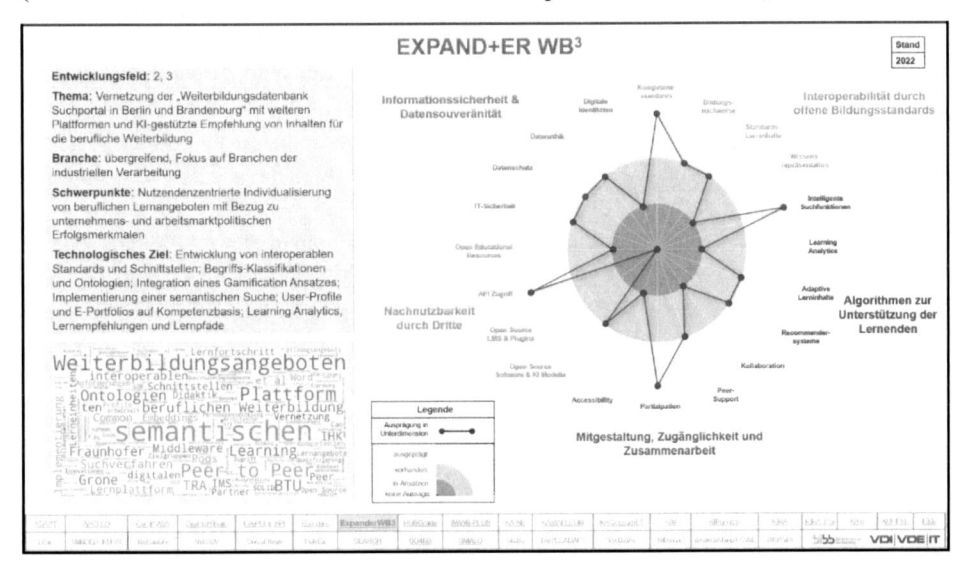

Abb.1: Perspektive *Projektebene*, Beispielprojekt EXPAND+ER WB[3] (Zwischenstand 11/2022)

Dieser qualitative Ansatz eignet sich zur Selbst- sowie zur Fremdeinschätzung und wird in unserer Arbeit für die Betrachtung von Entwicklungsverläufen und den Vergleich aus drei Perspektiven benutzt. (1) Die Perspektive *Projektebene* stellt neben den Eckdaten, wie technologischen Schwerpunkten, verwendeten Plattform(en) und Methoden, die Ausprägung der einzelnen (Unter-) Dimensionen in dem Projekt dar. (2) Die Perspektive *Programmebene* gibt einen Überblick aller Projekte und zeigt auf, wo Schwerpunkte und Randthemen liegen. Die kompakte Übersicht eignet sich zum themenbezogenen Clustering der Plattformen, da Gemeinsamkeiten schnell zutage treten. (3) Gleiches gilt auch für die Perspektive *Technologieebene*, bei der alle Projekte aus der Sicht einer Unterdimension betrachtet werden. Aus Platzgründen konzentrieren wir uns in diesem Beitrag auf die *Projektebene*. Die weiteren Darstellungen sind unter [Hu23] zu finden.

2.2 Einsatz der Matrix

Die Einschätzung der technologischen Projektschwerpunkte anhand des Bewertungsschemas erfolgte erstmals 2021 durch die Expert:innen der Digitalbegleitung auf Basis der Projektanträge und Projektsteckbriefe sowie später des Zwischenberichts 2021. Für jedes Projekt wurde eine grafische Darstellung auf *Projektebene* geschaffen (Abb. 1). Da die Einschätzung nur auf den vorliegenden Dokumenten beruhte, konnte ein gewisser Bias aufgrund der zwangsläufig nicht vollumfänglichen Darstellung nicht ausgeschlossen werden. In einem nächsten Schritt wurde daher die Einschätzung durch die Projekte selbst validiert und Änderungswünsche aufgenommen. So konnte die eventuelle Diskrepanz zwischen der Einschätzung der Digitalbegleitung (Fremdbild) und der Perspektive der Projekte (Selbstbild) aufgehoben werden. Auffallend war, dass die Einschätzung häufig nicht angepasst werden musste. Einzelne Änderungswünsche betrafen die Korrektur der Skala nach oben wie unten.

2.3 Technische Umsetzung

Die technische Umsetzung der Radarboards gliedert sich in mehrere Phasen. Zuerst wurden Wireframes entwickelt. Als Visualisierung kamen Netzdiagramme zum Einsatz. Im zweiten Schritt entwickelten wir auf dieser Basis einen Prototyp, welcher mit den Projekteinschätzungen befüllt wurde. Bei diesem Prototyp standen funktionale Aspekte im Vordergrund, fokussiert wurde die Lesbarkeit des Informationsgehalts unter Berücksichtigung von Designprinzipien. Im nächsten Schritt übertrugen wir die Projekteinschätzungen entlang der Dimensionen in ein JSON-basiertes Datenschema. Dazu wurden die Daten validiert, auf Vollständigkeit und Konsistenz hin überprüft und anschließend aggregiert. Dieses Datenschema bildet die Grundlage für eine in Entwicklung befindliche interaktive Anwendung. Die Webanwendung nutzt clientseitig JavaScript / CSS3 / HTML5 und für die Visualisierungskomponente ein Open Source Chart Framework. Einzelne technologische Dimensionen können gefiltert und Projektausprägungen verglichen werden. Der Einsatz eines „Zeitsliders" erlaubt die Betrachtung des Entwicklungsverlaufs eines Projekts oder des Förderprogramms von der Antragseinreichung bis zum Projektabschluss. Feedback-Mechanismen wie Tooltipps geben Aufschluss über das Begriffsverständnis und Leitfragen zu jeder der 20 Dimensionen. Ein Annotationstool erlaubt es, Kommentare und Anmerkungen direkt in der Webanwendung zu erstellen. Die generierten Visualisierungen können in Standardbildformaten (PNG, JPG und PDF) und die zugrundeliegenden Daten in Standarddatenformaten (JSON, CVS und XLS) exportiert werden.

3 Diskussion

Die Aspekte, die für Plattformanalysen in Frage kommen, können sehr unterschiedlich im Fokus und der Abstraktionsebene sein, daher betrachten wir hier zunächst ausschnitthaft

Literatur, die verwandte Dimensionen behandelt. Hein et al. [He20] nehmen ökonomische Aspekte und Governancefragen in den Blick, die in unserer technologischen Betrachtung nicht vorhanden sind. Mah und Hense [MH21] analysieren didaktisch-methodische Ansätze für Lernsettings, beispielsweise gewählte Medien oder vorhandene Betreuungsangebote. Dabei gibt es Überschneidungen zur Dimension *Algorithmen zur Unterstützung der Lernenden* der Radarboards. Rhode et al. [Rh21] betrachten dagegen bspw. mit Bezug auf KI-Systeme Nachhaltigkeitskriterien anhand des Lebenszyklus. Obwohl der Blickwinkel ein anderer ist, lassen sich gemeinsame Aspekte identifizieren (bspw. *Partizipation* - Inklusives und partizipatives Design). Sonnberger und Bruder [SB22] sowie Ehlers [Eh04] betrachten Anforderungen an die Qualität von E-Learning. Dieser sehr relevante Blick fokussiert allerdings ebenfalls nicht eine technologische Auseinandersetzung. [SB22] heben die Nutzung von Kriterienkatalogen zur Untersuchung der Qualität vor. Die vorliegenden Radarboards können in einem technologischen Kontext als ein solcher Kriterienkatalog verstanden werden.

Insgesamt offenbart der Blick in die Literatur, wie vielschichtig Abstraktionsebenen und Betrachtungswinkel von Bildungsplattformen sein können und müssen. Gleichzeitig sind den Autor:innen keine Quellen bekannt geworden, deren Fokus der vorliegenden Betrachtung technologischer Plattformmerkmale gleicht.

Folgende Erkenntnisse können wir bisher ableiten: Der wichtigste Schritt in der Anwendung der Radarboards erfolgt durch die Öffnung der Datengrundlage für die beteiligten Projekte. Auf diese Weise konnte die Außen- und die Innensicht auf die Projektgefüge synchronisiert werden, ein kohärentes und vor allem konsensbasiertes Bild erreicht werden. Es ist damit ein partizipatives Evaluationstool und ein Prozess entstanden, der für technologisch versierte Projekte eine Vergleichsmöglichkeit bietet.

Trotz der erreichten Kompaktheit und Verständlichkeit, sind die Dimensionen jedoch je nach gewünschter Perspektive nicht umfassend. Eine Herausforderung stellt hier bspw. der zentrale Aspekt der Nachhaltigkeit [vgl. Rh21] dar. Diese wird im Rahmen der Radarboards als implizite Dimension verstanden. Die technologischen Dimensionen sind so strukturiert, dass nachhaltige Aspekte in der Technologiegestaltung als Bestandteil der Dimensionen gesetzt sind (bspw. OER, Accessibility-Standard, Open Source). Da aber in der Betrachtung von Nachhaltigkeit solche ausschnitthaften Betrachtungen zu Verkürzungen führen können (bspw. Bereitstellung von OER, aber Erstellung unter unfairen Arbeitsbedingungen), sind die Radarboards in ihrer derzeitigen Fassung ungeeignet um Nachhaltigkeit abzubilden. Die gemeinsame Betrachtung von fachlichen Aspekten der beruflichen Weiterbildung auf Plattformen, wie bspw. Zugänglichkeit, Durchlässigkeit oder Betreibermodell sind für die Weiterentwicklung im Sinne der Nachhaltigkeit in Zukunft entscheidend.

4 Ausblick

Die in diesem Papier vorgestellten Dimensionen der Radarboards ermöglichen einen breiten Blick auf die unterschiedlichen Facetten zukunftsfähiger Bildungsplattformen, ohne dass jede Plattform zwingend alle Dimensionen im gleichen Umfang bedienen muss. Für unsere zukünftige Arbeit mit den Radarboards sind verschiedene Schritte geplant. Die Darstellung soll neben grundsätzlichen Usability-Aspekten interaktiver gestaltet werden, so dass unterschiedliche Betrachtungstiefen dargestellt werden können. Dies kann zum Vergleich zwischen Projekten und zur Betrachtung der Veränderung einzelner Projekte im Laufe der Zeit genutzt werden. Zudem werden die Radarboards in eine Webdarstellung eingebettet, so dass auch Förderprojekte oder Fördergeber sie zur Außendarstellung und zur Gesamtschau des Programms nutzen können. Jenseits der in diesem Papier beschriebenen Erfahrungen und Dimensionen können die Radarboards auch ganz konkret für eigene Analysen nachgenutzt werden, dafür ist die jeweils aktuelle Version und Zusatzmaterial unter [Hu23] zu finden. Zusätzlich ist geplant, dass den bisher technologisch motivierten Dimensionen die Analyse fachlicher Aspekte – auch im Sinne der Nachhaltigkeit - gegenübergestellt wird.

Literaturverzeichnis

[Bi23]   BIBB, Bundesinstitut für Berufsbildung, Innovationswettbewerb INVITE, https://www.bibb.de/de/120851.php, accessed: 08/02/2023.

[Eh04]   Ehlers, UD.: Erfolgsfaktoren für E-Learning: Die Sicht der Lernenden und mediendidaktische Konsequenzen. In (Tergan, SO., Schenkel, P., eds.): Was macht E-Learning erfolgreich?. Springer, Berlin, Heidelberg. https://doi.org/10.1007/978-3-642-18957-9_3, 2004

[GK19]   Gerdenitsch, C.; Korunka, C.: Digitale Transformation der Arbeitswelt. Springer Berlin Heidelberg, 2019.

[He20]   Hein, A. et al.: Digital platform ecosystems. In: Electron Markets 30, 87–98. https://doi.org/10.1007/s12525-019-00377-4, 2020.

[Hu23]   Hübsch, T. et al., Datensammlung zur Nachnutzung der Radarboards, https://github.com/Digitalbeg/radarboards, accessed: 10/03/2023.

[MH21]   Mah, DK.; Hense, J.: Zukunftsfähige Formate für digitale Lernangebote – innovative didaktische Ansätze am Beispiel einer Lernplattform für Künstliche Intelligenz. In: Digitalisierung in Studium und Lehre gemeinsam gestalten: Innovative Formate, Strategien und Netzwerke, 617-631, 2021.

[Rh21]   Rohde, F. et al.: Nachhaltigkeitskriterien für künstliche Intelligenz. In: Schriftenreihe des IÖW, 220, 2021.

[SB22]   Sonnberger, J.F.M.; Bruder, R.: Entwicklung von Qualitätsanforderungen an E-Learning-Angebote: transparent und zielgruppengerecht. In (Pfannstiel, M.A.; Steinhoff, P.FJ., eds.): E-Learning im digitalen Zeitalter, Springer Gabler, Wiesbaden, 2022.

Umgang der DELFI-Community mit Forschungsdaten und Softwareartefakten

Eine Erhebung auf Basis der Tagungsbände im Zeitraum 2018-2022

Wabi Melkamu Jate[1] und Michael Striewe [2]

Abstract: Um Forschungsergebnisse validieren und weiterverwenden zu können, ist ein möglichst umfassender Zugriff auf die zugrundeliegenden Forschungsdaten notwendig. Die FAIR-Prinzipien geben dazu Leitlinien, die für eine umfassende Veröffentlichung von Daten befolgt werden sollten. Der vorliegende Beitrag untersucht, in wie weit die Veröffentlichungen der DELFI-Tagungen von 2018 bis 2022 Forschungsdaten auffindbar und zugänglich machen. Das Ergebnis zeigt, dass bisher nur ein Bruchteil der Daten verfügbar ist, wobei Softwareartefakte tendenziell besser verfügbar sind.

Keywords: Open Science, Open Data, Open Source, FAIR-Prinzipien, DELFI-Community

1 Einleitung

Wissenschaftliche Tagungen dienen der Veröffentlichung von Forschungsergebnissen, um innerhalb der Fachcommunity inhaltliche und methodische Fortschritte zu erzielen, Erkenntnisse zu verbreiten und Resultate unabhängig zu validieren. Dafür, aber auch zum Aufgreifen und Fortführen existierender Ideen ist es notwendig, auf die bei Forschungsaktivitäten anfallenden Daten zuzugreifen. In diesem Kontext sind Daten in einem breiten Sinne zu verstehen und umfassen z. B. sowohl Messdaten als auch Gesprächsprotokolle und Softwareartefakte. Insbesondere Software und IT-Infrastruktur erfahren im Rahmen der Veröffentlichung von Forschungsergebnissen oft eine geringe Beachtung [KS22], obwohl gerade in einer interdisziplinären Fachcommunity wie die der DELFI-Tagung, in der u. a. Forschende aus Informatik, Fachdidaktik und Psychologie kooperieren, viele unterschiedliche Daten involviert sind. Um z. B. eine Technologie in einem veränderten Kontext zu erproben, muss die Software verfügbar sein; um Erprobungen aus verschiedenen Kontexten zu vergleichen, müssen die dabei entstandenen Log- und Erhebungsdaten verfügbar sein, und um eine Evaluationsmethode weiterverwenden zu können, müssen Befragungsbögen, Interviewfragen und ähnliches Material verfügbar sein.

Um die Veröffentlichung derartiger Daten zu fördern, wurden 2016 die sogenannten FAIR-Prinzipien veröffentlicht [Wi16], die konkrete Anleitung zur Veröffentlichung von

---

[1] Universität Duisburg-Essen, Universitätsstraße 2, 45141 Essen, wabi.melkamu-jate@stud.uni-due.de
[2] Universität Duisburg-Essen, paluno – The Ruhr Institut for Software Technology, Gerlingstraße 16, 45127 Essen, michael.striewe@paluno.uni-due.de, https://orcid.org/0000-0001-8866-6971

Daten geben, um sie für eine weitere Nutzung verfügbar zu machen. Das Akronym FAIR steht dabei für die Auffindbarkeit (Findable), Zugänglichkeit (Accessible), Interoperabilität (Interoperable) und Wiederverwendbarkeit (Reusable) von Daten.

Der vorliegende Beitrag konzentriert sich als erster Versuch einer summarischen Analyse auf die ersten beiden Aspekte und untersucht, wie Forschungsdaten in Publikationen auf der DELFI-Tagung verfügbar gemacht werden. Im Vordergrund steht daher die Frage, ob Forschungsdaten zu DELFI-Beiträgen leicht auffindbar sind (indem Beiträge direkt auf ihren Speicherort verweisen) und ob die Daten dort auch tatsächlich zugänglich sind (indem enthaltene Verweise auf Ressourcen zeigen, die ohne Einschränkung zugreifbar sind). Die Untersuchung beschränkt sich dabei auf die fünf DELFI-Tagungen der Jahre 2018 bis 2022 und deckt damit einen Zeitraum ab, in dem die FAIR-Prinzipien der DELFI-Community bekannt gewesen sein können. Eine detaillierte Analyse der Vollständigkeit und Qualität der bereitgestellten Daten sowie eine Aufschlüsselung nach Beitragsformen erfordert weiteren Aufwand und muss nachfolgenden Publikationen vorbehalten bleiben.

2 Methode

Für die Erhebung wurden alle Beitragskategorien der DELFI-Hauptkonferenz berücksichtigt. Beiträge zu den Workshops wurden nicht berücksichtigt. Alle Beiträge wurden vom Erstautor des vorliegenden Beitrags daraufhin untersucht, ob ihrem Inhalt Forschungsdaten zugrunde liegen. Als Indikatoren dafür wurde die Forschungsmethode (sofern beschrieben) auf Tätigkeiten überprüft, bei der Forschungsdaten anfallen. Ferner wurden die textuell beschriebenen Ergebnisse sowie Abbildungen (sofern vorhanden) daraufhin untersucht, ob sie Ausschnitte aus Forschungsdaten oder aggregierte Daten enthalten. Im Ergebnis wurde für jeden Beitrag festgehalten, ob ein unmittelbarer Bezug zu Forschungsdaten vorliegt. Die so gewonnenen Erhebungsdaten wurden vom Zweitautor des vorliegenden Beitrags in einer zweiten Sichtung aller Beiträge überprüft.

Für alle Beiträge, die Forschungsdaten enthalten wurde geprüft, ob im Beitrag Verweise auf den Veröffentlichungsort der Daten in Form einer URL, einer DOI oder eines Verweises auf eine andere schriftliche Publikation enthalten sind. Im Fall von URLs und DOIs wurde ferner geprüft, ob diese Verweise tatsächlich zu einer zugreifbaren Ressource führen. Bei schriftlichen Publikationen wurde überprüft, ob es eine solche Veröffentlichung gibt. Eine inhaltliche Prüfung der Vollständigkeit oder Qualität der referenzierten Daten wurde in keinem der Fälle vorgenommen. Es wurde allerdings erhoben, ob im Beitrag selbst Informationen dazu gegeben wurde, wenn nur ein Teil der Forschungsdaten über die genannten Referenzen verfügbar war, beispielsweise lediglich ein verwendeter Fragebogen, nicht jedoch alle darüber erhobenen Rohdaten.

Alle genannten Daten wurden in Form einer Excel-Tabelle[3] erhoben und wurden anschließend manuell ausgewertet, um einen summarischen Überblick zu erhalten. Da in

---
[3] Verfügbar unter https://doi.org/10.5281/zenodo.7774014

der Bildungstechnologie Softwareartefakten als Informatik-spezifische Form von Forschungsdaten eine besondere Rolle spielen, wurden diese in der Erhebung gesondert erfasst. In den nachfolgenden Ergebnissen meint „Forschungsdaten" daher alle Daten außer Softwareartefakte, die jeweils getrennt diskutiert werden.

3 Ergebnisse

Im Folgenden werden zunächst die Ergebnisse der Erhebung nach Jahren betrachtet und anschließend Beobachtungen über den Zeitverlauf zusammengefasst. Zuletzt werden weitere Beobachtungen aufgeführt, zu denen keine systematische Erhebung erfolgte.

3.1 Nach Jahren

Die Zahlen für Forschungsdaten ohne Softwareartefakte sind in Tab. 1 zusammengefasst. In gut 50% bis knapp 70% der Beiträge jedes Jahres konnten Forschungsdaten identifiziert werden. Insbesondere in Beiträgen der Kategorie „Demo" sind dabei in der Regel keine Forschungsdaten enthalten, da sich diese Beiträge auf die Vorstellung eines Softwareartefakts konzentrieren. Ebenso gibt es in jedem Jahrgang Beiträge, die Forschungskonzepte und theoretische Überlegungen vorstellen, die nicht durch Forschungsdaten untermauert werden. Während Forschungsdaten in 14 Fällen vollständig auffindbar und zugänglich sind, sind in 17 Fällen nur Teile auffindbar und zugänglich.

Jahr	Beiträge	enthalten	voll zugänglich	teilweise zugänglich	nicht zugänglich	Anteil voll oder tlw. zugänglich
2018	44	30 ≅ 68%	2 (1)	3 (2)	25	10%
2019	59	33 ≅ 56%	4	3 (2)	26	18%
2020	60	39 ≅ 65%	5	2	32	18%
2021	63	43 ≅ 68%	1	3	39	9%
2022	49	25 ≅ 51%	2	6	17	32%

Tab. 1: Anzahl der Beiträge, die Forschungsdaten enthalten und deren Zugänglichkeit. Zahlen in Klammern geben an, wie viele der per URL zugänglich gemachten Daten tatsächlich verfügbar sind. Bei fehlender Angabe in Klammern sind alle URLs noch verfügbar.

Die separat erfassten Zahlen für Softwareartefakte sind in Tab. 2 dargestellt. Knapp 60% bis etwa 70% der Beiträge jedes Jahres beziehen sich auf konkrete Softwareartefakte als Forschungsgegenstand. Dies trifft wie erwartet insbesondere auf Beiträge der Kategorie „Demo" zu. Regelmäßig anzutreffende Beiträge zu Erhebungen und Befragungen weisen dagegen zwar Forschungsdaten, aber keine Softwareartefakte auf. Anders als bei den Forschungsdaten ist die teilweise Zugänglichkeit von Softwareartefakten die deutliche Ausnahme und tritt nur in vier von insgesamt 59 Fällen zugänglicher Softwareartefakte auf.

Jahr	Beiträge	enthalten	voll zugänglich	teilweise zugänglich	nicht zugänglich	Anteil voll oder tlw. zugänglich
2018	44	31 ≅ 70%	7 (5)	2	22	23%
2019	59	34 ≅ 58%	9	0	25	27%
2020	60	36 ≅ 60%	10	1	25	31%
2021	63	40 ≅ 63%	19 (18)	0	21	45%
2022	49	34 ≅ 69%	10	1	23	32%

Tab. 2: Anzahl der Beiträge, die Softwareartefakte enthalten und deren Zugänglichkeit. Zahlen in Klammern geben an, wie viele der per URL zugänglich gemachten Artefakte tatsächlich verfügbar sind. Bei fehlender Angabe in Klammern sind alle URLs noch verfügbar.

3.2 Vergleich über die Jahre hinweg

Der Jahresvergleich zeigt keine starken Trends. Insbesondere bei den Forschungsdaten sind Schwankungen zu beobachten. Während 2019 und 2020 jeweils 18% der Beiträge und in 2022 sogar 32% der Beiträge Forschungsdaten zumindest teilweise auffindbar und zugänglich gemacht haben, trifft dies für 2018 und 2021 jeweils auf nur 10% der Beiträge zu. Bei den Softwareartefakten ist für die Jahre 2018 bis 2021 eine kontinuierliche Steigerung von 23% auf 45% der Beiträge zu erkennen, die Softwareartefakte auffindbar und zugänglich machen. Im Jahr 2022 sinkt dieser Anteil jedoch wieder auf 32% und liegt damit auf demselben Niveau wie bei den Forschungsdaten.

3.3 Weitere Beobachtungen

Die Nutzung dedizierter Dienste für die langfristige Verfügbarmachung von Forschungsdaten oder Softwareartefakten wurde nur selten beobachtet. Viermal wird eine DOI des Dienstes Zenodo[4] angegeben. Dreizehnmal wird auf GitHub[5] verwiesen, wobei dies nicht ausschließlich für Softwareartefakte der Fall ist. In allen anderen Fällen beziehen sich Verweise auf augenscheinlich projektspezifische URLs oder Webseiten von Hochschulen.

4 Diskussion

Zunächst muss festgestellt werden, dass eine eher geringe Auffindbarkeit und Verfügbarkeit von Forschungsdaten und Softwareartefakten gegeben ist. Mit Ausnahme von Software im Jahr 2021 liegt die Quote durchweg bei unter einem Drittel; bei den Forschungsdaten mit Ausnahme von 2022 sogar bei unter einem Fünftel. Als überraschend erwies sich, dass oft sogar bei Demo-Beiträgen, die explizit der Vorstellung eines Software-

---
[4] https://zenodo.org/
[5] https://github.com/

Artefakts dienen, keine Verweise zu finden waren, unter denen das Artefakt auffindbar und zugänglich gemacht wurde. In einigen dieser Fälle wurde zumindest der Name der Software genannt. Fraglich ist jedoch, ob alleine das (ggf. zuzüglich des Hinweises auf eine Verfügbarkeit im App-Store) als hinreichend für die Auffindbarkeit gelten sollte. Immerhin könnte auf diesem Weg inzwischen eine neuere oder auch gänzlich veränderte Version der Software verfügbar sein, als diejenige, die in dem Beitrag besprochen wird.

Ebenfalls kritisch zu beurteilen sind URLs, die auf interne Webseiten verweisen. Während die Notwendigkeit zur Registrierung der Zugänglichkeit nicht prinzipiell im Wege steht, ist dies anders, wenn Accounts nur an Angehörige einer bestimmten Organisation vergeben werden. Die betroffenen Daten sind damit über die URL zwar eindeutig auffindbar, faktisch aber für einen Großteil der Forschungscommunity nicht zugänglich.

Positiv zu bemerken ist die längerfristige Verfügbarkeit der Forschungsdaten. Nur in insgesamt sechs Fällen sind die Ziele von in Beiträgen angegeben URLs bereits nicht mehr erreichbar. Vier dieser Fälle liegen allerdings im Jahr 2018, so dass die Verfügbarkeit von Daten nach vier bis fünf Jahren möglicherweise spürbar abnimmt. Die Prüfung dieser Hypothese erfordert weitere Untersuchungen älterer Jahrgänge der Proceedings.

Bei der Auswertung erwies es sich in einigen Fällen als schwierig, Forschungsdaten und Softwareartefakte eindeutig zu klassifizieren bzw. eine klare Trennung zu ziehen, wann ein Softwareartefakt in einem so engen Bezug zum Beitrag steht, dass seine Auffindbarkeit und Verfügbarkeit sichergestellt werden sollte. Insbesondere zwei Sachverhalten scheinen im Kontext der DELFI-Community vermehrt aufzutreten:

- Die Forschungsdaten enthalten digitale Artefakte, die nur mit der zugehörigen Software nutzbar sind, bei denen die Software selber aber nicht primärer Gegenstand der Forschung ist. Ein Beispiel dafür sind Lerneinheiten in einem frei verfügbaren oder kommerziellen Lern-Management-System. In der vorliegenden Erhebung wurde in solchen Fällen jeweils die Auffindbarkeit und Zugänglichkeit einer lauffähigen Version im Sinne eines Softwareartefakts gewertet, da der Untersuchungsgegenstand ansonsten nicht nachvollziehbar ist.
- Es ist ein Softwareartefakt Gegenstand der Forschung, das selbst wiederum ein anderes Softwareartefakt als Grundsystem benötigt, um lauffähig zu sein. Beispiele dafür sind Plugins für Lern-Management-Systeme oder Erweiterungen für Spieleplattformen. In der vorliegenden Erhebung wurde in solchen Fällen jeweils nur das Plugin bzw. die Erweiterung als relevantes Softwareartefakt betrachtet, nicht jedoch das zugehörige Grundsystem. Dies geschah in der Annahme, dass der Forschungsgegenstand insgesamt nur für denjenigen Personenkreis relevant ist, dem das Grundsystem ohnehin zur Verfügung steht.

Beide Annahmen sollten für eine detailliertere Untersuchung ggf. überdacht oder die Kategorisierung von Forschungsdaten verfeinert werden.

Schließlich sollte bei der Beurteilung der Ergebnisse berücksichtigt werden, dass die DELFI-Tagung bisher keine explizite Policy hat, die Autorinnen und Autoren zur

Veröffentlichung von Forschungsdaten verpflichtet oder dafür formale Vorgaben macht. Beim Vergleich mit anderen Konferenzen muss daher auch berücksichtigt werden, ob es dort solche Policies gibt und ob diese ggf. sogar die Bereitstellung von Begleitmaterial zu einem Paper untersagen [KS23].

5 Fazit und Ausblick

Die Erhebung zeigt, dass in der DELFI-Community bereits Ansätze für die systematische Bereitstellung von Forschungsdaten existieren, indem in allen untersuchten Jahrgängen Beiträge aufgefunden wurden, die Forschungsdaten und Softwareartefakte vollständig auffindbar und zugänglich machen. Gleichzeitig kann festgestellt werden, dass derartige Beiträge in der Minderheit sind und dedizierte Dienste für die langfristige Bereitstellung von Forschungsdaten selten genutzt werden.

Die Untersuchung in diesem Beitrag ist keineswegs als abschließend zu betrachten. Es wurde insbesondere nicht untersucht, ob die verfügbaren Forschungsdaten vollständig und qualitativ geeignet sind, um die jeweilige Forschungsaktivität vollständig nachvollziehen zu können. Bei Softwareartefakten wurde nicht untersucht, ob die Artefakte lediglich zur Nutzung bereitstehen oder ob sie als Open Source Software verfügbar sind. Auch die Lauffähigkeit von Software sowie die Reproduzierbarkeit von aggregierten Ergebnissen auf Basis der veröffentlichten Rohdaten und Auswertungsskripte wurde nicht geprüft. Außerdem wurde auf eine Analyse von Metadaten für Forschungsdaten und Softwareartefakte gänzlich verzichtet. Alle diese Aspekte bieten Raum für zukünftige Erhebungen; letzterer insbesondere auch mit Blick auf den Entwurf eines Metadaten-Schemas, das für die Verfügbarmachung von Forschungsdaten im Fachgebiet der Bildungstechnologie dienlich ist. Dabei müssen auch die am Ende von Abschnitt 4 genannten Beobachtungen berücksichtigt werden, nach denen eine einfache Trennung zwischen reinen Softwareartefakten und sonstigen Forschungsdaten nicht ausreichend zu sein scheint oder gar nicht ohne weiteres möglich ist.

Literaturverzeichnis

[KS22] Kiesler, N., Schiffner, D.: On the Lack of Recognition of Software Artifacts and IT Infrastructure in Educational Technology Research. In: 20. Fachtagung Bildungstechnologien (DELFI). Bonn: Gesellschaft für Informatik e.V., S. 201-206, 2022. https://doi.org/10.18420/delfi2022-034

[KS23] Kiesler, N., Schiffner, D.: Why We Need Open Data in Computer Science Education Research. In: Proc. 28th annual ACM conference on Innovation and Technology in Computer Science Education (ITiCSE), 2023.

[Wi16] Wilkinson, M. et al.: The FAIR Guiding Principles for scientific data management and stewardship. Sci Data 3, 160018, 2016. https://doi.org/10.1038/sdata.2016.18

Conversational Systems und Virtual Reality

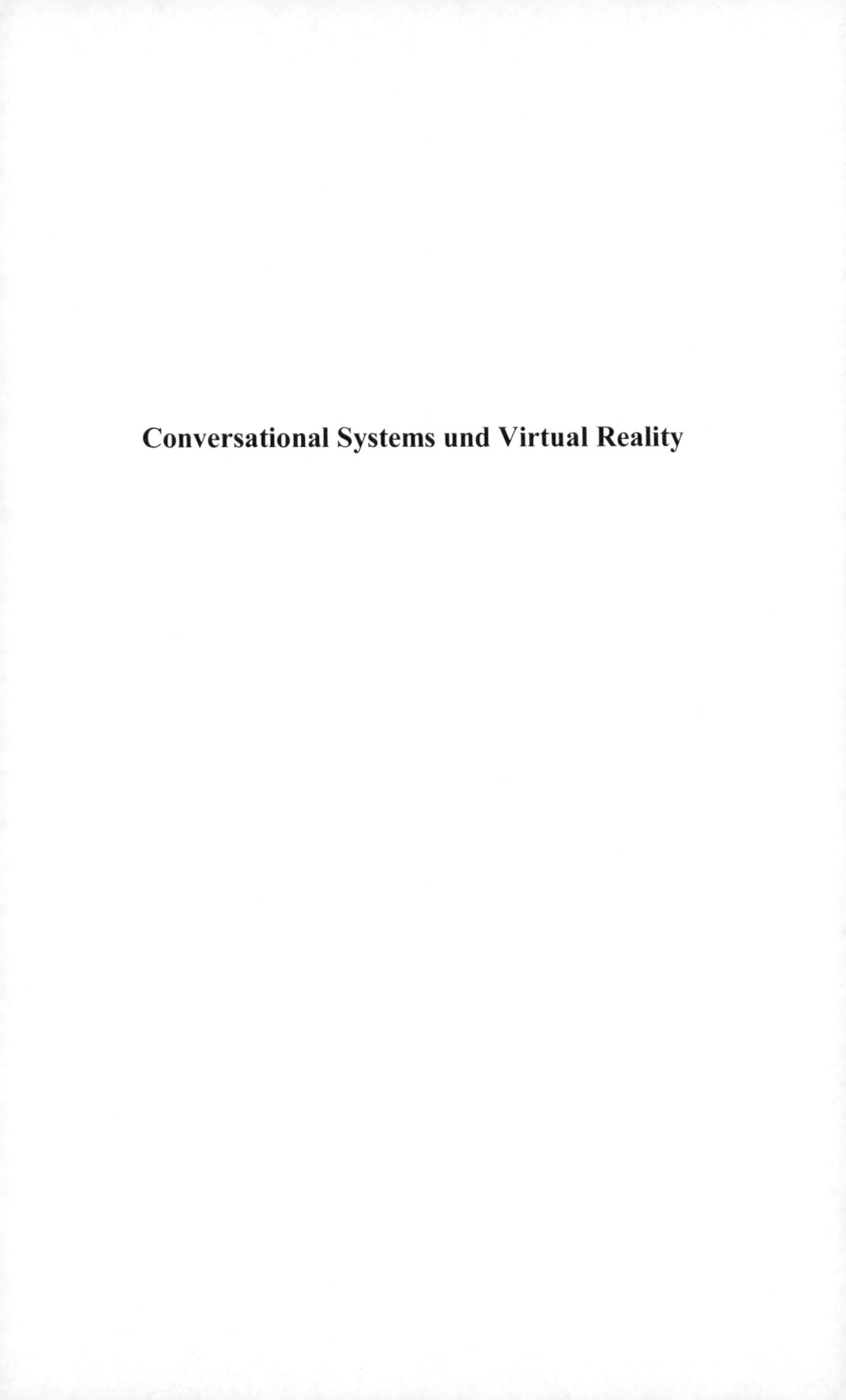

Einführungskriterien für Chatbots in der Kommunikation und der Lehre an Hochschulen

Chrysanthi Melanou[1], Andreas Bildstein[1], Bernd Dörr[1], Martin Lachmair[1], Blanche Schoch[2] und Martin Kimmig[1]

Abstract: Conversational User Interfaces (CUI), insbesondere Chatbots, versprechen vielseitige Einsatzmöglichkeiten sowohl im Bereich der Hochschullehre als auch in der Kommunikation zwischen Hochschule und Studierenden, Studieninteressierten und weiteren Partnern der Hochschule. Dieser Beitrag berichtet von den Erfahrungen, die bei der Einführung von Chatbots in der Hochschulkommunikation an der Hochschule gemacht wurden, und davon, wie diese Erkenntnisse sowohl hinsichtlich Technologie-einführung und -umsetzung als auch Nutzerakzeptanz in den Bereich der Lehre transferiert werden könnten. Neben der Anforderungserhebung für den Einsatz von Chatbots in der Hochschulkommunikation werden auch die Ergebnisse aus der Erprobungsphase dargestellt. Des Weiteren wird darauf aufbauend dargestellt, wie Chatbots als integraler Bestandteil sowohl unter technischen Aspekten als auch unter wirtschaftlichen und organisatorischen Aspekten in der Hochschullehre eingesetzt werden könnten.

Keywords: Chatbot, Hochschullehre, Hochschulkommunikation, Einführungskriterien

1 Einleitung

Die in weiten Bereichen der website-basierten Kommunikation von Unternehmen eingesetzten Chatbots erfüllen im Bildungskontext typischerweise die Rolle des Gegenübers im dialogischen Lernen mit der programmierten Absicht den Lernenden per "autonomer Kommunikation" [Ra21, S. 102] die Bandbreite von beantworteten Fragen bis hin zu Denkanstößen und Reflexionsanlässen zu liefern. Gleichzeitig ist die Technologie Bestandteil des Curriculums der Wirtschaftsinformatik und das auch mit dem Ziel, diese auf organisatorischer Ebene einzusetzen [La23]. Chatbots sind somit potenziell ein weiterer Bestandteil im Kanon digitaler (Bildungs-)angebote mit den bekannten Vorzügen der zeitlichen wie räumlichen Unabhängigkeit und der beliebigen Wiederholbarkeit der Nutzung.

In jüngerer Zeit wurden Studien mit Chatbots zum Einsatz an Hochschulen durchgeführt (z.B. [Pa19]). Einige dieser Studien befassten sich z.B. mit der Reduzierung des Workloads für Büromitarbeiter [Le19] oder mit der Nutzererfahrung und Akzeptanz der Technologie an sich [El21]. All diese Arbeiten, insbesondere die letztgenannte Studie,

---

[1] Duale Hochschule Baden-Württemberg Villingen-Schwenningen, Friedrich-Ebert-Straße 30, 78054 Villingen-Schwenningen, {melanou, bildstein, doerr, lachmair, kimmig}@dhbw-vs.de
[2] blanche.schoch@gmail.com

doi: 10.18420/delfi2023-28

weisen darauf hin, dass es sich lohnen kann, diese Technologie im Hochschulbereich sowohl organisatorisch als auch didaktisch einzusetzen.

Wir stehen am Standort Villingen-Schwenningen der Dualen Hochschule Baden-Württemberg (DHBW) noch am Anfang der Entwicklung eines Chatbots zur Nutzung sowohl in Verwaltung als auch Lehre. Im Rahmen des standortübergreifenden Forschungsprojektes der DHBW, Education Competence Network (EdCoN) stellen wir im Folgenden den aktuellen Projektstatus und die geplanten weiteren Einsatzgebiete vor.

2 Chatbot als Unterstützung für Hochschulkommunikation

Als erstes Teilprojekt soll die Erprobung von Chatbots in der Hochschulkommunikation dienen. Hier sollen Erfahrungen zur Funktionalität von Chatbots gesammelt und das Feedback der Anwender untersucht werden.

Ziel des Chatbot-Einsatzes soll das einfachere Auffinden der häufigsten (zielgruppenspezifischen) Inhalte und eine zeitliche Entlastung der Studiengangsekretariate sein. Daneben wird auch eine Verbesserung der Digitalisierung der Studienorganisation (Suche nach Vorlesungsterminen und –orten, Hilfe bei technischen Problemen, etc.) angestrebt [Me20].

Um Effektivität und Effizienz eines Chatbots quantitativ bewerten zu können [Ca20] bzw. die geeigneten Inhalte auszuwählen, wurden zuerst einige Kennzahlen der Kommunikation ermittelt (s. Tab. 1).

Man kann daraus erwarten, dass der Einsatz von Chatbots aufgrund deren Charakteristik hier erheblichen organisatorischen Nutzen und Mehrwert bringen wird. Zur Umsetzung wurden 2 Chatbots z.T. mit Referenzen im Hochschulbereich ausgewählt [Ku23, Cm23].

Kennzahl	Website	Studiengangsekretariate
Inhalte	**Anzahl Seiten gesamt:** ca. 300, davon im Menü 90 **Meist aufgerufene Webseiten:** Startseite (34 %) Bibliothek (10 %) Studiengänge (6 %) Wohnungsbörse (2 %) **Häufigste Suchanfragen** Hochschule (48 %) Notenschlüssel (27 %) Bibliothek (2 %)	**Auswahl Anfragen:** Wo finde ich die Klausurtermine? Welche sind die Voraussetzungen für das Studium? Wo finden wir die Studien- und Praxisphasen? Wann muss ich eine Krankmeldung bringen?
Anfragen	**Zugriffe:**	**Durchschnittliche zeitliche Belastung pro Tag:**

Kennzahl	Website	Studiengangsekretariate
	1.240 Zugriffe (Nutzer) / Woche, 4.400 Sitzungen / Woche **Anzahl Suchanfragen:** 16.400 pro Woche	51 Minuten (Umfang: 5 Studiengänge aus Fakultät Wirtschaft)

Tab. 1: Kennzahlen zu Kommunikationsanfragen (Stand 12.03.2023)

2.1 Ergebnisse

Auswahl der Inhalte

Die Themenliste des Chatbots wurde aus der Schnittmenge der 10-15 häufigsten Webseiten, Suchanfragen und den meisten Anfragen per Mail und Telefon gebildet: Studienangebot, Zulassungsvoraussetzungen, Bibliothek, Wohnungsbörse, usw.

Aufrufe und Zufriedenheit der Anwender

Zur Bewertung der Akzeptanz der Chatbots wurden Zugriffszahlen und Feedback der Anwender ermittelt (Tab. 2).

	Chatbot 1	Chatbot 2
Interaktionen (Zeitraum)	112 (+/- 24) Chats / Woche (09.02. -15.03.23)	156 (+/- 114) Chats / Woche (16.02.-15.03.23)
Zufriedenheit	57 % positives Feedback	47 % positives Feedback
Automatisierung	38 %	32 %

Tab. 2: Vergleich Chatbots im Betrieb

Funktionale Evaluation

Die Erprobung ergab eine Liste von Kriterien zur Auswahl und Bewertung der Funktionalitäten eines Chatbots (Tab. 3):

Kriterium	Beschreibung	Gewünschte Merkmale
Inhalte		
Anliegen (Intent)	Sammlung möglicher Fragestellungen, die ein Anliegen beschreiben	unbegrenzter Umfang, Erweiterbarkeit, einfache Verknüpfung von Anliegen und Antwort
Antwort (Response)	Antwort auf ein Anliegen	Textformatierung und Verknüpfung verschiedener Abschnitte möglich,

Kriterium	Beschreibung	Gewünschte Merkmale
		Schaltflächen und Grafiken einsetzbar, längere Unterhaltung umsetzbar
Formular	Anwender kann Informationen weiter- bzw. Feedback abgeben	Ausführliche Gestaltungs- und einfache Verarbeitungsmöglichkeiten
API-Schnittstelle	Zugriff auf Informationen externer IT-Systeme	Ausführliche Dokumentation, einfache Fehleranalyse
Veröffentlichung		
Training	Erkennung eines Anliegens erlernen	Geringer Zeitaufwand, Anliegen werden eindeutig erkannt, Analytik der Erkennung liegt vor
Vorschau	Testen der Antwort	Einfache Vorschaumöglichkeit für alle Funktionalitäten

Tab. 3: Kriterien für funktionalen Vergleich

2.2 Wirkungsanalyse und Diskussion

Aus den Zugriffszahlen von Tabellen 1 und 2 lässt sich der Anteil aller Nutzeranfragen in Form von Webseitenzugriffen berechnen, die auch erfolgreich mit dem Chatbot interagieren. Aus den Zugriffszahlen und den Lizenzkosten von Chatbot 1 ergeben sich mittlere Kosten pro Chatbot-Unterhaltung von rund 10 € (Tab. 4)

	Chatbot 1	Chatbot 2
Anteil Zugriffe Website pro Woche	1.240	1.240
Anteil Chatbot-Interaktion pro Webseitenzugriff	9 %	15 %
Automatisierung x pos. Feedbackrate	22 %	15 %
Kosten / Woche	235 € [Ku23]	-
Anteil Kosten / pos. Feedback	9,57 €	-

Tab. 4: Kosten eines erfolgreichen Chats

Demgegenüber stehen ca. 51 Minuten täglicher zeitlicher Belastung pro Studiengangsekretariat. Je nach Bruttostundenlohn sind die Kosten des Chatbots bei 2-3 beteiligten Sekretariatsstellen amortisiert. Allerdings muss der Chatbot dann auch die technisch schwierigen Inhalte der Studienorganisation beantworten können.

3 Didaktisches Konzept zur Integration in die Hochschullehre

Auf Basis der Erkenntnisse aus der Einführung von Chatbots in der Hochschulkommunikation wurden drei Möglichkeiten für die Integration dieser Technologie in der Lehre sowohl inhaltlich als auch funktional abgeleitet:

Technologische Betrachtung:

In den technisch orientierten Fächern der Hochschule können Chatbots unter dem Gesichtspunkt der technischen Umsetzung betrachtet werden. Insbesondere in Studiengängen wie Informatik oder Wirtschaftsinformatik eignen sich Chatbots als Anwendung im Kontext von Natural Language Processing (NLP) anhand derer die Studierenden die Arbeit mit Sprachmodellen und deren Auswertung umsetzen und praktisch erproben können. Dies wurde z.B. in einer Pilotstudie innerhalb des Integrationsseminars des Studiengangs Wirtschaftsinformatik hinsichtlich Akzeptanz und Qualität der von Teilnehmern des Seminars erstellten Chatbots untersucht [La23].

Betrachtung wirtschaftlicher und organisatorischer Aspekte:

Chatbots sind Software-Roboter (Bots), die Aufgaben übernehmen können, die typischerweise von Menschen im Rahmen ihrer täglichen Arbeit durchgeführt werden. Im Allgemeinen besteht das Ziel bei der Einführung von Chatbots in den Unternehmen darin, die menschlichen Arbeitskräfte von Routineaufgaben zu entlasten und damit Freiräume für höherwertige Tätigkeiten zu schaffen [Mü21]. Die hierfür notwendigen wirtschaftlichen und organisatorischen Aspekte lassen sich gut in wirtschaftlich orientierten Studiengängen, z.B. BWL oder Wirtschaftsinformatik, vermitteln.

Unterstützung Studierender im Rahmen der Lehre

Schließlich lassen sich Chatbots auch funktional als Anwendung im Lernprozess selber einsetzen. Beispielsweise können Chatbots Prüfungsfragen stellen und gegebenenfalls auch auswerten sowie als Tutor bei Übungsseminaren oder Planspielen eingesetzt werden [Ra21]. In diesen Szenarien können Chatbots sowohl substituierend oder auch ergänzend zu den Dozierenden wirken.

Idealerweise werden durch die Integration dieser drei Aspekte Synergieeffekte hinsichtlich Qualität, Support und Wartung erzeugt, so dass jeder Aspekt von den Erfahrungen der anderen Punkte profitiert.

4 Fazit & Ausblick

Die Einführung eines CUI erfordert die Unterstützung aller Ebenen der Hochschule, vor allem in Bezug auf Studienorganisation und Lehre. Auf der Grundlage der oben dargestellten Ergebnisse, planen wir die Einführung von CUI mit drei verschiedenen Schwerpunkten:

- Umsetzung und Evaluation des oben vorgeschlagenen didaktischen Konzeptes.
- Integration einer Chatbot-Lösung in ein Lernmanagementsystem (LMS) wie moodle.
- Untersuchung von neuen Sprachmodellen, sogenannte Large Language Modells (z.B. GPT), die im Dialog mit dem Menschen verblüffende Ergebnisse erzielen können [Br20].

Literaturverzeichnis

[Ca20] Casas, J.; Tricot, M. O.; Abou Khaled, O.; Mugellini, E.; Cudré-Mauroux, P.: Trends & methods in chatbot evaluation. In: Companion Publication of the 2020 International Conference on Multimodal Interaction, S. 280-286, 2020.

[Cm23] CM.com - Setting New Standards in Customer Experience, cm.com, Stand: 12.03.2023.

[Br20] Brown, T. B.: Language Models are Few-Shot Learners, arXiv:2005.14165 [cs.CL], 2020.

[Du23] DHBW-VS, www.dhbw-vs.de, Stand: 12.03.2023.

[El21] El Hefny, W.; Mansy, Y.; Abdallah, M.; Abdennadher, S.: Jooka: A Bilingual Chatbot for University Admission. In: World Conference on Information Systems and Technologies. Springer, Cham, S. 671-681, 2021.

[Ku23] Kundenkommunikation automatisieren mit AI Chatbots, moin.ai, Stand: 12.03.2023.

[La23] Lachmair, M.; Melanou, C.; Kimmig, M: Der Einsatz künstlicher Intelligenz in Form von Chatbots im Hochschulbereich. In (Hufnagel, J., Schnekenburger, C.; Ternes, D. Hrsg.): #Dual – ZHL-Schriftenreihe für die DHBW, Band 6, 2023, Im Druck

[Le19] Lee, K.; Jo, J.; Kim, J.; Kang, Y.: Can chatbots help reduce the workload of administrative officers? Implementing and deploying FAQ chatbot service in a university. In: International conference on human-computer interaction. Springer, Cham, S. 348-354, 2019.

[Me20] Meyer von Wolff, R.; Nörtemann, J.; Horbert, S.; Schumann, M.: Chatbots for the information acquisition at universities-a student's view on the application area. In: Chatbot Research and Design: Third International Workshop, CONVERSATIONS. 3. Springer International Publishing, S. 231 – 244, 2020.

[Mü21] Müller, A.; Schröder, H.; von Thienen, L.: Digineering. Springer Berlin Heidelberg. 2021.

[Pa19] Patel, N. P., Parikh D. R.; Patel, D. A.; Patel, R. R.: AI and Web-Based Human-Like Interactive University Chatbot (UNIBOT). In: 3rd International conference on Electronics, Communication and Aerospace Technology (ICECA), Coimbatore, India, S. 148-150, 2019.

[Ra21] Raunig, M.: Lernmedium Chatbot. In (Wollersheim, H.-W.; Karaponos, M.; Pengel, N. Hrsg.): Bildung in der digitalen Transformation; Medien in der Wissenschaft, Band 78. Waxmann Verlag GmbH, 2021.

Designing Pedagogical Conversational Agents in Virtual Worlds

Bijan Khosrawi-Rad[1], Heidi Rinn[2], Dominik Augenstein[3], Daniel Markgraf[2] and Susanne Robra-Bissantz[1]

Abstract: Pedagogical conversational agents (PCAs) are intelligent dialog systems that can support students as chatbots or voice assistants. However, many users find interactions with PCAs less engaging. One solution to increase learners' engagement is to embed the PCA in a virtual world, e.g., as a humanoid avatar that facilitates collaborative learning. Such a learning setting could be beneficial because virtual worlds positively affect fun and immersion. In this paper, we derive prescriptive design knowledge for PCAs in virtual worlds based on the results of nine expert interviews synthesized with findings from the literature. This design knowledge aims to enable the meaningful design of PCAs in virtual worlds. We contribute to research and practice by demonstrating how PCAs in virtual worlds can be designed to increase students' motivation to learn.

Keywords: Pedagogical Conversational Agent, Virtual World, Education, Design Principle.

1 Introduction and Motivation

Pedagogical conversational agents (PCAs) are intelligent dialog systems that support learners by processing natural language [HM19]. They can teach content, motivate learners, or moderate collaborative learning [Kh22a]. With AI advances, PCAs are getting better at helping learners with individual concerns, as the example of ChatGPT shows. However, users often perceive interactions with PCAs as not motivating, leading to the rejection of PCAs [Be22]. Combining PCAs with game approaches is one way to counteract this issue. This can be done by integrating PCAs as human-like avatars into virtual worlds (VWs) [GG16]. They can, for instance, guide learners through the VW while presenting them with lively challenges [KGR23]. Such VWs have been showing positive effects for years, such as immersion and collaborative learning [DMJ12]. Recent examples such as Roblox or Minecraft show that VWs can be fun for users. They can also be used for serious purposes such as education [HC22]. Hence, by combining both trends, PCAs and VWs, educators could benefit from the positive effects of both [KGR23]. Current literature reviews show that embedding PCAs in VWs is novel and that there does not yet exist prescriptive design knowledge on PCAs in VWs [KGR23, Kh22a]. However,

---

[1] TU Braunschweig, Institut für Wirtschaftsinformatik, Mühlenpfordtstraße 23, 38106 Braunschweig, b.khosrawi-rad@tu-bs.de; s.robra-bissantz@tu-bs.de
[2] AKAD, IDEA, Heilbronner Str. 86, 70191 Stuttgart, heidi.rinn@akad.de; daniel.markgraf@akad.de
[3] FAU Erlangen-Nürnberg, WiSo, Lange Gasse 20, 90403 Nürnberg, dominik.augenstein@hs-karlsruhe.de

doi: 10.18420/delfi2023-29

this design knowledge helps developers and educators implement PCAs in VWs. We address this research gap using the design science research methodology to derive design knowledge for PCAs. Hence, we address the following **research question (RQ):** *How to design PCAs in VWs to foster students' motivation to learn?* We follow the procedure of [He07] to answer our RQ. We derive design knowledge based on nine expert interviews. We aim to ensure scientific rigor and practical relevance by incorporating this body of expertise. We formulate the design knowledge as design principles (DPs), i.e., abstract requirements for PCAs in VWs [GCS20]. These are complemented by meta-requirements (MRs), design features (DFs), and overarching design guidelines (DGs). In this short paper, we report the results of our first design cycle as a tentative conceptual design.

2 Research Background

PCAs interact with their users either via text (as chatbots) or speech (as virtual assistants) [HM19]. They can take on different roles, which lead to different functionalities [Kh22a]: organizer, tutor, mentor, motivator, and moderator. PCAs, as organizers, support learners in navigating the learning environment. The tutor role focuses on imparting learning content. The mentor role goes beyond merely imparting learning content, so learners are accompanied in the long-term, e.g., through feedback and study tips. The PCA as a motivator serves to promote learners' engagement, e.g., through gamification. The moderator mediates collaborative learning or brainstorming. PCAs can be incorporated into VWs to guide learners in these human-like roles [GG16]. VWs are immersive 3D environments where avatars communicate with each other [DMJ12]. VWs promote immersion and contribute to a social presence experience, and learners thus enjoy learning [ibid.]. In classic game environments, virtual agents were usually implemented by non-player characters (NPCs). While these were not AI-based, PCAs, as an extension of NPCs, enable individualized communication [KGR23]. Moreover, AI allows learners to receive social and empathic support if the PCA acts as a friendly virtual companion [St22]. Some authors already propose design recommendations for PCAs, e.g., for argumentative writing support [WSL20]. However, there is yet no design knowledge for PCAs in VWs.

3 Study Design and Results

We conducted semi-structured interviews with nine experts from different research streams (psychology, computer science, information systems) and industry practitioners. All experts had prior experience with designing PCAs or VWs. The interview guide consisted of questions about design recommendations and desired features for PCAs in VWs. The interviews lasted between 42 to 64 minutes. We transcribed and analyzed all interviews based on a pre-defined coding guide in two coding cycles. The coding guide followed our interview guide and included categories on the benefits of PCAs in VWs and learners' challenges to be solved, the design of PCAs and VWs, the design of the PCA roles in the VW, and mentioned kernel theories. Following [Mö20], we synthesized the results with supporting literature and formulated MRs for PCAs in VWs. We then combined MRs that relate to each other into DPs and illustrated these DPs with example DFs [Mö20]. In formulating the DPs, we followed a unified scheme according to [GCS20]. We structured the DPs according to the PCA roles (see Chapter 2) so that each DP corresponds to a particular PCA role. We choose this approach because, according to social agency theory, different roles of human-like agents lead to varying expectations of users and functions to realize [Be22, MSM03]. Since the experts also mentioned aspects that apply to all roles, we furthermore formulated role-independent design guidelines (DGs). Figure 1 outlines the DGs and DPs, which we will explain in detail in the following. Our **digital appendix** contains a mapping diagram of all MRs, DPs, DFs, and DGs and information about the interviewees: https://doi.org/10.6084/m9.figshare.23538363.v1.

Role-Independent Design Guidelines (DGs)				
DG1: Multiple Social Cues	DG2: PCA as a Co-equal Companion	DG3: Balanced Level of Playfulness	DG4: Appropriate Size of the Virtual World	DG5: Playful Onboarding and Co-Creation
DG6: Context-Adapted Virtual World Design	DG7: Balance between PCA Proactivity and Autonomy	DG8: Choice of PCA Roles based on Application Goal	DG9: Avoidance of Intrusive PCA Behavior	DG10: Functionality, Transparency, and Security

Role-Dependent Design Principles (DPs)				
DP1: Supporting Organizer	DP2: Clever Instructor	DP3: Personal Guide	DP4: Motivating Sparring Partner	DP5: Moderating Mediator

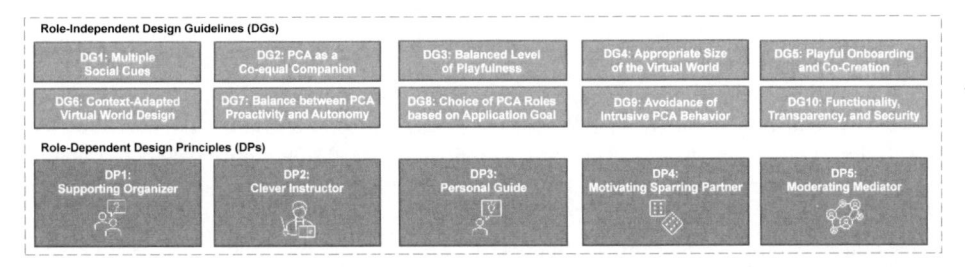

Fig. 1: Overview of Design Guidelines and Design Principles for PCAs in Virtual Worlds

Role-independent design guidelines: The experts emphasized that the PCA should have human-like "social cues" to exude social presence [Fe19] (DG1). E.g., the PCA can have a human-like name and a personality, greet learners, use emojis, and tell jokes to appear natural [Fe19, St22]. The experts addressed that the PCA should act as a co-equal companion to ensure learners' trust [St22] (DG2). However, the learning environment must have a balanced level of playfulness and an appropriate size so that learners do not get distracted (e.g., no open world) (DG3, DG4). Upon initial entry into the VW, learners should be welcomed and onboarded by the PCA. The experts emphasized that learners should set up the world with their classmates and lecturers in the first sessions to meet students' needs (co-creation) (DG5). The joint design of the VW might contribute to a sense of team cohesion. However, the design of the VW should fit the context, e.g., not be too fictional or playful (like a space world) but also not entirely true to reality (DG6). E.g., students could learn in a classroom with open windows and nature to simulate a relaxed learning atmosphere. If possible, the room's virtual objects should be included (e.g., to simulate processes). The PCA should act proactively but also leave freedom of decision. Hence, according to self-determination theory, learners can act autonomously, which is crucial for their motivation [RD00, St22]. E.g., they could choose between learning tasks and select the desired PCA role [Kh22b] (DG7). In addition, we suggest that practitioners base the choice of design elements and roles of the PCA on the application goal. Thus, we recommend deciding which DPs should be implemented (DG8). We suggest considering that it is also possible that a PCA in a VW takes on multiple roles [GG16]. However, role changes should be clearly communicated so that the PCA meets the learners' expectations. The experts emphasized that the PCA should not be intrusive (DP9) so that users perceive it as trustworthy. E.g., it should not constantly follow learners or get too close. The proximity can vary, depending on the use case. If the PCA acts as a mentor (see DP2), it could stand next to the learner, and as a moderator, it could be in a central location. For learners to accept this technology, basic prerequisites such as technical functionality or transparency on data security must be considered [Kh22b, St22] (DG10).

Role-dependent design principles: The first **DP1 (Supporting Organizer)** concerns the PCA as an organizer. The experts suggested the PCA explain the controls and navigation when learners first enter the VW so that they can find their way around and do not have technical hurdles (MR1). In doing so, the PCA should proactively explain the functions so that users have clear expectations [Kh22b, St22] (MR2). The PCA should be able to answer questions about the VW and relieve instructors if, e.g., users have technical problems logging into the VW (MR3). This onboarding by the PCA should be skippable if learners are already experienced (MR4). **DP2 (Clever Instructor)** focuses on the delivery of learning content. The PCA should explain content naturally and use VW objects for illustration (MR5). The PCA should support the human teacher and enable learners to ask questions anonymously, e.g., if they have not understood something and do not dare to ask them publicly. If the learners have difficulties in understanding, the PCA should explain the learning content step by step using "scaffolding (an established teaching technique) [Kh22b, VC78, WSL22] (MR6). In addition, the PCA should present the learners with tasks in which they test their knowledge [Be22, Kh2] (MR7). The interviewees recommended using troubleshooting tasks, e.g., identifying errors. To promote learners' understanding, they should be encouraged to explain circumstances on their own in dialog with the PCA to promote interactive learning [WSL22] (MR8). In addition, to be perceived in its role, the PCA should be positioned centrally to be visible to all (MR9). **DP3 (Personal Guide)** relates to the PCA going beyond the tutor role and becoming a mentor by accompanying students in the long term, for instance, by promoting the "how to learn" instead of only teaching content [Kh22b]. During the onboarding, the PCA should inquire about the current learning status and students' current challenges, e.g., using practice tests to identify knowledge gaps to support learners individually (MR10). Within the VW, the PCA should initiate the completion of learning tasks to let students gain practical experiences [Kh22b] (MR11). In addition, the PCA can provide hints to facilitate the completion of tasks (MR12). These hints could be adapted to the learning pace and, if desired, be anonymous to provide individual support and not expose learners. To ensure learning success, it is crucial that learners receive feedback, so the PCA should be able to point out errors and incomplete answers or recommend further learning content and paths [GG16, Kh22b, WSL20] (MR13). Moreover, the PCA might proactively initiate breaks to help students learn focused [Kh22b] (MR14). E.g., the PCA could use a "pomodoro timer" or allow learners to explore the VW while listening to relaxing music during breaks. To achieve long-term learning success, students should not only absorb the knowledge once but are also proactively reminded to repeat and apply it in practice tasks (MR15). **DP4 (Motivational Sparring Partner)** aims to promote learners' engagement.

Thus, the PCA should congratulate users for successes [GG16, Kh22b] (MR16). The PCA can also use methods from design thinking (e.g., warm-ups) to lighten the mood, make it clear to learners why group learning is important, and reward all participants for collaborative learning (MR17). In addition, the PCA can present learners with playful challenges, e.g., asking them to run a maze or solve quizzes [Be22, GG16] (MR18). Moreover, the PCA can reward learners to appreciate their performance, visualize their progress, and motivate them intrinsically and extrinsically [Be22, Kh22b, RD00] (MR19). Points can be awarded for completing individual units, and learners can receive achievements for longer-term successes [Be22]. The PCA could give these achievements to learners, keeping them in a "virtual display case." The further development of the world and the avatar was also particularly desired, e.g., possibilities to unlock additional features/furniture or to buy new avatar items. Rewards should be given both for fun activities in the VW and topic-related activities. Additionally, respondents recommended giving learners opportunities to compare themselves if actively desired (e.g., by who asked the most questions to the PCA) (MR20). **DP5 (Moderating Meditator)** refers to collaborative learning. The PCA should help to match learners with each other (Kh22b) (MR21). The PCA could, for instance, match learners with peers at a similar skill level and that are online in the VW simultaneously. Thereby, it is useful to form diverse teams, so teammates complement each other (MR22). For data protection reasons, they should be asked whether they would like to connect with others [St22] and the PCA should initiate the matching as a mediator (MR23). To do this, the PCA can, e.g., guide learners through the room to others or beam them to another location. To support collaborative learning, the PCA should contribute ideas when learners are stuck and suggest collaborative and creative methods (e.g., ABC method) (MR24). The experts recommended encouraging (introverted) learners to contribute knowledge, e.g., by the PCA sending a hint to learners to contribute more to the group (MR25). To do so, the PCA might analyze the group dynamics and emotions of the participants, e.g., who contributed how much (MR26).

4 Conclusion and Outlook

PCAs can be integrated into VWs to make learning immersive and motivating. We have derived design knowledge to assist researchers and practitioners in creating such learning scenarios. We are implementing these abstract conceptual considerations into a virtual design thinking training in the VW Unity that includes two PCAs to support learners, one using the chatbot service Rasa and one interfacing with ChatGPT. The Rasa-based PCA is to take over simple tasks like welcoming the learners to the VW and introducing them to the design thinking method. The ChatGPT-based PCA will take on more complex tasks, such as moderating the training, and generating creative ideas. We plan to evaluate our approach's effectiveness using focus group interviews with our target group.

Acknowledgements: This paper is part of the projects StuBu and AVILAB2, which the German Federal Ministry of Education and Research (BMBF) funded; Grant # 21INVI06 and # 16INB2005A.

Bibliography

[Be22] Benner, D. et.al.: Level-Up your Learning – Introducing a Framework for Gamified Educational Conversational Agents. In: WI2022 Proceedings. Nürnberg, 2022.

[DMJ12] Duncan, I.; Miller, A.; Jiang, S.: A Taxonomy of Virtual Worlds Usage in Education. British Journal of Educational Technology Bd. 43, Nr. 6, S. 949–964, 2012.

[Fe19] Feine, J. et.al.: A Taxonomy of Social Cues for Conversational Agents. International Journal of Human-Computer Studies, Bd. 132, Nr. 1, S. 138–161, 2019.

[GCS20] Gregor, S.; Chandra Kruse, L.; Seidel, S.: The Anatomy of a Design Principle. Journal of the Association for Information Systems Bd. 21, S. 1622–1652, 2020.

[GG16] Guo, Y.R.; Goh, D.H.: Evaluation of affective embodied agents in an information literacy game. Computers & Education Bd. 103, S. 59–75, 2016.

[HC22] Hwang, G.; Chien, S.: Definition, roles, and potential research issues of the metaverse in education: An artificial intelligence perspective. Computers & Education: Artificial Intelligence Bd. 3, 2022.

[He07] Hevner, A.: A Three Cycle View of Design Science Research. Scandinavian Journal of Information Systems Bd. 19, Nr. 2, S. 87–92, 2007.

[HM19] Hobert, S.; Meyer von Wolff, R.: Say Hello to Your New Automated Tutor – A Structured Literature Review on Pedagogical Conversational Agents. In: WI2019 Proceedings. Siegen, 2019.

[KGR23] Khosrawi-Rad, B.; Grogorick, L.; Robra-Bissantz, S.: Game-inspired Pedagogical Conversational Agents – A Systematic Literature Review. THCI Bd. 15, Nr. 2, 2023.

[Kh22a] Khosrawi-Rad, B. et al.: Conversational Agents in Education – A Systematic Literature Review. In: ECIS Proceedings. Timișoara, 2022.

[Kh22b] Khosrawi-Rad, B. et.al.: Design Knowledge for Virtual Learning Companions. In: ICISER Proceedings. Copenhagen, 2022.

[Mö20] Möller, F. et.al.: Towards a method for design principle development in information systems. In: DESRIST Proceedings. Kristiansand, 2020.

[MSM03] Mayer, R.E.; Sobko, K.; Mautone, P.D.: Social Cues in Multimedia Learning: Role of Speaker's Voice. Journal of Educational Psychology Bd. 95, Nr. 2, S. 419–25, 2003.

[RD00] Ryan, R.M.; Deci, E.L.: Intrinsic and Extrinsic Motivations: Classic Definitions and New Directions. Contemporary Educational Psychology Bd. 25, Nr. 1, S. 54–67a, 2000.

[St22] Strohmann, T. et.al.: Toward a design theory for virtual companionship. Human–Computer Interaction, S. 1–41, 2022.

[VC78] Vygotsky, L.S.; Cole, M: Mind in society: Development of higher psychological processes. Harvard university press, 1978.

[WSL20] Wambsganss, T.; Söllner, M.; Leimeister, J.M.: Design and evaluation of an adaptive dialog-based tutoring system for argumentation skills. In: ICIS Proceedings. Hyderabad, 2020.

"Don't drop the plane to fly the mic!" – Designing for Modern Radiotelephony Education in General Aviation

Peter Heinrich[1], Dagmar Hollerer[2], Christoph Karthaus[3] and Mario Gellrich[4]

Abstract: Learning to fly an aeroplane is a challenging endeavour; mastering the radio, i.e. talking to air traffic control (ATC) is considered by many students as an especially daunting activity. Using the correct voice procedures and phraseology is paramount for a smooth and safe aircraft operation in busy airspaces. However, training new general aviation pilots in radiotelephony is still a largely manual activity, where students and teachers engage in role-play to mimic the different ends of communication. The design of an aeronautical chatbot, capable of simulating ATC would provide students with plenty of additional training opportunities that they can conduct on their own and at their own pace. A detailed analysis of the voice input would provide feedback on the learning process. This paper reports on the preliminary proof-of-feasibility prototype design as well as synthetic language model training data generation.

Keywords: Aviation English, Computer Based Language Learning, Automatic Speech Recognition

1 Introduction

Pilot: "Tower, please call me a fuel truck." – Tower: "Roger! Sir, you are a fuel truck." [LU23]. Obviously, this is a fun joke, but it highlights the general problem of ambiguous communication with the aim to establish shared mental models. To avoid such ambiguities in aviation, a special (restricted) variant of the English language is used for communication over the radio specified by the International Civil Aviation Organization (ICAO). Although it is based on English, learning this language is comparable to learning a new language altogether as it has its own, restricted vocabulary, some special words as well as a precise grammar and order of information items given in each statement. Today, flight schools offer courses in radiotelephony, or RTF for short. These courses are synchronous interactions between a teacher and flight students that pretend to be flying. They can be held on premises or distant via some form of remote audio/video call. However, gaining the required practice outside of this training environment is difficult as no communication partner is available. Therefore, an overarching research question to answer would be: *"How can a radiotelephony learning environment for GA (student) pilots be designed to be an effective learning aid for building and maintaining RTF proficiency?"*. We answer

---

[1] ZHAW School of Management and Law, Theaterstrasse 17, Winterthur, 8401, Switzerland, heip@zhaw.ch
[2] fly-T GmbH, Rotackerstrasse 15, Jona SG, 8645, Switzerland, hello@fly-T.ch
[3] fly-T GmbH, Rotackerstrasse 15, Jona SG, 8645, Switzerland, hello@fly-T.ch
[4] ZHAW School of Management and Law, Theaterstrasse 17, Winterthur, 8401, Switzerland, gell@zhaw.ch

doi: 10.18420/delfi2023-30

this question by demonstrating an extensible prototype design and implementation to train one specific RTF procedure based on automatic speech recognition (ASR) with chatbot-like system interaction. These initial results are relevant to practices, first and foremost to companies building educational tools on radiotelephony and in the second line to private pilot students that prepare for the exams as well as for flight-schools and instructors as such technology can free them from repetitive tasks of re-training standard situation. Relevance for the scientific community is given by the identification and description of the research gap using literature review techniques as well as by the call for action and research agenda presented in the outlook.

2 Background

Correct mutual understanding between pilots and air traffic controllers is clearly a critical element of aircraft operation. The most prominent example probably is the 1977 Tenerife disaster that killed 583 people due to an uncleared take-off accompanied by a misunderstanding of the situation [WE90]. But even outside of controlled airspaces and airports, communication between pilots (e.g., local aerodrome traffic) needs to be concise and as short as possible as only one radio participant can talk at any given time. Official documents state that "The information and instructions transmitted are of vital importance in the safe and expeditious operation of aircraft" [IC07, p.2–1] and define the structure of communication from individual wording, pronunciation, and complete procedures (like departing and arriving at an airport). Although standard RTF voice is in English language, there are many special words and abbreviations like "WILLCO" (will comply) or "CAVOK" (ceiling and visibility ok), deliberate mispronunciation like "TREE" instead of "THREE" (because the "th" makes an unpleasant noise on the radio) or "NINER" instead of just "NINE" for the sake of clarity. Special formats for frequencies, time, altitudes etc. are specified. Additionally, although the rest is in English, local name (e.g.: cities, lakes and mountains) are pronounced in the local language.

Today, RTF is commonly trained in local flight schools in small group settings, sometimes using distance learning techniques but still most commonly in synchronous, on-site classroom settings. In Switzerland, there are 84 training organizations offering courses for obtaining a private pilot license (PPL for aeroplane or helicopter) and thus also on RTF training [FO23]. The Swiss Federal Office of Civil Aviation (FOCA) issued 431 light aircraft and private pilot licenses in 2022 [FE23]. Therefore, it is safe to assume that approximately 400 RTF exams are passed per year as well. Specific numbers are not publicly available but according to field experts, initial failure rates in RTF exams are in the range of 20 to 30% in Switzerland. This also raises the question on how private pilots maintain long-term RTF proficiency.

Thus, designing a virtual assistant based on ASR seems helpful for both initial training and for long term proficiency maintenance, but interestingly hardly any prior research on ATC simulation and only very few commercial virtual ATC products for private pilot training are available. Some of these products are even not covering ICAO language procedures sufficiently. Plenty of related work can be found on the training of new ATC controllers (where pilots need to be simulated) and also on operational support of ATC in the tower (e.g., [HE21, HE16]). Thus, there seems to be a research gap in the whole area of supporting pilot education on RTF procedures. The training of air traffic controllers is even more involved and expensive. While a student pilot just needs a single, simulated air traffic controller, training a controller requires several "pseudo-pilots" simulating airplanes in the relevant airspace [JAR20]. More general, this type of training is called human-in-the-loop-simulations and first studies have been conducted on the question of the potential of virtual agents replacing human actors [SDB19]. However, the potential of ASR in ATC application is not restricted to training situations but could also be used to assist active controllers. Use cases for ASR in the field of ATC range from call-sign-highlighting on radar screen to pilot readback error detection. One example is the large scale HAAWAII-EU Horizon 2020 project, exploring the applicability of ASR in real world settings with the aforementioned application areas [HE21]. Another example is the MALLORCA project aiming for automatic digitization of analogue, verbal communication to increase controllers' performance by extracting commands from the transcripts to check for plausibility and to predict next commands [HE20].

3 An Architecture and Prototype Implementation for Low-Cost ASR Training Tools

3.1 Prototype Training Scenario and General Requirements

To prototype, we selected one procedure, namely a CTR crossing. A CTR is a controlled region of airspace where a pilot must ask for permission for entering. Typically, such CTRs are established around controlled airports to ensure separation between all planes operating in this region. For this specific operation, the pilot would call the tower to make initial contact, state the current plane's position, altitude, and the intended route through the CTR. The tower would then either reject the request, grant the request or state further preparatory tasks (like selecting a specific transponder code). Instead of using one specific, existing CTR we opted to abstract from the real world and provide an artificial airspace for the students built around a fictional station called "Lilyfield Tower".

```
Pilot: Lilyfield Tower, HB-ABC, C172, Robinhill, 5500 ft, Request
to Cross CTR direct E, 5500 ft.
ATC: HB-ABC, Lilyfield Tower, Crossing Approved direct E,
Report Entering
Pilot: Crossing Approved direct E, WILLCO, HB-ABC
Pilot: HB-ABC, 5500 ft, Entering CTR
ATC: HB-ABC, Maintain 5500 ft, Report Overhead
Pilot: Maintain 5500 ft, next Overhead, HB-ABC
```

Figure 1: Partial transcript of the prototype's CTR crossing scenario

Figure 1 depicts the initial call of the pilot and parts of the further communication transcript. This conversation follows the typical request → response → readback structure. The readback is especially important as it aids as a verification step to the controller that the pilot has correctly understood his or her commands. Further, all message elements must appear in order, the numbers and letters ought to be correct. Additionally, the pilot must answer timely (no more than a couple of seconds delay) and at appropriate speed (expressed by words per minute). Hence, the training goal is to enable the student pilot to engage in radio communication timely and according to the standard procedure. Although these procedures are rigid in structure, the controller can request additional things anytime that require appropriate reaction, again.

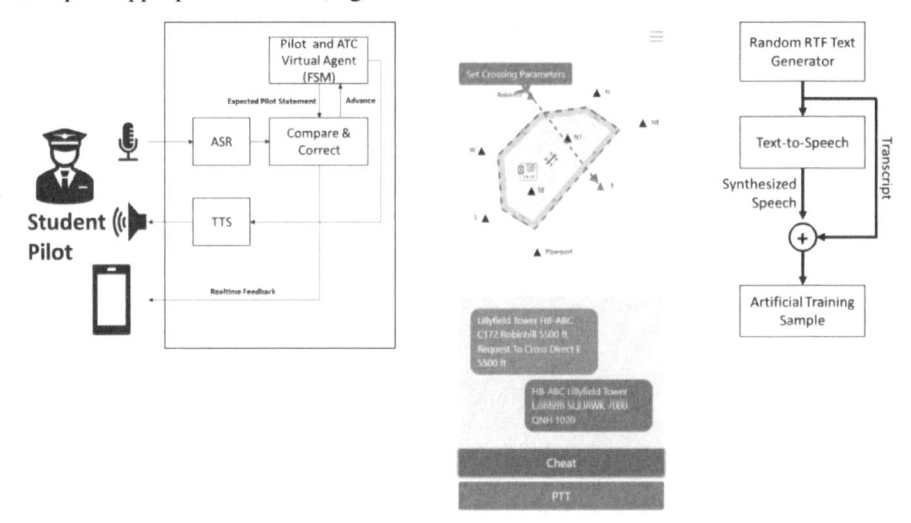

Figure 2: High level PoC backend system components (left) / Screenshot of prototype frontend (center) / Automated sample generation for custom langue model training flow (right)

3.2 Implementing a Pragmatic Conversational Learning Environment

As depicted in Figure 2 (left) we opted to simulate both Pilot and ATC using virtual agents (implemented as a finite state machine). A small, domain specific language expresses the dialog flow and its possible variations for both communication parties. As the XML-snippet (Listing 1) demonstrates, the structure of a message is encoded as a sequence of different message elements, expected in a specific radio transmission. Many of these "messages" together form the dialog of a complete procedure. Using a deterministic state machine, there always exists a predefined expected transmission from the student pilot. More specifically we applied an even stricter variant than the "Single Intent – Multi Turn"

[ZA20, S.203] chatbot interaction pattern that seems well suited for this kind of deterministic multi turn conversation. This strictness enables the system to give specific feedback on where the mistakes (missing elements, incorrect sequence, incorrect numbers or names) were made within a message statement. This 'shortcut' is possible as one single correct variant of a radio statement can be specified during pilot education – in contrast to practice where people sometimes deviate from the defined structures. Such situations are currently also not trained in traditional settings but leave options for later improvement.

```xml
<message role="pilot">
    <element type="Station"/>        <!-- Lilyfield Tower       -->
    <element type="CallSign"/>       <!-- HB-ABC                 -->
    <element type="Aircraft"/>       <!-- C172                   -->
    <element type="Location2D"/>     <!-- Robinhill              -->
    <element type="Altitude"/>       <!-- 4500 ft                -->
    <element type="Phrase" value="Request to Cross Direct" />
    <element type="Location2D"/>     <!-- E                      -->
    <element type="Altitude"/>       <!-- 4500 ft                -->
</message>
```

Listing 1: Procedure dialog excerpt matching the first statement listed in Figure 1

3.3 Generating Training Samples

In contrast to the deterministic nature of the dialog, automatic speech recognition needs supervised machine learning in order to achieve an acceptable recognition rate, given the number of deviations from standard English. The prototype uses Microsoft's Cognitive Speech services [MI23] for ASR and text-to-speech (TTS) synthesis. While language specialities can be implemented straight forward programmatically in TTS (encode "tree" vs. "three"), ASR needs training to create a custom speech model, tailored towards RTF dialect. However, large, annotated datasets of ATC communication are scarce and often also contain environment noises from cockpits or from the tower. From an ASR perspective however, these noises are not beneficial for language model training as students will typically train in quieter areas or in areas with noise sources different from cockpits. Such noises on the other hand could later be introduced in the TTS phase to make the training experience more realistic. Further, real-world data also include all miss-spellings and wording errors real pilots make. Therefore, special training datasets for ASR model training are required. Using the prototype system, we can create synthetic transcripts of random instances of the CTR crossing procedure. In this case, a random number generator sets all flight parameters (i.e. call sign, start, destination, crossing altitude) and by advancing the pilot-ATC state machine, a complete, syntactically and semantically valid transcript of a procedure is generated. The output of the automaton is plain text but by applying TTS synthesis, audio-data matching the transcript to 100% is generated. Using this approach, we synthesized 1400 text messages and generated the corresponding audio representation (.wav files; pilot, ATC using two different voices) to train a custom speech model (see Figure 2, right). This custom speech model is instantiated using Microsoft Cognitive Speech Services and then used for ASR within the prototype.

4 Outlook

Although a rigorous evaluation of the selected approach is still in planning, we could already demonstrate the feasibility of the concept with a first research prototype that implements a single procedure with a pragmatic approach. A next step would be to explore the effectiveness of different design options in real world settings with real student pilots as test subjects. Further research is additionally required on the synthetic learning dataset generation approach. Exploratory research using experimental techniques could be applied to determine the effects of varying the number of different synthetic voices, artificial noise addition and training data set size on ASR performance.

Bibliography

[FE23]   Federal Office of Civil Aviation FOCA: Statistics of Flight Personnel 2022, 2023

[FO23]   Federal Office of Civil Aviation FOCA: Training organisations (ATO/DTO): https://app02.bazl.admin.ch/web/bazl/en/#/facilities/search, accessed: 2023-03-30

[HE16]   Helmke, H. et.al.: Reducing controller workload with automatic speech recognition, In Proc. 35th Digital Avionics Systems Conference (DASC), 2016

[HE20]   Helmke, H. et.al.: Machine learning of air traffic controller command extraction models for speech recognition applications, In Proc. 39th Digital Avionics Systems Conference (DASC), 2020

[HE21]   Helmke, H. et.al.: Readback error detection by automatic speech recognition to increase ATM safety, In Proc. Fourteenth USA/Europe Air Traffic Management Research and Development Seminar, 2021

[IC07]   International Civil Aviation Organization ICAO: Manual of Radiotelephony, 2007

[JAR20] Juričić, B.; Antulov-Fantulin, B.; Rogošić, T.: Project ATCOSIMA–Air traffic Control Simulations at the Faculty of Transport and Traffic Sciences, Engineering Power: Bulletin of the Croatian Academy of Engineering 2/20, 2-9, 2020

[LU23]   Lufthansa on Twitter: https://twitter.com/lufthansa/status/263668108944891904, accessed: 2023-04-01

[MI23]   Microsoft Speech Services: https://azure.microsoft.com/en-us/products/cognitive-services/speech-services/, accessed: 2023-06-17

[SDB19] Schier, S.; Duensing, A.; Britze, S.: Sparring partners for human-in-the-loop simulations: The potential of virtual agents in air traffic simulations, CEAS Aeronautical Journal, 10, pp. 553–564, 2019

[WE90]   Weick, K.: The vulnerable system: An analysis of the Tenerife air disaster, Journal of management 3/1990, pp. 571-593, 1990

[ZA20]   Zamanirad, S. et.al.: State machine based human-bot conversation model and services, In Proc. 32nd International Conference on Advanced Information Systems Engineering, 2020

The tension between abstract and realistic visualization in VR learning applications for the classroom

Thiemo Leonhardt [1], Lanea Lilienthal [2], David Baberowski [3] and Nadine Bergner [4]

Abstract: While learning applications such as driving simulations aim for the most realistic experience possible, learning in other applications can be hindered by unintentional distractions. Similarly, VR learning applications with a high sense of presence address the learner's attention as well as the emotional component of learning. A high sense of presence can also evoke negative feelings in learners due to the emotional component and thus hinder the learning process. With this tension in mind, this paper analyses two different VR learning applications. The results show no effect of abstract visualization in contrast to realistic, high visualization on user preference and usability between both applications with constant high presence.

Keywords: Visualization, Presence, VR, Learning

1 Introduction

This paper describes the results of an ongoing research effort to develop VR applications for computer science education. Thereby we follow a design-oriented research approach. For VR applications to be used in the classroom, they must be able to be integrated into the flow of a lesson like comparable media. This requires that VR applications are designed for specific learning phases. One of the strengths of interactive simulations, especially in VR, is the representation of and interaction with abstract or even inaccessible places. In the didactics of computer science, it is possible to look into and interact with information technology systems such as computers and routers at different levels of abstraction, to visualize their internal processes and to learn their functionality interactively [De20], [LBB22]. Additionally, visualizations of abstract computer science content like regular automata are realized [De18]. In computer science didactics, conceptual models [GM00] are often implemented using notional machines [Gu19], [MSL21]. In this respect, the visual representation in such learning applications is an

---

[1] TU Dresden, Professur für Didaktik der Informatik, Nöthnitzer Str. 46, 01187 Dresden, thiemo.leonhardt@tu-dresden.de, https://orcid.org/0000-0003-4725-9776
[2] TU Dresden, Professur für Didaktik der Informatik, Nöthnitzer Str. 46, 01187 Dresden, lanea.lilienthal@tu-dresden.de, https://orcid.org/0000-0002-8508-9483
[3] TU Dresden, Professur für Didaktik der Informatik, Nöthnitzer Str. 46, 01187 Dresden, david.baberowski@tu-dresden.de, https://orcid.org/0000-0001-6308-4334
[4] TU Dresden, Professur für Didaktik der Informatik, Nöthnitzer Str. 46, 01187 Dresden, nadine.bergner@tu-dresden.de, https://orcid.org/0000-0003-3527-3204

doi: 10.18420/delfi2023-31

important area of research, since abstract content must be visualized that cannot be measured against real templates.

In this context, the design of VR applications for schools is still an under-researched area. The specific requirements for learning concentration and effective use of learning time need to be questioned and re-evaluated in the context of VR's strengths in motivating learning through immersion, presence, and interaction. To make these strengths of VR learning applications visible for the learning process, the design of the learning applications is of central importance. The extent to which abstract or realistic representations of learning content can influence learning outcomes, and the design decisions that can be derived from this, will be examined in more detail in this paper by comparing two VR learning applications.

2 Theoretical Background

The distinction and definition of immersion and presence is still part of the scientific discourse [BA19]. Slater defines immersion as an objective property of a system [Sl18] Less or more immersion is therefore to be specified as aspects such as display resolution, field of view, sound and similar relevant system components. Definitions of immersion in terms of user engagement or a state of flow [Pl21] should be rejected due to the strong interrelationship with psychological constructs and learning design. The creation of detailed virtual environments as well as the use of 3D models of low detail can certainly influence the effects of the VR learning application on the investigated factors, as an effect on the perception of presence can be expected here. Presence is defined as the impression of being part of the virtual environment [Ma21]. While Plotzky et al. found no scientific consensus on the influence of presence on learning effects [Pl21], they primarily attributed this to the small number of studies available. Learning theories suggest a positive relationship between the sense of presence and learning motivation and effectiveness.

Dengel investigates the relationships and effects between learner-specific variables (presence, motivation, cognition, and emotion), the level of immersion provided and learning outcomes in VR learning applications for teaching computer science [De20]. The model demonstrates an approach in which presence, which was influenced by immersion, cognitive ability, and achievement emotions, predicted learning outcomes along with the correlated factors of contextual motivation and cognitive ability, both of which also influenced learners' achievement emotions. While there was evidence that higher immersion was associated with higher learning outcomes, significant predictive effects were found between presence and learning outcomes.

Radianti et. al. [Ra20] found in a systematic mapping study that immersive VR technologies are considered a promising learning tool in higher education. However, most of the technologies described in the reviewed articles were still at an experimental stage, mainly tested for performance and usability. Similarly, only a few papers described in detail how VR-based instruction can be integrated into higher education curricula. Similar research on the use of VR in schools is scarce. Zender et al. [Ze22] argue that many questions regarding learning effectiveness, pedagogical and didactic design, as well as medical and ethical risks of use cannot yet be adequately answered for schools. Previous design specifications for VR learning applications do not specifically address the needs of schools. As part of his Multimedia Design Principles, Mayer formulates the *Immersion Principle*, which states that immersion does not necessarily improve learning, but that effective teaching methods in immersive virtual environments can improve learning, based on 35 studies from 2018 to 2021 [Ma21]. The main theoretical implication of the immersion principle in multimedia learning is that teaching methods can be used with immersive media to promote better learning. Research that has addressed the implications of instructional design in immersive learning environments is very limited. VR learning applications in particular show good results in teaching declarative and procedural knowledge [Ra20], [LBB22].

3 Applications Design

The *Inside the System* series, developed at the chair of Didactics of Computer Science at TU-Dresden, aims at the possibility to get inside computer systems and to understand and control their internal processes. Thus, the training of procedural knowledge about the internal processes of computer systems is built. To fit into a regular school lesson, the games were designed to have an average playing time of maximum 10 minutes. The implementation in VR assumes a higher motivation and activity of the learner and thus to produce good learning results. To compare the effect of abstract and realistic visualizations of VR learning applications, the two VR learning applications *Inside the Router* (ITR) and *Inside the CPU* (ITC) were designed differently.

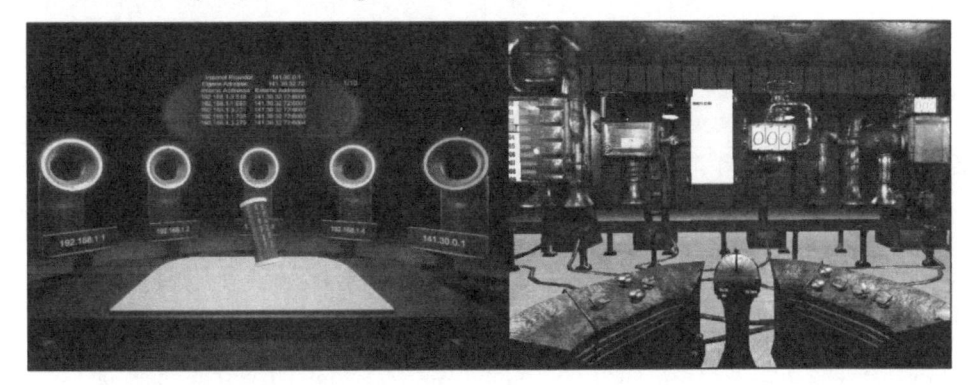

Fig. 1: First person views of *Inside the Router* (left) and *Inside the CPU* (right)

In ITR, the three main cases for routing IP packets in a home router that relate to everyday use cases are internal packets, outgoing packets, and incoming external packets. To practice an abstract task like routing, a metaphor is needed to haptically grasp the task. For Inside the Router, this metaphor is a pneumatic tube system in which the routes to the various network components are pipes. The IP packets are symbolized by capsules transported by these pipes. The main interaction as part of the game mechanics are the three steps: Catch, Decide, Throw. The didactic reduction following the German educational standards of CS for Inside the Router is described in detail in [LBB22]. The design of ITR follows an abstract visualization but high presence approach. Detailed representations of the pipes and packages were omitted and at the same time the virtual room was darkened so that the learner's attention is focused on the components relevant for learning. Thus, instead of implementing a detailed, more realistic representation of the visual component (electronic circuits and components), an abstract space was created. However, in order not to reduce the sense of presence at the same time, the learner is placed in the center of the room and all interactions are continuously performed by the learner. The darkened room should at the same time give the learners the feeling of being in an abstract space, which is only defined by the activity of sorting.

ITC places the user in an abstraction of a computer system, the Von-Neumann architecture of a computer. The player controls a machine made up of five components that relate to the components of the Von-Neumann model. As in the model, the machine's task is described by macrocode instructions in the RAM. The player retrieves these instructions and executes the corresponding microcode using control elements such as buttons and levers from a central console. The didactic reduction is equivalent to other widely accepted simulations for this topic in German secondary school CS education, such as Jhonny[5]. The steampunk-oriented design of ITC aims for a more realistic visualization and a high presence. The former is achieved by using highly detailed textures and complex 3D models for the main interactable objects. In contrast to ITR the background is also visible and uses detailed textures and factory ambient sounds. High presence is achieved by not using the input buttons of the VR controller, but by having the user grab and move the control elements on the central console. The components of the Von-Neumann machine are realistically animated and underlaid with sound effects which contribute to both immersion and presence, by linking the high detailed environment to user interactions. As in ITR the user is placed in the center of the room with all controls within reach, but in contrast to ITR the machine's components and surroundings are well illuminated and perceived in detail.

4 Comparative Analysis

Characteristics regarding VR of the application are considered in factors *immersion, presence,* and *interactivity*. The applications were tested with current high-end VR systems (HTC Vive Pro Eye, PICO 3 Pro) to compare the results. Accordingly, differences in immersion can only be attributed to the in-game representations. We use the Virtual

---

[5] https://sourceforge.net/projects/johnnysimulator/

Reality Learning Performance Model [LBB22] to measure the performance of the applications. The study was conducted with prospective teachers of computer science in their first semester. The two applications were tested separately with different subjects (ITR N=28; ITC N=13).

	ITC (N=13)		ITR (N=28)	
General Presence (IPQ)	M=4.86	SD=1.834	M=5.21	SD=.791
Spatial Presence	M=4.843	SD=1.216	M=5.36	SD=.791
Involvement	M=4.054	SD=1.190	M=4.47	SD=1.163
Experienced Realism	M=2.750	SD=.519	M=3.179	SD=1.128
Interactivity (IS)	M=1.476	SD=.566	M=1.571	SD=.753

Tab. 1: Mean (M) and standard deviation (SD) of both applications.

The IPQ (igroup presence questionnaire) to measure presence consists of 13 items on a scale between 1 to 6. 12 of the items are divided into 3 subscales (Spatial Presence 5 items, Involvement 4 items, and Experienced Realism 3 items). The last item (G1) loads on all three factors and simultaneously represents the General Presence factor. The Interactivity Scale (IS) consists of 3 Items on a scale between 1 and 7 where 1 corresponds to high interactivity. Accordingly, the VR-specific observation showed a strong sense of participant presence (high IPQ) and a high sense of interactivity regarding the IS scale analysis for both applications (see table 1). As the applications show the high levels of presence and interactivity expected from the design, a possible influence of realistic or abstract representations in the visual presentation on user preference and learning performance can now be measured. User preference can be surveyed via user experience (UEQ-S), usability (SUS) and VR specific motion sickness (MSAQ). Learning performance is investigated by considering flow experience in the learning process (FSS).

To measure the two independent samples, the non-parametric Mann-Whitney U-test for independent samples was performed on all scales and subscales. All requirements for the test[6] are met. No significant differences were found between the two applications on any of the scales (user experience, usability, VR specific motion sickness), so the null hypothesis of no difference in user preference and learning performance between ITR and ITC is maintained. The beta error was calculated to test the null hypothesis. No effect of abstract visualization in contrast to realistic, high visualization on user preference (1-β=.99) and usability (1-β=.92) with constant high presence could be demonstrated. For the MSAQ (1-β = .07) and the Flow (1-β=.12) the power is not sufficient to make a valid statement about the null hypothesis. To measure actual learning effects beyond the flow experience, the learning content must be comparable, therefore an abstract visualization version of the ITC application will be implemented in a follow-up study.

---

[6] Independence of measurements, independent variable is nominally scaled and has two expressions, dependent variable is at least ordinally scaled and distribution form of the two groups is approximately equal.

Bibliography

[BA19] Berkman, M. I.; Akan, E.: Presence and Immersion in Virtual Reality. In (Lee, N. Ed.): Encyclopedia of Computer Graphics and Games. Springer International Publishing, Cham, pp. 1–10, 2019.

[De18] Dengel, A.: Seeking the Treasures of Theoretical Computer Science Education: Towards Educational Virtual Reality for the Visualization of Finite State Machines: 2018 IEEE International Conference on Teaching, Assessment, and Learning for Engineering (TALE). IEEE, pp. 1107–1112, 2018.

[De20] Dengel, A.: Effects of Immersion and Presence on Learning Outcomes in Immersive Educational Virtual Environments for Computer Science Education. Dissertation, Passau, 2020.

[GM00] Greca, I. M.; Moreira, M. A.: Mental models, conceptual models, and modelling. International Journal of Science Education 1/22, pp. 1–11, 2000.

[Gu19] Guzdial, M. et al.: Notional Machines and Programming Language Semantics in Education (Dagstuhl Seminar 19281). 23 pages, 2019.

[LBB22] Leonhardt, T.; Baberowski, D.; Bergner, N.: Inside the Router: An interactive VR learning application to practice routing and network address translation. Gesellschaft für Informatik e.V, 2022.

[Ma21] Mayer, R. E.: Multimedia learning. Cambridge University Press, Cambridge, 2021.

[MSL21] Maass, W.; Storey, V. C.; Lukyanenko, R.: From Mental Models to Machine Learning Models via Conceptual Models. In (Augusto, A. et al. Eds.): Enterprise, Business-Process and Information Systems Modeling. Springer International Publishing, Cham, pp. 293–300, 2021.

[Pl21] Plotzky, C. et al.: Virtual Reality in Healthcare Skills Training: The Effects of Presence on Acceptance and Increase of Knowledge. i-com 1/20, pp. 73–83, 2021.

[Ra20] Radianti, J. et al.: A systematic review of immersive virtual reality applications for higher education: Design elements, lessons learned, and research agenda. Computers & Education 147, p. 103778, 2020.

[Sl18] Slater, M.: Immersion and the illusion of presence in virtual reality. British journal of psychology (London, England 1953) 3/109, pp. 431–433, 2018.

[Ze22] Zender, R. et al.: Virtual Reality für Schüler:innen. MedienPädagogik: Zeitschrift für Theorie und Praxis der Medienbildung 47, pp. 26–52, 2022.

Virtual Reality, Eye Tracking and Machine Learning: Analysis of Learning Outcomes in Off-the-Shelve VR-Software

Johannes Tümler [1], Juan Enrique Erazo Sanchez[1] and Christian Hänig [1]

Abstract: The combination of Virtual Reality (VR) and eye tracking allows to analyze how students use the presented VR content for learning. Here, we propose a novel approach to analyze eye tracking data in VR, even if no access to the VR software source code is given. This proof-of-concept leverages image classification methods to identify objects that captured the students' attention in VR. The method allows analysis of individual learning strategies and correlate those to individual learning outcomes.

Keywords: Virtual Reality, Education, Eye Tracking, Machine Learning, Image Classification

1 Introduction and Goals

Virtual Reality allows users to immerse in a completely computer-generated interactive experience in real-time. This makes it an ideal technology to let students learn and explore in a safe, controllable, reproducible environment. Because of its attractiveness for learning and teaching, there is a lot of research to apply VR in education. Especially important are studies of the effectiveness of VR implementations and as well as questions on how to embed such systems into regular teaching processes.

Eye tracking is a technology to *find spatial focus points of user's vision over time*. The combination of virtual reality and eye tracking consequently offers benefits to understand where users focus their view in a virtual environment. Clay et al. give insight on basic principles, limitations and application examples for eye tracking in VR [CKK19]. Rappa et al. analyzed papers that incorporated eye tracking in VR learning [Ra22]. Today, several VR headsets exist, that have included eye tracking capabilities. The best approach to carry out eye tracking studies in VR would be to embed it into the VR software source code for maximum flexibility. Unfortunately, most of the commercial VR learning software does neither offer eye tracking integration nor provide software source code. Therefore, an alternative approach would be helpful for eye tracking analysis in *off-the-shelve software*.

---

[1] Anhalt University of Applied Sciences, Bernburger Straße 55, 06366 Köthen, Germany, Ingenieurinformatik, johannes.tuemler@hs-anhalt.de, https://orcid.org/0000-0002-4788-2667
Master of Data Science student programme, juanenrique.erazosanchez@student.hs-anhalt.de
Artificial Intelligence, christian.haenig@hs-anhalt.de, https://orcid.org/0000-0001-7775-4386

doi: 10.18420/delfi2023-32

Here, we present a novel approach to analyze eye tracking in off-the-shelve VR software. The goal is to use machine learning to identify VR scene objects that the users have looked at. This allows teachers or researchers to analyze their student's gaze behavior in a post-intervention step. The research was conducted in form of a student project at Anhalt University of Applied Sciences in Köthen, Germany.

2 Data Acquisition

The data used here was recorded in a previous study [IT22]: Having biomedical curricula at our university, we used a biomedical software: ShareCare YOU VR[2] is a VR simulation to teach and learn the human body, anatomical structures, organs, and their functions (Figure 1). In consent with N=20 participants we took video recordings from a Varjo VR-2 headset during a thirty-minute virtual learning experience.

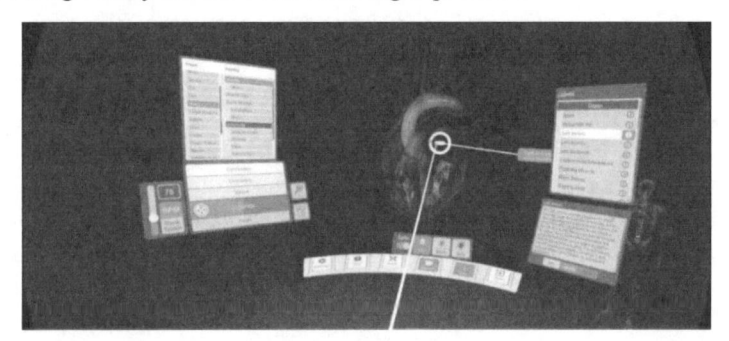

Figure 1: Screenshot of user's view in ShareCare YOU VR software. Billboards show a menu and additional text on the left and right side. A dock gives access to features at the bottom. The currently activated 3D object is visible in the center (here: human heart).

The study incorporated both a pre- and a post-intervention quiz to assess the participants' knowledge of human heart anatomy before and after using the VR learning software. Looking at the gained score percentage, exactly those with high/low starting knowledge scored a low/high absolute gain in score, corresponding to outcomes of Zinchenko et al. [Zi20]. Unfortunately, due to loss of data, not all the 20 participants' data sets were still available for our new analysis. Therefore, in the following approach we used only ten data sets (IDs 4, 5, 6, 7, 8, 9, 10, 11 ,17, 18) to provide a proof-of-concept.

---

[2] https://store.steampowered.com/app/724590/Sharecare_YOU_VR/

3 Method and Implementation

Data annotation provides the ground truth labels necessary for training and evaluation of machine learning models. In our study, we used the annotation tool makesense.ai to annotate the images in our dataset. From the existing video recordings, at first, we extracted each video frame as image and determined the user's 2D focus point using the existing eye tracking method. Second, we reduced the size of each image to the area around the user's focus point. The annotator has chosen a receptive field of 400x400 pixels, which provides enough visual information for the classification of the target classes. We identified six relevant classes based on the content of the videos: The virtual depiction of the human heart, three display types (left/right/main), the dock allowing users to control the simulation and the "booting screen" from before application start.

Each training image was assigned exactly one class, which was determined by the human annotator as the most relevant class. In total, we manually annotated 1978 images, resulting in a reasonably balanced dataset (see Table 1). While there is some variation in the number of samples per class, there are no classes that are significantly over- or under-represented (as in 1:100, 1:1000 or 1:10000 [CJK04]).

Class	Video 1	Video 2	Video 3	Video 4	Video 5	Video 6	Total
Boot Screen	63	108	68	29	23	29	320
Left Display	24	70	84	22	36	14	250
Right Display	119	161	103	72	179	58	692
Dock	5	23	4	3	27	16	78
Main Display	19	63	3	19	17	46	167
Heart	87	98	56	90	68	72	471
							1978

Table 1: Frequency of target classes on a per-video (user) level and in total.

To classify the images in our dataset, we experimented with ResNet models [He16] of different sizes. We based our choice on previous work in the field of computer vision, which has shown that ResNet architectures are parameter-efficient for comparable image classification tasks [Do20]. In all conducted experiments, we initialized our models with weights been pre-trained on the ImageNet1k dataset [Ru15] to benefit from robust features trained on a large dataset.

To train our ResNet models, we split our annotated dataset of 1978 images into train, validation, and test sets. Since our data comes from videos, we used a leave-one-out approach on video level for cross-validation [HTF09]. For each experiment, the training set was built from four videos, the validation and test set from one video each. We have chosen this approach over the well-established stratified n-fold cross-validation [ZM00] because this approach ensured that no frames from the same video were present in both the training and test sets. Temporally consecutive frames from the same video are very similar to each other, which would lead to an overestimation of our model's generalization ability if frames from the same video would be distributed among train and test sets. In total, we conducted 30 independent runs for each of the ResNet variants (18, 34, 50, 101, and 152 layers) and evaluated their performance on the held-out test set. After training and validating our ResNet models on the annotated dataset, we evaluated their performance using Precision, Recall, and F1-Score metrics [CH92] (Table 2). Based on our experiments, the ResNet34 model achieved the highest mean F1-Score of 0.9663, closely followed by the other models.

Model	Parameters	Mean F-Score	Min F-Score	Max F-Score	σ
ResNet18	11M	0.9638	0.8979	0.9830	0.0227
ResNet34	21M	**0.9663**	**0.9277**	**0.9906**	0.0207
ResNet50	23M	0.9635	0.8936	0.9843	0.0291
ResNet101	42M	0.9559	0.8809	0.9872	0.0295
ResNet152	58M	0.9620	0.8979	0.9872	**0.0200**

Table 2: Resulting F-Scores of all ResNet models (evaluated on test sets).

To gain a deeper understanding of the performance of our models, we analyzed misclassifications. Most were due to the presence of multiple objects in a single frame. In these cases, the model correctly predicted one of the visible objects, while the human annotator defined another object as the dominant and thus, correct one.

4 ML-based Analysis of the Previous Study Data

From previous experiments we able to assume that users focus points would not erratically jump back and forth between the target classes multiple times per second. Therefore, we extracted one frame per second from the VR eye tracking data to obtain a representative sample of participants' visual attention during their VR experience. Subsequently, we applied our trained ResNet34 model to classify the extracted frames, enabling us to identify the participants' focus objects among the object classes. We computed Pearson correlation coefficients between knowledge gain, the relative and absolute time spent on various classes (Table 3). For that, we excluded participants #4 and #17, because these had either a large or a very low previous knowledge.

Object Class	left_display	right_display	dock	main_display	heart
Average Viewing Time	14.4%	37.1%	6.6%	9.9%	32.0%
Correlation Coefficient	-0.72	-0.46	-0.02	0.39	0.72
Avg. Sec. per Participant	43	110	20	28	91
Correlation Coefficient	-0.30	-0.67	-0.40	-0.11	0.19

Table 3: Correlations between relative viewing time and gained knowledge (first two rows), correlations between absolute viewing time and gained knowledge (last two rows)

VR, Eye Tracking and ML: Analysis of Learning Outcomes in Off-the-Shelf VR-Software

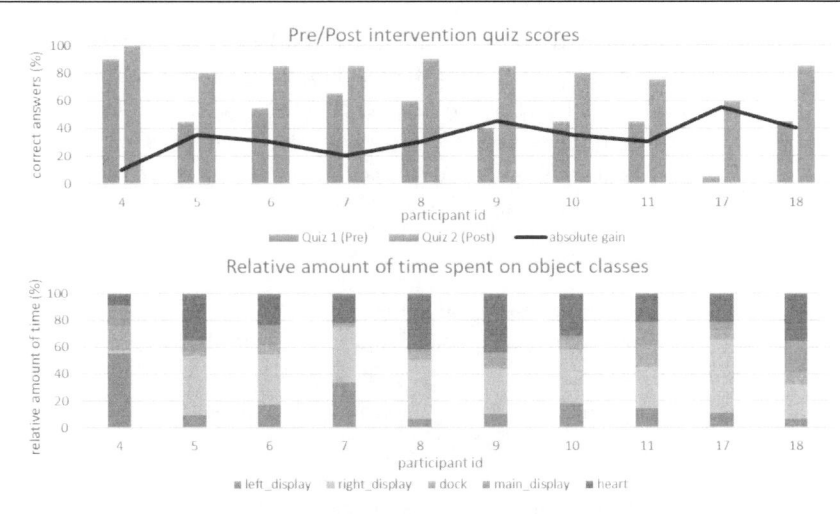

[Figure: Two charts. Top: "Pre/Post intervention quiz scores" bar chart showing Quiz 1 (Pre), Quiz 2 (Post) and absolute gain line across participant ids 4, 5, 6, 7, 8, 9, 10, 11, 17, 18. Bottom: "Relative amount of time spent on object classes" stacked bar chart with categories left_display, right_display, dock, main_display, heart for the same participant ids.]

Figure 2: Gained knowledge (top), relative amount of time spent with a certain object class per participant, retrieved using the novel machine learning-based method (bottom).

Figure 2 illustrates the distribution of attention across the five main object classes. The learning experience of the participants and the factors influencing their learning outcomes were analyzed, considering various aspects such as individual pre-existing knowledge, the use of different displays, and overall learning duration. For most participants, the left display exhibited a moderate to strong negative correlation with learning outcomes. This suggests that the left display may not have effectively conveyed information. Interactions with the 3D VR heart model positively correlated with learning outcomes, ranging from mediocre to strong associations. This implies that focusing on the key object of the virtual environment was beneficial for understanding of the subject. The absolute duration of learning had, at most, a weak influence on learning outcomes. This result emphasizes that the quality of the learning experience and engagement with relevant objects may be more crucial than the time spent in the virtual environment.

5 Summary and Discussion

This study has two main contributions: (1) A machine learning model was developed and successfully applied to identify specific gazed-at regions in an off-the-shelf VR software. (2) The result of the machine learning analysis was used to examine possible correlations between learner's viewing behaviour and learning outcome.

We aimed at a proof-of-concept for the method and therefore used a relatively low number of data sets and object classes. We found correlations between the knowledge gained and time spent on specific VR objects. Future research should aim to replicate these findings with a larger and more diverse participant pool to better understand factors influencing learning outcomes. The data used to create the image classification model was taken from real study videos. Therefore, the quality of the machine learning training data was not optimal. For future analyses, we suggest to first generate training data from a controlled dataset, for example by recording in-app videos with only known objects in sight and with controlled headset movements. Following our ideas, future research based on eye tracking data in off-the-shelve VR software may become easier.

Bibliography

[Ch92]   Chinchor, N.: MUC-4 Evaluation Metrics. In: Fourth Message Understanding Conference (MUC-4): Proceedings of a Conference Held in McLean, Virginia, June 16-18, 1992.

[CJK04] Nitesh, V. C.; Nathalie, J.; Aleksander, K.: Editorial: special issue on learning from imbalanced data sets. Sigkdd Explorations, 6(1), 1-6, 2004.

[CKK19] Clay, V.; König, P.; König, S.: Eye tracking in virtual reality. Journal of Eye Movement Research, vol. 12, no. 1, 2019. doi: 10.16910/JEMR.12.1.3

[Do20]   Dosovitskiy, A. et al.: An image is worth 16x16 words: Transformers for image recognition at scale. 2020. doi: 10.48550/arXiv.2010.11929

[He16]   He, K.; Zhang, X.; Ren, S.; Sun, J.: Deep Residual Learning for Image Recognition. In: 2016 IEEE Conference on Computer Vision and Pattern Recognition, 2016.

[HTF09] Hastie, T.; Tibshirani, R.; Friedman, J.: The Elements of Statistical Learning. Data Mining, Inference, and Prediction, Second Edition. Springer, New York, 2009. doi: 10.1007/978-0-387-84858-7

[IT22]   Igbudu, M.; Tümler, J.: Investigating Eye Tracking in 3rd Party Off the Shelve Software. Proceedings of DELFI Workshops 2022, pp. 47-55. Gesellschaft für Informatik e.V., 2022. doi: 10.18420/delfi2022-ws-14

[Ra22]   Rappa, N.A. et al.: The use of eye tracking technology to explore learning and performance within virtual reality and mixed reality settings: a scoping review. Interactive Learning Environments, vol. 30, no. 7, pp. 1338–1350, 2022. doi: 10.1080/10494820.2019.1702560

[Ru15]   Russakovsky, O. et al.: Imagenet large scale visual recognition challenge. International journal of computer vision, 115, 211-252, 2015. doi: 10.1007/s11263-015-0816-y

[Zi20]   Zinchenko, Y.P.; Khoroshikh, P.P.; Sergievich, A.A.; Smirnov, A.S.; Tumyalis, A.V.; Kovalev, A.I.; Gutnikov, S.A.; Golokhvast, K.S.: Virtual reality is more efficient in learning human heart anatomy especially for subjects with low baseline knowledge. New Ideas Psychol., vol. 59, 2020. doi: 10.1016/j.newideapsych.2020.100786

[ZM00]   Zeng, X.; Martinez, T. R.: Distribution-balanced stratified cross-validation for accuracy estimation. Journal of Experimental & Theoretical Artificial Intelligence, 12(1), 1-12, 2000. doi: 10.1080/095281300146272

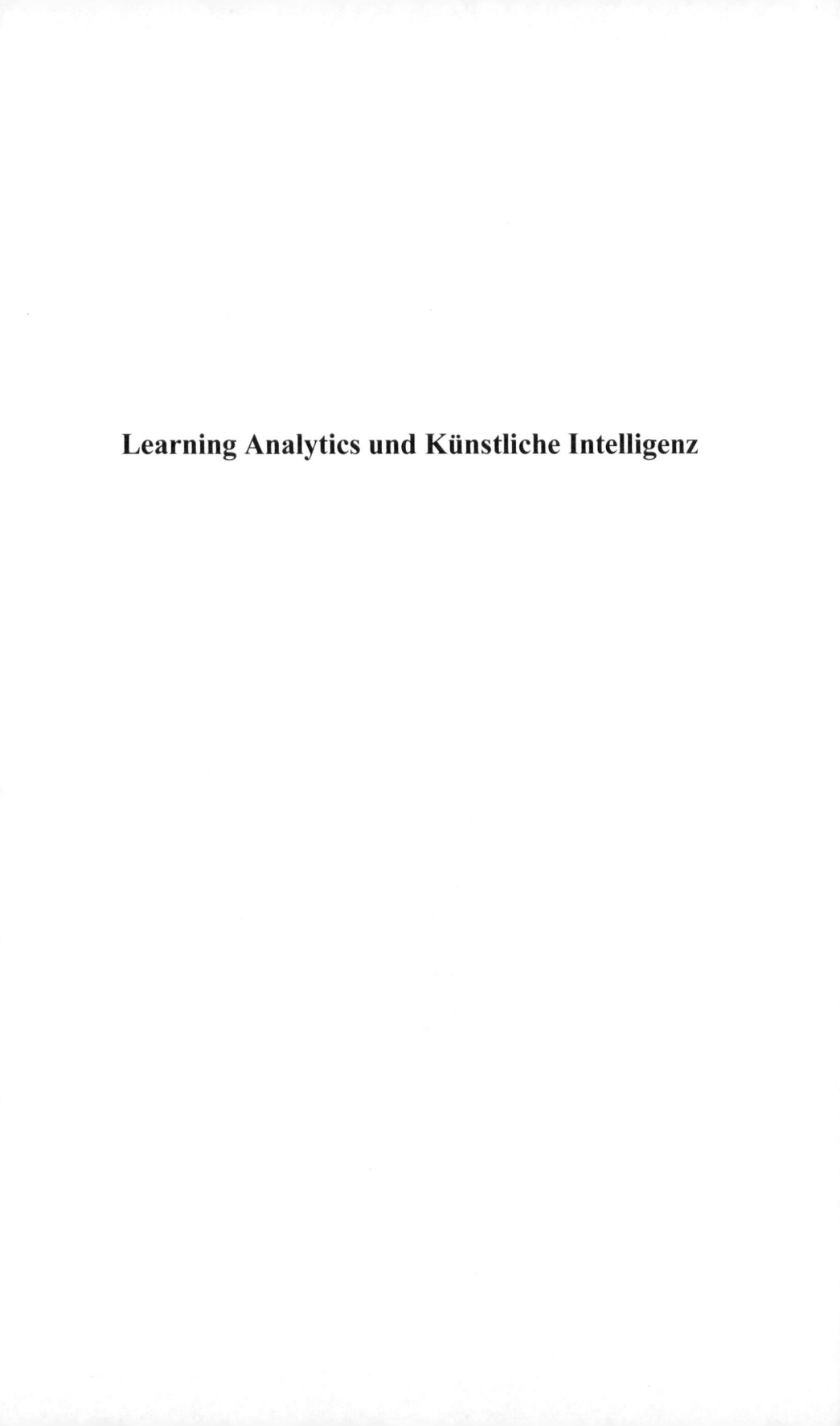

Learning Analytics und Künstliche Intelligenz

Automated alerts to avoid unfavourable interaction patterns in collaborative learning: Which design do students prefer?

Anja Hawlitschek [1], Galina Rudolf[2], Sarah Berndt[3] and Sebastian Zug[4]

Abstract: Longer phases without interaction or a later start into task processing are often related to problems in collaborative learning. Teams that exhibit such patterns of teamwork are more likely to underperform or fail in collaboration. Automated alerts are a way to contact such student teams, make them aware of unfavourable interaction patterns and offer support. An adequate design of such alerts is a basis for their efficacy. In this study, we investigated students' (N = 39) attitudes towards alerts and analysed which types of automated alerts students prefer. Based on findings of previous studies, we have designed three types of alerts – "impersonal-with response", "personal-with response" and "information only". Students in our study mainly preferred "personal-with response". However, in-depth investigation revealed restrictions. Based on results, we give recommendations for the design of automated alerts.

Keywords: automated alerts, design, teamwork

1 Introduction

Alerts from learning analytics systems could support students in digital collaboration, establish effective learning groups and facilitate lecturers work, especially in larger courses. Therefor observable indicators for successful digital teamwork are needed. One of these indicators is a continuous, timely cooperation without longer phases of no interaction and without a delay in task processing [DHH17]. This is not only important for efficient teamwork but also for performance. Studies show that there is a negative correlation between late submissions of assignments and course performance [Ce16; Yo15]. Continuous interaction is relevant for a positive group climate and team performance [KLJ14]. Automated alerts could help, to make students aware of unfavourable interaction patterns, to avoid delay or make the comparison with successful teams possible [DHH17; MES15; RHS17]. However, students perceive such interventions, not only as useful but also as potential invasion of their privacy, as unnecessary paternalism and as restriction of their autonomy [MES15; Ro16; RHS17]. Therefore, an adequate design and usage of alerts is a basis for

---

[1] Otto-von-Guericke-Universität, Universitätsplatz 2, 39106 Magdeburg, anja.hawlitschek@ovgu.de, https://orcid.org/0000-0001-8727-2364
[2] TU Bergakademie Freiberg, Akademiestraße 6, 09599 Freiberg, galina-rudolf@informatik.tu-freiberg.de
[3] Otto-von-Guericke-Universität, Universitätsplatz 2, 39106 Magdeburg, sarah.berndt@ovgu.de
[4] TU Bergakademie Freiberg, Akademiestraße 6, 09599 Freiberg, sebastian.zug@informatik.tu-freiberg.de

doi: 10.18420/delfi2023-33

their efficacy; however, there is limited research on students' perceptions of alerts and on their responses to different alert designs [HRM18]. This is especially true for team alerts. Hence our first research question is: How do students like the idea of alerts in GitHub that inform about unfavourable teamwork patterns? From literature we also identified open questions regarding the design of alerts: Those were, (1) do students like conversational/personal or formal/impersonal language style better? Results from a study indicate that students prefer automated alerts over personalized E-Mails from lecturer [RHS17]. Automated alerts are less likely perceived as restriction of autonomy and external control. However, it is not clear whether this preference goes hand in hand with a preference for an impersonal language style in the alerts. Studies on multimedia learning indicate that a conversational instead of a formal language style increases learning performance – the so-called personalization principle [GMM13]. However, in a study of [HRM18] no significant difference was found between a more personalized message and a more formal message in terms of impact on students. (2) Do students prefer to get only the information about unfavorable interaction patterns or to also get the option to interact with lecturers? Studies suggest, that giving learner information that should make them aware of problems is not enough, because students often do not know how to improve learning processes [Ji17]. Students on the other hand, highlight the relevance of the implementation of some kind of communication channel to contact lecturers [RHS17]. However, for alerts that transport a relatively simple message (e.g., inform teams that they are not continuously working) this could be different. In a study on alerts designed to enhance attendance in a family support program, the simplest message providing only a reminder of the date and the time of the workshop was most effective [Pa22]. Taking these findings into account, it might be effective to simply combine awareness alerts with the option for students to contact the lecturer.

2 Methods

The alerts were implemented as issues in GitHub. We used github2pandas - a python package that allows an automatic screening of GitHub repositories. The automatically running script evaluates the changes in the projects regarding new versions, reviews, or test results. In the event that no activity was observed for a specific interval, the action automatically generated an issue using the predefined texts.

Three types of alerts were developed by our team, to be used in the current study. For issue 1 ("impersonal-with response"), we implemented a formal/impersonal language style, the note, that it is an automatically created message and the possibility to ask for lecturer's support: "This is an automatically created message: The last commit in team [team name] was on [date, time]. Does the team need ... ☐ content support from lecturers? ☐ support in organizing the team's work?." For issue 2 ("personal-with response") we implemented a more personal/conversational language style with the possibility to ask for lecturer's support but also the possibility to mark the issue as unnecessary: "Dear Team [team name], your last commit was on [date, time]. That was a while ago. What's going on? Do you need support? ▢We need content support and would love to hear from lecturers. ▢ We need support in organizing the teamwork and would be happy to be contacted by the lecturers. ▢ We can do it on our own! ▢ We do not want to work on the task at all." For issue 3 ("information-only"), we implemented the same formal information as in issue 1 but without the possibility to ask for support.

The survey took place at a German university in a course on embedded systems. 39 students took part and filled out a paper-pencil questionnaire. The sample is composed of 56 percent computer scientists (N 22) and 44 percent engineers (N 17). We first asked the students with open-ended questions about their general perceptions of automated alerts regarding teamwork in GitHub. The coding and analysis of the answers on the open-ended questions was carried out by two scientists according to principles of content analysis [Ku18]. The coding manual was created inductively. The inter-rater reliability (Cohen's kappa) was 0.84 and can thus be rated as very good.

After the open-ended questions we presented the three issues. With a five-point semantic differential scale we surveyed students' perceptions towards each issue. We used the following six pairs of adjectives: useless - helpful, unpleasant – pleasant, demotivating – motivating, controlling – supporting, intrusive – unintrusive, not appealing – appealing. A last question asked which of the three issues students would prefer. They could choose one of the issues or none. Students who choose "none" had the possibility to explain their answer in a text box.

3 Results

The coding resulted in a total of 92 codes (Coder 1) within 4 categories – overall evaluation (N = 35), reasons for usefulness (N = 13), reservations (N = 25), conditions (19). Multiple answers to a code by the same person were counted only once. With few exceptions, the students perceived the idea of creating automated alerts in case of unfavourable interaction patterns positively (N = 32). In particular, the reminder and motivation function are emphasized (N = 8), but also the decreasing hurdle to seek support (N = 5). However, from the students' point of view, the positive evaluation of automated issues is linked to conditions (N = 19). Students stated the importance of sending alerts not too frequently (N = 3) and not too fast (N = 4). In particular, students recommend the usage of alerts "only once per task" and "only just before deadline", so that the team has enough time to deal with the task itself. Students emphasize that multiple reminders per assignment are perceived as spam. Students also mention prior instruction in GitHub as essential for the usage of alerts, since they perceive the environment as challenging, especially for beginners (N = 3). Furthermore, students consider it important that the issues are only used in large projects (N = 2), are automated/anonymous (N = 3) and don't force a reaction on the part of the students. They also recommend accompanying alerts by supportive materials or links (N = 3) without reveal solutions (N = 1). However, there are also reservations about the automated issues (N = 25). Students don't like to get unnecessary alerts, e.g., if the student group don't like to work on the task at all or if lack of time is the reason for a delay (N = 6). They also perceive alerts as invasive (N = 5), especially if they were sent to often or unnecessary. In particular students criticise the intrusion in their time planning (N = 4) and the underlying assumption that students need support in scheduling. Therefore, from students' perspective, alerts can have negative effects such as pressure (N = 4). Furthermore, the general usefulness of such automated alerts in GitHub is questioned (N = 6). It is argued that students do not notice the issues, ignore them, or deactivate the corresponding mail notifications.

Confronted with the three implementations of the alerts, most students prefer the "personal-with response"-variant (46%, Issue 2), followed by the "impersonal-with response"-variant (39%, issue 1). In contrast, only 8 percent of students prefer an "information only"-alert (issue 3) or none of the three issues. Despite students' preference for issue 2, the evaluation of issue 1 is better in five of six individual aspects (see Fig. 1).

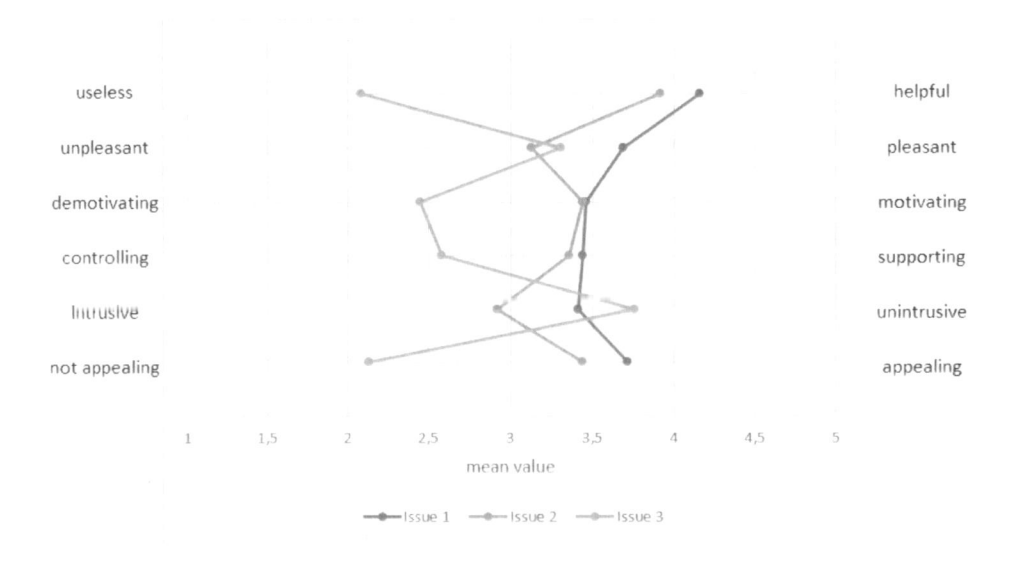

Fig. 1: Semantic differential: Students' perceptions of the alerts

Findings in particular indicate that students perceive issue 2 as more intrusive than issue 1. The evaluation of issue 3, is clearly more negative compared to issue 1 in five out of six items and to issue 2 in four out of six items. In particular, students perceive issue 3 as rather useless. The only item, where issue 3 is rated better than both other issues, is "unintrusiveness".

4 Discussion

Students overall evaluated the idea to use automated alerts to inform about unfavorable interaction patterns positively. They especially liked the function as reminder but also the nudge to seek help. However, students made clear that alerts must be designed in a way that they are not perceived as invasive and as control mechanism. Against this background, students pointed on the importance of anonymous alerts where a reaction from students is completely voluntary. Students especially had reservations regarding an intrusion in their time management. Students emphasized time and amount as important pre-conditions for the usefulness and non-invasiveness of alerts. They prefer a one-time reminder shortly before the deadline. From a didactic point of view, it would be better not to remind students just before the deadline, to avoid a deadline rush. A solution to bring these two views together might be, to transparently communicate students when and why an alert will come or to jointly define the rules for when and how often to alert. The exact timing should also depend on the amount of work students have to invest to complete the task. This goes hand in hand with students' wish to avoid unnecessary alerts, in particular in the cases if students don't have the time to work on the assignment. That students perceive their time resources as too scarce for the requirements of the course is indeed a valuable information for lecturers. We believe that this problem should be included as feedback option in the alerts. Based on such feedback, lecturer could contact student teams and inquire about what are reasons for problems with time management and look for ways to help students with this. In addition, students wanted additional help within the alerts, such as links to explanations. This result is in line with previous research [RHS17]. Within our descriptive data, we found clear evidence that the alert which contains information-only was not favored by students – students rated this alert as rather useless, demotivation und unappealing. The potential to interact with the lecturer is of clear value for our students. Concerning our research question on language style, we did not find clear answers. We found that students in our study overall prefer issue 2 ("personal-with response") just ahead of issue 1 ("impersonal-with response"). However, we cannot say for sure whether students liked the conversational and personal language style in issue 2 or the two more possibilities of interaction they had in this alert. That two students explicitly wished to implement the response options of issue 2 into the header of issue 1 can be interpreted according to the latter. Also, that we found more positive evaluations of the individual characteristics of issue 1 compared to issue 2 points in that direction. Students seem to perceive the language style of issue 2 as more intrusive than issue 1.

Our study has limitations: (1) It is a small scale, exploratory study with a homogenous sample where all students were enrolled in one specific course. (2) It might be that the perception of the three alert types is different when they are given in an actual teamwork situation as opposed to a what-if scenario. Further studies are needed to examine the generalizability of the findings as well as the effects of different designs of alerts on learning behaviour, learning performance or teamwork.

Bibliography

[Ce16]   Cerezo, R. et. al.: Students' LMS interaction patterns and their relationship with achievement: A case study in higher education. Computers & Education 96, pp. 42-54, 2016.

[DHH17]   Doberstein, D., Hecking, T., & Hoppe, H. U.: Sequence patterns in small group work within a large online course. In: Collaboration and Technology: 23rd International Conference, Saskatoon 2017. Springer International Publishing, Cham, pp. 104-117, 2017.

[GMM13]   Ginns, P., Martin, A. J., & Marsh, H. W.: Designing instructional text in a conversational style: A meta-analysis. Educational Psychology Review 25/4, pp. 445-472, 2013.

[HRM18]   Howell, J. A., Roberts, L. D., & Mancini, V. O.: Learning analytics messages: Impact of grade, sender, comparative information and message style on student affect and academic resilience. Computers in Human Behavior 89, pp. 8-15, 2018.

[Ji17]   Jivet, I., Scheffel, M., Drachsler, H., & Specht, M.: Awareness is not enough: Pitfalls of learning analytics dashboards in the educational practice. In (Lavoué, É., Drachsler, H., Verbert, K., Broisin, J. & Pérez-Sanagustín, M., eds.): Data driven approaches in digital education. EC-TEL 2017. Lecture Notes in Computer Science, Springer, pp. 82–96, 2017.

[Ku18]   Kuckartz, U.: Qualitative Inhaltsanalyse. Methoden, Praxis, Computerunterstützung. Beltz, Weinheim, 2018.

[KLJ14]   Kwon, K., Liu, Y. H., & Johnson, L. P.: Group regulation and social-emotional interactions observed in computer supported collaborative learning: Comparison between good vs. poor collaborators. Computers & Education 78, pp. 185-200, 2014.

[MES15]   Martin, J., Edwards, S. H., & Shaffer, C. A.: The effects of procrastination interventions on programming project success. In: Proceedings of the eleventh annual International Conference on International Computing Education Research, pp. 3–11, 2015.

[Pa22]   Patnaik, A. et. al.: Impact of text message reminders on attendance at healthy marriage and relationship education workshops. Family Relations, 2022.

[Ro16]   Roberts, L. D. et. al.: Student attitudes toward learning analytics in higher education: "The fitbit version of the learning world". Frontiers in psychology 7, 2016.

[RHS17]   Roberts, L.D., Howell, J.A. & Seaman, K.: Give Me a Customizable Dashboard: Personalized Learning Analytics Dashboards in Higher Education. Tech Know Learn 22/3, pp. 317–333, 2017.

[Yo15]   You, J. W.: Examining the effect of academic procrastination on achievement using LMS data in e-Learning. Educational Technology & Society 18/3, pp. 64-74, 2015.

Anwendung von Process Mining zur kontinuierlichen Lernpfadidentifikation in Lernmanagementsystemen

Lars Quakulinski[1], Sven Judel [2], Miriam Wagner [3] und Ulrik Schroeder [2]

Abstract: Learning Analytics Anwendungen, die mittels Process Mining die Lernpfade von Studierenden identifizieren, machen dies meist nach Kursabschluss auf den vollständigen Daten. Von diesen gewonnenen Kenntnissen und eventuell folgenden Kursanpassungen profitieren jedoch frühestens die Teilnehmenden der nächsten Kursdurchführung. Lehrenden bereits während der Kursdurchführung Einsichten zu geben bietet die Möglichkeit frühzeitig auf eventuelle Probleme zu reagieren. Studierende können ihren eigenen Lernpfad reflektieren und bei Bedarf anpassen. In diesem Beitrag wird eine Anwendung vorgestellt welche einmal täglich die als xAPI Statements gesammelten Daten der letzten 24 Stunden aus dem Lernmanagementsystem Moodle analysiert und die Lernpfade der einzelnen Kurse erweitert. Um eine skalierende Lösung bereitzustellen, werden Techniken des Streaming Process Minings angewandt.

Keywords: Educational Process Mining, Streaming Process Mining, Learning Analytics, xAPI

1 Einleitung

Learning Analytics beschreibt die Sammlung, Messung, Analyse von sowie das Berichten über Interaktionen von Lernenden und deren Kontext mit dem Ziel das Lernen zu verstehen und zu optimieren [Co11]. Datenquellen für solche Analysen sind unter anderem Event Logs aus Lernmanagementsysteme wie Moodle. *Educational Process Mining* (EPM) bezeichnet die Analyse solcher Event Logs um z. B. Einsichten in das Lernverhalten von Studierenden zu gewinnen [SK22]. Bisherige Arbeiten analysieren meist jedoch erst am Ende eines Kurses den vollständigen Datensatz [JZR19]. Um Lehrenden und Lernenden die Vorteile des EPMs schon während einer Kursdurchführung zugänglich zu machen, braucht es eine Infrastruktur, welche die Analysen periodisch durchführt und die Ergebnisse kontinuierlich bereitstellt. Für größeren Universitäten mit mehreren 10.000 Studierenden muss eine gute Skalierung der Infrastruktur gegeben sein. Im Folgenden werden zunächst die theoretischen Grundlagen von EPM und eine geeignete Analyseinfrastruktur vorgestellt sowie die Auswahl eines Algorithmus' für die Lernpfaderkennung begründet. Abschließend wird das Dashboard, in dem die Analyseergebnisse dargestellt werden, vorgestellt und fortführende Arbeiten diskutiert.

---

[1] RWTH Aachen, lars.quakulinski@rwth-aachen.de
[2] RWTH Aachen, Lerntechnologien, {judel, schroeder}@cs.rwth-aachen.de, https://orcid.org/{0000-0002-0424-0402, 0000-0002-5178-8497}
[3] RWTH Aachen, PADS, wagner@pads.rwth-aachen.de, https://orcid.org/0000-0002-6941-037X

doi: 10.18420/delfi2023-34

2 Process Mining und Learning Analytics

Educational Process Mining (EPM) wurde vielfach erfolgreich auf Event Daten aus Lehr- und Lernsituationen, oft aus Moodle, angewandt [SK22]. Dabei werden unter anderem geplante Lernpfade mit real genommenen abgeglichen [Á16] oder das Verhalten während Moodle Quizzes analysiert [JZR19]. Als Modelle für Lernpfade werden im EPM meist Directly Follows Graphen (DFGs) oder Petri Netze verwendet [SK22]. In den bisherigen Arbeiten werden die Analysen jedoch erst nach Abschluss eines Kurses, auf den vollständigen Event Logs durchgeführt. Es gab somit keine Rückmeldungen während der Kursdurchführung, sodass Teilnehmende nicht von eventuellen Kursanpassungen profitieren. Auch Lehrende können nicht rechtzeitig intervenieren, wenn Probleme schon früher erkennbar sind. Um dies zu ermöglichen muss zunächst eine Infrastruktur für periodische Datenverarbeitungen und kontinuierliche Ergebnisbereitstellung geschaffen werden. Tools wie Celonis[4] oder Disco[5] eignen sich aufgrund ihrer kommerziellen oder Closed Source Umsetzung nicht, da die eigenen Anwendung Open Source umgesetzt werden soll.

Analyseinfrastruktur: Eine geeignete Infrastruktur stellt Excalibur LA dar. Verschiedene Systeme können Event Daten als xAPI Statements an diese schicken, sodass sie in einem Learning Record Store (LRS) speichern und mit Analytics Engines verarbeitet werden. Die Ergebnisse werden kontinuierlich über eine REST API bereitgestellt. [JS22] Für Moodle existiert bereits ein Plugin, welches Moodle Events sowie clientseitige Interaktionen in xAPI Statements überführen und verschicken kann [JSS22], welche alle für die angedachten Analysen benötigten Informationen enthalten. Ein Dashboard zur Darstellung der Ergebnisse in Moodle ist ebenfalls gegeben, muss jedoch um eine geeignete Visualisierung für die Lernpfade erweitert werden. Die Existenz dieser Tools sowie deren Erweiterbarkeit und Skalierbarkeit stellen eine gute Grundlage für periodisches EPM dar.

Streaming Process Mining: Trotz der skalierenden Infrastruktur hat EPM auf dem Event Logs aller Kurse Grenzen. Bisherige Erfahrungen an der RWTH Aachen mit mehr als 47.000 Studierenden zeigen, dass etwa 2 Millionen xAPI Statements pro Tag von Moodle erwartbar sind. Das Abrufen der Statements einer Woche dauert bereits über 13 Stunden. Die Datenmenge stellt auch für den Arbeitsspeicher eine Herausforderung dar, da in einem Semester mindestens 347,6 GB an Statements zu verarbeiten sind. Die Literatur nennt einige Techniken zum Umgang mit solchen Mengen wobei die meisten, wie z. B. Dekompositionstechniken [LFVdA18], immer noch den vollständigen Datensatz benötigen. Einzig *Streaming Process Mining* Techniken benötigen nicht die Gesamtheit an Daten [Bu22]. Hierbei wird der Event Log erst in eine abstrakte, deutlich kompaktere, Repräsentationsform, wie z. B. ein DFG [VVV18], überführt, auf dessen Basis anschließend Prozess Modelle, wie das Petri Netz, konstruiert werden können. Beim Verarbeiten neuer Events ist es ausreichend, die abstrakte Repräsentation zu aktualisieren und darauf ein neues Petri Netz zu identifizieren.

---

[4] https://www.celonis.com/, abgerufen am 18.06.2023
[5] https://fluxicon.com/disco/, abgerufen am 18.06.2023

3 Streaming Process Mining in Excalibur

Während der Fuzzy Miner simplere Modelle [Sa21], was Lesen und Interpretieren erleichtert, erzeugen kann, schnitt der Inductive Miner (IM) im Vergleich mit unter anderen dem Heuristic und Inductive Miner am besten ab [BCR18]. Die nur auf dem DFG operiende Variante des IM [VdA16] ist für Streaming Process Mining geeignet, sodass diese für Excalibur gewählt wurde. Da Analytics Engines in Python implementiert werden, wurden zunächst bestehende PM Packages evaluiert. Das Open Source Package PM4Py[6] unterstützt den Inductiver Miner auf DFGs und gibt das resultierende Modell maschinenlesbar aus, sodass es sich am besten für den Anwendungsfall eignet. Um die Darstellungen von DFG und Petri Netz im Dashboard zu ermöglichen, wird die Detektion der Lernpfade durch zwei Engines umgesetzt. Entsprechend konstruiert und speichert die erste Engine, der *DFG Discoverer*, für jeden Kurs den DFG als abstrakte Repräsentation des Event Logs eines Tages und reichert zusätzlich einen kumulierten DFG über alle bisherigen Events des jeweiligen Kurses an. Primär sollen die Lernpfade die Daten der gesamten Kursdauer widerspiegeln. Um aber auch Verhaltensänderungen zwischen verschiedenen Zeiträumen erkennen zu können, soll es möglich sein, die Lernpfade zeitlich einzuschränken. Wird später ein kleinerer Zeitraum gefiltert, können die DFGs der ausgewählten Tage verbunden und darauf ein neues Petri Netz erstellt werden. Die zweite Engine, der *LP Discoverer*, generiert aus diesem kumulierten DFG die Lernpfade in Form eines Petri Netzes.

Um einen Plattformwechsel zu vermeiden, werden DFG und Petri Netz in einem in Moodle integriertes Dashboard dargestellt. Abbildung 1 zeigt beide Visualisierungen. Über ein Toggle-Element können Nutzende selbst bestimmen, was ihnen angezeigt wird und sowohl das Zeitinterval als auch, im Falle des DFGs, die Kantengewichte filtern.

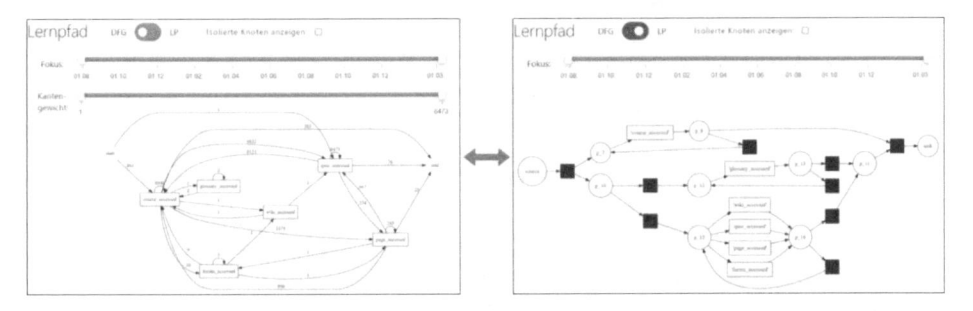

Abb. 1: Darstellung von DFG und Petri Netz sowie der Interaktionsmöglichkeit im Dashboard

Die dargestellten Modelle wurden aus Realdaten[7] eines Kurses mit 365 Teilnehmenden ermittelt. Dabei wurden die Zugriffe auf Kursinhalte, basierend auf Objekttyp und Verb, betrachtet, was zu einer übersichtlichen Darstellung führt. Im DFG (links) ist anhand der

---

[6] https://pm4py.fit.fraunhofer.de/, abgerufen am 18.06.2023
[7] Die Autoren bedanken sich bei Niels Seidel von der FernUniversität Hagen für die Aufbereitung und Bereitstellung dieser Daten.

Kantengewichte erkennbar, dass Glossar, Wiki und Forum kaum genutzt wurden, Textseiten und Quizze hingegen deutlich öfter. Da die Hauptseite des Kurses (*course_accessed*) häufig zur Navigation zwischen Kursinhalten genutzt wird, sind die hohen Werte erwartbar. Das Petri Netz (rechts) erlaubt Einsichten in die Parallelitäten der Zugriffe. Während jedes Mal der Kurs aufgerufen wird, ist zu erkennen, dass entweder das Glossar oder einer der anderen vier Objekttypen aufgerufen wurde. Dabei ist keine Navigation von diesen vier Objekttypen und dem Glossar möglich. Diese Einsichten sind noch limitiert, bereiten aber eine Grundlage für weitere Analysen und Interpretationen (siehe Abschnitt 4).

Abbildung 2 zeigt die gemittelte Laufzeit der einzelnen Analyseschritte, die auf 2,4 Millionen Statement mehrfach ausgeführt wurden. Dabei sind die ersten vier Schritte (blaue Balken) Teil der DFG und die unteren beiden (violette Balken) Teil der LP Discoverer Engine. Die horizontale Linie trennt die unteren drei Schritte ab, da diese sowohl in den Engines auch in den Endpoints ausgeführt werden um den angeforderten, zeitlich gefilterten DFG und das zugehörige Petri Netz zu konstruieren und auszuliefern. Das Gruppieren der Statements und deren Mapping auf Events brauchen die meiste Zeit. Die anschließende Konstruktion der DFGs erfolgt sehr schnell. Gemessen wurde dies für Aktivitäten, die aus Objekttyp und Verb zusammengesetzt wurden. Eine geringe Laufzeit ist speziell in den letzten drei Schritten wichtig, um den Dashboard-Nutzenden schnell die angeforderten, gefilterten Daten auszuliefern und eine gute Nutzbarkeit zu unterstützen. Die abgebildeten Messwerte wurden für die Operationen auf den DFGs aller 3000 Kurse erhoben. Im Durchschnitt dauerte die Petri Netz Konstruktion also nur 2,4 Millisekunden.

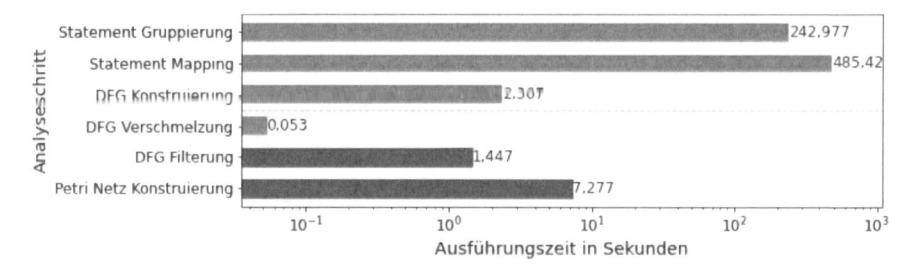

Abb. 2: Benötigte Zeit für die einzelnen Analyseschritte.

Neben der Laufzeit wurde die Qualität der resultierenden Petri Netze evaluiert. Als Aktivitäten wurden sowohl die Kombination von Objekttyp und Verb (OT-V), als auch Objektinstanz und Verb (OI-V) genutzt. Für beide Aktivitätsdefinitionen ist die Fitness mit 98,03% (OT-V) und 98% (OI-V) sehr hoch. Die DFG Variante und die optionalen Filter führen zum Verlust der perfekten Fitness [VdA16]. Die Präzision ist mit 22,69% für OT-V und 1,19% für OI-V vergleichsweise gering. Laufzeit und Modellqualität sind vielversprechend. Negativ fällt nur die Präzision bei der Verwendung von OI-V als Aktivität auf. Dem Dashboard können Ergebnisse in einer angemessenen Zeit ausgeliefert werden. Auch die zeitintensiven Analyseschritte verarbeiten große Datenmengen in nur wenigen Minuten, was für die nachts ausgeführten Analysen als angemessen angesehen wird.

4 Diskussion und weitere Arbeiten

Die umgesetzten Engines und Darstellungsmöglichkeit sind eine gute Grundlage für weitere Arbeiten. Zur Beantwortung konkreter Fragen von Lernenden und Lehrenden können fokussierte Engines entwickelt werden, die sich z. B. auf bestimmte Objekttypen konzentrieren, ähnlich den Quiz-Analysen von [JZR19]. Weitere Engines können auch die vorgeschlagene Kombination von EPM Ergebnissen mit denen anderer Analysen umsetzen. Zusätzlich können nicht nur tägliche DFGs für Kurse, sondern auch für Studierende jeden Kurses erstellt werden. Dies eröffnet das Potential, Studierenden ihren eigenen Pfad aufzuzeigen und individuelle Rückmeldungen zu geben. Manche Rückmeldungen, wie z. B. das Einhalten angedachter Lernpfade, wie in [Á16], erfordern zudem initialen Input durch Lehrende. Die Anwendung von *Streaming Conformance Checking* ermöglicht Fitness und Präzision ebenfalls periodisch zu bestimmen und kontinuierlich im Dashboard anzuzeigen. Dies schafft mehr Transparenz und erlaubt die dynamische Filterung des DFGs nach den häufigsten Aktivitäten und Pfaden. Dies kann zwar bereits mit der aktuellen Implementierung realisiert werden, allerdings kann durch die fehlenden Fitnesswerte die Qualität der Modelle nicht eingeschätzt werden. Korrektes und verständliches Feedback könnte die Akzeptanz von EPM erhöhen. Lernenden die Vorteile des EPM zu vermitteln könnte ihre Bereitschaft, der notwendigen pseudonymen Datensammlung zuzustimmen, erhöhen. Die Engines sind so umgesetzt, dass xAPI Statements beliebiger Plattformen analysiert werden können. Studienverlaufsdaten wie z. B. die Belegungsreihenfolge von Modulen, wie in [Wa23], ebenfalls mit dem IM, skizziert, können untersucht werden. Einzig die DFG Discoverer Engine muss dahingehend angepasst werden, dass sie nach Studiengang oder Kohorte statt Kurs gruppiert.

5 Zusammenfassung

Periodisches Educational Process Mining (EPM), z. B. zur Erkennung von Lernpfaden, kann Einsichten in und Feedback zum Lernverhalten der Studierenden bieten. Während viele Arbeiten Anwendungsfälle und Vorteile von EPM durch die Analyse von Event Logs nach Abschluss eines Kurses demonstrieren, wurden in dieser Arbeit eine Möglichkeit zur Bereitstellung von Ergebnissen noch während der Kursdurchführung vorgestellt. Analytics Engines für die Learning Analytics Infrastruktur Excalibur LA analysieren xAPI Statements aus Moodle und erzeugen Directly Follows Graphen sowie Petri Netze. Zur Verarbeitung großer Datenmengen in angemessener Zeit, werden Techniken des Streaming Process Minings angewandt. Die Laufzeit der Analysen ist gut und auch die Operationen, die z. B. beim zeitlichen Filtern der Ergebnisse ausgeführt werden, sind performant. Zwar kann keine perfekte Fitness der Ergebnisse mehr garantiert werden, jedoch sind 98% im gegebenen Kontext ein guter Wert. Die geringe Präzision wiederum muss verbessert werden. Die Analyse von Realdaten zeigt, dass die Visualisierungen von DFGs und Petri Netzen abhängig von der Wahl der Aktivitätserstellung schnell komplex werden und damit schwierig zu lesen sind. Hier könnte ein Fokus auf ausgewählte Aktivitäten mehr Nutzen bringen. Die vorgestellten Engines sind leicht für solche Spezialisierungen anpassbar und auf die Analysen von Logs anderer Plattformen übertragbar. Zusätzlich können weitere Engines geschrieben und in die vorgestellte Infrastruktur integriert werden, welche Ergebnisse des EPMs und anderer Analysen zusammenführt um Lehrenden und Lernenden weitere Rückmeldungen zu geben.

Literaturverzeichnis

[BCR18] Bogarín, A.; Cerezo, R.; Romero, C.: Discovering learning processes using Inductive Miner: A case study with Learning Management Systems (LMSs). Psicothema, (30.3):322–329, 2018.

[Bu22] Burattin, A.: Streaming process mining. Process Mining Handbook, 349, 2022.

[Co11] Conole, G. et al.: Proceedings of the 1st International Conference on Learning Analytics and Knowledge. 2011.

[JS22] Judel, S.; Schroeder, U.: EXCALIBUR LA - An Extendable and Scalable Infrastructure Build for Learning Analytics. In: 2022 International Conference on Advanced Learning Technologies (ICALT). IEEE, S. 155–157, 2022.

[JSS22] Judel, S.; Schnell, E.; Schroeder, U.: Performantes xAPI Logging in Moodle. In: 20. Fachtagung Bildungstechnologien (DELFI), S. 159–164, 2022.

[JZR19] Juhaňák, L.; Zounek, J.; Rohlíková, L.: Using process mining to analyze students' quiz-taking behavior patterns in a learning management system. Computers in Human Behavior, 92:496–506, 2019.

[LFV18] Leemans, S.; Fahland, D.; Van der Aalst, W.: Scalable process discovery and conformance checking. Software & Systems Modeling, 17:599–631, 2018.

[Sa21] Saint, J. et al: Using process mining to analyse self-regulated learning: a systematic analysis of four algorithms. In: LAK21: 11th International Learning Analytics and Knowledge Conference. ACM, S. 333–343, 2021.

[SK22] Sypsas, A.; Kalles, D.: Reviewing Process Mining Applications and Techniques in Education. Artificial Intelligence & Applications, 13(1):83–102, 2022.

[VdA16] Van der Aalst, W.: Process Mining: Data Science in Action. Springer, 2016.

[VVV18] van Zelst, S.; van Dongen, B.; van der Aalst, W.: Event Stream-Based Process Discovery using Abstract Representations. Knowledge and Information Systems, 54(2):407–435, 2018.

[Wa23] Wagner, M. et a.: A Combined Approach of Process Mining and Rule-Based AI for Study Planning and Monitoring in Higher Education. In (Montali, M.; Senderovich, A.; Weidlich, M., Hrsg.): Process Mining Workshops, S. 513–525. Springer, 2023.

[Á16] Álvarez, P. et al.: Alignment of teacher's plan and students' use of LMS resources. Analysis of Moodle logs. In: 2016 15th International Conference on Information Technology Based Higher Education and Training (ITHET). S. 1–8, 2016.

Energy Consumption of AI in Education: A Case Study

Marlene Bültemann[1], Nathalie Rzepka[1], Dennis Junger [2], Katharina Simbeck[1] and Hans-Georg Müller[3]

Abstract: Although the utilization of AI in education has grown considerably in the last decade, its environmental impact has been disregarded thus far. In this paper, we examine the energy consumption of Artificial Intelligence (AI) in education, which is employed, for instance, in adaptive learning. We measured the energy requirements of four AI implementations used on the student learning platform orthografietrainer.net. We found that two of the implementations have notably low energy and CPU demands in comparison to the baseline, while in two other implementations, these parameters are significantly higher. We conclude that more attention should be paid to whether the comparable performance of AI in education can be achieved with lower energy consumption.

Keywords: Green IT, Artificial Intelligence in Education, Sustainable Learning Analytics

1 Introduction

The significance of sustainability within the Information and Communication Technology (ICT) industry has increased in recent years. The sector was responsible for 9% of the world's energy consumption in 2018, and this figure is estimated to rise to 20% by 2025 [MGC21]. The reason for this increase is the persistent expansion of the ICT industry which outpaces growth in other sectors [BE18]. Therefore, the amount of processed data as well as the number of (intelligent) applications grows and results in more energy that is needed to run these. For instance, the computing power to train the largest deep learning models has increased by the factor of 300,000 in six years [Be21].

The number of applications using machine learning in education is rising sharply as well [RV20]. To this point, only the learning benefits have been taken into consideration, which include variables e.g., learning success, dropout rate, etc. Several studies have focused on the energy consumption of the application of AI in general, revealing large resource demands [FLM22, SGM19]. However, we did not find any that covered the use of energy of AI in education in particular. We aim to fill this gap by measuring the use of energy in prediction models that are applied on the AI-based adaptive learning platform

---

[1] University of Applied Sciences Berlin, Computing and Society, Wilhelminenhofstraße 75A, 12459 Berlin, Germany, marlene.bueltemann@student.htw-berlin.de, {rzepka, simbeck}@htw-berlin.de
[2] University of Applied Sciences Berlin, Industrial Environmental Informatics Unit, Wilhelminenhofstraße 75A, 12459 Berlin, Germany, dennis.junger@htw-berlin.de
[3] Department of German Studies, University of Potsdam, Am neuen Palais 10, 14469 Potsdam, Germany, hans-georg.mueller@uni-potsdam.de

orthografietrainer.net by using a measurement setup as proposed by [JWK22], which is described in detail in section 3. We evaluate different options for transforming a digital learning platform into an adaptive learning platform by using machine learning models and interventions. The reflections concerning energy consumption are secondary to the learning impact; however, it is crucial to discuss the trade-off between learning benefits and the use of energy. Given the same learning benefit, the lower energy-consuming technology should be preferred.

Therefore, our research question is: By how much does the local resource utilization differ across different AI models used on a learning platform?

The structure of this paper is organized into several sections. Firstly, we will present some background information. After, we will describe the platform and test setup, followed by an analysis of our results and a discussion.

2 Background

Dick et al. define sustainable software as "software whose direct and indirect negative impact on economy, society, human beings, and the environment resulting from development, deployment, and usage of the software is minimal and/or has a positive effect on sustainable development" [DNK].

When measuring the actual consumption of energy in software, one can use a software-based or hardware-based approach. A software-based approach uses software tools to measure energy consumption while software is executed. Since the consumption is only estimated, inaccuracies might occur. On the other hand, a hardware-based measurement uses physical energy meters that are connected to PC hardware. This approach is more expensive but provides more accurate results [MGC21].

An adaptive learning environment is defined as a learning environment that uses AI to adapt to a user's unique level of skills in real-time to support the learning process using educational data [Me19].

3 Methodology

Orthografietrainer.net, the platform we analyze, is a learning platform for German grammar and spelling exercises, addressing students from 5th grade. Ever since it has been established in 2008, the platform has been accessed by more than 1.2 million users and more than 12 million tasks have been completed. Elements of gamification are used and tasks that were answered incorrectly are asked again[4]. Four different AI models (decision tree, logistic regression, support vector machine (SVM), and multilayer perceptron (MLP)

---

[4] https://orthografietrainer.net/

have been trained on datasets that have been recorded in 2020 and applied in an experiment on the platform for four months to predict the probability of solving a task correctly [Rze23]. The models perform differently with regard to accuracy and precision as shown in Table 1, suggesting that decision tree and MLP reveal marginally higher results than Logistic Regression and SVM.

	DT	LR	SVM	MLP
Accuracy (in %)	97.04	96.94	96.62	97.09
Precision (in %)	97.75	97.76	97.38	97.97

Table 1 Model performance (DT: Decision Tree, LR: Logistic Regression)

To measure energy consumption accurately, we use a measurement protocol described by [JWK22]. Before every measurement, the computer is rebooted to minimize the number of programs running in the background or using local storage. The setup measurement consists of a System Under Test and an energy data aggregator is started as well as the Workload Generator, resource management, and energy data collection. In addition, a Network Time Protocol server is set up to provide an accurate time for the measurement environment and finally assigns the measurement data in the evaluation, while the energy data aggregator queries and logs the energy data via Simple Network Management Protocol. To analyze the results, the OSCAR tool (Open Source Software Consumption Analysis and Reporting) is being accessed by the control and evaluation station. To avoid measurement errors and inaccuracies due to user interaction, a script is run to perform tasks and measurements.

Because of the model requirements, we use two different Python versions: version 3.7 for the decision tree, logistic regression, and SVM and version 3.10 for the MLP. Since calling the SVM requires more time than other models, we use a separate measuring time for this model (600 seconds for the model and 60 seconds for cool down), while all other models are measured in 120 seconds and 60 seconds for cool down. The measurements are run 30 times and the average is calculated over these values [JWK22]. We compare our measurements to baseline measurements (new set-up computer with nothing but Windows installed) and idle mode (having all software requirements for the measurements installed) measurements. We utilize a t-test as a statistical tool to analyze our results in comparison to the baseline.

4 Results

We find differences to baseline and idle with regards to CPU intensity and consumption of electric energy in Watt hours (Wh) and power in Watt.

In Table 2, the results for baseline and idle measurements are presented. One can see that the differences across the parameters displayed are minor which suggests that the installed software does not cause a large additional load.

	BL 120 + 60	Idle 120 + 60	BL 600 + 60	Idle 600 + 60
Mean el. power in W	32.47	32.43	32.29	32.29
Mean el. work in Wh	1.08	1.09	5.38	5.38
Average CPU load	2.26%	1.71%	1.33%	1.08%

Tab. 2: Baseline and Idle Measurements (BL: Baseline)

Table 3 presents the results of our measurement runs. The average power measurements of decision tree, logistic regression, and MLP is between 32.32W and 33.48W, showing only a slight change to the baseline value of 32.47W and the idle time measurement of 32.43W. On the other hand, the SVM measurement has a power demand of 42.4W, which is a significant increase from the measurement of 32.39W in both the baseline and idle run. We can also see that the short-running measurements have a low electric work in Watt hours (Wh) compared to baseline and idle measurements, only the MLP has slightly higher values. On the other hand, the SVM measurement results in relatively higher values as the electric work increases by 156,04% in comparison to the baseline and 154,61% in comparison to the idle measurement.

Looking at the CPU utilization, we see that it moves between 2.32% in the decision tree and 2.37% in the logistic regression, showing only a slight increase to baseline and idle measurements that is not statistically significant. We found a CPU load of 5.5% in the MLP while the SVM had a higher average CPU usage of 13.14%, making this highly statistically significant compared to the baseline values.

	Measurement Results	t-Test	Delta % baseline	Delta % idle
Mean el. power in W DT	32.36	2.22 (*)	-0.34%	-0.22%
Mean el. work in Wh DT	1.09	-	0.93%	0.00%
Av. CPU load DT	2.32%	-0.05 (n.s.)	2.65%	35.67%
Mean el. power in W LR	32.32	1.16 (n.s.)	-0.44%	-0.32%
Mean el. work in Wh LR	1.09	-	0.93%	0.00%
Av. CPU load LR	2.37%	-0.54 (n.s.)	4.87%	38.60%
Mean el. power in W MLP	33.48	-11.41 (***)	3.11%	3.23%

	Measurement Results	t-Test	Delta % baseline	Delta % idle
Mean el. work in Wh MLP	1.15	-	6.48%	5.50%
Av. CPU load MLP	5.50%	-15.47 (***)	143.36%	221.64%
Mean el. power in W SVM	42.40	-135.15 (***)	31.14%	31.18%
Mean el. work in Wh SVM	7.07	-	156.04%	154.61%
Av. CPU load SVM	13.14%	-135.12 (***)	522.44%	705.54%

Tab. 3: Measurement Results (DT: Decision Tree, LR: Logistic Regression; ***: highly significant result, **: moderately significant result, *: marginally significant result, n.s.: not significant)

5 Discussion

Our results show differences between the models, suggesting that the choice of a specific model does have an impact on local energy and system requirements. While decision tree and logistic regression hardly use more energy than the baseline, we found that the increase of using energy and CPU utilization in the MLP and SVM is highly significant. This correlates with the general findings of [SGM19], who look at the energy consumption of training and developing different Natural Language Processing algorithms and find that power use and training time differs across models. However, we measure other models than these researchers used and look at implementations of AI in education in particular.

We can only measure the local energy consumption since we do not have access to data centers. We only consider the energy consumed while running the software and do not take manufacturing emissions into account. Also, using different Python versions might influence the results.

We run the measurements in a standard setup on a reset computer using 30 iterations including cool-down time to get the best possible results. Nevertheless, we cannot exclude measurement errors due to unforeseen background activities. As this is a standard setup that does not apply to every user of this application, we assume that the accurate values vary between users. Nevertheless, they provide strong implications on which data model is rather a resource efficient or intensive.

To verify the results, we suggest rerunning the experiment with either a different dataset and/or a different measurement setup.

6 Conclusion

Our study suggests that decision tree and logistic regression models in the implementation of AI in education have the lowest impact in terms of energy and system requirements. Although the differences seem rather small, they do have an impact on an application frequently used by many people. To address the ICT sector's emissions reduction requirements and contribute to climate change mitigation efforts, implementing energy-conscious AI technology should be a priority on educational platforms. However, uncertainties remain. Due to the scarcity of previous works in this area, this case study should be rerun to confirm the results.

Overall, we see that the choice of a specific algorithm has an impact on the resources consumed. Therefore, we encourage developers to not only consider accuracy and performance but also the environmental impact of software.

Literaturverzeichnis

[BE18] Belkhir, L.; Elmeligi, A.: Assessing ICT global emissions footprint: Trends to 2040 & recommendations. Journal of cleaner production 177, pp. 448–463, 2018.

[Be21] Bender, E. et al.: On the Dangers of Stochastic Parrots: Proceedings of the 2021 ACM 2021, pp. 610–623, 2021.

[DNK] Dick, M.; Naumann, S.; Kuhn, N.: A Model and Selected Instances of Green and Sustainable Software. In (Berleur, J.; Hercheui, M. D.; Hilty, L. M. Eds.): What Kind of Information Society? Governance, Virtuality, Surveillance, Sustainability, Resilience. Springer Berlin Heidelberg, Berlin, Heidelberg, pp. 248–259, 2010.

[FLM22] Frey, N. C. et al.: Benchmarking Resource Usage for Efficient Distributed Deep Learning: 2022 IEEE High Performance Extreme Computing Conference (HPEC). IEEE, pp. 1–8, 2022 - 2022

[JWK22] Junger, D.; Wohlgemuth, V.; Kammer, E.: Conception and test of a measuring station for the analysis of the resource and energy consumption of material flow-oriented environmental management information systems (EMIS). In (Wohlgemuth, V. et al. Eds.): EnviroInfo 2022. Gesellschaft für Informatik e.V, Bonn, p. 211, 2022.

[Me19] Meier, C.: KI-basierte, adaptive Lernumgebungen, 2019.

[MGC21] Mancebo, J.; García, F.; Calero, C.: A process for analysing the energy efficiency of software. Information and Software Technology 134, p. 106560, 2021.

[RV20] Romero, C.; Ventura, S.: Educational data mining and learning analytics: An updated survey. WIREs Data Mining and Knowledge Discovery 3/10, 2020.

[Rze23] Rzepka, N.: Transforming First Language Learning Platforms towards Adaptivity and Fairness: Models, Interventions and Architecture [Unpublished doctoral dissertation]. Humboldt-Universität zu Berlin, 2023.

[SGM19] Strubell, E.; Ganesh, A.; McCallum, A.: Energy and Policy Considerations for Deep Learning in NLP. arXiv, 2019.

Supporting Individualized Study Paths Using an Interactive Study Planning Tool

Sven Judel [1], Rene Roepke [1], Maximilian Azendorf[2] and Ulrik Schroeder [1]

Abstract: In addition to various subject-related challenges, students face diverse organizational challenges, including the planning of their own study path while considering individual and organizational circumstances or constraints. While examination regulations usually provide an exemplary study plan, it may only fit as long as no adjustments have to be made. If students fail exams or postpone modules, an individual study plan is needed to keep track of the own study path. With growing enrolment numbers and increasing heterogeneity of study profiles and paths, staff resources in student counselling or mentoring can only provide limited support. As such, this paper presents an interactive, web-based study planning tool, which enables students to plan their individual path using a visual representation of subject areas and modules, while also highlighting module requirements and dependencies. A first evaluation provides positive feedback, a good user experience, but also feature suggestions for further development.

Keywords: Interactive Study Planning, Study Paths, Assistance, User Experience

1 Introduction

When starting at a university in Germany, students usually choose a study program and get presented with a set of compulsory and elective modules to complete over the duration of their studies. Encapsulated in the examination regulations with an accompanied module handbook, students are recommended to follow an exemplary study plan outlining which modules to start with and how to successfully complete a study program in order to get a degree. While this exemplary plan and its adaptations all try to outline suitable paths through the study program, they usually do not account for any kind of deviation. If students fail exams or postpone modules, an individual study plan is needed to keep track of the own study path. Especially with the limitations introduced by module cycles (i.e. modules which are offered only once a year), order requirements (i.e. when module A needs to be passed before module B) or expected workload, study planning can become a challenge as soon as students diverge from the recommended plan. Alongside subject-related challenges, the organizational challenge of planning their own studies may burden students and hinder study success. The question arises of how students can be supported in planning and reflecting on their study paths.

---

[1] RWTH Aachen University, Learning Technologies, {judel, roepke, schroeder}@cs.rwth-aachen.de, https://orcid.org/{0000-0002-0424-0402, 0000-0003-0250-8521, 0000-0002-5178-8497}
[2] RWTH Aachen, maximilian.azendorf@rwth-aachen.de

doi: 10.18420/delfi2023-36

With growing enrolment numbers and increasing heterogeneity of study profiles and paths, staff resources in student counselling or mentoring can only provide so much support, as time and resources are limited. Meanwhile, students may utilize tools and provided information to plan and reorganize their studies as they see fit. Unfortunately, this approach is error-prone as students can make mistakes, e.g., if they do not consider certain module dependencies when planning their upcoming semesters and cannot take the final exam due to missing requirements. As a solution to both, a digital tool supporting individualized study planning could be considered.

This paper presents an interactive, web-based study planning tool for students in university. The tool enables students to create their individual plan for a study program using a visual representation of the study program's subject areas and modules, while also highlighting module requirements and dependencies. It provides feedback on invalid plans as well as warnings if module dependencies and requirements are violated. In a first user evaluation of the prototype, participants responded with positive feedback, but also feature suggestions for further development.

2   Related Work

When it comes to study plans included in examination regulations, often tabular depictions or list structures are used to visualize an exemplary path towards completing a study program. Figure Fig. 1 shows an excerpt of the sample study plan for a German Bachelor program in Computer Science (CS). It demonstrates that depicting flexibility might result in a more complex plan which is harder to read and understand. The different arrows (blue or red, solid or dashed line) show possible adjustments to the order in which modules can be completed but need a lengthy explanation to be understood the first time. Despite its complexity, the plan still fails to present relevant information on module requirements (e.g., *Proseminar* has to be passed before a student is allowed to take a *Seminar*) or module cycles. This information is often provided in additional documents (e.g., module handbooks), where students have to make sure to use the correct version suitable to their study program's examination regulations. All this specific information gathering and long-term maintenance puts a lot of effort on the students and could instead be supported by a comprehensive tool. Further, given its PDF-format, students cannot use this plan directly to adapt it to their needs but have to use other tools to recreate and adjust the plan (e.g., spreadsheet software). Here, the potential for interactive tool support visualizing module dependencies but also allowing users to adapt the plan to their individual circumstances has not been explored.

To support students in study planning as well as dealing with various organizational issues in their studies, universities often provide academic advisory services or (peer) mentoring systems. As such, counselling sessions, office hours or email services are offered to students for asking questions and getting individual support. With increasing enrolment numbers and limiting personnel, technology is introduced to provide scalable services, e.g., through the use of intelligent mentoring system [KSI19] or chatbots [Kl20]. Furthermore, digital study assistants [Ka21] and recommender systems [We22, Ha22, BRH14] have been introduced to guide students' module choices or the use of learning materials. Related work shows the potential of educational technology supporting these tasks, however, interactive tool support for individual study path planning compared to inflexible exemplary plans in examination regulations has not been presented.

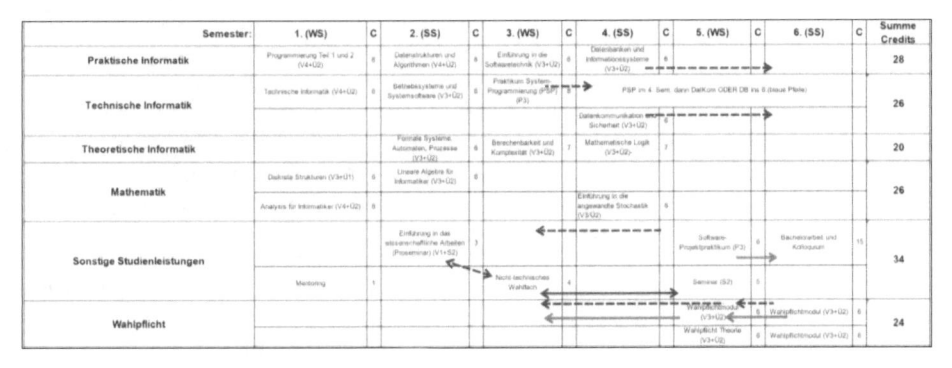

Semester:	1. (WS)	C	2. (SS)	C	3. (WS)	C	4. (SS)	C	5. (WS)	C	6. (SS)	C	Summe Credits
Praktische Informatik	Programmierung Teil 1 und 2 (V4+Ü2)	8	Datenstrukturen und Algorithmen (V4+Ü2)	8	Einführung in die Softwaretechnik (V3+Ü2)	6	Datenbanken und Informationssysteme (V3+Ü2)	6					28
Technische Informatik			Technische Informatik (V4+Ü2)	8	Betriebssysteme und Systemsoftware (V3+Ü2)	6	Praktikum Systemprogrammierung (PSP) (P3)	6	FSP im 4. Sem. dann DatKom ODER DB im 6 (neue Plans)	6			26
									Datenkommunikation und Sicherheit (V3+Ü2)	6			
Theoretische Informatik					Formale Systeme, Automaten, Prozesse (V3+Ü2)	8	Berechenbarkeit und Komplexität (V3+Ü2)	7	Mathematische Logik (V3+Ü2)	7			20
Mathematik	Diskrete Strukturen (V3+Ü1)	6	Lineare Algebra für Informatiker (V3+Ü2)	8			Einführung in die angewandte Stochastik (V3+Ü2)	6					26
	Analysis für Informatiker (V4+Ü2)	6											
Sonstige Studienleistungen			Einführung in das wissenschaftliche Arbeiten (Proseminar) (V1+S2)	3					Software-Projektpraktikum (P3)	6	Bachelorarbeit und Kolloquium	15	34
							Nicht technisches Wahlfach	4					
	Mentoring	1							Seminar (S2)	5			
Wahlpflicht									Wahlpflichtmodul (V3+Ü2)	6	Wahlpflichtmodul (V3+Ü2)	6	24
									Wahlpflicht Theorie (V3+Ü2)	6	Wahlpflichtmodul (V3+Ü2)	6	

Fig. 1: Sample Study Program Plan

3 Requirements for an Interactive Study Planning Tool

First, some general requirements for the tool were gathered and evaluated with a group of seven students, as they are the primary target group of an interactive study planning tool. In general, the tool should be provided as a web application for easy access and it should integrate into the university's user account system, i.e. authentication via single sign-on. It should store individual study plans as well as the recommended exemplary plan from the examination regulations. The interactivity should be intuitive and a plan's design linked to the tabular form known by most students. Moving modules with the mouse (referring to drag and drop) was directly suggested by students for intuitive ways to rearrange a plan. Besides moving modules between semesters, the tool should allow to add more semesters to the plan if needed.

The tool should be able to manage multiple study plans per student, e.g., when considering to pursue their Master's at the same university. Further, students of combinatorial study programs (e.g., teacher training) need to coordinate individual plans for multiple subjects. Thus, the tool should support to manage multiple concurrent plans and adjust them individually while also tracking some overall reports, e.g., number of credits per semester. Since some study programs have options of specialization (e.g., choosing application areas or elective minors), the tool should also provide support in the selection as well as visualization of options in the planning process. Finally, the tool should visualize a plan's progress, i.e. passed modules should be marked as such and failed or postponed ones should automatically be moved to the next possible semester.

4 Design and Implementation

Most of the tool's functionality is included in the frontend. A database persists the students' plans which can be retrieved via a backend, also taking care of the account management. To ease the development of the powerful frontend and ensure good maintainability, it was decided to use a popular frontend framework. From the most popular ones, Angular was chosen due to its flexibility, high performance and large community. Due to its limited functionality, no special requirements were set on the backend technology. To use the same programming language, Node.js was chosen. More requirements were given for the database. As study plans and paths are quire flexible, a relational database with preset columns was not suitable, and instead, a document-oriented database should be used. Here, MongoDB is the best option, as it performs good on big and often changing data while also allowing to set indices to speed up queries [So21].

The design of the tool aimed at capturing the look of the exemplary plans known by the students. As such, it also uses a tabular form and shows the different modules sorted into their respective module areas and recommended semesters based on the exemplary plan (see Fig. 2). But instead of looking flat and static, modules are displayed in a way that transmits the option to interact with and move them. Working with colors presents an intuitive style communicating what can be done. For example, the first two semesters in Fig. 2 are depicted using grey scale colors as they are in the past and modules cannot be moved there anymore. Current or future semester display modules in various colors, highlighting different module areas of the study program. This way, study progress as well as not yet completed parts of the study plan can be distinguished.

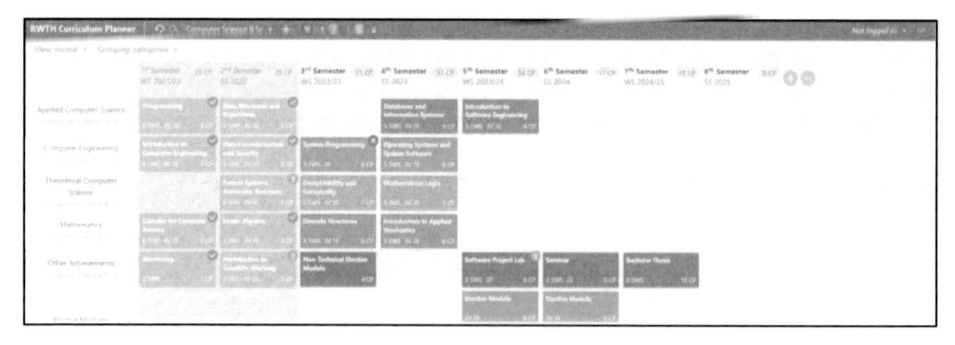

Fig. 2: Cropped screenshot of the interactive study planning tool showing an individual study plan for a Bachelor in Computer Science, first started in the winter semester 2021/22.

To further visualize study progress, green check marks on past modules indicate successful completion while orange question mark icons indicate missing information on the module status. When a student provides the missing information, a module is either completed or moved to the next possible semester while considering module cycle information. To keep track, failed courses are still shown in the related semester but hidden by default.

Two types of indicators are used to display module dependencies: (1) *recommendations* include suggestions to take a module before another one as, e.g., prior knowledge and skills might be recommended but not required, while (2) *requirements* present hard conditions that have to be fulfilled before taking a module. Upon mouse-over on a module, all module recommendations and requirements are depicted using arrows to linked modules. To provide feedback in the planning process, violations are depicted by either an orange exclamation mark icon (for recommendations) or a red cross mark icon (for requirements) as shown for Software Project Lab and System Programming in Fig. 2. Further, all reported violations can be reviewed by a mouse-over on the icons or clicking on the icons in the header tool bar.

5 Evaluation Setup

To evaluate the first version of the interactive study planning tool, with the aim to gather first user feedback and quantify its user experience, we conducted a user study with 12 CS students. After a brief introduction, the participants were first asked to complete two open tasks using the interactive study planning tool:

1. A persona of a CS student in their third semester was described for whom the participants had to create a suitable, adapted study plan while considering the student's study history and a reasonable workload.
2. The participants were asked to model their own studies as well as their future study plans (considering both Bachelor and a consecutive Master study program).

During both tasks, the participants were asked to voice their thoughts, opinions and question according to the think-aloud method. Furthermore, silent observation and screen and voice recording were used to gather user feedback. After completing the tasks, participants were asked to fill out the User Experience Questionnaire[3] (UEQ), in order to quantify the perceived attractiveness as well as pragmatic and hedonic qualities of the experience with the tool.

6 Discussion of Results and Future Work

Overall, the idea of providing an interactive, visual representation of a study plan received good feedback: requirement violations are reported, module cycles respected when moving modules to other semesters and the estimated workload based on credits per semester is displayed. These features enable students to plan their course of study on their own without requiring additional staff resources in student counselling or mentoring. Instead, these resources can be used to help students with more in-depth issues.

---

[3] https://www.ueq-online.org/, last accessed on 2023-04-02

During the evaluation, minor bugs were detected, that were immediately fixed after the sessions. More noticeable is that some participants had issues selecting the correct year that the course of study was started in task 1, as the winter semester spans beyond New Year's Eve. One participant selected the later year while still being able to fulfill the given task successfully. In terms of user experience feedback, participants reported that they would prefer a list of available elective modules to select from, rather than adding names manually. Besides that, the user experience was perceived as good and the UEQ shows very good results, as both *Attractiveness* and *Pragmatic Quality* received values above 2 and the *Hedonic Quality* a value of 1,45 (all on a scale between -3/worst and 3/best).

Furthermore, a lot of feature suggestions could be collected during the evaluation. Although undo and redo buttons were given, one participant wished for an option to reset the plan to the exemplary one, allowing to start over. Another request was to select multiple modules at once to move them simultaneously. Finally, many participants wished for an automatic planning option, based on some input by them, including past performance, a maximum number of credits per semester and even the desire to align their plan to the plans of their peers.

As for future work, we consider the suggested features and improvements for development and plan on evaluating the tool in both more iterative user evaluation to validate the tool's fit to users' requirements as well as summative evaluation in the field, measuring its acceptance, usage and influence on study progress and success. The ease of creation and management of study plans will be considered to include more study programs and keep their plans up-to-date.

Bibliography

[BRH14] Bittner, P., Ritter, C.; Hildmann, T.: Get Your Study Plan. In: INFORMATIK 2014. Bonn, pp. 1861-1872, 2014.

[Ha22] Hagemann, N.: Navigating Academia – Recommender Systems for Module Exploration. Doctoral dissertation, University College Dublin, 2022.

[Ka21] Karrenbauer, C. et al.: Individual Digital Study Assistant for Higher Education Institutions: Status Quo Analysis and Further Research Agenda. In: Innovation Through Information Systems: Volume III, Springer, Cham, pp. 108-124, 2021.

[KSI19] Kravčík, M.; Schmid, K.; Igel, C.: Towards requirements for intelligent mentoring systems. In: ABIS 2019. ACM Press, pp. 19-21, 2019.

[Kl20] Klamma, R. et al.: Scaling Mentoring Support with Distributed Artificial Intelligence. In: Intelligent Tutoring Systems. Springer, Cham, pp. 38-44, 2020.

[So21] SocialCompare: NoSQL Document Database comparison. https://socialcompare.com/en/comparison/nosql-databases-solution-cassandra-mongodb-couchdb, 02.04.2023

[We22] Weber, F. et al.: A Web-Based Recommendation System for Higher Education: SIDDATA. Emerging Technologies in Learning, 17(22), pp. 246-254, 2022.

Towards a Creativity Support Tool for Facilitating Students' Creative Thinking on Writing Tasks

Swathi Krishnaraja[1], Thiemo Wambsganss[2], Paola Mejia[3] and Niels Pinkwart[4]

Abstract: Creative thinking is one of the key skills of human intelligence that leads to the generation of valuable and novel ideas. It is also considered essential for developing students' capabilities and their cognition. While recent advances in artificial intelligence and machine learning technologies have been shown to promote critical thinking, learner interfaces that support the 'creative thinking' of students are scarce. In this work, we present a design system for facilitating students' creative writing abilities. We follow a learner-centered design methodology, and evaluate the design system functionally, visually, and for accessibility, with a group of twelve students as representative users. The results show that designing alongside the target audience helps to rapidly identify user needs, individual preferences, and diverse viewpoints, and shows that the designed system performs better in all tested aspects including learner satisfaction, ownership, and self-efficacy.

Keywords: Creative Thinking, Educational Technology, Adaptive Writing Support

1 Introduction

Creative thinking is an innate ability that is shown to have a positive influence on students' academic performances and their personal development. This way of thinking lets the student engage in a thought process that allows them to explore distinct ideas in an unconventional way. According to Torrance [To72], four main components are essential for creative behavior: fluency (the total number of relevant ideas generated); flexibility (the number of different categories of ideas); originality (the rarity of the ideas generated); and elaboration (the amount of detail in the ideas). In this rapidly evolving landscape of technology-enhanced learning, teaching methods have either been directly/indirectly adapted from conventional pedagogy into the technological pedagogical environment. In this transition, the importance to promote creative thinking skills has been disoriented. However, a few learner interfaces [WJL22, Fr19] retain the importance of promoting creative thinking skills in combination with other skills such as domain knowledge. However, previous research [Fr19] has shown us that transferring conventional methods into a technological environment does not render the same educational benefits. Especially, technological environments struggle, to react promptly to learners'

---

[1] Humboldt University of Berlin, Department of Computer Science, swathi.krishnaraja@hu-berlin.de
[2] Swiss Federal Institute of Technology in Lausanne, thiemo.wambsganss@epfl.ch
[3] Swiss Federal Institute of Technology in Lausanne, paola.mejia@epfl.ch
[4] Humboldt University of Berlin, Department of Computer Science, pinkwart@hu-berlin.de

interactions. Nevertheless, research efforts are currently taking place to understand the most-valued components in creativity support tools.

In this paper, we aim to address this gap, by designing a creativity support intervention together with students following a learner-centered design. We present a holistic design cycle including the design thinking methodologies used in our study. To this end, we first conducted design interviews with a representative population of students and set up two different design systems with the same functionalities but with a different user interface design (i.e. design components, informational components, and navigational components). We used the two design prototypes to conduct a within-subject experimental study, in which we investigated what influence they have on user experience, creative performance, and immersion.

2   Related Work

Recent research has shown to closely investigate the different aspects (such as user experience, immersion, and performance ratio) of digital technological environments [Pa22]. An experiment conducted by Palani et al. [Pa22] with creativity practitioners revealed that the most valued components of a creativity support tool (CST) are the CST's features and functionalities, performance, interface, and user experience. Furthermore, Hillmayr et al. [Hi20] highlights how digital tools could impact learning and how different methods of representation creates an educational impact. Several design principles and heuristics are followed in CST research showing the importance of building effective design solutions. Resnick et al. [Re05] proposed design principles that align with 'low thresholds, high ceilings, and wide walls'; support many paths and many styles; support collaboration; support open interchange; and make it as simple as possible and choosing the black boxes of explorability carefully. Shneiderman [Sh07] proposed similar design recommendations that focus on supporting exploration, and collaboration, and includes low thresholds, high ceiling, and wide walls. In a more recent work [WJL22], it is reported that technology-enhanced learning could benefit students' creativity positively. At the same time, the authors also point out that there have been no or few studies that explored the connection between technological capabilities and their impact on students' creativity, and learning performances [OH19]. These prior works led us to investigate different representations of creative writing support tools.

3   Design Process of the Creativity Support Tool for Writing

Following a learner-centered design process, we designed and implemented our adaptive support tool capable of supporting students' creative writing. We describe the design process involved.

(i) *Deriving Requirements from Literature.* We searched the literature in the field of educational technology (EdTech), human-computer interaction (HCI), and creativity-supporting nterventions. The keywords used were: creativity AND EdTech, creativity AND HCI, creativity AND support intervention. The initial search criteria led us to 123 papers from the following databases: Google Scholar, ACM digital library, ScienceDirect, and Elsevier, which were then filtered based on their relevance to our current research and their quality. During the final scan, we included 24 papers with the following inclusion criteria: papers that include (i) creativity theories, (ii) conventional methods for creativity assessment (e.g. creativity support index), (iii) design principles for creativity support tools, and (iv) successful implementations of learning support interventions. Further screening was conducted based on the relevance to education (educational tools), language (English), and accessibility (open access or accessible via institution). We then collected the literature issues and formed the basis for literature-driven design requirements (see figure 1) for our design system.

(ii) *Deriving Requirements from Representative Sample of Learners.* We followed a learner-centered design approach and conducted twelve semi-structured interviews with a representative sample of students (university students who could benefit from our educational tool) to obtain an initial understanding of the requirements. Each interview lasted for an average of 29.7 minutes (SD = 13.6 minutes) and consisted of 27 questions. The interviewees (Male=5; Female=7) were between the age group of 22 - 33 (M=24.9; SD=3.1) and studied linguistics, computer science, or engineering. 20 pre-determined questions were discussed with the students in a semi-structured manner, where we allowed students to express their opinions on technology-based learning systems, their perceptions of existing learning systems in use, and the importance of creative skills in university education. Following this, we included questions from the well-established technology acceptance model (TAM) [VB08] to further gain an understanding of the system needs (e.g. performance and technical needs) and system requirements (e.g. functional requirements, design requirements) for fostering creative writing. The interviews were recorded, manually transcribed by two coders, and were used for qualitative content analysis.

(iii) *Mapping User Stories into Design Principles.* From the transcribed data, we mapped each user requirement into user scenarios with the intention of converting users' descriptions into realistic situations relevant to the design of a solution. At the end of the mapping process, we derived 33 scenarios with different goals and objectives. The priority of each scenario was set based on the number of occurrences (i.e. the number of times different users mentioned the same scenario). At the end of the coding process, we derived 8 scenarios that were mentioned more than thrice. We aggregated the meta-/user-requirements (see figure 1) that were identified from the literature and user interviews. The aggregated requirements were then coded into six design principles, forming the basis for designing our creative writing-support tool.

(iv) *Prototyping.* Based on the derived design principles, we designed two low-fidelity prototypes of the creativity writing-support tool. We conducted a follow-up study with university students (n=4) to test different design hypotheses and validate our design principles. For example, design principle one described that receiving feedback with highlighted parts of texts to show the strengths of the learner (highly creative parts), and weaknesses or inconsistencies (less creative parts) of the learner will help students identify creative parts of their writing. These design principles (see Figure 1) formed the basis for the design of our creative writing-support tool.

Literature Issues and User Stories	Meta/User Requirements	Design Principles
LI1: Divergent thinking (Guilford, 1968)	MR1: Presenting open-ended tasks leading to numerous and varied responses	DP1: To design an effective writing-support tool for fostering students creative skills, highlight parts of texts to show the strengths of the learner (highly creative parts), and weaknesses or inconsistencies (less creative parts) of the learner
LI2: Machine-in-the-loop creative writing support interventions (Clark et al., 2018)	MR2: Support wide range of creative explorations	
LI3: Principles for design of creativity support tools (Shneiderman et al., 2010)	MR3: Easy-to-use for novices	DP2: To design an effective writing-support tool for fostering students creative skills, support learners with scaffolds/prompts in order to promote creative behavior in learners
LI4: Adaptive learning support interventions (Wambsganss et al., 2022)	MR4: Self-regulated learning through adaptive feedback-provision mechanisms	
LI5: Effective pedagogical approaches across contexts (Bolden et al., 2019)	MR5: Support self-assessment and self-reflection	DP3: To design an effective writing-support tool for fostering students creative skills, visualize students' creative progress to track their performance over time
US1: As a creative writing student I would like to see my creativity score on different dimensions to help me improve in those areas	UR1: Feedback on different dimensions of creativity to help learner identify and to improve.	DP4: To design an effective writing-support tool for fostering students creative skills, provide a feature to explain the dimensions used for creativity measurement in order for learners to stay informed and to promote transparency of the system
US2: As a creative writing student I would like to get feedback on my weaknesses/inconsistencies to help me improve and not deviate from the topic	UR2: Feedback on the correctness and incorrectness of the solution.	
US3: As a creative writing student I would like to see how correct the solution is to understand my strength	UR3: Suggestions must be abstract and derived from another conceptual space.	DP5: To design an effective writing-support tool for fostering students creative skills, provide adaptive, sensible and individual feedback to improve creative thinking
US4: As a creative writing student I would like to see highlighted parts of my essay and reason to see areas that were creative and not creative	UR4: Feedback on learner's progress over time and over tasks	DP6: Design a creativity support tool as a web-based application allowing open-ended solutions with an easy-to-use and simple interface
US5: As a creative writing student I would like to receive topic-specific feedback but vague and general at the same time to help me think differently within a topic	UR5: Present information on what is being measured, and how it is measured	
US6: As a creative writing student I would like to get feedback on my progress over time and over tasks to see my performance and past works		
US7: As a creative writing student I would like to see general guidelines on what is being measured to help me trust the system		

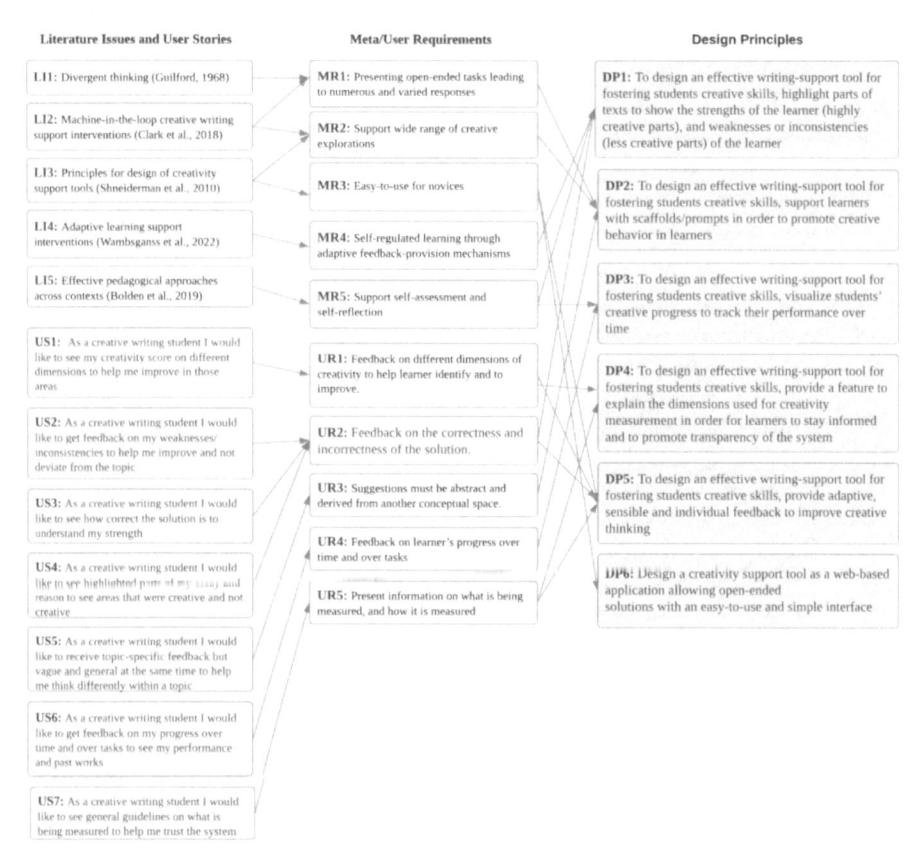

Fig 1: Overall design thinking process from gathering requirements to deriving design principles.

4 Results

User Interface Designing. Based on the design principles, we created paper prototypes and tested them with four representative students. We then validated and aggregated the design requirements and derived a final design prototype (see Figure 2). Our design system provides a simple user interface (DP6) with a simple text input field in which the students are allowed to write, edit, or modify an essay. The user interface also allows students to navigate to the start page (where a description of the tool is provided), and an information page (where detailed information of the internal working of the design system is provided). The students are allowed to submit the essay at any stage in order to receive adaptive feedback throughout their writing process. The creativity learning dashboard provides individual feedback (DP1) by highlighting the strengths and weaknesses in the essay. Additionally, it analyzes the creativeness of an essay (DP3) based on three aspects [To72]: fluency (the ability of students to come up with varied ideas), flexibility (the ability of students to make novel connections between ideas), and originality (the ability of students to come up with unique and unexplored ideas). These three aspects are visualized through a progress indicator, below which a hover feature is provided to support transparency of the creativity measurement process (DP4). Further, the creativity learning dashboard provides a visualization of individual ideas extracted from the student's essay. In order to support design principle two, the tool provides scaffolds of topics relevant to the student's essay (DP2) to invoke new connections in their essay. These design principles were integrated with prior design recommendations in mind [Cl18],[Sh07].

Fig. 2: Screenshot of an adaptive writing support tool for creativity (where DP stands for design principles). Left: A student writes an essay on a particular topic in the text editor and receives adaptive feedback on their creative level through a creativity learning dashboard. Right: Creativity learning dashboard provides scaffolds and guides students to write unexplored ideas in an essay.

5 Conclusion and Outlook

Designing intuitive learner interfaces can be challenging for educational technology developers. There are still open questions to address on the connection between technological design and capabilities, and its impact on students' creative performance and learning experiences [OH19]. In this work, we explored the potential of creative writing support and designed a learning tool considering learner-centered design methodologies, and existing design recommendations for addressing writing-related learning tasks. Our results from the prototype testing phase revealed that co-designing with students helps to rapidly improve the learning interface instantly based on their critical needs, preferences, and viewpoints. Despite the efforts to understand a new interface, the general conclusion from user testing is that the designed learning interface is intuitive, and promotes learner satisfaction, ownership, and self-efficacy. In future work, we plan to investigate the effectiveness of the designed learner interface in real-time incorporating intelligent AI techniques to support creative behavior, alongside a baseline study interface as a between-subject study design. Furthermore, we plan to evaluate the creative performances of students using our creativity support tool, with students using the baseline method, in a longitudinal study. This work can serve as a useful guideline for educational technology practitioners to incorporate similar design aspects and features for creativity support tools in different educational domains.

Bibliography

[Cl18]   Clark, E.; Ross, A.S.; Tan C.; Ji Y.; Smith N.A.: Creative Writing with a Machine in the Loop: Case Studies on Slogans and Stories. In: 23rd International Conference on Intelligent User Interfaces. IUI '18, Association for Computing Machinery, New York, NY, USA, p. 329–340, 2018.

[Fr19]   Frich, J.; MacDonald Vermeulen, L.; Remy, C.; Biskjaer, M. M.; Dalsgaard, P.: Mapping the Landscape of Creativity Support Tools in HCI. In: Proceedings of the 2019 CHI Conference on Human Factors in Computing Systems. CHI '19, Association for Computing Machinery, New York, NY, USA, p. 1–18, 2019.

[Hi20]   Hillmayr, D.; Ziernwald, L.; Reinhold F.; Hofer S.I.; Reiss K.M.: The potential of digital tools to enhance mathematics and science learning in secondary schools: A context-specific meta-analysis. Computers Education, 153:103897, 2020.

[OH19]   Oppenlaender, J.; Hosio, S.: Design Recommendations for Augmenting Creative Tasks with Computational Priming. In: Proceedings of the 18th International Conference on Mobile and Ubiquitous Multimedia. MUM '19, Association for Computing Machinery, New York, NY, USA, 2019.

[Pa22]   Palani, S.; Ledo, D.; Fitzmaurice G.; Anderson F.: Ï Don't Want to Feel like I'm Working in a 1960s Factory": The Practitioner Perspective on Creativity Support Tool Adoption. In: Proceedings of the 2022 CHI Conference on Human Factors in Computing Systems. CHI '22, Association for Computing Machinery, New York, NY, USA, 2022.

[Re05]   Resnick, M.; Myers, B.; Nakakoji K.; Shneiderman B.; Pausch R.; Selker T.; Eisenberg M.: Design Principles for Tools to Support Creative Thinking. Report of Workshop on Creativity Support Tools, 20, 2005.

[Sh07]   Shneiderman, B.: Creativity Support Tools: Accelerating Discovery and Innovation. Communications of the ACM, 50(12):20–32, 2007.

[To72]   Torrance, E Paul: Predictive validity of the Torrance tests of creative thinking. The Journal of creative behavior, 6(4):236–252, 1972.

[VB08]   Venkatesh, V.; Bala, H.: Technology acceptance model 3 and a research agenda on interventions. Decision sciences, 39(2):273–315, 2008.

[WJL22] Wambsganss, T.; Janson, A.; Leimeister J.M.: Enhancing Argumentative Writing with Automated Feedback and Social Comparison Nudging. Comput. Educ., 191(C), dec 2022.

Positionspapiere

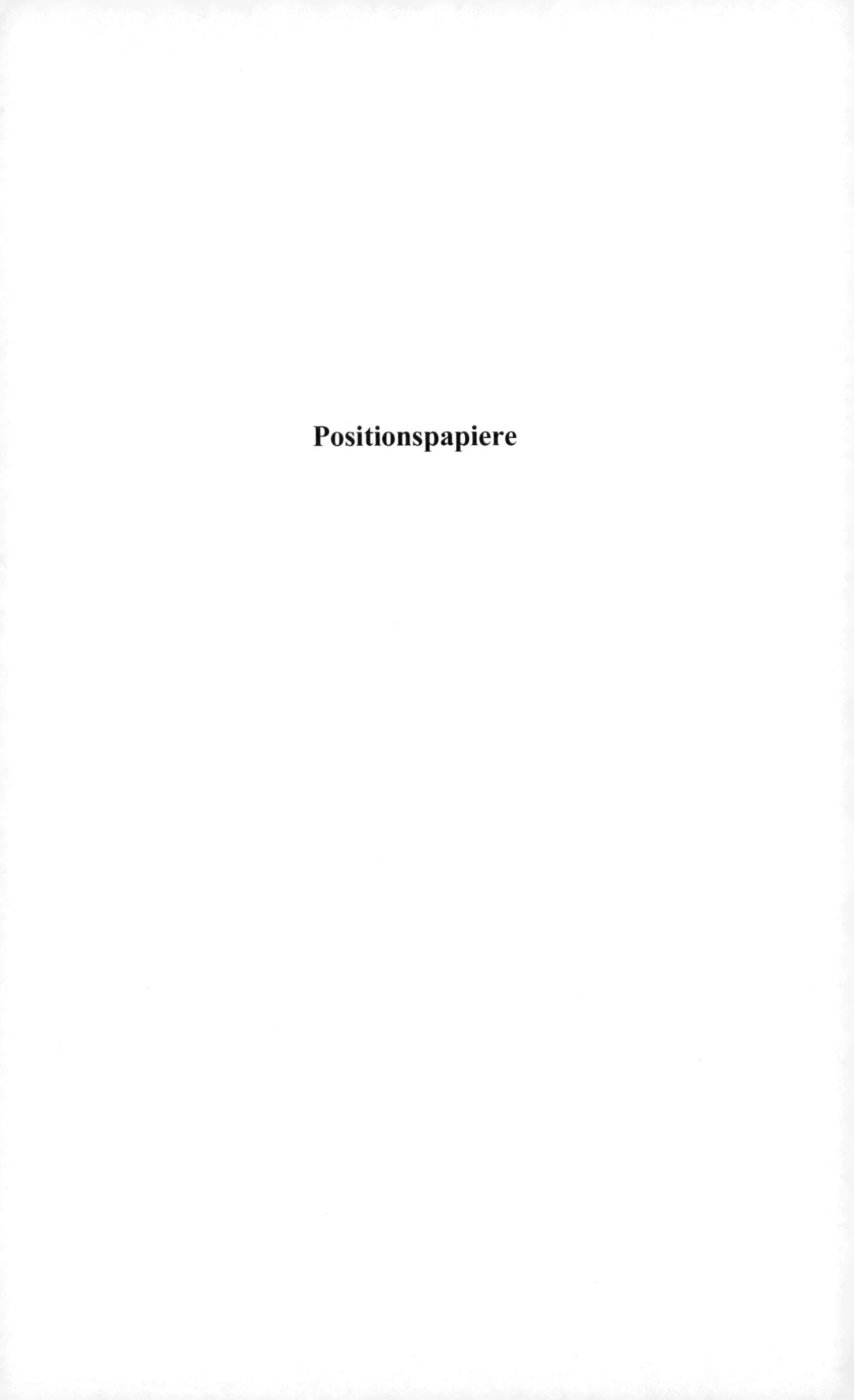

Mitigating Educational Challenges Through Unlearning

Marco Di Maria[1], David Walter[1], Paul-Ferdinand Steuck and Ralf Knackstedt[1]

Abstract: The rapid growth and obsolescence of knowledge cause uncertainty for university actors, such as students, teachers, administrative staff, and technology vendors. They must find new ways of dealing with hindering assumptions, and behaviors toward learning and teaching. To overcome these and achieve educational goals, it is essential to question ineffective ways of teaching and learning, adopt new education processes, and discard inadequate beliefs and procedures. This process is known as unlearning. In this position paper, we explore the potential of unlearning for mitigating educational challenges through unlearning. From a socio-technical perspective, we highlight the value of unlearning as a tool for tackling different challenges in university contexts. Finally, we identify central problem spaces stimulating further discussions.

Keywords: Unlearning, Educational Challenges, Socio-Technical System, Knowledge

1 Educational challenges for the university system

As the field of education is continuously evolving, new challenges arise daily. For instance, the next shock to the university system is already waiting in the wings – ChatGPT and generative artificial intelligence. It is more than obvious that we cannot stay passive given the disruptions in the university environment. To a large degree, these challenges are reinforced by hindering assumptions, outdated beliefs, inappropriate routines, and inhibiting behavioral patterns that prevent universities from adapting to changing circumstances. 'Unlearning' is a promising approach to mitigate these. It can be understood as a process of intentionally letting go of old beliefs, assumptions, biases, and behavioral patterns that are no longer effective or relevant in addressing new educational challenges – i. e. cognitive, beahvioral, and social knowledge [EL11]. It differs from related concepts such as 'absorptive capacity' or 'conceptual change' as it does focus neither on internalizing new, valuable information nor on mental, cognitive knowledge. These knowledge-related challenges can be grasped better, if we view the university as a socio-technical system (see Fig.1) consisting of two sub-systems, i.e. social system (structure, people), and technical system (technology, tasks):

People. Teachers, students, and administrative staff use technology for teaching and learning. However, they may not have sufficient experience in using new technologies, which can impact their learning success. Digital competencies are often not adequately taught in teacher training programs, and this gap has become problematic during the

---

[1] Universität Hildesheim, Institut für Betriebswirtschaft & Wirtschaftsinformatik, Universitätsplatz 1, Hildesheim, {maria; walter002; steuckp; knacks}@uni-hildesheim.de

COVID-19 pandemic, where digital teaching is essential [St23]. All internal roles in the university are affected by disruptions caused by technology or other factors. Thus, they are forced to update their knowledge and adapt to novel demands, if they want to or not.

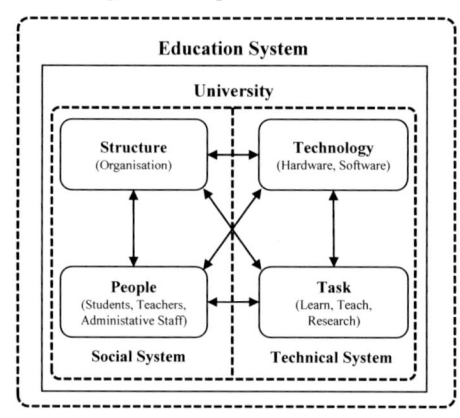

Fig. 1: University system as a socio-technical system

Structure. Universities need flexible structures to support both research and teaching, but their rigid and inflexible routines make it hard to adapt quickly to change, e.g., through COVID-19. Stu.diCo [Tr20] found that students struggled with the increased workload and inadequate IT infrastructure of universities during the pandemic, resulting in poorer support and student success. This highlights the need for more adaptable structures and provisioning to support digital learning – a case for unlearning routines.

Task. Traditional teaching methods can be challenging to transfer to the digital space, as they are often rooted in long-held beliefs and assumptions about how students should learn. Stu.diCo [Tr20] suggests that many students still prefer in-person classes due to the importance of social interaction, but there is also a desire for more digital options. This suggests that there is no single "right" approach to the digital shift in education and that the role of teachers may need to evolve to meet the demands of a changing world.

Technology. Outdated technology can hinder teaching and learning, as IT infrastructure may not be sufficient to support flexible and scalable teaching. Universities struggle to keep up with the speed of technological change, and there is no uniform approach to digital teaching across institutions [CLL21]. This makes it challenging to deliver effective digital teaching, and there is no one-size-fits-all solution to the challenges faced in digitalizing higher education. Actors need to become familiar with new technology first before they can productively adopt it. As with physical infrastructure, there will always be constraints on providing proper technology for teaching and learning.

As these examples illustrate, challenges are inherently complex as human needs and technical intricacies are interwoven in a non-trivial fashion. Accordingly, appropriate knowledge from various actors needs to be combined and refreshed – from students, teachers, administrative staff, and technology providers – and all roles need to act in unison to tackle these challenges. Therefore, our central question is the following: *How can we unlearn hindering beliefs, assumptions, and behavioral patterns to collaboratively construct a resilient education system?* In this position paper, we argue that unlearning can be a powerful tool for universities seeking to address the challenges of rapid knowledge growth and obsolescence. By unlearning outdated or irrelevant knowledge (e.g., mental models, routines, norms), teachers and administrators can create space for new ideas and perspectives, enabling them to adapt more quickly to changing circumstances. We demonstrate how unlearning can be used as a strategy for knowledge management in higher education in times of change – planned and unintentional.

2 Unlearning hindering knowledge as a catalyst for change

We will now suggest how universities can utilize unlearning to address the previously outlined educational challenges. Thus, universities need to organize effective knowledge management orchestrating knowledge-related activities of creation, sharing, and utilization. However, the overwhelming growth of knowledge causes a constant stream of new information that is generated within the university system and beyond. This knowledge explosion requires the university and its actors to deliberately decide which knowledge to retain and which knowledge to unlearn. Thus, all university actors need to learn, unlearn and relearn to always keep the most valuable and useful stock of knowledge for the organization as a whole.

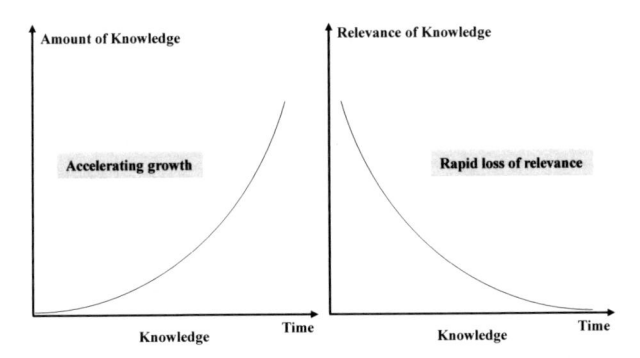

Fig. 2: Knowledge growth and loss of relevance

If everybody has the right knowledge – implicit and explicit – in place, the university will strive. This is easier said than done as knowledge underlies a dynamic process of accelerated growth followed by loss of relevance over time (see Fig. 2). As knowledge grows, it becomes increasingly specialized and complex. At the same time, the relevance of previously acquired knowledge may diminish as new technologies, theories, and practices emerge. Consequently, universities need to continuously (re-)evaluate the value of constituent knowledge to achieve educational goals in novel situations and decide which knowledge to keep and which to discard, i.e. unlearn (see Fig. 3).

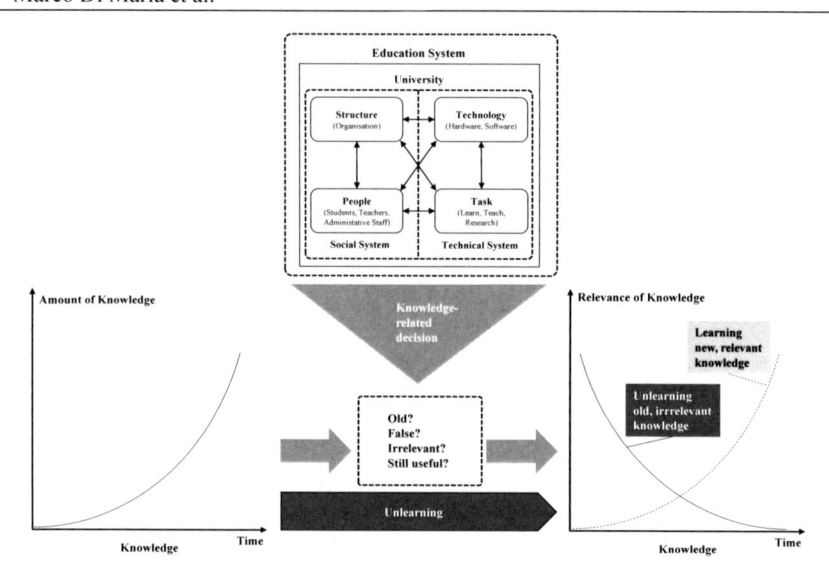

Fig. 3: Dynamic unlearning in the education system

For all actors, it is essential to continuously update their knowledge and adapt their teaching methods to keep up with the latest developments in their field. For *teachers*, this requires ongoing learning and professional development to ensure that they can effectively prepare students for their careers. Similarly, *students* must be equipped with the necessary skills, adaptability, and lifelong learning mindset to navigate the dynamic nature of knowledge in their chosen field. They must be prepared to continuously update their knowledge and adapt to new technologies, theories, and practices as they emerge. *Administrative staff* plays a crucial role in supporting both faculty and students in this process. They may need to adapt their procedures and practices to keep up with the latest developments in their field, and they must provide support and guidance to faculty and students as they navigate these changes. Apart from these, external actors, such as *technology providers*, cannot simply push their solutions into universities, e.g., ZOOM. Instead, they must work collaboratively with teachers, students, and administrative staff to ensure that their solutions meet the specific needs of each role and support the overall success of the university.

Again, this makes clear how entrenched knowledge structures may prevent universities from effectively addressing disruptions caused by technology or other factors. In our role as university teachers, we perceived a lack of critical reflection on the part of some university actors in the light of the shift to digital education due to the COVID-19. There has been little deliberate analysis of the situation and few collaborative efforts to design effective (educational) processes, task fulfillment, and technology use. This lack of reflection has resulted in a situation where the outcome has been "somehow" successful but not as a result of a planned process that takes into account all relevant perspectives. Furthermore, while there has been some recognition of the potential and pitfalls of digital education, there has not been a thorough and honest discussion between students, teachers, and administrative bodies about how to address these issues (in the future). As a result, there is a need for more deliberate and collaborative efforts to reflect on the knowledge-related challenges – cognitive and behavioral – and opportunities of digital education to design effective strategies that meet the needs of all university actors.

This exemplary reflection of universities' COVID-19 behavior, framed as an unlearning problem, shows that over-focusing on one component of the university system might not be the best advice to mitigate knowledge-related challenges today and in the future.

3 Solution spaces

Three solution spaces can help address unlearning challenges in university education:

Joint sensing: To be able to anticipate changes and trends in the education system, all stakeholders should actively participate in joint sensing [MN17]. This involves sharing perceptions of shifts and trends. Inside the university, it is crucial to listen to each other's perceptions of change and discuss them openly and honestly. Looking outside the university, it can be advantageous to establish a process of constant environmental scanning [Pa96]. In doing so, universities are always aware of changes within the organization and outside. To identify existing structures that block the adaption process, technology can be used as an aid, such as an early warning system. Therefore, we claim that all university actors should engage in joint sensing to better cope with disruptions as they are constantly aware of the utility of their knowledge.

Educational unlearning spaces: Creating educational unlearning spaces is critical to foster experimentation with new knowledge. It involves developing new perspectives, trying out new behaviors, and collectively experiencing and evaluating their effectiveness. Their value has already been proven in different contexts, such as entrepreneurship [CSC11]. Therefore, we think that unlearning spaces for experimentation with new ideas, frames of reference, and behaviors can foster universities' resilience, too. Thereby, all actors can experience the value of new knowledge and the disadvantages of keeping the old knowledge structures in place.

Collaborative, open reflection: All stakeholders should have a safe space to voice their opinions on the disadvantages of existing assumptions, behaviors, and routines. This creates an environment where the advantages of new approaches can be openly reflected and adjustments can be initiated [Ma18]. On the level of teachers, there is already evidence for the utility of collaborative reflection with open minds [Mc20]. Thus, we reckon that if all actors are encouraged to participate in collaborative, open reflection, universities as a whole, as well as their sub-systems, are better equipped to unlearn old knowledge that might act as obstacles in the context of environmental dynamism.

4 Conclusion

Adopting a socio-technical lens, we highlighted the importance of a balance between the human side to enhance educational processes and technology-focused approaches. We presented detailed examples of collaboration between main actors, such as students, teachers, administrators, and technology vendors. In doing so, we exemplified that unlearning – as part of an overall learning process – can support renewing our educational systems by focusing on the knowledge-related tasks of processing new knowledge (e.g., ideas, technology) and discarding outdated knowledge (e.g., beliefs, assumptions, routines). By deliberately unlearning existing cognitive and procedural patterns, new space can be opened up to jointly explore new avenues for learning and teaching in the 21st century as currently unknown demands unfold. Lastly, we provided guardrails for thinking in the form of unlearning-related solutions spaces.

Acknowledgments. We thank the NBank and the ESF+ for supporting our research project ProXHybrid (ZAM 3 – 87002690).

Bibliography

[CLL21] Chiu, T. K., Lin, T. J., Lonka, K.: (2021). Motivating online learning: The challenges of COVID-19 and beyond. *The asia-pacific education researcher*, *30*(3), 187-190.

[CSC11] Cegarra-Navarro, J. G., Sánchez-Vidal, M. E., Cegarra-Leiva, D.: Balancing exploration and exploitation of knowledge through an unlearning context: An empirical investigation in SMEs. Management Decision 49.7, S. 1099-1119, 2011.

[Ed17] Edmondson, A. C. et al.: Understanding psychological safety in health care and education organizations: a comparative perspective. Research in Human Development 13.1, S. 65-83, 2016.

[EL11] Easterby-Smith, M., & Lyles, M. A. (2011). In praise of organizational forgetting. *Journal of Management Inquiry*, *20*(3), 311-316.

[Ma18] Matsuo, M.: Effects of team unlearning on employee creativity: The mediating effect of individual reflection. Journal of Workplace Learning 30.7. S. 531-544, 2018.

[Mc20] McLeod, K. et al.: Principles for a pedagogy of unlearning. Reflective Practice, 21(2), S. 183-197, 2020.

[MN17] Morais-Storz, M.; Nguyen, N.: The role of unlearning in metamorphosis and strategic resilience. The Learning Organization, 24(2), S. 93-106, 2017.

[Pa96] Pashiardis, P.: Environmental scanning in educational organizations: uses, approaches, sources, and methodologies. International Journal of Educational Management, 10.3, S. 5-9, 1996.

[St23] Stifterverband, https://www.hochschulbildungsreport2020.de, zugegriffen: 31/03/2023.

[Tr20] Traus, A. et al. Stu diCo.–studieren digital in zeiten von Corona. 2020.

Demobeiträge

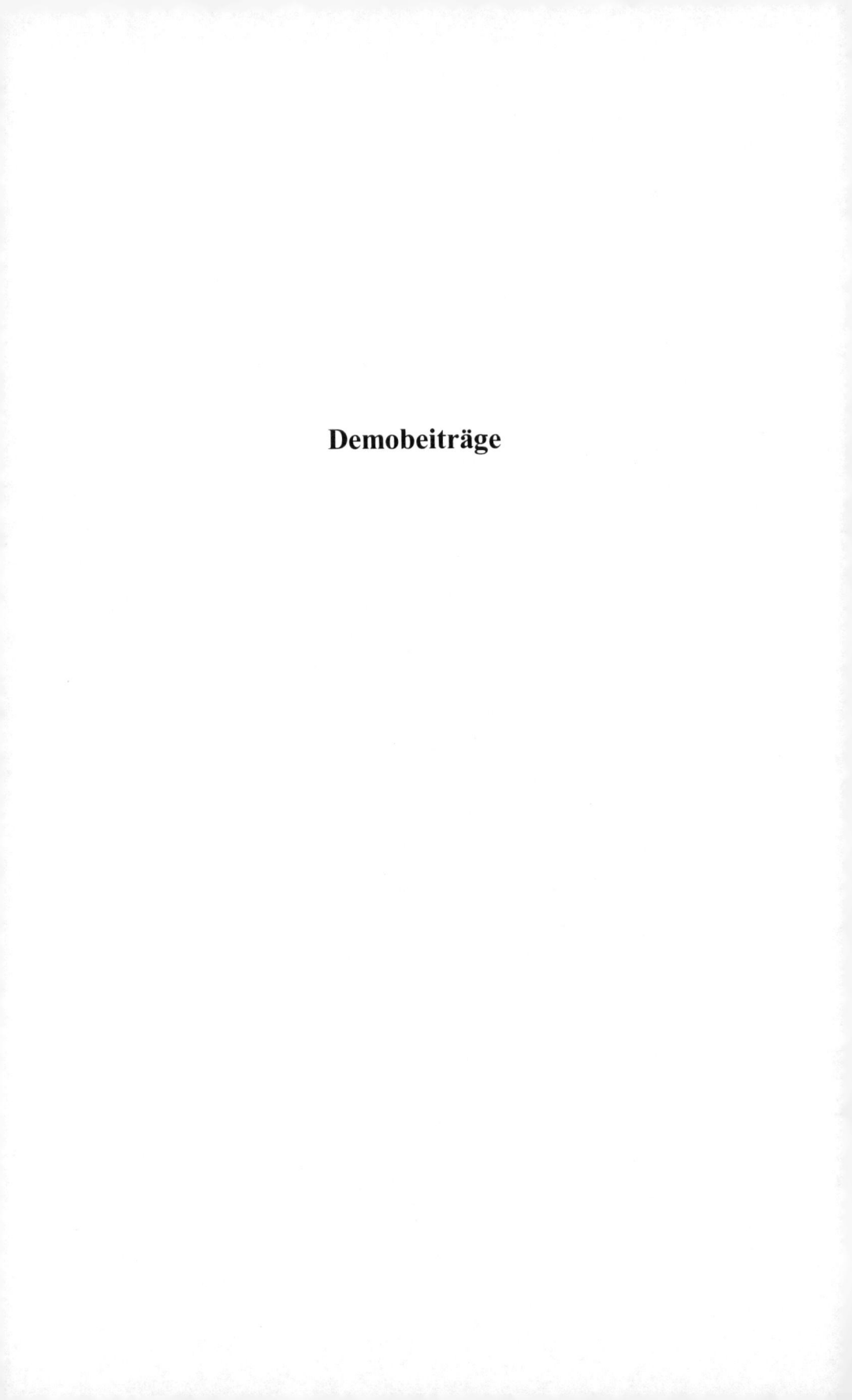

Steigerung von Lernerfolg und Motivation durch gamifizierte Mathematik-Aufgaben in Lernmanagementsystemen

Malte Neugebauer [1] und Jörg Frochte [2]

Abstract: Da Mathematik-Kompetenz entscheidend für Studierende ist und die Punkte in Studieneingangstests sinken, ist eine gesteigerte Motivation zum Lernen nötig. Gamification kann helfen, jedoch sind viele Lösungen aufwändig und nicht erweiterbar. Eine skalierbare, quelloffene Lösung, die mit LMS-Aufgabensammlungen kompatibel ist, wäre ideal. Ein Gamification-System wird in Moodle und ILIAS mittels JavaScript integriert, und automatisch generierte Lerndaten werden als Lernpfade visualisiert. Eine Pilotierung (n=115) zeigt erhöhte Motivation und Lernerfolg bei Vorkurs-Mathematik-Aufgaben. Der Ansatz eignet sich auch für höhere Mathematik.

Keywords: Mathematik, Gamification, Lernmanagementsystem, E-Learning

Mathematik-Kompetenz von Studierenden ist entscheidend für Erfolg im Fachstudium, besonders in den MINT-Fächern. Der Erfolg ist hierbei maßgeblich von der Motivation, mathematische Fertigkeiten aufzufrischen, abhängig [BM22]. Insbesondere in der Studieneingangsphase führen lückenhafte Mathematik-Kenntnisse trotz Interesse am Fachgebiet zu Frustration oder gar zum Studienabbruch [He17]. Sinkende Punktzahlen in entsprechenden Mathematik-Tests [Kn18, Kn12] weisen auf die Notwendigkeit von Maßnahmen hin, welche die Bereitschaft zur Auseinandersetzung mit mathematischem Lernen erhöhen. Gamification ist eine Möglichkeit, diese Bereitschaft zu erhöhen [WH20]. Es nutzt Spielelemente, um Motivation und Lernerfolg zu steigern. Da nahezu alle Hochschulen in Deutschland webbasierte Lernmanagementsysteme (LMS) wie Moodle oder ILIAS nutzen, ist es naheliegend, diese bestehenden Systeme zur Motivationssteigerung zu gamifizieren. Sie können mithilfe von JavaScript-Code derart modifiziert werden, dass Gamification-Elemente eingebaut werden, ohne dass serverseitige Änderungen (wie zum Beispiel die Installation eines Plugins) vonnöten wären. Auf diese Weise können gamifizierte Mathematik-Aufgaben auch von Lehrenden erstellt werden.

Im offenen Repositorium (https://bit.ly/3HRpyu0) steht eine Basis-Implementierung für das LMS Moodle (getestet ab Version 3), der Code und ein Analysewerkzeug zur freien Verfügung. Diese niedrigschwellige Technologie ermöglicht es Hochschullehrenden, ihre Studierenden zu mathematischem Lernen zu motivieren.

---

[1] Hochschule Bochum, Fachbereich für Elektrotechnik und Informatik, Kettwiger Str. 20, 42579 Heiligenhaus, malte.neugebauer@hs-bochum.de, https://orcid.org/0000-0002-1565-8222
[2] Hochschule Bochum, Fachbereich für Elektrotechnik und Informatik, Kettwiger Str. 20, 42579 Heiligenhaus, joerg.frochte@hs-bochum.de, https://orcid.org/0000-0002-5908-5649

In der ersten Umsetzung wurden kritische Mathematikbereiche in der Studieneingangsphase ermittelt und 28 zugehörige Aufgaben entwickelt. Der Fragentyp STACK ermöglicht es Lernenden, mathematische Eingaben per Tastatur zu machen, die von einem Computer-Algebra-System geprüft werden, um spezifische Fehler wie Vorzeichenfehler oder falsch erweiterte Brüche aufzuzeigen. Ein Skript integriert die Rückmeldung des Systems als Sprechblase neben einem Avatar. In einem Moodle-Test wurden die Aufgaben dann sachlogisch in aufsteigendem Schwierigkeitsgrad angeordnet. Die letzten und damit schwersten Aufgaben jedes Bereichs wurden als Endgegner gekennzeichnet. Die Aufgaben können beliebig oft wiederholt werden, wobei jede aus mehreren Varianten besteht. Dadurch können Lernende die gleiche Aufgabe mit anderen Zahlen üben, nachdem der Avatar die Lösung oder einen Hinweis auf den spezifischen Fehler gegeben hat.

Im Test mit 115 Vorkurs-Teilnehmenden lässt sich erkennen, dass Lernende signifikant häufiger die Endgegner-Aufgaben wiederholen. Unter Ausschluss anderer Wirkfaktoren (zum Beispiel besteht kein Zusammenhang zur Aufgabenschwierigkeit) lässt sich dieses Verhalten auf eine gesteigerte Motivation zurückführen. Ergebnisse eines standardisierten Fragebogens zur Einstellung der Lernenden zum Übungsraum stützen diesen Befund. Untersucht man die Punktzahlen, die die Lernenden durch die Wiederholungen der Endgegner-Aufgaben erreichen, lässt sich außerdem ein Lernfortschritt feststellen. Mehr als die Hälfte aller Fehlversuche werden durch Wiederholungen verbessert. Das Aufgabendesign führte also nicht nur zu einer höheren Wiederholungsrate der schwierigsten Aufgaben, sondern auch zu einer messbaren Verbesserung bei diesen Aufgaben [NTF23].

Literaturverzeichnis

[BM22]   Büchele, S.; Marten, C.: Math Skill Growth and Learning Differences in Higher Education. Can Lower-Skilled Students Catch up?. MAGKS Joint Discussion Paper Series in Economics 15, Marburg, S. 1-33, 2022.

[He17]   Heublein, U. et al.: Zwischen Studienerwartungen und Studienwirklichkeit, Ursachen des Studienabbruchs, beruflicher Verbleib der Studienabbrecherinnen und Studienabbrecher und Entwicklung der Studienabbruchquote an deutschen Hochschulen. Wiesbaden, DZHW, 2017.

[Kn12]   Knospe, H.: Zehn Jahre Eingangstest Mathematik an Fachhochschulen in Nordrhein-Westfalen. In: Proc. 10. Workshop Mathematik in ingenieurwissenschaftlichen Studiengängen, Mühlheim a.d. Ruhr, Hochschule Ruhr-West, S. 19-24, 2012.

[Kn18]   Knospe, H.: Erhebliche Mathematikdefizite bei Studienanfängern. Ergebnisse einer 15-Jahres Studie. https://www.nt.th-koeln.de/fachgebiete/mathe/knospe/aktuelles.html, 13.06.2023.

[NTF23] Neugebauer, M.; Tousside, B.; Frochte, J.: Success Factors for Mathematical e-Learning Exercises Focusing First-Year Students. In (Jovanovic, J. et al. Hrsg.): Proc. 15th Int. Conf. on Computer Supported Education, Prag 2023. Scitepress, S. 306-317, 2023.

[WH20]   Werbach, K.; Hunter, D.: For the Win, Revised and Updated Edition The Power of Gamification and Game Thinking in Business, Education, Government, and Social Impact. Pennsylvania, Wharton School Press, 2020.

Weiterentwicklung eines Dashboards zur digitalen Betreuung wissenschaftlicher Schreibprozesse

Joshua Martius[1], Sergej Görzen[2], Sven Judel[2] und Ulrik Schroeder[2]

Abstract: Eine hohe Auslastung in der Studierendenbetreuung schränkt Zeit und Mittel für Individualbetreuung von Seminar- und Abschlussarbeiten ein, was negative Auswirkungen auf die Qualität der Ergebnisse haben kann. Dem entgegenwirkend wurde die Webanwendung SWOFI entwickelt, welche Lehrende und Studierende mit simplen, zeitlich abgestimmten Handreichungen zum wissenschaftlichen Arbeitsprozess, einem zentralisierten und beidseitigem Kommunikationskanal, sowie der Abgabenverwaltung direkt im Browser unterstützt. SWOFI ist seit 2018 erfolgreich im Einsatz. Lehrende berichten von Zeitersparnissen bei gleichbleibender Qualität der Arbeitsergebnisse. Gleichzeitig wurden konstant Wünsche nach Anpassungen und neuen Features gesammelt. Auf diesen aufbauend wurde dieses Jahr eine neue Version des Lehrenden-Dashboards veröffentlicht, welche in dieser Demo präsentiert werden soll. Das Update ermöglicht einen einfacheren Überblick über alle Prozessdetails und schnelleren Zugang zu den wichtigsten Verwaltungselementen.

Keywords: Wissenschaftliches Schreiben, Digitale Betreuung, Interface Design, SWOFI

Motivation und Vorstellung

Zur Entlastung der Studierendenbetreuung in Seminaren wurde *SWOFI* entwickelt. Es besteht aus einem Tool Set für Lehrende und Studierende. Aus der bisherigen Nutzung auch über die RWTH hinaus gab es überwiegend positives Feedback. [Uc22] Kritik der Lehrenden, wie zum Beispiel ein Overhead in der Tooleinarbeitung und das initiale Einrichten der eigenen Kursprozesse, und Gespräche mit potenziellen zukünftigen Nutzern stellen neue Anforderungen für die Weiterentwicklung dar. In einer systematischen Befragung von vier Stammnutzern und einem Interessenten wurden Lösungsideen erhoben und anschließend in einem neuen Prototyp umgesetzt, welcher in dieser Demo vorgestellt wird.

Die größte Erneuerung war der Wechsel von statischen Templates ohne JavaScript zum React Framework. Dies ermöglicht einen modularen Aufbau mithilfe dynamischer Komponenten, die mit einer standardisierten und skalierbaren Schnittstelle zu den Daten über eine REST API kommunizieren. Damit ließen sich gezielt neue Lösungsideen umsetzen und gleichzeitig bewährte Elemente beibehalten. Abbildung 1 zeigt beispielhaft

---

[1] RWTH Aachen, joshua.martius@rwth-aachen.de
[2] RWTH Aachen, Lerntechnologien, {goerzen, judel, schroeder}@informatik.rwth-aachen.de,
https://orcid.org/{0000-0003-3853-2345, 0000-0002-0424-0402, 0000-0002-5178-8497}

doi: 10.18420/delfi2023-40

das Übersichtsdashboard eines Kurses. Der Fokus des neuen Prototyps liegt auf erhöhter Interaktivität. So geht bspw. bei der Bearbeitung von Kursinformationen (rot) und bei der Einladung von neuen Teilnehmern (gelb), ein Fenster innerhalb der Applikation auf. Direkte Aktionen (z. B. das Kontaktieren eines Teilnehmers) sind durch kleine Icons in der jeweiligen Zeile möglich. Prozessschritte lassen sich zudem via Drag'n'Drop, statt wie zuvor durch Buttons, in der Reihenfolge, aber auch in ihrer Phase (übergeordnete Gruppe) verschieben. Neben einer interaktiven Gestaltung von Prozessen, können Sprechstunden organisiert werden. Abgaben der Studierenden können in einer direkten PDF-Vorschau vom Betreuenden annotiert und bewertet werden. Da SWOFI bereits erfolgreich in der Betreuung von Seminaren eingesetzt wurde, wird es aktuell mithilfe der generalisierten Prozessgestaltung auf Abschlussarbeiten erweitert. Die Überarbeitung soll neuen Betreuenden eine geringere Einstiegshürde bieten und deckt mit neuen Features, wie zum Beispiel individuelle Deadlines für Abgaben, weitere Anforderungen ab. Das neue Dashboard soll weiterhin iterativ und nutzerzentriert evaluiert werden, um zukünftige Anforderungen zu ermitteln und die aktuellen Umsetzungen zu verbessern.

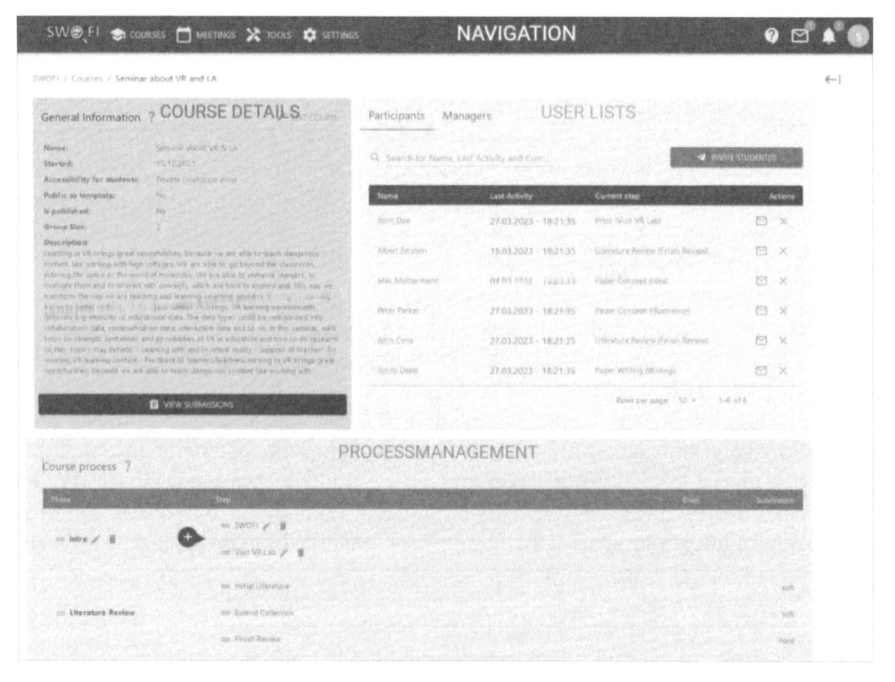

Abb. 1: Kursansicht von SWOFI für Lehrende: Kursdetails in Rot, Kursteilnehmer in Gelb und Prozessgestaltung in Cyan farblich hervorgehoben.

Literaturverzeichnis

[Uc22] Uckelmann, D. et al.: Structured Digital Writing Lab: Workflow, Application and Evaluation. International Journal of Online and Biomedical Engineering (iJOE), 18(14), S. 133–146, 2022.

AdLer: 3D-Lernumgebung für Studierende

Antonia Dörringer[1], Marco Klopp[1], Lukas Schaab[1], Marvin Hochstetter[1], Daniel Glaab[1], Paula Bartel[2], Jörg Abke[1], Jens Elsebach[1], Raphael Rossmann[1] und Georg Hagel[2]

Abstract: Mit Hilfe des AdLer-Autorentools können Lehrende virtuelle 3D-Lernumgebungen konzipieren und generieren, in welchen Studierende nach den Prinzipien des Game-based Learning mit Lerninhalten interagieren können.

Keywords: 3D-Lernumgebung, Game-based Learning, Serious Game

Ziele des AdLer-Projekts

Das *AdLer-Projekt*[3] (**A**daptive **d**igitale **Ler**nräume) hat zum Ziel ein frei verfügbares Instrument zu entwickeln, mit welchem Lehrende virtuelle 3D-Lernumgebungen erstellen und in ihrer Lehre in unterschiedlichen Formen (in der Präsenzlehre, rein digitale Lehre oder als Blended Learning) einsetzen können. Eine Zielgruppe sind somit die **Lehrenden**, welche mit Hilfe des AdLer-Autorentools bei der Konzeption und Erstellung von 3D-Lernumgebungen unterstützt werden. Da Lehrende in der Regel keine Expert:innen für die Gestaltung von virtuellen Lernumgebungen sind und in diesem Bereich wenig Wissen mitbringen, wird bei der Entwicklung des AdLer-Autorentools, im Sinne des „end-user development" [Me17, S. 359], insbesondere dessen Benutzerfreundlichkeit und leichte Erlernbarkeit berücksichtigt, sodass sich das Tool auch ohne technisches Hintergrundwissen und Fähigkeiten in Programmierung oder Multimediagestaltung bedienen lässt. Dadurch können Lehrende auf schnellem und einfachem Weg eigene digitale 3D-Lernumgebungen erstellen sowie nach ihren individuellen Vorstellungen hinsichtlich der spezifischen Bedingungen der eigenen Lernszenarien und Lehrziele konfigurieren. Mit Hilfe eines Plug-ins wird nicht nur eine 3D-Lernumgebung, sondern parallel dazu auch ein passender Moodle-Kurs mit den identischen Inhalten generiert. Dieser kann von den Studierenden als zusätzliche oder alternative Lernmöglichkeit genutzt werden (für mehr Informationen zum AdLer-Autorentool und der Erstellung der 3D-Lernumgebung siehe [Kl23]). In der 3D-Lernumgebung können **Studierende** als

---

[1] Technische Hochschule Aschaffenburg, Fakultät Ingenieurwissenschaften, Würzburger Straße 45, 63743 Aschaffenburg, {antonia.doerringer, marco.klopp, lukas.schaab, marvin.hochstetter, daniel.glaab, joerg.abke, jens.elsebach, raphael.rossmann}@th-ab.de
[2] Hochschule Kempten, Fakultät Informatik, Bahnhofstraße 61, 87406 Kempten, {paula.bartel, georg.hagel}@hs-kempten.de
[3] Die vorliegende Arbeit wurde im Rahmen des Projekts „Adaptive digitale Lernräume" (AdLer) von der Stiftung Innovation in der Hochschullehre (StIL) gefördert. Die Verantwortung für den Inhalt dieser Veröffentlichung liegt bei den Autor:innen.

doi: 10.18420/delfi2023-41

zweite Zielgruppe von AdLer, nach den Prinzipien des Game-based Learning erkundungsorientiert und interaktiv lernen. Serious Games stellen ein vielversprechendes Beispiel von Game-based Learning dar, um die Lernmotivation der Studierenden zu adressieren. Hierbei geht es darum, Mechaniken (digitaler) Spiele zu verwenden, „um einen zielgerichteten Wissenserwerb zu ermöglichen, der unterschwellig und zeitgleich motivierend verpackt ist" [St09, S. 14]. Anknüpfend daran haben Immersionseffekte das Potential in Kombination mit durchdachten didaktischen Settings digitale Hochschullehre für Studierende ansprechend und abwechslungsreich zu gestalten sowie deren Motivation und Flow-Erleben zu erhöhen [Hoe13]. Um dies zu erreichen, können Studierende mittels eines selbst gewählten, virtuellen Avatars die AdLer-3D-Lernumgebung betreten und verschiedene Handlungsmöglichkeiten wahrnehmen. Sie können sich frei in dieser Lernumgebung bewegen und unterschiedliche Lernangebote (z.B. die Bearbeitung von Lernelementen, wie H5P, Text und Video) durchführen. Um die Motivation der Studierenden weiter zu fördern, sollen zukünftig bei der Konzeption von 3D-Lernumgebungen weitere Spielemechaniken und -elemente, wie z.B. Badges, Ranglisten, NPCs und eine Storyline, verwendet werden können. Abbildung 1 zeigt die Benutzeroberfläche des AdLer-Autorentools und Abbildung 2 zeigt ein Beispiel für die AdLer-3D-Lernumgebung.

Abb. 1: AdLer Autorentool   Abb. 2: AdLer 3D-Lernumgebung

Literaturverzeichnis

[Me17]   Menestrina, Z.; De Angeli, A.: End-user development for serious games. In: Paternò, F.; Wulf, V. (Hrsg.): New Perspectives in End-User Development, Cham, Springer, S. 359–383, 2017.

[Kl23]   Klopp, M. et al.: Development of an Authoring Tool for the Creation of Individual 3D Game-Based Learning Environments; In: Proceedings of the 5th European Conference Software Engineering Education (ECSEE), Kloster Seeon, ACM, S. 204-209, 2023.

[St09]   Staudacher, N.: Digitale Spiele und ihr Potenzial als Bildungs- und Lernräume. In: Gruber, E.; Schmid, K. (Hrsg.): Lern- und Bildungsräume, Magazin erwachsenenbildung.at.- Ausgabe 35/36, Wien, 2019.

[Hoe13]   Höntzsch, S. et al.: Simulationen und simulierte Welten. Lernen in immersiven Lernumgebungen. In: Ebner, M. et al. (Hrsg.): L3T. Lehrbuch für Lernen und Lehren mit Technologien (2. Aufl.), 2013.

COREFLECTOR – Prototyp zur Unterstützung von Verlernen beim analytischen Lesen für Studierende

Marco Di Maria[1], David Walter[1], Fabian Segieth[1] und Ralf Knackstedt[1]

Abstract: In diesem Beitrag stellen wir die Webanwendung COREFLECTOR zur Unterstützung von Studierenden beim analytischen Lesen vor. Sie unterstützt das Verlernen hinderlicher Verhaltensmuster beim Lesen und Verstehen wissenschaftlicher Texte, z. B. von vorne bis hinten durchlesen. Studierende identifizieren dabei Schwächen in ihrem bestehenden Leseverhalten, lernen eine neue Technik für das analytische Lesen kennen und reflektieren eigene (Ver-)Lernerfahrungen und die anderer Studierender. Erste explorative Anwendungen deuten darauf hin, dass Studierende durch gemeinsames Reflektieren und Experimentieren eher dazu neigen, sich mit eigenen Verständnisproblemen und Techniken des analytischen Lesens auseinanderzusetzen.

Keywords: Unlearning, Peer Unlearning, Digital Learning, Kollaborative Reflexion, Tool Support

1 Konzept und Implementierung

Studierende müssen in verschiedenen Lehrveranstaltungen mit wissenschaftlichen Texten (u. a. Konferenzbeiträgen, Fachbüchern) arbeiten. Sie beginnen dabei oft ohne Vorbereitung und lesen vollständig von vorne bis hinten. Das führt jedoch häufig nicht zum erhofften Textverständnis, was Unzufriedenheit und Motivationsverlust zur Folge hat [St10]. Im Sinne des Verlernens (engl. *Unlearning*) liegt hier ein Problem aufgrund störenden Wissens vor [FO17]. Studierende rufen ein gelerntes Leseverhalten ab, das sie durch Erfahrung beim Lesen nicht-wissenschaftlicher Texte aufgebaut haben. Dieses hindert sie daran wissenschaftliche Texte zu verstehen. Techniken des analytischen Lesens [Ha98] und der Reflexion [SSK23] können beim Verlernen ungeeigneter Vorgehensweisen helfen [Ma18]. COREFLECTOR (siehe Abb. 1) unterstützt Studierende zunächst durch eine Abfrage des Kenntnisstandes zum Lesen wissenschaftlicher Texte mittels eines Quizzes. Danach wird die Technik des Analytischen Lesens nach Hart [Ha98] präsentiert, sowie die Quizergebnisse. Studierende sollen so fehlerhafte Einschätzungen identifizieren. Anschließend erproben sie die Lesetechnik an einem konkreten Beispiel. Dabei erhalten sie für jeden Schritt Unterstützung zum erwarteten Vorgehen, u. a. per Video. Danach können sie sich nochmals vergewissern, wie andere Studierende vorgegangen sind. Dazu werden Ergebnisse anderer Studierender für diese Aufgabe präsentiert. Dann reflektieren Studierende ihr eigenes Vorgehen sowie das anderer [Ma18] und führen nochmals das

---

[1] Universität Hildesheim, Institut für Betriebswirtschaft & Wirtschaftsinformatik, Universitätsplatz 1, Hildesheim, {maria; walter002; segieth; knacks}@uni-hildesheim.de

doi: 10.18420/delfi2023-42

Quiz durch, um die neu gewonnene Sicht auf das analytische Lesen zu sichern. Zum Abschluss formulieren sie persönliche Merksätze, um einen Rückfall in alte, falsche Muster zu vermeiden.

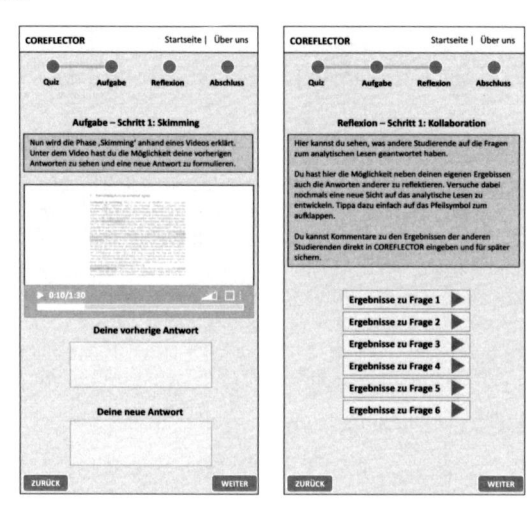

Abb. 1: Komponenten des analytischen Lesens und der kollaborativen Reflexion

Bei einem Experiment mit vier Studierenden half COREFLECTOR bei der Identifikation hinderlicher Annahmen, u.a. durch das Quiz und das Reflektieren anhand der Lösungwege anderer Studierender. Der Einfluss störender Verhaltensmuster konnte so reduziert und Verlernen ermöglicht werden. Wir planen COREFLECTOR in Tutorien einzusetzen, um mittels Digital Peer Unlearning die Lesekompetenz Studierender zu fördern. Der Quellcode kann hier eingesehen werden: https://github.com/dawalt/CoReflector.

Danksagungen. Wir danken der NBank und dem ESF+ für die Förderung des Forschungsprojekts ProXHybrid mit Fördernummer: ZAM 3 – 87002690.

Literaturverzeichnis

[FO17]   Fiol, C. M.; O'Connor, E. J.: Unlearning established organizational routines–Part II. *The Learning Organization* 24.2, S. 82-92, 2017.

[Ha98]   Hart, C.: Doing a literature review. Releasing the Social Science Research Imagination SAGE Publications, 1998.

[Ma18]   Matsuo, M.: Effects of team unlearning on employee creativity: The mediating effect of individual reflection. *Journal of Workplace Learning* 30.7. S. 531-544, 2018.

[St10]   Steinhoff, T.: Wissenschaftliche Textkompetenz: Sprachgebrauch und Schreibentwicklung in wissenschaftlichen Texten von Studenten und Experten. Walter de Gruyter, 2010.

[SSK23] Schoormann, T., Stadtländer, M., & Knackstedt, R. (2023). Act and Reflect: Integrating Reflection into Design Thinking. *Management Information Systems*, *40*(1), 7-37.

Modulare und konfigurierbare Remote Labore mit Edrys

André Dietrich[1], Karl Fessel[1] und Sebastian Zug[1]

Abstract: Das Konzept der Remote-Labore kombiniert eine hohe Verfügbarkeit von Lehrmaterialien mit relevanten Herausforderungen realer Applikationen. Damit bilden sie einen Baustein zur Flexibilisierung und Studierendenzentrierung der Lehre. Gegenwärtige Implementierungen setzen diese Ziele mit statisch konfigurierten und auf individuelle Lernziele zugeschnittenen, serverbasierten Applikationen um. Das im Rahmen des CrossLab-Projektes weiterentwickelte Framework Edrys, realisiert konzeptionell einen interpreterbasierten Ansatz. Der Lehrende definiert die Lehrinhalte und Konfigurationsparameter des Remote-Labors in einer Beschreibungsdatei. Dazu implementiert Edrys ein parametrisierbares und modulares Konzept (für Code-Editoren, interaktive Visualisierungen, Formate für Lehrinhalte) und bettet diese in eine Gesamtspezifikation ein.

Keywords: RemoteLab; OER

1 Motivation

Für die Vermittlung von MINT-Fächern ist praktische Lernerfahrung im Laborkontext unerlässlich. Mit dem spezifischen Zuschnitt und dem beschränkten Zugang steht der praktische Laborunterricht aber im Kontrast zu den Visionen eines offenen und selbstbestimmten Lernens. So werden Labore mit ähnlichem Inhalt parallel an unterschiedlichen Bildungseinrichtungen mit viel technischem und didaktischen Aufwand vorbereitet, um sie dann für wenige Übungen zu nutzen. Die Konzepte der Remote-Labore, die das reale Experiment online zugänglich machen sollen (e.g., [HdlTD16]), zielen zwar auf eine organisatorische Öffnung, überlassen aber neben technischen Herausforderungen eines konkreten Labors und die Erstellung der zugehörigen Materialien aber dem jeweiligen Lehrenden. Ansätze zur kollaborativen Erarbeitung von Lehrmaterialien und die übergreifende Nutzung ähnlicher Setups ist nicht vorgesehen. Gegenwärtige Remote-Labore stellen damit monolithische Einzellösungen dar, die in anderen Lernkontexten nur begrenzt nutzbar sind.

2 Remote-Labore als Open Educational Ressources

Das Open-Source-Projekt Edrys, das unter anderem von Mitgliedern des CrossLab-Projekt [AZD22] weiterentwickelt wird, zielt darauf, diese methodische Lücke zu

---

[1] TU Bergakademie Freiberg, Fakultät für Mathematik und Informatik, Bernhard-von-Cotta-Straße 2, 09599, Freiberg, Germany. {andre.dietrich, karl.fessel, sebastian.zug}@informatik.tu-freiberg.de

doi: 10.18420/delfi2023-43

schließen. Es versteht sich als Konfigurationswerkzeug für die Kombination und Parametrisierung von Modulen, die in ihrem Gesamtkontext ein Remote-Labor mit den technischen und didaktischen Elementen darstellen [Ed].

Ein Modul kann ein Editor sein, ein Videochat, ein Zeichenprogramm, ein LiaScript online-Kurs [Di19], aber auch ein Terminal oder eine beliebige andere Anwendung sein, die den Zugriff auf "Remote"Ressourcen und Geräte erlaubt. Jedes Modul ist einzeln konfigurierbar und unterschiedliche Module können in einem Klassenraum kombiniert werden. Diese Klassenräume können über ein einfaches Beschreibungsformat (JSON[2], YAML[3]) exportiert und importiert werden. Diese Klassenraum-Konfigurationen können dann selbst als OER[4]-Projekt, unter einer freien Lizenz, anderen zur Verfügung gestellt und verändert werden.

Aus der Konfigurationsdatei wird das eigentliche Interface für die Studierenden ge-neriert. Dieses greift auf unterschiedliche Module zu, die als verteilte Anwendung direkt im Browser ausgeführt werden. Aus Sicht des Remote-Labors ist dabei der sogenannte Station-Mode wichtig, der den Zugriff auf eine oder mehrere lokale Ressourcen erlaubt. Dieser Zugriff wird direkt über Web Serial[5]-API des Browsers zur Verfügung gestellt oder lokal über eine Server-Appt, mit der die Station direkt kommunizieren kann.

3 Demonstrator

Um zu demonstrieren, wie einfach es ist, mit Edrys lokale Ressourcen zu teilen, werden wir verschiedene Klassenraumkonfigurationen für die Programmierung eingebetteter Systeme laden, diese anpassen (zum Beispiel das Code-Editor Modul durch ein Blockly-Modul ersetzen oder die LiaScript basierten Instruktionen verändern) und den Zugriff auf Mikrocontroller in virtuellen Klassenräumen teilen.

Literaturverzeichnis

[AZD22] Aubel, Ines; Zug, Sebastian; Dietrich, André et al.: Adaptible Digital Labs – Motivation and Vision of the CrossLab Project. In: IEEE GeCon 2022. S. 1-6, 2022.

[Di19] André Dietrich: A Domain-Specific-Language for Interactive Online Courses. In: IADIS International Conference e-Learning 2019. S. 186-194, 2019.

[Ed] Edrys: Next Genration Remote Teaching Plattform. https://edrys.org, accessed: 31.3.2023.

[HdlTD16] Heradio, Ruben; de la Torre, Luis; Dormido, Sebastian: Virtual and remote labs in control education: A survey. Anual Reviews in Control, 42:1-10, 2016.

---

[2] JavaScript Object Notation: https://de.wikipedia.org/wiki/JavaScript_Object_Notation
[3] YAML Ain't Markup Language: https://de.wikipedia.org/wiki/YAML
[4] Open Educational Resource: https://de.wikipedia.org/wiki/Open_Educational_Resources
[5] https://developer.mozilla.org/en-US/docs/Web/API/Web_Serial_API

Ansätze um der Darstellungsflüchtigkeit in Virtual Reality entgegenzuwirken

Birte Heinemann [1], Sergej Görzen [1], Daniel Gotzen [2] und Ulrik Schroeder [1]

Abstract: Darstellungsflüchtigkeit ist ursprünglich ein Konzept aus dem Geometrieunterricht, welches auch in Virtual Reality Lernanwendungen zutreffen kann. Lernende erarbeiten etwas und können anhand des Resultates nicht mehr strategisch über ihr Vorgehen bei Problemlösung reflektieren. Diese Demo stellt eine Möglichkeit vor, wie Lernende in Virtual Reality Anwendungen Zugriff auf Zwischenergebnisse und Ergebnisse von sich selbst und anderen Lernenden bekommen können. Das Konzept lässt sich ebenfalls auf weitere Lernszenarien in virtueller Realität übertragen und kann so einen Beitrag zur Unterstützung von Reflektion und Strategieentwicklung leisten.

Keywords: Darstellungsflüchtigkeit, Virtual Reality, Usability, Bedienkonzepte, Geometrieunterricht, Computergrafik

Kontext und Inhalt der Demo

Das Konzept der Darstellungsflüchtigkeit wurde ursprünglich im Geometrieunterricht der Mathematik beschrieben [Hu13]. Es beschreibt die Schwierigkeit von Lernenden, strategisch über ihr Vorgehen bei der Problemlösung nachzudenken, nachdem sie ein Ergebnis erzielt haben. Das eigene Vorgehen und Strategien nachzuvollziehen ist besonders dann schwierig, wenn die Lernenden sich nicht aktiv auf den Prozess fokussieren und deshalb nicht über ihre eigenen Methoden reflektieren können. Dieses Phänomen kann ebenso in vielfältigen Feldern außerhalb des Geometrieunterrichts beobachtet werden, z.B. lässt es sich auf informatikdidaktische Potenziale unter anderem für die Computergrafik Lehre übertragen, bei der Prozesse und Zwischenprodukte ebenfalls nicht zugänglich sind.

Diese Problematik tritt in analogen Lerngelegenheiten sowie digitalen Lernumgebungen und verschiedenen Technologien, z.B. Virtual Reality (VR) auf. Lernende können aber insbesondere in digitalen Lernumgebungen im Austausch und der Reflektion über eigene diagnostische Maßnahmen gefördert werden, da verschiedene Hilfen bei Problemlöseprozessen angeboten werden können, z.B. beschrieben in [BHE20].

Die vorgestellte Demo zeigt eine Möglichkeit, wie Lernende in VR Anwendungen auf Zwischenergebnisse und Ergebnisse von sich selbst und anderen zugreifen können, um

---

[1] RWTH Aachen, Lerntechnologien, {heinemann, goerzen, schroeder}@cs.rwth-aachen.de, https://orcid.org/{0000-0002-7568-0704, 0000-0003-3853-2435, 0000-0002-5178-8497}
[2] RWTH Aachen, daniel.gotzen@rwth-aachen.de

doi: 10.18420/delfi2023-44

ihre Strategien zu reflektieren und verbessern zu können. Die Grundlage dieser Demo sind ringförmige 3D Objekte, die verschiedene Interaktionsmöglichkeiten aufweisen. Das Konzept vereinigt Eigenschaften von interaktiven Fenstern/Portalen, durch die eine Beobachtung des Lösungsprozesses ermöglicht wird, und bekannten Interaktionsmechanismen, wie einer gestenbasierten Änderung der Größe der Fenster (welche entstehen, wenn die Ringe groß gezogen werden). Die nötigen Funktionalitäten wie die Aufnahme von Interaktionen, die Darstellung der vergangenen Interaktionen und die Navigation innerhalb der Aufnahmen, wurden so entworfen, dass sie möglichst intuitiv nutzbar sein sollten, um die kognitive Belastung durch die zusätzlichen Funktionalitäten möglichst gering zu halten. Das Konzept nutzt die besonderen Möglichkeiten der VR um komplexe Funktionalitäten nutzerfreundlich in Lernumgebungen zu integrieren.

Die Demo zeigt drei verschiedene Szenarien, in denen das Konzept der interaktiven Fenster getestet werden kann und welche verschiedene Anwendungsbeispiele vorstellen. Neben dem in diesem Beitrag vorgestellten Anwendungskontext, der Reduktion von Darstellungsflüchtigkeit durch eine Visualisierung der Aufgabenlösung, können die interaktiven Fenster auch in anderen pädagogischen Anwendungsfällen genutzt werden, z.B. dem Einblenden zusätzlicher, eventuell optionaler Informationen oder versteckter Objekte, zur Verwaltung verschiedener Ebenen/Varianten von Lernumgebungen oder zum Wechsel zwischen verschiedenen Zuständen. Die in der Demo vorgestellten Szenarien haben der Evaluation der Interaktionsmechanismen gedient, welche zunächst in einer Proof of Concept Studie mit acht Versuchspersonen getestet wurden [Go22] und im Sommersemester 2023 in einer größeren Studie evaluiert werden.

Das vorgestellte Interaktionskonzept kann in verschiedenen Lernszenarien in virtueller Realität genutzt werden, dazu beitragen, die Reflektion und Strategieentwicklung zu fördern und weitere didaktische Möglichkeiten eröffnen. Die Demo soll Feedback aus der DELFI Community ermöglichen und den Diskurs über Interaktionskonzepten für Lehre in VR voranbringen.

Literaturverzeichnis

[BHE20] Beyer, S., Huhmann, T., & Eilerts, K.: Nutzung von Hilfen in Problemlöseprozessen – am Beispiel einer analogen und einer digital gestützten Lernumgebung zu Pentominos. In S. Ladel, R. Rink, C. Schreiber, & D. Walter (Eds.), Forschung zu und mit digitalen Medien (1st ed., pp. 119–133). WTM-Verlag, Münster, 2020

[Be22] Beyer, S.: Innovieren unter Druck: Qualitative Exploration von Lernwegen und Entwicklung eines Chatbots zur Unterstützung von schulpraktischen Erprobungen im Kontext einer Lehrkräftefortbildung. Herausforderung Lehrer*innenbildung - Zeitschrift zur Konzeption, Gestaltung und Diskussion, 5(1), 2022

[Go22] Gotzen, D.: Rewatching and analyzing local scenes through interactive windows in extended reality. RWTH Publications, Aachen, 2022

[Hu13] Huhmann, T.: Einfluss von Computeranimationen auf die Raumvorstellungsentwicklung. Springer Spektrum, Wiesbaden, 2013

Semi-assisted Module Handbook Content Extraction for the Application of Curriculum Analytics

Rene Roepke [1], Maximilian Nell[2] and Ulrik Schroeder [1]

Abstract: Alongside examination regulations, module handbooks provide overview of a study program, including information like workload, learning goals, examinations. They provide guidance to students, but can also be a valuable information source to curriculum analytics, e.g., the identification of trends and patterns across modules, the assessment of course content coherence, and data-driven decision-making regarding curriculum design and revision. This paper introduces a tool for semi-assisted module handbook content extraction, which uses natural language processing and text mining techniques to extract all properties and relevant details from module handbooks, allowing instructors and curriculum designers to efficiently identify key information. As module handbooks between institutions may look very different, fully automated extraction is difficult and error-prone. By allowing users to verify and correct extraction results in a semi-assisted manner, higher accuracy and reliability of module data can be achieved.

Keywords: Curriculum Analytics, Natural Language Processing, Text Mining, Module Handbooks

Motivation and Prototype Workflow

For the analysis of study programs and curricula, the contents of module handbooks and examination regulations as well as student activity data are considered valuable input. Covered under the umbrella term *curriculum analytics* [Hi22], a subdomain of learning analytics, the beforementioned data can provide meaningful insights to detecting patterns, trends and evidence to guide data-driven decision-making regarding curriculum design and revision. A crucial step in curriculum analytics is the data collection and pre-processing. Here, module handbooks provide an overview of a study program, including information like workload, learning goals, examinations. As module handbooks between institutions may look very different, fully automated information retrieval is difficult and error-prone. Here, a user-assisted approach for module handbook content extraction could support the process and introduce manual data correction cycles to improve data quality. This demonstration paper presents a first prototype of a content extraction tool[3] using natural language processing (NLP) and text mining techniques to extract all properties and relevant details from module handbooks and prepare them for curriculum analytics.

While the content seems unstructured at first, a module handbook consists of a list of modules described by a set of properties. Each property can be described using a key-

---
[1] RWTH Aachen University, Learning Technologies, {roepke, schroeder}@cs.rwth-aachen.de, https://orcid.org/{0000-0003-0250-8521, 0000-0002-5178-8597}
[2] RWTH Aachen University, maximilian.nell@rwth-aachen.de
[3] https://git.rwth-aachen.de/learntech-lufgi9/mhb-extractor, last accessed 15.06.2023

doi: 10.18420/delfi2023-45

value pair, where the key is the *abstract* property name and the value is the assigned content, e.g. a property for module duration called "Moduldauer" and its value "1 Semester". These characteristics of the document structure can be exploited with the help of an NLP model [Ta20] and text mining [FT21]: On the one hand via a simple frequency analysis and on the other hand via the language model itself, recognizing certain strings in the document. In the first step, according to the motto *divide and conquer*, a term or string always appearing at the beginning of a module description is searched for, e.g., "Modulname". If not detectable by means of the model, it can also be recognized over a customizable Regular expression. Next, each module start is marked and the document is automatically split into one PDF per module. Now, for the recognition of the property keywords and their values, a predefined set of synonyms for module properties is evaluated and marked in the PDF using the NLP model. In addition, we extract a list of bold strings in the PDF and compare them with the keywords of the model. Under the assumption that keywords are printed in bold in many module handbooks, this heuristic is particularly well suited to supplementing the model. In a semi-assisted manner, the user then checks all marked key-value pairs for one module in order to correct markings and add missing properties and values. By allowing users to verify and correct extraction results, higher accuracy and reliability can be achieved. Based on similarities in the module description structure and repetitively used keywords, checking one marked module allows for adapting the model to detect properties in all. Here, corrected and verified key-value pairs may serve as training data for model improvement.

Overall, while the semi-assisted approach still needs user input and is therefore costly compared to fully automated approaches, the quality of the extraction results is crucial to its further use in curriculum analytics. With the development of a module handbook content extraction tool, we are able to retrieve comparable information from different module handbooks of different institutions and provide rich input data to the application of curriculum analytics. Potential analyses include the identification of trend topics for similar study programs or the generation of competency profiles, depending on students' module choices. Of particular interest is module handbook data for study path planning, e.g., by constructing a knowledge graph and recommend modules with connected topics or to foster specific competencies. Since NLP is already used in the extraction process, another interesting direction would be using curriculum data for mentoring and guidance tools, e.g., a generative AI-based chatbot for choosing a study program or elective courses.

Bibliography

[FT21]   Föll, P.; Thiesse, F.: Exploring Information Systems Curricula – A Text Mining Approach. Business & Information Systems Engineering, 63, pp. 711-732, 2021.

[Hi22]   Hilliger, I. et al.: Lessons learned from designing a curriculum analytics tool for improving student learning and program quality. Journal of Computing in Higher Education, 34(3), pp. 633-657, 2022.

[Ta20]   Tarcar, A. K. et al.: Healthcare NER Models Using Language Model Pretraining. In: Health Search and Data Mining Workshop (HSDM 2020). CEUR, pp. 12-18, 2020.

Ein Assistenzsystem zur Annotation von Learning Analytics Reports

Sven Judel[1], Paul Nitzke[2] und Ulrik Schroeder[1]

Abstract: Die verschiedenen Reports, die in Learning Analytics Dashboards aufbereitet werden, sollen Nutzende befähigen lehr- und lernbezogene Entscheidungen zu treffen. Dazu müssen diese Reports gelesen, verstanden und interpretiert werden. Wissen über die Lehr- und Lernsituationen, in denen Daten erhoben und analysiert wurden, kann dabei essenziell sein. Es kann eine zusätzliche kognitive Last bedeuten dieses Wissen während der Arbeit mit den Reports im Kopf oder anderweitig außerhalb des Dashboards präsent haben zu müssen. Diese Demo stellt ein Assistenzsystem vor, das Nutzenden erlaubt durch direkte Interaktionen mit Visualisierungen zusätzliche Informationen einzubinden. Das System ist in ein Learning Analytics Dashboard in Moodle integriert und erlaubt datumsbasierte Diagramme mit Daten oder Zeitspannen zu annotieren. Zusätzlich zu eigenem Wissen kann das System, basierend auf u. a. dem Moodle Kalender, eigene Vorschläge für Annotationen machen und auf potentiell relevante Ergebnisse hinweisen. Annotationen können mit anderen Nutzenden geteilt werden um eigenes Wissen oder eigene Erkenntnisse zu kommunizieren.

Keywords: Learning Analytics, Dashboard, Annotation, Assistenz

1 Einleitung

Die verschiedenen Reports, die als Visualisierungen oder textuelles Feedback in Learning Analytics (LA) Dashboards aufbereitet werden, sollen Nutzende befähigen lehr- und lernbezogene Entscheidungen zu treffen [Oc15]. Jedoch ist der Prozess der Datennutzung um informierte, bildungsbezogene Entscheidungen zu treffen nicht trivial. Vom LA Dashboard bereitgestellte Reports müssen in Wissen überführt und zur Anwendung gebracht werden. Wise und Jung leiteten aus der Literatur über die Nutzung von LA Dashboards ein Modell dieses Prozesses ab. Der Dateninterpretation ordnen sie die zwei Schritte des Lesens der Daten und des Erklärens von Mustern unter. Bei letzterem wird das Einordnen in einen Kontext als Teilschritt gelistet. [WJ19]

Solches Kontextwissen in die Reports zu integrieren kann eine kognitive Entlastung für die Nutzenden darstellen, da das Wissen nicht weiterhin im Kopf oder anderweitig präsent gehalten werden muss. Eine Möglichkeit dieser Integration wird in dieser Demo durch ein Assistenzsystem für ein LA Dashboard in Moodle vorgestellt.

---

[1] RWTH Aachen, Lerntechnologien, {judel, schroeder}@informatik.rwth-aachen.de, https://orcid.org/{0000-0002-0424-0402, 0000-0002-5178-8547}
[2] RWTH Aachen, paul.nitzke@rwth-aachen.de

2 Learning Analytics Kontext Assistenz

Abbildung 1 zeigt die zweite Version des Assistenzsystems während der Annotation eines Tages. Diese entstand basierend auf Rückmeldungen von potentiellen Nutzern während einer Evaluation der ersten Version. Neben den Rückmeldungen zum Interface wurden positive Rückmeldungen zur Idee der Annotation selbst gesammelt.

Zur Annotation stellt ein frei positionierbares Modal Nutzenden in einem chatähnlichen Interface zunächst die gegebenen Funktionalitäten vor. Durch einen Klick in das Diagramm kann ein Tag oder auch ein Zeitfenster zur Annotation ausgewählt werden. In der Abbildung sind die Kurszugriffe am ausgewählten Tag im Vergleich zu den Mustern der anderen Wochen besonders hoch. In der Beispielveranstaltung wurde an diesem Termin das freiwillige, kursbegleitende Projekt besprochen, zu dem Studierende sich anschließend im Moodle Kursraum zusätzlich registrieren mussten. Damit erklären sich die Lehrenden diesen Hochpunkt und könnten den Tag z. B. mit *Projektorga* annotieren.

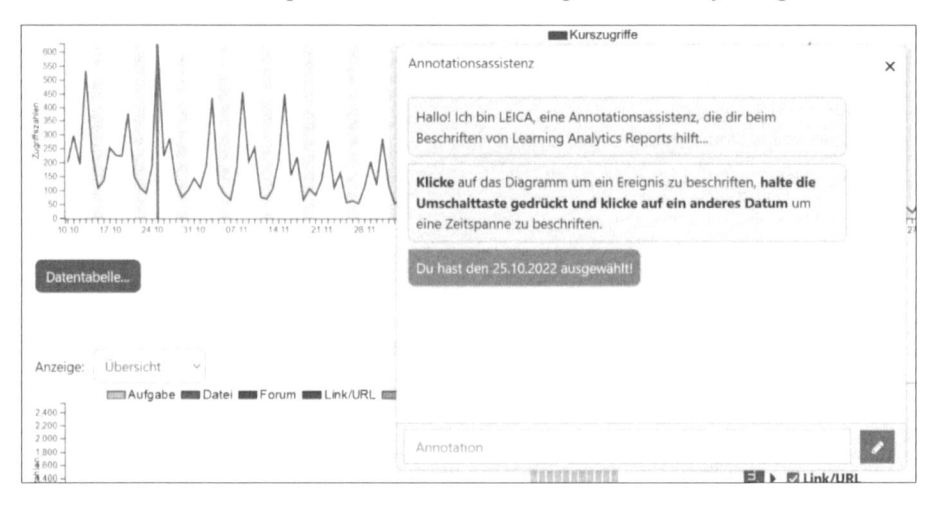

Abb. 1: Beispiel der Annotation eines Tages im Assistenzsystem

In der Demo können Interessierte die Annotationsoptionen selbst ausprobieren. Weiterhin möchten wir in Diskussionen Anregungen für weitere annotierbare Reports, sowie weitere Arten von Kontextinformationen, die in Reports integriert werden können, sammeln.

Literaturverzeichnis

[Oc15] Ochoa, Xavier: Visualizing Uncertainty in the Prediction of Academic Risk. In: Proceedings of the First International Workshop on Visual Aspects of Learning Analytics co-located with 5th International Learning Analytics and Knowledge Conference (LAK 2015). Poughkeepsie New York, 2015.

[WJ19] Wise, Alyssa Friend; Jung, Yeonji: Teaching with Analytics: Towards a Situated Model of Instructional Decision-Making. Journal of Learning Analytics, 6(2), Juli 2019.

DMT-Magic: Interaktives E-Assessment in der Datenbank-Lehre mit Jupyter Notebooks

Martin Petersohn[1], Konrad Schöbel[2] und Andreas Thor[3]

Abstract: Dieser Beitrag demonstriert DMT-Magic, ein System für interaktives E-Assessment im Fachgebiet Datenbanken unter Verwendung von Jupyter Notebooks. DMT-Magic fungiert dabei als Jupyter Magic Command, das dynamisch E-Assessment-Aufgaben in Jupyter Notebooks integriert. Die Aufgaben stammen dabei vom E-Assessment-Tool DMT (Data Management Tester), das auch die Bewertung der eingegebenen Lösung inklusive Feedback-Generierung realisiert. Dazu steuert DMT-Magic die Kommunikation mit DMT und erzeugt dynamisch das User Interface direkt im Jupyter Notebook. Unterschiedliche Aufgabenformate decken dabei typische Datenbankübungen ab. Die Demonstration illustriert den Einsatz von DMT-Magic sowohl für interaktive Vorlesungen als auch innerhalb digitaler Übungsblätter für Studierende.

Keywords: Jupyter Notebook, E-Assessment, Data Management Tester

DMT-Magic ist ein System für interaktives E-Assessment im Fachgebiet Datenbanken unter Verwendung von Jupyter Notebooks. Es ermöglicht die Integration eines interaktiven Assessments während des Bearbeitungszyklus, d.h. Lernende können das Notebook bearbeiten, z.B. in einer Zelle Quellcode entwickeln, und ohne Unterbrechung bzw. Systemwechsel ihre Lösung zu einer Aufgabe in einer anderen Zelle bewerten lassen. Diese Form ermöglicht es auch, E-Assessment in einer interaktiven Vorlesung direkt in der Lehrveranstaltung einzusetzen. DMT-Magic integriert dabei das E-Assessment-Tool DMT (Data Management Tester) [TK21], das die automatische Bewertung strukturierter Ergebnisse, die häufig als Lösung von Aufgaben in der Datenbank-Lehre entstehen, ermöglicht. Die Ergebnisformate umfassen u.a. SQL-Anfragen und die Spezifikation von Tabellen.

DMT-Magic ist dabei als ein Jupyter Magic Command implementiert, die durch ein Präfix (%) gekennzeichnet werden und eine einfache Möglichkeit bieten, die Funktionalität des Kernels zu erweitern[4]. Bei der Ausführung einer Zelle, z.B. `%dmt bibliothek:5` in Zelle [3] von Abb. 1, sendet DMT-Magic einen Request an DMT und erhält Informationen zur Aufgabe, die durch eine eindeutige Id (`bibliothek:5`) referenziert wird. Daraufhin erstellt DMT-Magic ein passendes User Interface im Output der Zelle, was neben der textuellen Ausgabe der Aufgabenstellung je nach Aufgabentyp z. B. eine Textbox für SQL-Anfragen (Zelle [3]) oder eine tabellarische Eingabe (Zelle [4]) enthält. Zusätzlich wird

---

[1] Hochschule für Technik, Wirtschaft und Kultur Leipzig, martin.petersohn@stud.htwk-leipzig.de
[2] Hochschule für Technik, Wirtschaft und Kultur Leipzig, konrad.schoebel@htwk-leipzig.de
[3] Hochschule für Technik, Wirtschaft und Kultur Leipzig, andreas.thor@htwk-leipzig.de
[4] Für weitere technische Details zu DMT-Magic sei auf [PST23] verwiesen.

doi: 10.18420/delfi2023-47

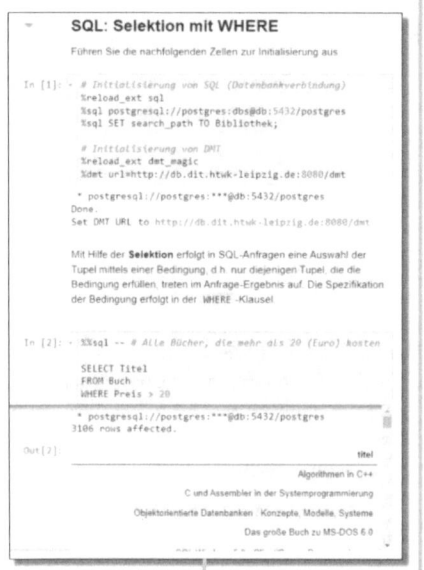

Abb. 1: Jupyter Notebook mit interaktiven Aufgaben unter Verwendung von DMT-Magic.

ein Button *Abgabe überprüfen* dargestellt, der die eingegebene Lösung an DMT zur Überprüfung sendet und die erhaltene Bewertung inklusive Feedback darstellt.

Die Demonstration illustriert die Nutzung von DMT-Magic am Beispiel einer interaktiven Vorlesung im Fachgebiet Datenbanken mit einem Notebook analog zu Abb. 1. Dazu wird die Magic zunächst im Notebook geladen (`%reload_ext dmt_magic`) und die Verbindung zu DMT hergestellt (`%dmt url=...`). Mit Hilfe einer Datenbankverbindung (`%sql`) lassen sich SQL-Anfragen formulieren, deren Ergebnis als Output der jeweiligen Notebook-Zelle erscheint und inspiziert werden kann. Im Beispiel von Abb. 1 ist das die Anfrage nach Büchern, die mehr als 20€ kosten (Zelle [2]), als einfaches Beispiel für die Selektion in SQL. Basierend auf dieser Einführung kann nun DMT-Magic für eine andere Anfrage verwendet werden (*Alle Bücher, die vor 1980 erschienen sind.*), bei der Lernende ihre Kompetenz selbst überprüfen können. Darüber hinaus kann die Kompetenz auch mit anderen Aufgabentypen überprüft werden, z. B. in dem Lernende für eine gegebene SQL-Anfrage das Ergebnis in Tabellenform angeben (Zelle [4]). Bei fehlerhaften Lösungen wird unterhalb des Buttons auch das Feedback von DMT angezeigt (*Unterschiedliche Anzahl an Zeilen*), so dass Lernende zur Überarbeitung ihrer Lösung angeregt werden.

Literaturverzeichnis

[PST23] Petersohn, M.; Schöbel, K.; Thor, A.: Kopplung von Jupyter Notebooks mit externen E-Assessment-Systemen am Beispiel des Data Management Testers. In: 21. Fachtagung Bildungstechnologien (DELFI). 2023.

[TK21] Thor, A.; Kirsten, T.: Das E-Assessment-Tool DMT. Datenbank-Spektrum 21/1, 2021.

Code and Consequences - an Educational Game about Social Scoring

Thiemo Leonhardt [1], Johanna Walther[2], Jens Podeyn[2] and Anne Hamann[1]

Abstract: In this demo we present the serious game Code and Consequences. The learning application is implemented as a point and click adventure and discusses the possible influence of social scoring on society in a school context. The educational game was developed using the Escoria framework of the Godot Engine.

Keywords: Point-and-Click, Serious Games, Social Scoring

1 Concept and Design

In this paper we present the point-and-click learning application *Code and Consequences*. The goal of Code and Consequences is to experience the social and societal consequences of IT solutions, in this case social scoring systems, and to reflect on their possible effects. The target group of the learning application is students in grades 8 to 10. As is typical for point-and-click adventures, the actions and reality of the main character's life are to be reflected through interactions with non-player characters (NPCs). The player experiences different scenarios with social relevance, is asked to perceive negative as well as positive effects of technology in connection with social scoring systems and reflects them in his own perception.

The story follows Aristotle's common three-act structure (see Tab. 1), which is often used in game productions [Sc20]. After an introductory tutorial, the character spends the first act experiencing and navigating the world under the influence of a social scoring system. In the second act, the system's problems and benefits become increasingly apparent, culminating in a decision against a perceived injustice. In the third act, the problem is solved by the main character. The plots are humorous without satirizing the serious core of the story. The technical implementation as well as the aesthetics of the learning

---

[1] Technische Universität Dresden, Professur für Didaktik der Informatik, Nöthnitzerstraße 46, 01187 Dresden, {thiemo.leonhardt | anne.hamann}@tu-dresden.de, https://orcid.org/0000-0003-4725-9776.
[2] Technische Universität Dresden, Professur für Didaktik der Informatik, Nöthnitzerstraße 46, 01187 Dresden, {johanna-walther | jens.podeyn}@mailbox.tu-dresden.de.

doi: 10.18420/delfi2023-48

application implemented in the bachelor thesis by Selina Natschke [Se23] in the Godot Engine[3] and the Escoria Framework[4].

Type	Location	Goal
Tutorial	Classroom	Practice game interaction
Act 1: Everyday life in school	School (7 rooms)	Achieve a good social scoring value
Act 2: The world outside of school	City (5 rooms)	Manipulate the social scoring algorithm
Act 3: Chaos in the school	School (7 rooms)	Unraveling the chaos

Tab. 1: Storyline

The learning application is based on the content area *Informatics, Man and Society* of the *Recommendations for Educational Standards in Informatics for Secondary Level* of the German Informatics Society [Ge08]. Students should be able to describe the changes in their own actions at school and in their free time, comment on automated processes and evaluate their implementation, and evaluate the effects of automation in the workplace. The basis for a reflective discussion is the specialized knowledge of computer science that students are taught in computer science classes to be able to discuss interactions between computer systems and their social embedding. The learning application should therefore be embedded in the computer science classroom, where it should be discussed and reflected upon. The approach of introducing the social effects of computer systems through point-and-click adventures and thus making them usable as a medium in the classroom is the goal of our further research.

Bibliography

[Ge08]   Gesellschaft für Informatik e.V.: Grundsätze und Standards für die Informatik in der Schule: Bildungsstandards Informatik für die Sekundarstufe I, 2008.

[Sc20]   Schell, J.: Die Kunst des Game Designs. Bessere Games konzipieren und entwickeln [The Art of Game Design. Design and Develop better Games]. mitp, Frechen, 2020.

[Se23]   Selina Natschke: Code and Consequences - Visuelle Gestaltung eines Serious Games zum Thema Social Scoring [Code and Consequences - Visual Design of a Serious Game on the Topic of Social Scoring]. Bachelorarbeit, Dresden, 2023.

---

[3] https://godotengine.org/
[4] https://gamefromscratch.com/escoria-point-click-adventure-game-framework-for-godot/

Inside the CPU - eine interaktive VR-Lernanwendung zur Von-Neumann-Architektur

Thiemo Leonhardt [1], Karl Wenzel[2] und David Baberowski [3]

Abstrakt: In diesem Demobeitrag wird eine VR-Lernanwendung zur Von-Neumann-Architektur vorgestellt, die als Lernmittel in Schul- und Hochschulszenarien eingesetzt werden kann.

Keywords: Von-Neumann-Architektur, VR, Lernanwendung

1 Konzept und Design

Die Von-Neumann-Architektur als Referenzmodell für einen Computer ist ein Lerngegenstand der Informatik, sowohl in der Schule als auch in der Hochschule. Zur Vermittlung des Referenzmodells und der Funktionsweise eines Rechners insgesamt, werden konzeptuelle Modelle [GM00] zur Funktionsweise eines Rechners definiert, die dann didaktisch reduziert in Form von *notional machines* [So13] an die Lerngruppe angepasst vermittelt werden. Der Johnny-Simulator ist eine häufig verwendete *notional machine* für die Von-Neumann-Architektur, für die es bereits zahlreiche Übungen und Materialien für den Informatikunterricht[4] gibt. An der TU Dresden wird dieser Ansatz im ersten Semester des Lehramtsstudiums Informatik verwendet, um die Grundlagen der Schulinformatik darunter auch das Thema Netzwerke zu wiederholen. In der entsprechenden Lehrveranstaltung *Grundlagen der Informatik* schneiden die Studierenden jedoch trotz des Einsatzes des Johnny-Simulator seit 2019 in der Klausur bei dem Thema Rechnerstruktur im Vergleich zu den anderen Themen unterdurchschnittlich ab.

Als Lernziele sollen die Studierenden 1. die Aufgaben der Komponenten der Von-Neumann-Architektur erklären, 2. den Datenfluss über den Bus innerhalb der Von-Neumann-Architektur nachvollziehen und 3. vorgegebene Makrocode-Befehle als Microcode-Befehle ausführen können. Da der Ansatz über den Johnny-Simulator nicht für alle Studierenden ausreichend ist, wurde die VR-Lernanwendung *Inside the CPU*[5] entwickelt. In der Lernanwendung wurde der Schwerpunkt auf die Vermittlung der

---

[1] TU Dresden, Professur für Didaktik der Informatik, Nöthnitzer Str. 46, 01187 Dresden, thiemo.leonhardt@tu-dresden.de, https://orcid.org/0000-0003-4725-9770
[2] TU Dresden, Professur für Didaktik der Informatik, Nöthnitzer Str. 46, 01187 Dresden, karl.wenzel@mailbox.tu-dresden.de
[3] TU Dresden, Professur für Didaktik der Informatik, Nöthnitzer Str. 46, 01187 Dresden, david.baberowski@tu-dresden.de, https://orcid.org/0000-0001-6308-3634
[4] https://www.inf-schule.de/rechner/johnny
[5] Der Sourcecode ist unter der GNU GPLv3 lizenziert unter https://gitlab.com/ddi-tu-dresden/vr/vr-router

doi: 10.18420/delfi2023-49

Abläufe innerhalb der Von-Neumann-Architektur gelegt, indem ein vorgegebener Makrocode im RAM-Speicher durch die Ausführung des entsprechenden Mikrocodes abgearbeitet wird. In der Single-Player-Lernanwendung steuern die Lernenden die Busse zwischen den Komponenten. Die Ästhetik orientiert sich an einer Steampunk-Optik und versetzt die Lernenden in eine Industriehalle vor eine große Maschine mit mehreren Komponenten (siehe Abb. 1). Das Spiel besteht aus zwei Modi. Im ersten Modus werden die Komponenten der Maschine, sowie die Busse an einer Steuerkonsole mit Schaltern und Hebeln bedient. Im zweiten Modus müssen die Daten zwischen den Komponenten von den Spielenden selbst transportiert werden.

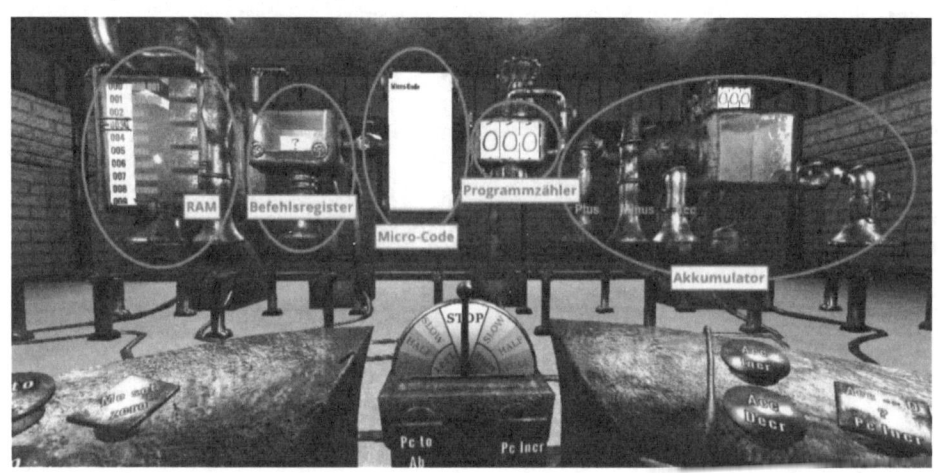

Abb. 1: Repräsentation der Von-Neumann-Architektur und deren Komponenten, sowie ein Ausschnitt der Steuerkonsole in der VR-Anwendung *Inside the CPU*

Durch den Einsatz der VR-Technologie soll die Motivation der Studierenden erhöht werden, sich mit dem Lerngebiet auseinanderzusetzen. Weiterhin wird durch das gesteigerte Präsenzempfinden in VR-Anwendungen im Gegensatz zu Desktopanwendungen eine erhöhte Lernleistung für bestimmte Personengruppen erhofft. Ob der Einsatz der zusätzlichen VR-Anwendung eine Steigerung der Lernleistung der Studierenden insgesamt erzeugen kann, wird eine aufbauende Evaluationsstudie zeigen.

Literaturverzeichnis

[GM00] Greca, I. M.; Moreira, M. A.: Mental models, conceptual models, and modelling. International Journal of Science Education 1/22, S. 1–11, 2000.

[So13] Sorva, J.: Notional machines and introductory programming education. ACM Transactions on Computing Education 2/13, S. 1–31, 2013.

Flowboard: Visual Flow-Based Embedded Programming for Young Learners

Anke Brocker[1] and Simon Voelker[1]

Abstract: Through beginner-friendly environments like the Arduino IDE, embedded programming has become an essential part of STEM education. Learning embedded programming demands coding knowledge as well as basic electronics skills. To explore if a different programming paradigm can help with learning, we developed Flowboard, which uses Flow-Based Programming (FBP) rather than the usual imperative programming paradigm. This way, users code using processing nodes arranged in a graph instead of command sequences. Flowboard consists of a visual flow-based editor on an iPad, an Arduino board in the hardware frame and two breadboards next to the iPad, letting learners connect their visual graphs seamlessly to the electronics. Graph edits are implemented directly, making Flowboard a live coding environment.

Keywords: Embedded Development Environments, Young Learners, Learning Tools

1 Introduction

Embedded development environments like the Arduino IDE enable makers and novices to develop interactive artifacts [PGJ00]. However, learning embedded programming is challenging as it requires an understanding of (a) basic electronics, (b) coding, and (c) the connections between hardware and software [Mc01]. The traditional *imperative programming* paradigm is widespread. Users mostly need to type source code in text, which may lead to syntax errors. *Block-based* environments like Scratch replace textual source code with a graphical editor to assemble code from visual programming blocks. That avoids syntax errors but is still the imperative programming paradigm. We wanted to understand if a different programming paradigm, called *flow-based programming (FBP)*, can help learners even more. In FBP, data flows through a network of nodes that process the data. This paradigm closely resembles electronic signal processing circuits. Unlike in imperative programming, parallel processes in one program are straightforward [WMR02]. FBP development environments such as Microflo or XOD have been available for a few years. These systems are missing two aspects that motivated us to design and build our own hardware and software: 1) *Liveness:* Program graphs can process incoming data and reflect changes directly. These live programs, like analog circuits, can respond immediately to incoming electronic signals, without an Edit-Compile-Run cycle. 2) *Seamlessness:* The points where electrical signals flow into and out of the program graph have a direct correspondence both in the visual graph and as hardware I/O pins.

---

[1] RWTH Aachen University, brocker@cs.rwth-aachen.de, voelker@cs.rwth-aachen.de

doi: 10.18420/delfi2023-50

2 System Design

The user creates her program graph using a visual, flow-based multitouch editor (cf. https://hci.rwth-aachen.de/flowboard) running an iOS app on a 12.9" iPad Pro. Touch-based interfaces also support more natural interactions that can support learning [Ho04]. Flowboard contains an Arduino Uno board and a custom printed circuit board that also holds the "switchboard": a second microcontroller and 18 electronic switches. The iPad editor talks to the Arduino and the switchboard controller via Bluetooth. The Arduino is running our modified version of the Firmata protocol. Firmata allows the iPad editor to set and read the Arduino pins through serial commands sent via Bluetooth. With a real-time protocol like Firmata Flowboard is a live system as the iPad editor interprets the graph continuously, sending Firmata commands to the Arduino to achieve the appropriate behavior. We provide all files open source. The user has access to all Arduino's I/O pins twice, once on each side of the iPad. Pins are always active and detect plugged-in components automatically. Below the screen, a hardware toggle switch allows disconnecting power from the breadboards to reduce the risk of short circuits while building them. The Flowboard case has three layers, the bottom layer contains the custom circuit board, switchboard controller, and cables. The middle layer holds the breadboards and the iPad. The top layer contains the breadboards, the external pin row connectors, and a power switch. The user drags nodes onto the canvas from the node menu and connects them by drawing virtual wires between them. Both sides of the editor show virtual representations of the input resp.~output pins aligned with the hardware pins on each side of the iPad. Active pins show a green LED and are not greyed out on the screen. The node menu includes nodes for basic mathematical and logical functions as well as nodes to work with more complex electronic components, such as servo motors. We believe that our *Flowboard* prototype using FBP, liveness and seamlessness may increase students' understanding of the interaction between embedded hardware and software code. We hope to facilitate the mental model of students in terms of what programming an electronic component involves and would like to study what students are able to translate of their gained knowledge to non-graphical IDEs. More about the project can be found on https://hci.rwth-aachen.de/flowboard.

Bibliography

[PGJ00]   Papavlasopoulou, S.; Giannakos, M.; Jaccheri, L. (2016). Empirical Studies on the Maker Movement, a Promising Approach to Learning: A Literature Review. Entertainment Computing. 18. doi: 10.1016/j.entcom.2016.09.002.

[Mc01]   McGrath, W. et al: 2018. WiFröst: Bridging the Information Gap for Debugging of Networked Embedded Systems. In Proc. ACM UIST '18. 447–455.

[WMR02]   Wesley M. Johnston, J. R. Paul Hanna, and Richard J. Millar. 2004. Advances in dataflow programming languages. ACM Comput. Surv. 36, 1 (March 2004), 1–34.

[Ho04]   Hornecker, E. et al.: 2008. Collaboration and interference: Awareness with mice or touch input. In Proc. CSCW '08. 167–176.

Adapting RDMO for the Efficient Management of Educational Research Data

Natalie Kiesler [1], Daniel Schiffner [1] and Axel Nieder-Vahrenholz[1]

Abstract: Research data management has become a core element of research projects in educational technology research. Tools like the Research Data Management Organiser (RDMO) offer support to researchers by gathering metadata of (planned) projects, studies and their output in a structured manner. It further facilitates machine actionable components so that metadata and information can be exchanged by connecting metadata, repositories, and institutions. In this demo, we present a use case of RDMO at a German research data center. Therein, we adapt RDMO's export plugin so that it generates JSON in the data structure of the German Network of Educational Research Data, and thus allows the export of metadata from RDMO to research data centers. This proof-of-concept thus presents an application scenario of RDMO, and how it can contribute to an improved data management process in educational technology research.

Keywords: Research Data Management Organiser, metadata, export, interoperability

1 Einleitung

The Research Data Management Organiser (RDMO) is a tool that supports the structured planning and management of research projects and their data [Kl23]. RDMO further provides researchers with machine actionable data management plans (maDMPs) which enable a basic interoperability between RDMO [Mi20] and, for example, research data centers archiving data. This interoperability is crucial to support the full data life cycle of research, especially after its completion. Research data centers such as those within the German Network of Educational Research Data (GNERD) help with the long-term availability and accessibility of research data, thereby increasing its FAIRness, provenance, etc. [KS22]. Fortunately, RDMO offers export options in XML or CSV format by default. Moreover, maDMPs and their export as JSON files are supported. However, the maDMP default structure is less detailed so that it does not match the metadata scheme used within GNERD (e.g., project attributes, see Fig. 1). As a consequence, researchers willing to share their data with the network would have to enter and submit the entire metadata of their research into another system than RDMO.

---

[1] DIPF | Leibniz Institute for Research and Information in Education, Information Center Education, Rostocker Straße 6, 60323 Frankfurt am Main, {kiesler, schiffner, a.nieder-vahrenholz}@dipf.de, https://orcid.org/0000-0002-6843-2729, https://orcid.org/0000-0002-0794-0359

doi: 10.18420/delfi2023-51

2 Adapting and Extending RDMO's Export Options

To avoid this repetitive and error-prone procedure, we adapted RDMO's Python code for the generation of the JSON files so that it represents the GNERD structure and metadata scheme. To be precise, the following tasks were conducted:

- Utilize the Python code generating maDMP's JSON scheme as template [Mi20],

- Adapt structure and metadata scheme of the generated JSON to reflect those of GNERD,

- Map RDMO's standard DMP with the metadata and attributes required by GNERD, and include controlled vocabularies.

To conclude, this new export option helps researchers in the context of education to manage their data after a project's end, especially with regard to long-term storage. It further proves the interoperability of RDMO and its contribution to a more sustainable research data management in educational technology research and related fields. This proof-of-concept opens the possibility for multiple research questions in the maDMP context: a) Does a unified tool actually avoid the repetitive and error-prone procedure of re-entering metadata; b) What metadata can be filled automatically by extracting it from either the user or the data; c) Can this be used as an iterative approach to update existing DMPs or research objects? We will investigate these questions in the near future.

Fig. 1: Excerpt of the newly generated JSON file reflecting the GNERD metadata scheme.

```
▼ project:
    title:              "Metadata Export (in work)"
    ▼ subtitle:         "In scheme of German Network of Educational Research Data"
    acronym:            "XP-VFDB"
    duration_from:      "2022-11-09"
    duration_to:        "2023-05-31"
    funding_code:       "DFG-0815"
    funding_agency:     "German Research Foundation"
    ▼ programme:
        acronym:        "EBF"
    ▼ description:      "Export a Data Management Plan from RDMO tool in the JSON scheme of GNERD"
    comment_external:   "(just a dummy comment)"
```

Bibliography

[Kl23]   Klar, J., https://github.com/rdmorganiser/rdmo, accessed 27/03/2023.

[KS22]   Kiesler, N.; Schiffner, D.: On the Lack of Recognition of Software Artifacts and IT Infrastructure in Educational Technology Research. In Henning, P. A., Striewe, M. & Wölfel, M. (Hrsg.): 20. Fachtagung Bildungstechnologien (DELFI) 2022. Gesellschaft für Informatik e.V., Bonn, S. 201-206, 2022. https://doi.org/10.18420/delfi2022-034

[Mi20]   Miksa, T., https://github.com/RDA-DMP-Common/RDA-DMP-Common-Standard, accessed 27/03/2023.

Strukturformeln für Moleküle zeichnen und differenziertes Feedback erhalten: Eine integrierte Lösung im Rahmen des E-Assessment-Systems JACK

Michael Striewe [1]

Abstract: Zu den Kompetenzen in der organischen Chemie gehört das Zeichnen von Strukturformeln für Moleküle und Reaktionsmechanismen. Existierende Werkzeuge dazu erwiesen sich als zu umständlich oder nicht leistungsfähig genug, um anspruchsvolle Übungen digital zu unterstützen. Die neue Integration eines web-basierten Molekül-Editor in das E-Assessment-System JACK mit Funktionen zur Analyse der Eingaben erwies sich in einer ersten Erprobung als besser nutzbar.

Keywords: E-Assessment, Feedback, Zeichenaufgabe, Organische Chemie.

1 Einleitung und Stand der Technik

Das Zeichnen von Strukturformeln einzelner Moleküle sowie von Reaktionsmechanismen sind Kompetenzen, die Schülerinnen und Schüler in der Oberstufe sowie Studierende in Lehrveranstaltungen zur organischen Chemie erwerben sollen. Um Übungen mit einem E-Assessment-System zu unterstützen, muss für die Eingabe ein Werkzeug verfügbar sein, das es ermöglicht, anspruchsvolle Aufgaben (z. B. unter Beachtung stereochemischer Eigenschaften von Molekülen) zu bearbeiten und das zugleich leicht bedienbar ist. Die Auswertung muss unwichtige zeichnerische Details ignorieren und verschiedenartige Abweichungen von den erwarteten Lösungen mit individuellem Feedback versehen können.

Eine einfache Umsetzung entsprechender Aufgaben ohne integrierte Lösung ist möglich, indem Lernende Strukturformeln in einem externen Werkzeug zeichnen, als Zeichenkette in Form des standardisierten InChI-Codes[2] exportieren und diese in herkömmliche Lückentextaufgaben einfügen, so dass das genutzte Übungssystem diese Eingaben mit erwarteten Eingaben vergleichen und mit Hilfe regulärer Ausdrücke auf verschiedene Eigenschaften hin untersuchen kann. Das Vorgehen ist jedoch auf Seiten der Lernenden äußerst umständlich und auf Seiten der Auswertung auf eine reine Zeichenanalyse ohne Berücksichtigung der chemischen Semantik des InChI-Codes beschränkt.

Integrierte Lösungen sind durchaus seit vielen Jahren verfügbar [Jo15], aber auf Seiten der Eingabe zu limitiert, um anspruchsvolle Aufgaben aus universitären Lehrveranstaltungen umsetzen zu können. Zudem besteht auch hier weiterhin das Problem der

---

[1] Universität Duisburg-Essen, paluno – The Ruhr Institute for Software Technology, Gerlingstraße 16, 45127 Essen, michael.striewe@paluno.uni-due.de, https://orcid.org/0000-0001-8866-6971
[2] https://www.inchi-trust.org/

doi: 10.18420/delfi2023-52

Auswertung, wenn nicht sogar eine rein grafische Speicherung der Eingabe erfolgt, für die gar keine automatische Bewertung zur Verfügung steht.

2 Integrierte Lösung

Die neue, integrierte Lösung basiert auf dem E-Assessment-System JACK, dessen Architektur für fachspezifische Erweiterungen gut geeignet ist [PS19] und für das mit der Lösung eine neue Anwendungsdomäne erschlossen wird. Für die Eingabe wurde der webbasierten Editor Kekule.js[3] ausgewählt, da er von allen frei verfügbaren Werkzeugen den größten Funktionsumfang bietet. Er ist zudem gut konfigurierbar, so dass die verfügbaren Funktionen individuell auf die jeweilige Aufgabe sowie die Fähigkeiten der Lernenden eingestellt werden können. Für die Auswertung wird die Eingabe im proprietären Format des Editors, im standardisierten „molfile"-Format und als InChI-Code gespeichert, so dass Semantik- und Layout-Informationen erhalten bleiben. Lehrende können Prüffunktionen auf die Eingabe anwenden und somit gezielt beispielsweise die stereochemischen Eigenschaften einer Einreichung überprüfen und mit Feedback versehen. Für die Umsetzung der Prüffunktionen wurde u. a. das Chemistry Development Kit (CDK)[4] integriert, das die chemische Semantik der Eingabe berücksichtigen kann.

3 Erprobung und Verbesserungsmöglichkeiten

Die integrierte Lösung wurde im SS 2022 als Prototyp und im WS 2022/23 regulär im Lehrbetrieb in zwei universitären Vorlesungen der Uni Bonn sowie im Rahmen eines Projekts im Lehramtsstudium auch in einem Oberstufenkurs in Bonn eingesetzt. In der qualitativen Evaluation wurde insbesondere das sofortige Feedback positiv hervorgehoben. Die Eingabemöglichkeiten wurden einerseits als bequem und schnell, andererseits aber auch bei vollem Funktionsumfang des Editors als schwierig zu bedienen bewertet. Daher wurden im SS 2023 Möglichkeiten zur aufgabenspezifischen Beschränkung des Editors umgesetzt. Lernende und Lehrende wünschten sich zudem weitere Möglichkeiten für noch differenzierteres Feedback, die in kommenden Versionen umgesetzt werden.

Literaturverzeichnis

[Jo15]   Jobst, C.: Potenziale neuer Fragetypen für die Naturwissenschaften. In: Grundfragen Multimedialen Lehrens und Lernens (GML² 2015). S. 145-152, 2015.

[PS19]   Pobel, S.; Striewe, M.: Domain-Specific Extensions for an E-Assessment System. In: Advances in Web-Based Learning - ICWL 2019, Springer, Cham. S. 327-331, 2019.

---

[3] http://partridgejiang.github.io/Kekule.js/
[4] https://cdk.github.io/

E-Assessment für Entity-Relationship-Diagramme mit FEEDI

Erik Morawetz [1], Nadine Hahm [2] und Andreas Thor [3]

Abstract: Dieser Beitrag demonstriert den Einsatz von FEEDI (Feedback im Diagramm-Assessment) für Entity-Relationship-Diagramme. FEEDI ist eine E-Assessment-Lösung, welche studentische ER-Diagramme automatisiert bewertet und Feedback auf eingereichte Lösungen gibt. Die Demonstration illustriert, wie Lehrende ihre Musterlösung hochladen und mittels einer GUI annotieren können. Für die Bewertung einer studentischen Lösung wandelt FEEDI die Diagramme zunächst in eine interne Graph-Repräsentation um und ermittelt mittels Graph-Matching die größtmögliche Passung. Aus dem Ergebnis des Matchings wird dann eine Bewertung sowie für fehlende bzw. falsche Aspekte der studentischen Lösung ein Feedback ausgegeben. FEEDI eignet sich als Übungs-System für Diagramme und grafische Modellierungen für Studierende im MINT-Bereich.

Keywords: E-Assessment, Entity-Relationship-Diagramm, Feedback

1 Demonstration von FEEDI für ER-Diagramme

FEEDI (Feedback im Diagramm-Assessment) ist ein E-Assessment-System für MINT-Fächer in der Hochschullehre, um studentische Diagramme und andere grafische Repräsentationen automatsch zu bewerten und Feedback zu diesen zu generieren. FEEDI nutzt eine verallgemeinerte Beschreibung von Diagrammen, um eine studentische Lösung (SL) mit einer oder mehreren Musterlösungen (ML) abzugleichen. Möglichst viele Prozessschritte sind generalisiert und auf eine Vielzahl an Eingabeformaten und Diagrammtypen im MINT-Bereich übertragbar, und werden hier am Beispiel von Entity-Relationship-Diagrammen (ER-Diagrammen) vorgestellt. In PowerPoint oder Diagrams.net (draw.io) erstellte ER-Diagramme können bereits für den Einsatz mit FEEDI genutzt werden, während die Erkennung von Pixelgrafiken noch in Arbeit ist. FEEDI verteilt Punkte für korrekte Elemente der SL (numerisches Feedback), wie z.B. Entitäten, etc., die mit denjenigen der ML übereinstimmen. Es markiert inkorrekte oder fehlende Elemente, sowie strukturelle Fehler wie falsche Beziehungen der Elemente (grafisches Feedback). Letztendlich formuliert FEEDI Hinweise auf Fehler, oder gibt Erklärungen aus (textuelles Feedback), ganz nach Spezifikation. Auch die ML selbst kann als zusätzliches Feedback angezeigt werden.

---

[1] Hochschule für Technik, Wirtschaft und Kultur Leipzig, erik.morawetz@htwk-leipzig.de
[2] Hochschule für Technik, Wirtschaft und Kultur Leipzig, nadine.hahm@htwk-leipzig.de
[3] Hochschule für Technik, Wirtschaft und Kultur Leipzig, andreas.thor@htwk-leipzig.de

doi: 10.18420/delfi2023-53

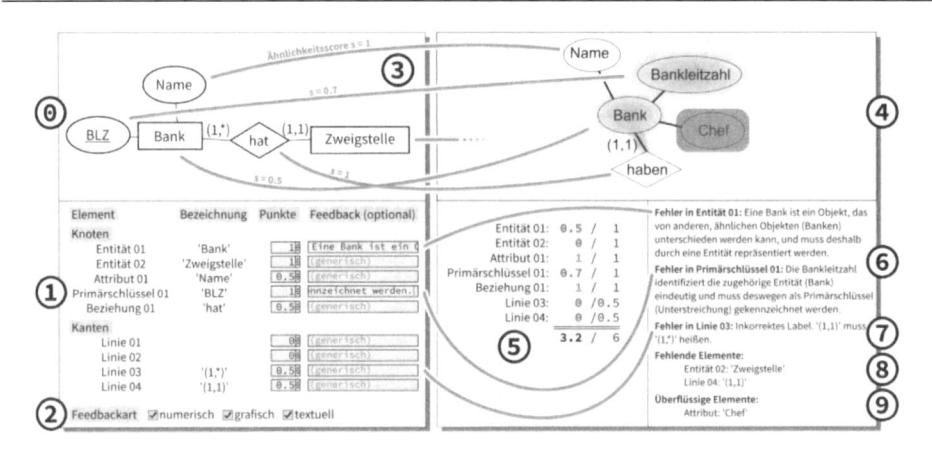

Abb. 1: User Interface des FEEDI-Prototyps. Links: Eingabemaske für Lehrende, um Feedback und Bepunktung in der Musterlösung zu spezifizieren. Rechts: Ausgabe des Feedbacks zu der studentischen Lösung, gemäß enthaltener Fehler und Spezifikation durch die Lehrperson.

Abb. 1 zeigt das User Interface zur Annotation der ML und die Ausgabe von Feedback zur SL von FEEDI. Lehrende erstellen eine ML in einem externen Programm und lassen diese von FEEDI einlesen ⓪. FEEDI erkennt die enthaltenen Bildelemente (*Knoten*) und ihre Beziehungen zueinander (*Kanten*) und gibt diese als Liste aus ①. FEEDI trifft Vorannahmen zu Bepunktung (z.B. 1 Punkt je Bildelement) und Feedback (Zusammenfassung des Fehlers). Die Lehrperson kann nun tiefer gehendes Feedback formulieren, das im Falle eines Fehlers ausgegeben werden soll, und Punktwertungen anpassen. Auch lässt sich die Art des Feedbacks festlegen ②.

In Abb. 1 rechte Seite wird das Feedback an Studierende exemplarisch aufgezeigt. Das Diagramm wurde mit der ML abgeglichen und das *beste Mapping* [MHT23] aufeinander identifiziert ③. Aus den *Ähnlichkeitsscores* der *Matches* ergibt sich, ob ein Fehler vorliegt. Im ersten Fall ist ein Element in der SL, aber nicht in der ML enthalten. Dieses wird rot in der SL markiert ④, und kann auch textuell gelistet werden ⑨. Grafisches Feedback kann auch gegeben werden, wenn Bildelemente Fehler enthalten – hier hellrot markiert ④. Es werden alternative Eingaben/Synonyme berücksichtigt, die in der Musterlösung hinterlegt wurden. Zu diesen Fehlern wird nach Angaben in der ML Feedbacktext generiert. Ist ein Feedbacktext spezifiziert worden, so wird dieser ausgegeben ⑥. Bleibt die Einstellung auf generisch, so produziert FEEDI eine simple Zusammenfassung ⑦. Elemente, die in der ML enthalten sind, aber nicht in der SL, werden als Liste ausgegeben ⑧. Letztendlich bepunktet FEEDI die SL, indem es die Punktewertung für jedes Element der ML mit dem Ähnlichkeitsscore des entsprechenden Matches multipliziert ⑤.

Literaturverzeichnis

[MHT23] Morawetz, E.; Hahm, N.; Thor, A.: Automatisierte Bewertung und Feedback-Generierung für grafische Modellierungen und Diagramme mit FeeDi. In: 21. Fachtagung Bildungstechnologien (DELFI). 2023.

Multimodales kooperatives Lernen mit einem digitalen Stift im inklusiven Unterricht

Kensuke Akao[1]

Abstract: Im Zuge der Digitalisierung im Bildungsbereich können moderne Technologien ein Umfeld ermöglichen, in dem Lernende mit Behinderung aktiver in die Kollaboration mit anderen Lernenden eingebunden werden. Der digitale Stift, der mit mikroskopischen 2D-Codes verbundene Audiodateien wiedergibt, wurde bereits in der sonderpädagogischen Praxis verwendet, um Kindern mit Förderbedarf visuelle Inhalte akustisch zugänglich zu machen. Unser Projekt zielt darauf ab, mit dem digitalen Stift Lernenden mit Sehschädigung die Teilhabe an Gruppenarbeiten zu ermöglichen. In diesem Beitrag stellen wir drei Pilotideen vor, die den aktuellen Stand des laufenden Forschungsprojekts reflektieren.

Keywords: Inklusion, Adaptives Hilfsmittel, Audio-Augmented-Reality, Kooperatives Lernen

Konzeption für inklusives kooperatives Lernen

Ein Schwerpunkt der aktuellen Bildungspolitik liegt auf der Digitalisierung, insbesondere wird die Umsetzung dieser Forderung mit kollaborativem Lernen und der Inklusion verknüpft [KMK21]. Wir erforschen die Möglichkeiten moderner auf dem Markt erhältlicher digitaler Geräte, um so zum Abbau der Barrieren für die Teilhabe von Menschen mit Sehschädigung in kollaborativen Lernsituationen beizutragen. Nach Prince bezieht sich kollaboratives Lernen auf alle gruppenbasierten Lehrmethoden im aktiven Lernen als Alternativ zum traditionellen, passiven Frontalunterricht von Lehrkräften [Pr04]. *Kooperatives Lernen*, das basierend auf erreichbaren Zielen und Ergebnissen für gemeinsames Lernen optimal strukturiert wird [2], ist außerdem hilfreich, um eine erfolgreiche Kollaboration in inklusiven Lerngruppen zu fördern [JJH93]. Beim Abbau von Barrieren kommt Assistive Technology (AT) zum Einsatz und sie ermöglicht zum Beispiel Lernenden mit Sehschädigung die Aufnahme der Informationen hauptsächlich durch haptische oder akustische Reize. Die beiden Sinnesorgane stellen jedoch einen Trade-off dar - zwischen einem tiefen Verständnis der Inhalte mit hohem Zeitaufwand auf der einen Seite und einem oberflächlichen Verständnis mit schnellem Zugang auf der anderen Seite [LHW21]. Um ein Umfeld für inklusives, kooperatives Lernen zu schaffen, liegt unsere Priorität darauf, den Lernenden mit Sehschädigung bei der Kommunikation während Gruppenaktivitäten nicht zurückzulassen. Deswegen basiert unser Ansatz auf der

---

[1] Technische Universität Dortmund, Zentrum für Hochschulbildung, Bereich Behinderung und Studium (DoBuS), Emil-Figge-Straße 50, 44227 Dortmund, kensuke.akao@tu-dortmund.de
[2] Als Kriterium des kollaborativen Lernens sind die *PIGS-Face-Basiselementen* von Johnson & Johnson [JJH93] und die *PIES-Prinzipien* von Kagan [KK09] bekannt.

doi: 10.18420/delfi2023-54

akustisch-optischen Multimodalität mit zusätzlicher haptischer Repräsentation bei Bedarf. Zu diesem Zweck ist die Audio-Augmented-Reality anwendbar. Beispielsweise wurde der digitale Stift, der mit mikroskopischen 2D-Codes verbundene Audiodateien wiedergibt, bisher für das Vorlesen von Lehrbüchern und Arbeitsblättern in der sonderpädagogischen Praxis erfolgreich eingesetzt [Ik20]. Unser Konzept für eine kooperative Lernsituation sieht vor, dass der Stift nicht nur bei Lernenden mit Behinderung, sondern auch bei allen Lernenden der Gruppe eingesetzt wird. Abb. 1 zeigt drei Pilotideen von uns für kooperatives Lernen mit dem Stift: das Programmierkartenspiel (Links), das 3D-Modell der Schaltungslogik (Mitte) und der Brainstormingzettel, mit dem die Aussagen auf dem Stift gespeichert werden können (Rechts). Damit solche Materialien im kooperativen Lernen umgesetzt werden, werden sie z. B. mit den Methoden von *Kagan-Strukturen* [KK09] oder *Methode 635* [Ro69] eingesetzt. Im nächsten Schritt müssen diese Pilotideen einen Zyklus der Erprobung, Evaluation und Verbesserung durchlaufen, um sie schrittweise für die Inklusion zu optimieren.

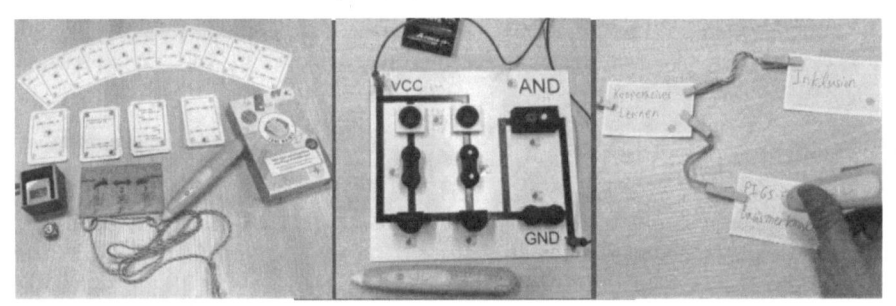

Drei Pilotideen mit einem digitalen Stift

Literaturverzeichnis

[Ik20] Ikuta, S. et.al.: School Activities for Disabled Students Using Self-Made Contents With Multimedia-Enabled Dot Codes. In: Society for Information Technology & Teacher Education International Conference. AACE, Waynesville, NC, S. 1990-1999, 2020.

[JJH93] Johnson, D.; Johnson, R. T.; Holubec, E. J.: Circles of learning: cooperation in the classroom. 4th Edition, Interaction Book Co, Edina, Minn, 1993.

[KK09] Kagan, S.; Kagan, M.: Kagan Cooperative learning. Kagan, San Clemente, CA, 2009.

[KMK21] Kultusministerkonferenz (KMK): Lehren und Lernen in der digitalen Welt - Ergänzung zur Strategie der Kultusministerkonferenz „Bildung in der digitalen Welt". 2021.

[LHW21] Lang, M.; Hofer, U.; Winter, F.: The Braille reading skills of German-speaking students and young adults with visual impairments. In: British Journal of Visual Impairment. Vol. 39 (1), S. 6-19, 2021.

[Pr04] Prince, M.: Does Active Learning Work? A Review of the Research. In Journal of Engineering Education. Vol. 93 (3), S. 223-231, 2004.

[Ro69] Rohrbach, B.: Kreativ nach Regeln – Methode 635, eine neue Technik zum Lösen von Problemen. In: Absatzwirtschaft. Vol.12 (19), S. 73-76, 1969.

Getch: a Web App for Personalized and Cooperative Learning Path Documentation

Julia Frohn [1], Frank Wehrmann [2] and Dominik Bechinie [3]

Abstract: In order to reduce the cognitive load of students, the web app *getch* supports documenting, structuring and presenting individual or joint learning paths using different types of media (recordings, writings, photographs, videos, formulas or files) depending on a learner's individual preferences. In addition, it allows for various forms of cooperative and co-constructive learning. It was designed to help balance the field of tension between personalized and cooperative learning that is constitutive for inclusive as well as digital learning settings. Due to its conceptual openness, *getch* can be used across subjects and supports participative learning processes.

Keywords: Learning App, Personalized Learning, Cooperative Learning, Cognitive Load, Inclusion

1 Aims and frameworks in the development of the app *getch*

In response to various recent educational challenges, there is a growing need to effectively integrate different existing educational approaches. One such example is the emergence of a research field that combines educational inclusion and digitalization (e.g., [FS21]), which holds increasing significance for educational research and practice. The web app *getch* is based on the theoretical premise that the tension between personalized and cooperative learning is constitutive for both discourses: digitalization and inclusion [Fr23]. Developed in the project "FDQI-HU-MINT"[4], *getch* can be accessed through the project website, where further explanations can be found (www.hu-berlin.de/fdqi).

The central goal of the app is to document individual or joint learning paths using different types of media, allowing students to create a multi-medial record of their learning path through a combination of their own images, texts, videos, or audio recordings. Among other things, this reduces the cognitive load in order to create more mental resources for the actual learning process (cognitive load theory, [CS91]). Based on their documentation,

---

[1] Humboldt-Universität zu Berlin, Professional School of Education, Hausvogteiplatz 5-7, Berlin, 10117, julia.frohn@hu-berlin.de, https://orcid.org/0000-0003-1060-3094
[2] Humboldt-Universität zu Berlin, Institut für Informatik, Rudower Chaussee 25, Berlin, 12489, frank.wehrmann@hu-berlin.de, https://orcid.org/0009-0007-5774-5045
[3] Humboldt-Universität zu Berlin, Mathematik in der Primarstufe, Schönhauser Allee 10, Berlin, 10119, dominik.bechinie@hu-berlin.de, https://orcid.org/0009-0008-8740-349X
[4] This project is part of the "Qualitätsoffensive Lehrerbildung", a joint initiative of the Federal Government and the Länder which aims to improve the quality of teacher training. The programme is funded by the Federal Ministry of Education and Research. The authors are responsible for the content of this publication.

doi: 10.18420/delfi2023-55

students can arrange the individual contents regardless of their medial representation in a suitable sequence using a grid – individually, in groups, and, if necessary, with the support of a teacher. This way, the learners themselves arrange the material in a way that is meaningful to them. Due to the conceptual openness of *getch*, the app can be used in various subjects as well as across subjects, for example, as part of interdisciplinary project work. In this sense, *getch* aims at facilitating learning through self-design and in dialogue with oneself and with others [see SWG19].

2 *Getch's* Features for personalized and cooperative learning

The app's features for personalized learning include *flexible forms of representation* (learners can utilize different types of media), *a participative design* (the basic setup initially shows an empty "stage" on which users fill and arrange the fields depending on their own inclinations), *individual customization options* (according to UDL-principles), and a possible *support for individual learners* (teachers or co-students can assign predefined interfaces).

Features for cooperative learning follow Wocken's [Wo98] definition and address *coexistent, communicative, subsidiary* and *cooperative learning situations*. Using the "group stage" function, users can collaborate in content work while exchanging information through the app's integrated chat function. *Getch* allows for both, successive cooperation (e.g. the think-pair-share method: individual documenting, joint sorting) as well as combined workflows from the beginning.

Bibliography

[CS91]   Chandler, P.; Sweller, J.: Cognitive Load Theory and the Format of Instruction. Cognition and Instruction 8/4, pp. 293–332. https://doi.org/10.1207/s1532690xci0804_2, (1991)

[Fr23]   Frohn, J.; Bechinie, D.; Vieregg, N.; Wehrmann, F.; Eilerts, K. Inklusion und Digitalisierung im Spannungsfeld von Personalisiertem und Kooperativem Lernen: Anforderungen an inklusionsorientierte digitale Lernumgebungen am Beispiel der App Getch. Medienpädagogik (in print).

[FS21]   Filk, C.; Schaumburg, H.: Editorial: Inklusiv-mediale Bildung und Fortbildung in schulischen Kontexten. MedienPädagogik 41, pp. i–viii. https://doi.org/10.21240/mpaed/41/2021.02.09.X, 2021.

[SW-G19] Schratz, M.; Westfall-Greiter, T.: Das Dilemma der Individualisierungsdidaktik. Plädoyer für personalisiertes Lernen in der Schule. journal für schulentwicklung 12 (1): 18–31. 2010.

[Wo98]   Wocken, H.: Gemeinsame Lernsituationen. In (Hildeschmidt. A.; Schnell; I., eds.). Integrationspädagogik. Auf dem Weg zu einer Schule für alle. Juventa, pp. 37-52, 1998.

Prototyping a Virtual Tutor with Modular Teaching Styles

Andrea Linxen[1], Simone Opel[2], Stephanie Ebbing[3] and Christian Beecks[4]

Abstract: Digitization and artificial intelligence (AI) have entered education in several different ways. While the current development of large language models enables students to access vast knowledge, virtual tutors offer a more tailored approach and better support for time-independent and individualized learning. As several AI systems have become more common in higher education, we developed a concept to implement a virtual tutor with different teaching styles, using the conversational AI platform Rasa. This tutor teaches students basic Exploratory Data Analysis in linear, free, and modular learning phases. In the future, we will conduct comprehensive studies to determine the ability of the virtual tutor to support successful learning.

Keywords: Virtual Tutor, Rasa Framework, NLP, chatbot, learning phases, learning analytics

1 Introduction

Exploratory Data Analysis (EDA) is utilized by data scientists to investigate datasets and discover new insights. Teaching this skill to data science students can be challenging as mastering EDA requires both theoretical understanding and practical experience. While data science programs strive to offer training opportunities, individual tutoring in higher education is restricted by large group sizes and scheduling constraints. Intelligent tutoring systems can help educators to overcome these challenges by offering highly personalized training at convenient times and locations. We developed a concept for a virtual tutor for EDA and implemented a prototype with modular teaching styles with the Rasa framework.

While numerous frameworks are currently available for implementing chatbots, the Rasa framework is particularly suitable for the creation of task-based systems. A task-based virtual tutor is capable of querying user input and processing the information into actions, such as calculating the statistical characteristics of a dataset. Furthermore, the Rasa framework can support the requirements for a virtual tutor, which we identified by analyzing existing tutoring systems [GJ19], [Ho19]: The virtual tutor offers students the opportunity to explore the dataset independently while aiding struggling students. If necessary, the virtual tutor can teach the theory of EDA and provide constructive feedback to students. By monitoring the progress and keeping track of the predefined goals, the virtual tutor can personalize the support for each student.

---

[1] FernUniversität Hagen, Data Science, Universitätsstr. 11, 58097 Hagen, andrea.linxen@fernuni-hagen.de
[2] FernUniversität Hagen, Fakultät M+I, Universitätsstr. 11, 58097 Hagen, simone.opel@fernuni-hagen.de
[3] FernUniversität Hagen, Data Science, Universitätsstr. 11, 58097 Hagen, stephanie.ebbing@fernuni-hagen.de
[4] FernUniversität Hagen, Data Science, Universitätsstr. 11, 58097 Hagen, christian.beecks@fernuni-hagen.de

doi: 10.18420/delfi2023-56

2 The Virtual Tutor

The prototype of the virtual tutor guides students through an exploration of an open-access dataset containing sales figures from 45 Walmart stores. The virtual tutor is targeted towards students with an intermediate level of competency in Python. Students analyze the fluctuation of weekly sales figures and develop a hypothesis on how the trend correlates to other variables such as holidays or unemployment numbers. The exploration is performed in three steps: data discovery, hypothesis formulation and hypothesis testing.

Corresponding to the three steps of the data analysis, three separate learning phases with three different teaching styles of the virtual tutor are provided. During the *first learning phase*, students familiarize themselves with the provided data and develop a basic understanding of the contained information. The virtual tutor guides them through the data discovery on a linear path with five predefined steps and offers appropriate support using an integrated back-end dictionary. In the *second learning phase*, students explore the data in an iterative approach: they examine the connection between the weekly sales figures and other variables to formulate a hypothesis. The virtual tutor adjusts to a new teaching style to allow students more independence. Instead of structured guidance, the tutor offers hints if a corresponding intent is detected. The second phase ends with a short quiz, to verify the hypothesis of the student. Students test their hypotheses in the *final learning phase* by gaining new insights from the dataset. The virtual tutor focuses on interacting as naturally as possible and offering feedback on the students' progress. The tutor observes the intent of the students' inquiries about the dataset and selects appropriate actions such as feedback. When students indicate the conclusion of their research, the virtual tutor verifies the completion of each goal and either comments on other possible tasks or initiates the finishing.

We examined the viability of the tutor in a user survey. The tutor received positive feedback regarding the different teaching styles, especially the invitation to explore the dataset freely was well received. One user indicated that "[...] the reaction of the tutor depends a lot on asking a question, while it did struggle with requests not formulated as a question." This problem will be resolved in the next version by adding more detailed intents. The virtual tutor is nevertheless the first step towards a powerful tool that supports students' self-directed learning. The prototype was able to meet the proposed requirements for the virtual tutor. The findings from the usability survey indicate that the task-based system of the Rasa framework is capable of hosting a virtual assistant to assist independent learning. In the future, we plan to conduct studies to examine learning success for data science education in a university setting. Furthermore, we will conduct comprehensive studies to determine the ability of the virtual tutor to support successful learning. In addition, we will continue to develop the virtual tutor and integrate it into a blended learning environment.

Bibliography

[GJ19]   Godinez, J.; Jamil, H.: Meet Cyrus. Proceedings of the 34th ACM/SIGAPP Symposium on Applied Computing, New York, 2019.

[Ho19]   Hobert, S.: Say Hello to 'Coding Tutor'! Fortieth International Conference on Information Systems, Munich, 2019.

A Fusion of XR Technology and Physical Objects to Increase Citizens Participation in Urban Planning

Sam Sabah [1], Imran Hossain [2], David Weiss [3] and Alexander Tillmann [4]

Abstract: Extended Reality (XR), comprising Augmented Reality (AR), Virtual Reality (VR), and Mixed Reality (MR) technologies have the potential to enhance urban planning with immersive and interactive experiences, but there learning cost hinders citizen participation. XR development requires technical knowledge, limiting individual engagement in urban planning. On the other hand, physical models offer tangible visualization for urban planning but lack features compared to software applications. Combining physical objects with XR technology poses challenges but holds the potential to promote citizen participation. This article introduces the concept of the city planner app, an application that integrates XR technology and physical objects in a mixed-reality setting. This app aims to leverage the strengths of both worlds and overcome their limitations to facilitate the involvement of citizens and students in urban planning.

Keywords: Social citizenship, Urban Planning, Citizens Participation, Extended Reality (XR), Augmented Reality (AR), Virtual Reality (VR), Mixed Reality (MR)

1 Motivation and Background

Active participation of civil society in urban planning is challenging due to citizens' rational ignorance and the perceived costs outweighing the benefits of involvement [Kr05]. Extended Reality (XR), technologies, can revolutionize urban planning by visualizing the unseen. XR models enable flexible and functional representation of urban environments, aiding by visualization of the unseen furthermore, tangible interfaces can be more inviting and more conducive to collaborative interaction [THF06] but have size and scale limitations and may be seen as toys. They also lack features compared to software applications [Ma18]. Mixing the appeal of tangible with the benefits of XR technology has the potential to increase the active participation of citizens in urban planning.

---

[1] University of Frankfurt, studiumdigitale, Eschersheimer Landstr. 155-157, 60323 Frankfurt am Main, Germany, sabah@sd.uni-frankfurt.de, https://orcid.org/0009-0009-5111-3068
[2] University of Frankfurt, studiumdigitale, Eschersheimer Landstr. 155-157, 60323 Frankfurt am Main, Germany, hossain@sd.uni-frankfurt.de, https://orcid.org/0009-0009-1272-2688
[3] University of Frankfurt, studiumdigitale, Eschersheimer Landstr. 155-157, 60323 Frankfurt am Main, Germany, weiss@sd.uni-frankfurt.de, https://orcid.org/0000-0002-7689-7833
[4] University of Frankfurt, studiumdigitale, Eschersheimer Landstr. 155-157, 60323 Frankfurt am Main, Germany, tillmann@sd.uni-frankfurt.de, https://orcid.org/0000-0001-7230-7042

doi: 10.18420/delfi2023-57

2 Implementation

The city planner app comprises six components: Gameboard: a portable surface for placing physical objects to create a virtual model of the city for planning. Physical objects: Elementary 3D objects representing real-world elements, to allow customization and experimentation in urban planning. Stakeholders: Inclusive involvement of diverse individuals and groups in urban planning. Monitoring system: Tracks and records user changes on the gameboard in real-time, providing information to the authoring component. Authoring component: Translates data from the monitoring system into immersive XR experiences (VR, MR, or AR) using UEmbed [HWV23] and Unreal Engine. Viewing Device: Users can immerse themselves in virtual city models using VR or overlay AR objects on real-world locations to explore planning scenarios and understand urban planning impacts. These components work together to simplify urban planning and enable users to explore different planning scenarios and understand the impacts of various strategies.

3 Conclusions and Future Work

Despite the potential benefits of Extended Reality (XR) technology, the road to develop such applications remains a challenge for many. The city planner app overcomes this hurdle by automating urban planning development process, utilizing tangible interfaces, object detection techniques and Augmented and Virtual Reality to create an immersive Mixed reality (MR) environment. Our approach aims to assess the effectiveness of citizen involvement in urban planning and further investigate the benefit of XR applications in urban planning, as well as help students develop spatial citizenship skills. Which in turn allows users to explore and make informed decisions about the future of their city.

Bibliography

[HWV23] Hossain, I.; Weist, L.; Voß-Nakkour, S.: UEmbed: An Authoring Tool to Make Game Development Accessible for Users Without Knowledge of Coding, S. 31-36, 2023.

[Kr05] Krek, A.: Rational ignorance of the citizens in public participatory planning. In: 10th symposium on Information-and communication technologies (ICT) in urban planning and spatial development and impacts of ICT on physical space, CORP. Jgg. 5, S. 420, 2005.

[Ma18] Maquil, V.; Leopold, U.; De Sousa, Luís Moreira; Schwartz, Lou; Tobias, Eric: Towards a framework for geospatial tangible user interfaces in collaborative urban planning. Journal of Geographical Systems, 20:185–206, 2018.

[THF06] Thompson, E. M.; Horne, M.; Fleming, D.: Virtual reality urban modelling an overview. 2006.

OnePageLayout für Lehrinhalte & -szenarien in ILIAS

Entwicklung und Implementierung eines benutzerfreundlichen, responsiven, CI-konformen und vernetzenden Layouts (Baukasten) für Lehrinhalte, respektive Lehrszenarien, inklusive multimedialer, formativer oder kollektiver Assessments samt Lernstandskontrolle

Ulrich Hofmann-von Kap-herr[1]

Abstract: Formative Assessments können mit diversen Softwareprodukten Realisierung finden und müssen, um den Lernerfolg abbilden zu können, kontextualisiert werden. Das entwickelte Layout integriert unterschiedliche Lehr-/Lern-Bausteine sowie Medien (Übungen, Filme mit Kontextfragen, Upload von Abgaben, kollaboratives Schreiben, Umfragen usw.) und setzt diese in ILIAS - unter Verwendung der *Funktion* Lernerfolgskontrolle - in Beziehung. Der modulare Aufbau ermöglicht es Lehrszenarien individualisiert und semesterunabhängig zu unterstützen. Alle Elemente sind individuell anpassbar, das Layout erweiterbar. Das Design ist responsiv, das Interface nimmt Bezug zu den Inhalten (Ikons) auf.

Keywords: Formative Assessments, Design, Baukasten, One-Page-Layout, ILIAS, LMS, Responsivität, Individualisierbarkeit, Modularität, Lehrinhalte, Lehrszenarien

Formative Assessments können mit diversen Softwareprodukten Realisierung finden und müssen, um den Lernerfolg abbilden zu können, kontextualisiert werden. Das entwickelte Layout integriert unterschiedliche Lehr-/Lern-Bausteine sowie Medien (Übungen, Filme mit Kontextfragen, Upload von Abgaben, kollaboratives Schreiben, Umfragen usw.) und setzt diese in ILIAS - unter Verwendung der *Funktion* Lernerfolgskontrolle - in Beziehung. Der modulare Aufbau ermöglicht es unterschiedliche Lehrszenarien individualisiert und semesterunabhängig zu unterstützen. Voraussetzung für das Erstellen formativer Assessments ist die Fragmentierung bzw. Implementierung der Lehrunterlagen, welche anschließend nach Themen bzw. Unterthemen geordnet und mit formativen Assessments (Übungen, Panopto, iMathAS, Etherpad, Particify usw.) angereichert werden können. Für diesen Anwendungsfall existiert keine einheitliche, intuitive, CI-konforme Benutzeroberfläche. Die Hochschule nutzt gegenwärtig zwei LMS. Formative Elemente finden sich in beiden Systemen – darüber hinaus nutzen Lehrende externe Lösungen. Insbesondere Navigation und Organisation unterscheiden sich erheblich - inhomogene

---

[1] Hochschule RheinMain, Fachbereich Architektur und Bauingenieurwesen, Kurt-Schumacher-Ring 18, 65197 Wiesbaden, Ulrich.Hofmann-vonKap-herr@hs-rm.de

doi: 10.18420/delfi2023-58

und inkonsistente Benutzeroberflächen stehen sich gegenüber. Das Layout fasst Lerninhalte zusammen, definiert das Lehrszenario / die Gruppierung der Fragmente und ist in der Lage die Komponenten miteinander in Beziehung zu setzen. Das Design unterliegt den Rahmenbedingungen (rollenbasierter Zugriff) von ILIAS und beinhaltet lediglich Verknüpfungen. Die Links wurden als Element *Block* erstellt, um die Anwendbarkeit zu vereinfachen, die Benutzerfreundlichkeit zu erhöhen und Eingabefehler zu reduzieren. Zusätzlich zu den Lehrinhalten werden Verknüpfungen zu den unterstützenden Serviceleistungen angeboten, um die hochschulinterne Vernetzung zu stärken.

Eine enge Zusammenarbeit, die ein gewisses Investment unbedingt einbringen muss, ist für das Gelingen formativer Assessments in der Lehre unabdingbar. Das Design orientiert sich an den Anforderungen der Lehrperson und ist individuell konfigurierbar. Alle formativen Elemente lassen sich integrieren und in einer Lernerfolgskontrolle zusammenführen, wodurch die fragmentierten Elemente selbst zu Assessment-Elementen werden. Layout und Inhalte sind Teil des LMS ILIAS und können modular organisiert werden. Das Design ist klar, verständlich, ikonographisch (Unterstützung der Barrierefreiheit) sowie responsiv. Um Fehler in der Benutzerführung zu vermeiden, wurden editierbare Elemente auf ein Minimum reduziert und die Benutzerfreundlichkeit durch die Ausbildung von *Blöcken* erhöht. Lediglich das Erstellen der *Blöcke* an sich ist aufgrund der Menüführung in ILIAS sowie u.a. defekter Funktionen erklärungsbedürftig bzw. zu optimieren.

Alle Werkzeuge, welche formatives Assessment unterstützen sind willkommen. In diesem Zusammenhang sind Lizenzierung, Implementierung und Support nicht zu unterschätzen. Für z.B. mathematische Assessments erscheint aktuell das Tool iMathAS das gegenwärtige Optimum zu sein – allerdings ist für die Erstellung dieser Assessmentart ein:e Informatiker:in erforderlich. Grundsätzlich wäre eine Ausweitung der Fragenarten innerhalb des *Test*-Moduls oder die globale Bearbeitbarkeit von Inhaltselementen innerhalb von ILIAS sehr förderlich. Der Prototyp befindet sich im Aufbau und wurde bislang zu Demonstrationszwecken eingesetzt. Aktuell implementierte Projekte sind: Baugeschichte I, Mathematik für Ingenieur:innen, Bautechnische Grundlagen, Facility Management, Qualitätsmanagement und Computer Media & Networking I & II.

Literaturverzeichnis

[BW09] Black, P., & Wiliam, D.: Developing the theory of formative assessment. Educational Assessment, Evaluation and Accountability S. 5–31, 2009.

[WT08] Wiliam, D., & Thompson, M.: Integrating assessment with learning: What will it take to make it work? In C. A. Dwyer (Hrsg.), The future of assessment: Shaping teaching and learning, S. 53–82, 2008.

[MY17] McLaughlin, T., & Yan, Z.: Diverse delivery methods and strong psychological benefits: A review of online formative assessment. Journal of Computer Assisted Learning, 33(6), 562–574, 2017.

Posterbeiträge

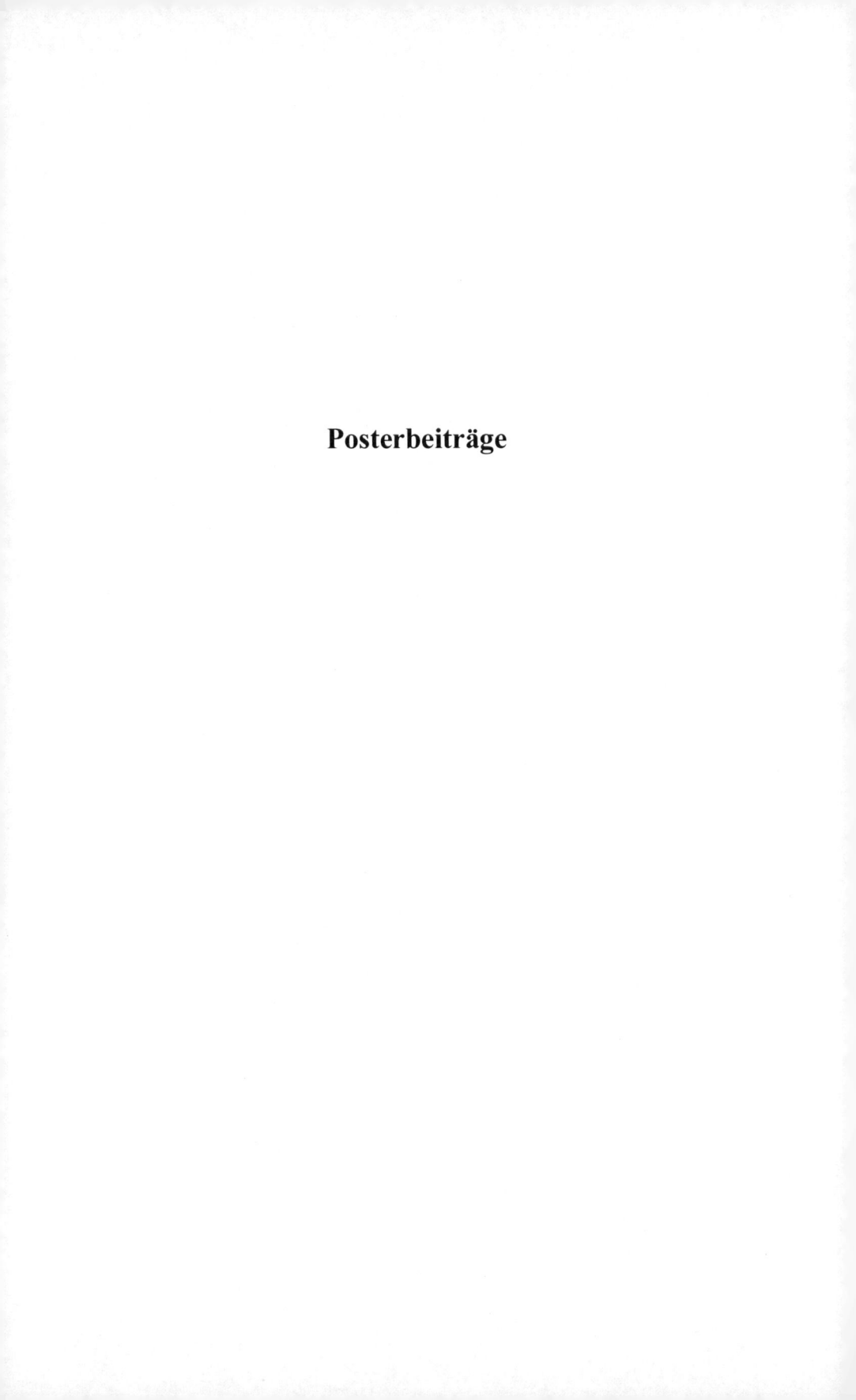

Show me the numbers! - Student-facing Interventions in Adaptive Learning Environments for German Spelling

Nathalie Rzepka[1], Katharina Simbeck[1], Hans-Georg Müller[2], Marlene Bültemann[1] and Niels Pinkwart[3]

Abstract: Our work presents the result of an experiment conducted on an online platform for the acquisition of German spelling skills. We compared the traditional online learning platform to three different adaptive versions of the platform that implement machine learning-based student-facing interventions that show the personalized solution probability. We evaluate the different interventions with regards to the error rate, the number of early dropouts, and the users' competency. Our results show that the number of mistakes decreased in comparison to the control group. Additionally, an increasing number of dropouts was found. We did not find any significant effects on the users' competency. We conclude that student-facing adaptive learning environments are effective in improving a person's error rate and should be chosen wisely to have a motivating impact.

Keywords: Adaptive Learning, Adaptive Intervention, Learning Analytics.

1 A Large Scale Online-Controlled Experiment

Since adaptive learning comes in many shapes and sizes, it is crucial to find out which adaptions can be meaningful for which areas of learning. One possibility to implement an intervention in an adaptive learning environment may be to show the student his or her performance data [WL18]. In their review, Bodily and Verbert review student-facing learning analytics reporting systems, that directly show students' performance data [BV17]. In their review, they found 14 articles that measured the effects of student-facing reports on student achievements. Of these, eight articles showed significant improvement in student achievements while five had no significant results.

In this contribution, we specifically investigate adaptive learning interventions for acquisition of spelling skills in German. For this purpose, we transformed a learning platform (Orthografietrainer.net) into an adaptive learning platform and implemented a machine learning-based prediction model on which the interventions are based. Our interventions are all student-facing interventions, i.e., information is displayed to the user in the user interface. The online-controlled experiment was carried out from the 21st of June to the 31st of October in 2022. During this time, all users in the student user group who performed

---

[1] HTW Berlin, Treskowallee 8, 10318 Berlin, {rzepka,simbeck}@htw-berlin.de,
[2] Universität Potsdam, Am neuen Palais 10, 14469 Potsdam, hgmuelle@uni-potsdam.de,
[3] Humboldt-Universität, Unter den Linden 6, 10117 Berlin, pinkwart@hu-berlin.de

capitalization tasks were randomly assigned to the control group or one of three intervention groups. All three intervention groups adapt to the user based on the prediction of the users' performance. The experiment was pre-registered at the OSF[4] and its setup is extensively described in [Rz22]. A more detailed version can be found online[5]. In total 8,121 users took part in the experiment answering 687,386 exercise sentences. We compared the control group to three intervention groups and calculate the error rate, number of dropouts and user competency. Interventions 1 and 2 are student-facing interventions where users are shown their prediction results. In Intervention 1, the prediction result is shown verbally, in intervention 2 it is shown as a percentage. Intervention 3 does not show the prediction results. Instead, for users whose prediction result is below 50%, the suitable spelling rule is displayed.

2 Results & Conclusion

Our results showed that all three interventions led to a decreasing error rate for the users in comparison to the control group. Here, interventions 1 and 2 result in an effect size of 0.11 and 0.12, while intervention 3 produces an effect size of 0.09 and is therefore negligible. An analysis of the number of dropouts showed significantly higher dropouts in comparison to the control group in all intervention groups, however, the effect sizes are negligible. The calculation of the users' competencies with the Rasch model did not show significant results. In summary, we found that student-facing machine learning-based interventions lead to fewer errors in German spelling learning environments. However, it can also demotivate users leading to more dropouts.

Bibliography

[BV17]   Bodily, R.; Verbert, K.: Review of Research on Student-Facing Learning Analytics Dashboards and Educational Recommender Systems. IEEE Transactions on Learning Technologies 4/10, pp. 405–418, 2017.

[Rz22]   Rzepka, N. et al.: An Online Controlled Experiment Design to Support the Transformation of Digital Learning towards Adaptive Learning Platforms: Proceedings of the 14th International Conference on Computer Supported Education. SCITEPRESS - Science and Technology Publications, 2022.

[WL18]   Wong, B. T.; Li, K. C.: Learning Analytics Intervention: A Review of Case Studies. In (Wang, F. L. Ed.): 2018 International Symposium on Educational Technology. ISET 2018 31 July-2 August 2018, Osaka, Japan proceedings. IEEE, Piscataway, NJ, pp. 178–182, 2018.

---

[4] https://doi.org/10.17605/OSF.IO/3R5Y7
[5] https://doi.org/10.48550/arXiv.2306.07853

Studierende und die Studienplanung: Untersuchung von Herausforderungen und Entwicklungsperspektiven eines digitalen Studienplanungsassistenten

Tobias Hirmer [1], Michaela Ochs [1] und Andreas Henrich [1]

Abstract: Das Poster stellt ausgewählte Ergebnisse einer Online-Umfrage zur aktuellen Situation der Studienplanung an der Universität Bamberg vor. Dabei werden Herausforderungen für Studierende in der Studienplanung identifiziert und Potentiale und Grenzen zur Adressierung dieser Faktoren durch einen Studienplanungsassistenten vorgestellt.

Keywords: Studienplanung, Digitaler Studienassistent

1 Herausforderung Studienplanung

Die Planung des Studiums ist ein multioptionaler und komplexer Entscheidungsprozess, welcher Studierende vor Herausforderungen stellt. Vor dem Hintergrund der fortschreitenden Digitalisierung der Hochschulen erfährt die Forschung rund um digitale Studienassistenten (DSA) in den letzten Jahren ein steigendes Interesse [KKB21]. Verschiedene Projekte und Systeme teilen dabei den zentralen Gedanken, Studierende bei der Planung und Organisation des Studiums auf unterschiedliche Art und Weise zu unterstützen.

Trotz des steigenden Interesses an DSA sind empirische Untersuchungen im Kontext der Studienplanung selten. Um den Status Quo der Studienplanung an der Universität Bamberg durch die Einschätzung von Studierenden aus verschiedenen Fachbereichen zu ermitteln, wurde im November 2022 eine universitätsweite Online-Umfrage *(n = 375)* durchgeführt.[2] Teil dieser Online-Umfrage waren u. a. offene Fragen zu den größten Störfaktoren. Diese wurden mittels qualitativer Inhaltsanalyse nach Kuckartz [KR22] ausgewertet. Zusammengefasst wurden als Störfaktoren insbesondere die Informationsbereitstellung, die universitären Systeme und relevanten Quellen zur Semester- und Studienplanung[3] sowie die Vielfalt an Quellen und Systemen von den Studierenden kritisiert. Weitere Kritikpunkte adressieren die Unübersichtlichkeit und Komplexität der Studienplanung.

---

[1] Universität Bamberg, Lehrstuhl für Medieninformatik, An der Weberei 5, 96047 Bamberg,
{tobias.hirmer, michaela.ochs, andreas.henrich}@uni-bamberg.de, https://orcid.org/0000-0002-5281-0342, https://orcid.org/0000-0002-3850-8585, https://orcid.org/0000-0002-5074-3254

[2] Eine ausführlichere Beschreibung und Diskussion der Ergebnisse findet sich unter:
https://doi.org/10.5281/zenodo.8037697

[3] Hierunter fallen u.a. das Lehrveranstaltungsverwaltungssystem, das Prüfungsverwaltungssystem, Studienordnungen, Modulhandbücher oder planungsrelevante Informationen auf der universitären Webseite.

Die Ergebnisse der qualitativen Analyse und ihre Implikationen werden umfassend auf dem Poster dargestellt und diskutiert.

2 Entwicklungsperspektiven eines Studienplanungsassistenten

Begleitend zu der Online-Umfrage wird an der Universität Bamberg im Rahmen von zwei Projekten[4] derzeit ein DSA entwickelt [HEH22]. Das Konzept und die Funktionen des Systems werden ausführlicher auf dem Poster dargestellt und vor dem Hintergrund der analysierten Herausforderungen diskutiert. Der DSA hat zum Ziel, Studierende sowohl in der kurzfristigen Semesterplanung als auch in der langfristigen Studienplanung zu unterstützen und relevante Informationen transparent darzustellen.

Die analysierten Störfaktoren werden im DSA derzeit insbesondere durch die möglichst nahtlose Anbindung bestehender Systeme und Materialien adressiert, sofern dies technisch möglich ist. Zudem wird im DSA versucht, vorhandene Materialien studierendenfreundlicher abzubilden, z. B. durch die Darstellung eines interaktiven Modulhandbuchs, in dem Module gesucht und Gruppierungen und Filter angewendet werden können. Im Hinblick auf die Anbindung anderer Systeme fehlen insbesondere zum Prüfungsverwaltungssystem hin adressierbare Schnittstellen, um eine automatische Integration zu ermöglichen. Durch solche Schnittstellen könnten von Studierenden häufig erwartete Funktionalitäten eines DSA, wie die Integration der Lehrveranstaltungsanmeldung oder die automatische Übernahme des Studienverlaufs ermöglicht werden. Viele der genannten Störfaktoren sind jedoch nicht allein durch einen DSA adressierbar. Hier braucht es u. a. organisatorische Anpassungen, deren Bedarf jedoch durch die Auseinandersetzung mit einem DSA klarer identifiziert werden kann. Die Ergebnisse der Umfrage sind vor dem Hintergrund der untersuchten Hochschule zu interpretieren, die Übertragbarkeit der Störfaktoren sowie der Möglichkeiten und Grenzen eines DSA auf andere Hochschulen sind jedoch denkbar und sollten in Zukunft konkreter diskutiert werden.

Literaturverzeichnis

[HEH22] Hirmer, T.; Etschmann, J.; Henrich, A.: Requirements and Prototypical Implementation of a Study Planning Assistant in CS Programs. In: 2022 International Symposium on Educational Technology (ISET). S. 281–285, 2022.

[KR22] Kuckartz, U.; Rädiker, S.: Qualitative Inhaltsanalyse. Methoden, Praxis, Computerunterstützung. 5. Auflage, 2022.

[KKB21] Karrenbauer, C.; König, C. M.; Breitner, M. H.: Individual Digital Study Assistant for Higher Education Institutions: Status Quo Analysis and Further Research Agenda. In: Innovation Through Information Systems: Volume III. Springer, S. 108–124, 2021.

---

[4] Der DSA wird im Rahmen der folgenden Projekte konzipiert: „Digitale Kulturen in der Lehre entwickeln (DiKuLe)" und „Von Lernenden Lernen (VoLL-KI)", gefördert von der Stiftung Innovation in der Hochschullehre sowie der Förderinitiative „Künstliche Intelligenz in der Hochschulbildung" des BMBF.

Was wirkt? Eine Literaturstudie zur Wirksamkeit von Systemeigenschaften in Mathematik-Lernumgebungen

Berit Blanc[1], Insa Reichow[1] und Benjamin Paaßen[1]

Abstract: Diese Literaturstudie untersucht die Lernwirksamkeit typischer Systemeigenschaften digitaler Mathematik-Lernumgebungen wie bettermarks, nämlich: (A) Vollständigkeit der Aufgaben und Inhalte, (B) Intelligente Interaktionswerkzeuge, (C) Mikro-Adaptivität, (D) Makro-Adaptivität und als Rahmenbedingung (E) Einsatz im Klassenverbund. Die Auswertung ergab besonders starke Evidenz für elaboriertes und adaptives Feedback bei der Bearbeitung von Aufgaben (C), reichhaltige Interaktionswerkzeuge (B), eine feine Auflösung von Aufgabenschritten und Feedback (A) sowie die Einbindung der Lehrkräfte (E). Eine Forschungslücke besteht hinsichtlich der Wirksamkeit makro-adaptiver Strategien (D).

Keywords: Schule, Mathematik, Digitale Lernumgebungen, bettermarks, Intelligente Tutoring-Systeme, Wirksamkeitsforschung, Evaluationsstudien

Digitale Lernumgebungen gewinnen zunehmend in Bedeutung. Beispielsweise ist *bettermarks* eine Lernumgebung für Mathematik in den Klassenstufen 4-10, die nach Unternehmensangaben von rund 500.000 Schüler*innen genutzt wird. Bei der Gestaltung und Beurteilung solcher Lernumgebungen stellt sich die Frage: Welche Eigenschaften machen die Plattform lernwirksam? Bisherige Metastudien (z.B. [KF16, RKS21]) untersuchen zwar die Lernwirksamkeit, differenzieren aber nur hinsichtlich weniger und einzelner Systemeigenschaften. Diese Arbeit versucht, die Lernwirksamkeit *aller* Kern-Systemeigenschaften einer digitalen Lernumgebung für Mathematik zu beurteilen.

Als Ausgangspunkt dient die *bettermarks*-Plattform, die als Kerneigenschaften definiert: (A) Vollständigkeit der Aufgaben und Inhalte, (B) Intelligente Interaktionswerkzeuge, (C) Mikro-Adaptivität (also adaptive Hilfe bei der Bearbeitung von Aufgaben) und (D) Makro-Adaptivität (also adaptive Hilfe bei der Auswahl von Aufgaben) [Sp23]. Zusätzlich beziehen wir (E) den Einsatz im Klassenverbund mit ein. Die Ergebnisse sind auch auf andere Lernumgebungen übertragbar, weil die bettermarks-Systemeigenschaften den best practices in der Gestaltung von Lernumgebungen folgen (z.B. [So13, Va06]) und die eingeschlossenen Studien eine große Breite von Systemen abdecken.

Durchsucht wurden Metastudien zur Wirksamkeit digitaler Mathematik-Lernumgebungen (13), Wirkungsstudien zu populären Mathematik-Lernumgebungen (87) und

---

[1] Deutsches Forschungszentrum für Künstliche Intelligenz, Educational Technology Lab, Alt-Moabit 91c, 10559 Berlin, {berit.blanc,insa.reichow,benjamin.paassen}@dfki.de. Die Durchführung der Literaturrecherche wurde von bettermarks finanziert.

doi: 10.18420/delfi2023-61

Wirkungsstudien zu intelligenten Mathematik-Tutoring-Systemen allgemein (39). Die volle Liste der eingeschlossenen Studien ist hier (https://doi.org/10.5281/zenodo.8047423) zu finden. Die Ergebnisse waren:

A: Keine Studie untersucht direkt die Wirkung der Vollständigkeit von Inhalten, aber mehrere Studien betrachten Vollständigkeit als Qualitätsmerkmal. Deutliche Wirkungsevidenz legt nahe, Aufgaben feinschrittig zu modellieren (z.B. [KF16]).

B: Reichhaltige Eingabewerkzeuge, z.B. für Texte und Diagramme, sind laut Metastudien lernwirksamer als einfache Aufgabentypen wie multiple/single-choice (z.B. [Pr22]).

C: Mehrere Metastudien vergleichen herkömmliche Übungssysteme (Computer-aided instruction) mit Tutoring-Systemen (mit adaptivem Feedback) und weisen für letztere eine höhere Wirksamkeit nach (z.B. [KF16]). Zusätzlich ist elaboriertes Feedback effektiver als schlichtes Richtig-/Falsch-Feedback (z.B. [Pr22]).

D: Obwohl Adaptivität bei der Auswahl der Aufgaben als Kerneigenschaft vieler Tutoring-Systeme gilt [Va06], konnten wir keine Studie finden, die kausale Evidenz für die Wirksamkeit dieser Systemeigenschaft beibringt. Die Theorie spricht eindeutig für die Wirksamkeit, aber im empirischen Nachweis sehen wir eine Forschungslücke.

E: ITS ergänzend zu herkömmlichem Unterricht sind effektiver als ITS allein oder herkömmlicher Unterricht allein (z.B. [KF16, RKS21]). Die Erfahrung bzw. Kompetenz der Lehrkräfte in der ITS-Nutzung ist für die Wirksamkeit entscheidend [KF16].

Ausgehend von den Ergebnissen empfehlen wir vor allem mikro-adaptives, elaboriertes Feedback (C), reichhaltige Interaktionswerkzeuge (B), feinschrittige Aufgabenmodellierung (A) und eine starke Einbindung der Lehrkräfte (E).

Literaturverzeichnis

[KF16]   Kulik, J.; Fletcher, J.D.: Effectiveness of Intelligent Tutoring Systems: A Meta-Analytic Review. Review of Educational Research, 86/1, S. 42-78, 2016.

[Pr22]   Prihar, E.; Syed, M.; Ostrow, K.; Shaw, S.; Sales, A.; Heffernan, N.: Exploring Common Trends in Online Educational Experiments. In (Cristea, A.; Brown, C.; Mitrovic, A.; Bosch, N. Hrsg.): Proc. Int. Conf. on Educational Data Mining, 2022

[RKS21] Ran, H.; Kim, N. J.; Secada, W. G.: A meta-analysis on the effects of technology's functions and roles on students' mathematics achievement in K-12 classrooms. Journal of Computer Assisted Learning, 38(1), S. 258–284, 2021.

[So13]   Sottilare, R.; Graesser, A.; Hu, X.; Holden, H.: Design recommendations for intelligent tutoring systems: Volume 1. US Army Research Laboratory, Orlando, FL, USA, 2013.

[Sp23]   Speroni, C.: Aus Fehlern lernen – Das Konzept hinter bettermarks, https://de.bettermarks.com/konzept-bettermarks/, abgerufen am 24.02.2023.

[Va06]   VanLehn, K.: The Behavior of Tutoring Systems. IJAIED, 16(3), S. 227-265, 2006.

Künstliche Intelligenz in der öffentlichen Bildungsförderung

Arno Wilhelm-Weidner[1], Annika Fünfhaus[2], Stefanie Brzoska[3], Marcel Dux[4] und Andrea Vogt[5]

Abstract: Das Poster stellt verschiedene Ansätze vor, wie Künstliche Intelligenz die Forschung, Anwendung und Dissemination der Hochschullehre im Rahmen einer vo Bundesministerium für Bildung und Forschung (BMBF) geförderten Projektträgerschaft inhaltlich ausgestaltet und öffentlich gefördert wird. Damit informiert das Poster Lehrende und Lernende über aktuelle, für sie relevante Entwicklungen und schafft Raum zum Austausch. Gleichzeitig bietet die Vorstellung der inhaltlichen Themenschwerpunkte die Möglichkeit Synergien zu identifizieren und für die eigene Lehre aufzugreifen. Zur konkreten Veranschaulichung werden einzelne Projekte referenziert, um greifbare Eindrücke von den Möglichkeiten der Verbindung von Hochschullehre und Künstlicher Intelligenz zu erhalten.

Keywords: Künstliche Intelligenz, Hochschulbildung, öffentliche Förderung, Transfer.

1 Themenfelder der Förderung zu KI

Um Deutschland zu einem führenden Standort für die Anwendung von Künstlicher Intelligenz (KI) zu machen, bedarf es einer sehr gut ausgebildeten Fachkräftebasis, der Schaffung von Experimentierräumen und dem zielgerichteten Einsatz von Technologien. Hochschulen sind ein zentraler Ort, um die notwendigen KI-Kompetenzen, deren Anwendungsfelder und Entwicklungsmöglichkeiten zu vermitteln. Im Rahmen der Projektträgerschaft "Digitale Hochschulbildung" und der Bund-Länder-Initiative "KI in der Hochschulbildung" werden daher verschiedene Einsatzbereiche von KI in der Hochschule gefördert: von der Vermittlung von KI-Kompetenzen, über die Entwicklung von Technologien und den Aufbau konkreter Infrastruktur vor Ort für den Einsatz in der Lehre bis hin zur Nutzung von KI zur Verbesserung von Betreuungs- und Verwaltungsprozessen. Die öffentliche Förderung des KI-Einsatzes in Hochschulen bietet die Chance, Rahmenbedingungen zu schaffen, die ethischen und datenschutzrechtlichen Standards gerecht werden, eine nachhaltige und kontrollierte Nutzung von Systemen ermöglichen und dabei die Abhängigkeit von großen internationalen Firmen und Service-

---

[1] VDI/VDE-IT, Bildung und Wissenschaft, Steinplatz 1, 10623 Berlin, arno.wilhelm-weidner@vdivde-it.de, https://orcid.org/0000-0003-2604-3367
[2] VDI/VDE-IT, Bildung und Wissenschaft, Steinplatz 1, 10623 Berlin, annika.fuenfhaus@vdivde-it.de,
[3] VDI/VDE-IT, Bildung und Wissenschaft, Steinplatz 1, 10623 Berlin, stefanie.brzoska@vdivde-it.de,
[4] VDI/VDE-IT, Bildung und Wissenschaft, Steinplatz 1, 10623 Berlin, marcel.dux@vdivde-it.de,
[5] VDI/VDE-IT, Bildung und Wissenschaft, Steinplatz 1, 10623 Berlin, andrea.vogt@vdivde-it.de

doi: 10.18420/delfi2023-62

Providern möglichst reduzieren.

Das Poster stellt drei von uns als Projektträger betreute Initiativen vor, die vom BMBF beauftragt wurden und den Einbezug von Künstlicher Intelligenz in die Hochschullehre auf unterschiedliche Arten unterstützen:

Eine Förderlinie der Projektträgerschaft widmet sich der Erforschung von Möglichkeiten und Effekten des (unterstützenden) Einsatzes von Big Data und Künstlicher Intelligenz (KI) in der Hochschulbildung. In vier Einzel- und acht Verbundprojekten werden innovative Lehr- und Lernszenarien (beispielsweise [Bl20]) mit starkem Blick auf Ethik und Datenschutz erforscht und umgesetzt.

Mit der Bund-Länder-Initiative "KI in der Hochschulbildung" werden sowohl Maßnahmen zur Entwicklung von Studiengängen oder einzelnen Modulen zur KI als auch der Aufbau KI-gestützter Systeme an den Hochschulen gefördert. Dazu gehören etwa intelligente Assistenzsysteme oder KI-basierte Lern- und Prüfungsumgebungen. Wir betreuen als Projektträger 14 Verbund- sowie 40 Einzelvorhaben für eine Laufzeit von bis zu vier Jahren. Die Fördermittel werden dafür im Verhältnis 90:10 von Bund und Ländern getragen.

Mit der Förderung der offenen Lernplattform "KI-Campus" werden zudem innovative, digitale Lernangebote zum Aufbau von KI-Kompetenzen für alle Interessierten bereitgestellt. Die Materialien sind frei lizenziert und können damit sowohl zum Lernen als auch zur Unterstützung der Lehrvorbereitung für Lehrende verwendet werden.

Vier Anwendungsfälle für den Einsatz von Künstlicher Intelligenz (KI) in der Hochschulbildung geben auf dem Poster Einblick in die Bandbreite der geförderten Projekte:

- Simulationen: Klinische Kompetenzen und medizinische Maßnahmen werden mit einer KI-basierten virtuellen Lernumgebung trainiert,
- Tutorielle Systeme: Teilautomatisierte Analyseverfahren unterstützen Studierende und Lehrende durch personalisiertes Feedback, von der Orientierungsphase bis hin zum Abschluss von Studienleistungen
- Feedback-Assistenten: Der Einsatz von Chatbots begleitet die individuelle Studienberatung und entlastet das Hochschulpersonal
- Studiengangsentwicklung: Ein neuer Bachelorstudiengang verbindet KI- und Ingenieurausbildung und bereitet zukünftige Ingenieure auf die Arbeitswelt von morgen vor.

Literaturverzeichnis

[Bl20] Blattgerste, J. et al.: The Heb@ AR App–Five Augmented Reality Trainings for Self-Directed Learning in Academic Midwifery Education. 20. Fachtagung Bildungstechnologien (DELFI), 2022.

Tool-Support for Managing Technostress in Hybrid Learning Settings

David Walter[1], Marco Di Maria[1] and Ralf Knackstedt[1]

Abstract: Increasing use of technology in education can be a major concern for students as this can lead to technostress. To mitigate this, we develop a mobile application aimed at reducing techno-overload and techno-invasion, two stressors causing technostress. To do so, we suggest the features: goal management, rewarding, and reflection.

Keywords: Technostress, App Development, Digital Well-Being

1 Problem, Motivation and Implementation

Students increasingly use digital technology for educational reasons, which can lead to stress, especially in hybrid teaching and learning environments. If stress is caused primarily by technology, it is referred to as technostress [AGP11]. As previous research has shown, technostress can have a detrimental effect on students' learning effectiveness [UV21], such as knowledge acquisition or skills development. Against this backdrop, we develop a mobile app designed to mitigate the elevated levels of technostress caused by two of the dominant types of stressors: techno-overload (e.g., students are forced to do more work because of technology) and techno-invasion (e.g., technology invading students' privacy). We focused on these stressors because they have become more prominent since the COVID-19 pandemic and the subsequent transition to hybrid learning settings, which have intensified students' workload and blurred the conventional borders between learning and privacy even more. We aim to prevent students from experiencing strains, such as decreased motivation and reduced academic performance

Against this backdrop, we develop a mobile app using a design-based research (DBR) approach [KR14], suggesting features such as goal management, reward system, and reflection.

Goal management. *Students should be able to set and track technostress reduction goals.* The app enables students to establish personalized daily goals and monitor their progress towards achieving these goals by breaking down larger goals into manageable tasks, and providing reminders and notifications. The goals can be related to personal learning success or specifically directed towards mitigating techno-overload/-invasion and

---

[1] Universität Hildesheim, Institut für Betriebswirtschaft & Wirtschaftsinformatik, Universitätsplatz 1, Hildesheim, {walter002; maria; knacks}@uni-hildesheim.de

enabling unlearning of harmful behavior. For example, students can create personalized plans to establish daily routines that include physical exercise or meditation to help them manage their stress levels and improve their overall well-being. Overall, goal management should support in reducing cognitive overload, allowing users to focus on achieving their goals in a more structured and manageable way.

Reward system. *Students should be incentivised to achieve their personal goals.* By making use of gamification elements, the app will reward students for fulfilling set tasks. It does so by, e.g., virtual badges or points, personalized feedback and encouragement, and progress tracking, to create a positive and engaging user experience. This can be a way to mitigate technostress in e-learning contexts, e.g., [Fa21]. One specific idea would be to present challenges, e.g., abstaining from mobile phone distractions for a set amount of time and getting points for subsequent fulfilment. Finally, the reward system should support students in sustainably follow plans to reduce technostress in the long term.

Reflection. *Students should be encouraged to reflect on their behavior after experiencing technostress.* The app should provide tools to reflect on their goal achievement, personal behavior in situations of technostress, and its impact, as indicated by [AGP11]. Students can record their thoughts and reflections in a digital journal inside the app. Based on their insights, students can adapt their personal stance and behavior related to technostress. Thus, our app fosters a more mindful and intentional approach to cope with technostress.

To evaluate the utility of our app, we plan to conduct workshops with university students. The abstracted knowledge obtained during app design and workshop evaluation should serve as starting points for the the design of further learning applications. Thereby, we hope to support students in hybrid learning settings by providing guidance for technostress-mitigating design of apps in education.

Bibliography

[AGP11]   Ayyagari, R; Grover, V; Purvis, R.: Technostress: Technological Antecedents and Implications. MISQ 35/831, pp. 931-858, 2011.

[Fa21]   Fajri, F. A.; Haribowo R. Y. K.; Amalia, N.; Natasari, D.: Gamification in e-learning: The mitigation role in technostress. International Journal of Evaluation and Research in Education. 10/606, pp. 606-614, 2021.

[KR14]   McKenney, S.; Reeves, T. C.: Educational Design Research. In: Handbook of Research on Educational Communications and Technology. pp. 131-140. Springer New York, New York, 2014.

[UV21]   Upadhyaya, P.; Vrinda: Impact of technostress on academic productivity of university students. Education and Information Technologies, 26, pp. 1647-1664, 2021.

Virtual Reality für den Schulunterricht?!

Raphael Zender [1], Caterina Schäfer [2], Thiemo Leonhardt [3], Nadine Bergner [4], Josef Buchner [5] und David Wiesche [6]

Abstract: Virtual Reality (VR) gilt bereits seit einigen Jahren als vielversprechende Bildungstechnologie in allen Bildungsbereichen. Allerdings bleiben viele Fragen bezüglich der Lernwirksamkeit, der pädagogischen und didaktischen Gestaltung sowie medizinischer und ethischer Risiken noch unbeantwortet. Gerade im Schulunterricht haben diese Fragen jedoch eine besonders hohe Relevanz, da Kinder als Schutzbefohlene gelten. Dieses Poster präsentiert eine interdisziplinäre Initiative der Arbeitskreise "VR/AR-Learning" und "Informatik in Schulen" der Fachgruppe Bildungstechnologien, die sich unter Einbeziehung praktizierender Schullehrkräfte der praxisnahen Untersuchung von Chancen, Herausforderungen und Einsatzempfehlungen für VR im Schulunterricht widmet.

Keywords: Virtual Reality, Interdisziplinär, Schulunterricht, Lehrkräfte

1 Einführung

Eine Vielzahl von Projekten und Studien hat in den vergangenen Jahren die Stärken von VR (Virtual Reality) als ernstzunehmende Bildungstechnologie in verschiedenen Bildungsbereichen bestätigt [Ra20] [Mu23]. Dazu gehören z.B. die Möglichkeiten der 3D-Visualisierung sowie die Simulation real räumlich und sozial schwer herzustellender Lernsituationen. Diese Potentiale sind im Schulunterricht jedoch aufgrund einer Vielzahl von medizinischen, ethischen, pädagogischen, organisatorischen und technischen Herausforderungen des praktischen Einsatzes nur bedingt abrufbar.

Die interdisziplinäre Initiative "Virtual Reality für Schulkinder" aus Vertreter:innen der genannten Fachdisziplinen hat sich innerhalb der Arbeitskreise "VR/AR-Learning" und

---

[1] Humboldt-Universität zu Berlin, Institut für Informatik, Unter den Linden 6, Berlin, 10099, raphael.zender@hu-berlin.de, https://orcid.org/0000-0001-9866-9455
[2] Universität Duisburg-Essen, Institut für Sport- und Bewegungswissenschaften, Gladbecker Str. 180 / 182, Essen, 45141, caterina.schaefer@uni-due.de, https://orcid.org/0000-0002-3085-271X
[3] Technische Universität Dresden, Institut für Software- und Multimediatechnik, Dresden, 01062, thiemo.leonhardt@tu-dresden.de, https://orcid.org/0000-0003-4725-9776
[4] Technische Universität Dresden, Institut für Software- und Multimediatechnik, Dresden, 01062, nadine.bergner@tu-dresden.de, https://orcid.org/0000-0003-3527-3204
[5] Pädagogische Hochschule St. Gallen, Institut ICT & Medien, Müller-Friedbergstrasse 34, Rorschach, 9400, Schweiz, josef.buchner@phsg.ch, https://orcid.org/0000-0001-7637-885X
[6] Universität Duisburg-Essen, Institut für Sport- und Bewegungswissenschaften, Gladbecker Str. 180 / 182, Essen, 45141, david.wiesche@uni-due.de, https://orcid.org/0000-0002-6086-1406

doi: 10.18420/delfi2023-64

"Informatik in Schulen" der GI-Fachgruppe Bildungstechnologien seit 2021 der Erarbeitung der Bedenken und Risiken von Virtual Reality in der Schule gewidmet. Das Ziel ist dabei nicht die Verhinderung des schulischen VR-Einsatzes, sondern vielmehr dessen sensibilisierte und reflektierte Gestaltung und Durchführung unter Berücksichtigung der technologisch-inhärenten Chancen und Herausforderungen. Daher wurden ebenfalls erste Gestaltungsempfehlungen für die folgenden am schulischen Bildungsprozess beteiligten Akteur:innen vorgeschlagen.

- schulische Lehrkräfte
- Schüler:innen und deren Eltern
- Bildungsinstitutionen (z.B. Schulen)
- VR-Entwickler:innen
- politische und weitere Akteur:innen

In einem ersten Artikel [Ze22] wurden diese Ergebnisse zur Diskussion gestellt und anschließend in zwei Workshops ausgebaut und mit weiteren praktischen Einblicken untermauert.

2 Poster

Dieses Poster stellt die Initiative selbst sowie die bisherigen Erkenntnisse aus den Workshops in der DELFI-Community zur Diskussion. Dadurch wird das Thema in die fachwissenschaftliche Breite getragen und durch neue Perspektiven, auch über den schulischen Bereich hinaus, bereichert

Weiterhin wird durch das Poster versucht neue Akteur:innen für die Mitwirkung in der Initiative "Virtual Reality für Schulkinder" zu gewinnen, um im nächsten Schritt ein gemeinsames "Living Document" online zur Verfügung zu stellen, in dem die aktuellen Bedenken, Risiken und Empfehlungen zusammengetragen, kontinuierlich aktualisiert und durch Erfahrungsberichte aus der Schule ergänzt werden.

Literaturverzeichnis

[Mu23] Mulders, M. et al.: Immersives Lehren und Lernen mit Augmented und Virtual Reality - Teil 2 (Empirische Studien). Heft 52 der Zeitschrift für Theorie und Praxis der Medienbildung (MedienPädagogik), 2023.

[Ra20] Radianti, J. et al.: A Systematic Review of Immersive Virtual Reality Applications for Higher Education: Design Elements, Lessons Learned, and Research Agenda. In Computers & Education, 147, 2020.

[Ze22] Zender, R. et al.: Virtual Reality für Schüler:Innen – Ein ‹Beipackzettel› für die Durchführung Immersiver Lernszenarien im schulischen Kontext. In MedienPädagogik: Zeitschrift für Theorie und Praxis der Medienbildung, 47, pp. 26-52, 2022.

Immersive und interaktive Lernerfahrungen in der schulischen Bildung mit 360°-Videos

Frederic Maquet[1], Jean-Pierre Sterck-Degueldre[2] und Matthias Ehlenz[3]

Abstract: Immersive und interaktive Lernerfahrungen mit 360°-Videos bieten den Vorteil, dass sie durch die vorhandene Infrastruktur großer Videoplattformen und eine breite Auswahl an Abspielgeräten problemlos im schulischen Bildungsbereich einsetzbar sind. Beinahe alle Schüler*innen haben (spätestens) ab der weiterführenden Schule ein Smartphone, es gibt zunehmend mehr Tabletklassen. Somit bieten 360°-Videos eine praxisrelevante Skalierbarkeit dieser Lernerfahrung über VR-Leuchtturmprojekte hinaus. Im vorgestellten Projekt geht es darum, Lehrer*innen zu befähigen, ansprechendes 360°-Material didaktisch zielführend einzusetzen und selbst zu entwickeln. Perspektiven auf immersive Lernumgebungen, OER und Skalierbarkeit werden in diesem Projekt vereint. Als konkretes Anwendungsbeispiel wird das Kooperationsprojekt „Vor ORt" vorgestellt, in dem didaktisch aufbereitete 360°-Aufnahmen von sakralen Räumen aller Weltreligionen erstellt werden, die den Lernenden anderweitig nicht zugänglich sind. Die Aufnahmen werden Lehrkräften mit begleitendem Unterrichtsmaterial und didaktischem Kommentar zur Verfügung gestellt und evaluiert. Anschließend werden Lehrkräfte in die Erstellung eigener 360°-Videos eingeführt. Die abgeleiteten Erfahrungen werden aufbereitet und fächerübergreifende Fortbildungskonzepte und zielgruppenspezifische Tools entwickelt.

Keywords: 360°-Videos, Skalierbarkeit interaktiver und immersiver Lernerfahrungen, OER, Autorentools, Lehrkräftefortbildung, Schule.

Das Pilotprojekt „Vor ORt"

Viele Leuchtturmprojekte haben bereits ansprechende und mit VR-Technik kompatible Inhalte für die schulische Bildung hervorgebracht. Ein flächendeckender Einsatz bleibt ihnen jedoch aufgrund der fehlenden Geräteinfrastruktur verwehrt. Ebenso stockt die Verbreitung der Geräte aufgrund der in der Anzahl limitierten Inhalte. Dieser Posterbeitrag stellt ein Projekt vor, in dem Inhalte erstellt werden, die auf eine bereits vorhandenen Geräte- und Softwareinfrastruktur zurückgreifen, aber in Zukunft mit VR-Headsets abgespielt werden können: 360°-Videos. Als Anwendungsbeispiel dient das

---

[1] RWTH-Aachen, Lehrerbildungszentrum, MediaLab Lehramt, Karmanstraße 17-19, 52062 Aachen, maquet@lbz.rwth-aachen.de,
[2] Bistum Aachen, Katechetisches Institut, Religionspädagogische Fort-, Aus- und Weiterbildung, Eupener Str. 132, 52066 Aachen, jean-pierre.sterck-degueldre@bistum-aachen.de.
[3] RWTH-Aachen, Lehrerbildungszentrum, MediaLab Lehramt, Karmanstraße 17-19, 52062 Aachen, ehlenz@lbz.rwth--aachen.de.

doi: 10.18420/delfi2023-65

Projekt „Vor ORt". 360°-Videos von lokalen sakralen Räumen, wie Kirchen, Synagogen und Moscheen sollen didaktisch aufbereitet und kernlehrplankonform den Weg in die Schulen finden.[4] Thematische Schwerpunkte bilden die Kirchenraumpädagogik und das interreligiöse Lernen. Dabei werden die Betrachter*innen der 360°-Videos in einer ersten Phase von einem ortskundigen, menschlichen Guide geführt und im Anschluss in eine explorative Phase entlassen, in der sie sich in Ruhe ohne Störfaktoren in den Räumen umschauen können. Elemente von Interesse werden vorab fotografiert bzw. gefilmt und in die Videos eingefügt. Auch Tonspuren mit Gesängen oder Gebeten, die die Immersion steigern, können eingefügt werden. Das Material lässt sich so in individueller Weise und individueller Geschwindigkeit erschließen. Passendes Unterrichtsmaterial sowie ein didaktischer Kommentar werden frei verfügbar im Sinne der OER veröffentlicht. Nach einer Phase der Evaluierung und Überarbeitung der Endprodukte durch den Praxiseinsatz, werden darauf aufbauend Fortbildungen erstellt. Lehrkräfte werden befähigt, eigene 360°-Inhalte zu erstellen. 360°-Videos bieten je nach genutztem Endgerät einen geringeren oder größeren Anteil an Immersion und Interaktivität. Sie können per Smartphone/Tablet und Gyrosensor, aber auch per VR-Headset betrachtet werden. Verschiedene Videoplattformen bieten die notwendige Softwareinfrastruktur, die gemeinsam mit der Vielfalt der Endgeräte für eine hervorragende Skalierbarkeit dieser Lernerfahrung sorgen. Die Befähigung von Lehrkräften und perspektivisch auch Schüler*innen sowie die in Relation günstige Ausstattung zur Erstellung der Inhalte tun ihr Übriges. Das Poster stellt das Projekt in seinen Grundzügen dar, legt den Fokus jedoch auf das Element der Skalierbarkeit. Entscheidend ist, dass Lehrkräfte nachhaltig befähigt werden, solche Videos zu drehen und zu bearbeiten. Neben der Videobearbeitung ist hier perspektivisch ein Open-Source-Autorentool notwendig, welches sich bereits in Entwicklung befindet. Der Fokus des Tools liegt auf dem Einfügen von interaktiven Hotspots in 360°-Bilder und -Videos, welche Bilder, Videos, Texte, Audiospuren und Hyperlinks beinhalten können. Bei einer hinreichend großen Anzahl von Materialien aller Fächer ist auch sichergestellt, dass Lehrkräfte bei einer Investition in VR-Technik an Schulen auf bereits vorhandenes Material zurückgreifen können, ohne neue Möglichkeiten aus dem Blick zu verlieren.

Literaturverzeichnis

[Ke11]   Kernlehrplan Sekundarstufe I Gymnasium in NRW Katholische Religionslehre. https://www.schulentwicklung.nrw.de/lehrplaene/upload/klp_SI/kathol_Religionslehre/KLP_GY_KR.pdf

---

[4] Z. B. Katholische Religionslehre Sekundarstufe I, Inhaltsfelder 5+6. Vgl. KLP NRW KR Sek I.

Potenziale von Virtual Reality für inklusive Schulbildung

Frank Wehrmann [1] und Raphael Zender [2]

Abstract: Virtual Reality hat großes Potenzial für die inklusive Bildung. Dieser Beitrag verdeutlicht, wie VR-Anwendungen zur Förderung inklusiver Bildung beitragen können. Ein theoretischer Rahmen aus der Inklusionsforschung wird benutzt um eine Analyse inklusiver Prozessmerkmale in VR Lehr- und Lernanwendungen durchzuführen. Exemplarische Anwendungen zeigen, wie die Prozessmerkmale in VR umgesetzt werden können und unterstreichen das Potenzial von VR in diesem Bereich. Darüber hinaus bedarf es der Entwicklung grundlegender Gestaltungsprinzipien für inklusive VR-Anwendungen im schulischen Kontext.

Keywords: Virtual Reality, Inklusion, Schule

1 Inklusive Potenziale von VR Lehr- und Lernanwendungen

Das Potenzial für inklusive Schulbildung durch Virtual Reality (VR) wird vermehrt wahrgenommen [Sc23]. Das Ziel der schulischen Inklusion besteht darin, dass alle Lernenden unabhängig von ihrer Ausgangslage und möglichen Beeinträchtigungen in der Schule ihre individuellen Entwicklungspotenziale entfalten können [Fr19]. VR ermöglicht eine immersive Interaktion mit virtuellen Welten und kann dadurch vielfältige Inhalte auf neue Art erlebbar machen und im digitalen Raum diverse Zugänge schaffen. Doch es fehlen klare Konzepte zur Gestaltung inklusiver VR-Lehr- und Lernanwendungen. Dieses Poster zielt darauf ab den Inklusionsgehalt von beispielhaften VR-Anwendungen und den Bedarf für die Entwicklung grundlegender Gestaltungsprinzipien für inklusive VR-Lehr- und Lernanwendungen darzustellen.

Das didaktische Modell für inklusives Lehren und Lernen [Fr19] bietet einen geeigneten theoretischen Rahmen und operationalisiert vier Prozessmerkmale inklusiver Bildung: Partizipation, Kommunikation, Reflexion und Kooperation. Diese lassen sich in exemplarischen VR-Anwendungen nachweisen: „ChemGerLab" ermöglicht gefahrloses Experimentieren im virtuellen Labor, diese Anwendung fördert Partizipation und reduziert physikalische Barrieren [Fl22]. „CalcFlow" [Di21] unterstützt das Sprechen über mathematische Sachverhalte, während „Keep Talking and Nobody Explodes" die fremdsprachliche Kommunikation fördert [SM21]. Vermehrt in Museen und Gedenkstätten verwendete historische VR-Anwendungen wie z.B. „StasiVR" bieten

---

[1] Humboldt-Universität zu Berlin, Institut für Informatik, Unter den Linden 6, Berlin, 10099, frank.wehrmann@hu-berlin.de, https://orcid.org/0009-0007-5774-5045
[2] Humboldt-Universität zu Berlin, Institut für Informatik, Unter den Linden 6, Berlin, 10099, raphael.zender@hu-berlin.de, https://orcid.org/0000-0001-9866-9455

doi: 10.18420/delfi2023-66

Möglichkeiten zur kritischen Auseinandersetzung mit Medien und Geschichte, dadurch, dass die Perspektive des Medienrezipienten bewusster Teil des Unterrichtsprozesses werden kann [Le22], dies fällt unter das Prozessmerkmal Reflexion. Darüber hinaus hat eine Studie gezeigt, dass sowohl asymmetrische als auch symmetrische Kooperations- und Kollaborationsformate in VR-Anwendungen ko-konstruktive Lernprozesse ermöglichen können [Dr22], es ist also erkennbar, dass VR-Anwendungen diverse Zugänge zur Kooperation bieten. Diese Anwendungen zeigen bereits inklusive Mehrwerte, auch wenn sie nicht explizit für Inklusion konzipiert sind. Eine inhärente Tendenz zur Inklusion ist in allgemeindidaktischen Ansätzen zur Verwendung von VR in der Schule erkennbar. Es gilt, diese Tendenz strukturiert zu nutzen.

2 Gestaltungsprinzipien für inklusive VR Lernanwendungen

Es besteht ein Bedarf zur Entwicklung von Gestaltungsprinzipien für inklusive VR Lehr- und Lernanwendungen. Ein zu diesem Poster gehöriges Promotionsprojekt zielt darauf ab, die Aspekte der Inklusion zu maximieren, Barrieren zu minimieren und Entwickelnde von VR-Anwendungen sowie Lehrende mit Design- und Verwendungskonzepten auszustatten, die den inklusiven Ansprüchen gerecht werden. Das Ziel ist es, eine strukturierte und absichtsvolle Förderung von Inklusion durch VR-Anwendungen zu ermöglichen.

Literaturverzeichnis

[Di21]   Dilling, F.: Die App Calcflow. In: Begründungsprozesse im Kontext von (digitalen) Medien im Mathematikunterricht. Springer Spektrum, Wiesbaden, S. 231-268, 2022.

[Dr22]   Drey, T. et al.: Towards Collaborative Learning in Virtual Reality: A comparison of Co-Located Symmetric and Asymmetric Pair-Learning. In: CHI Conference on Human Factors in Computing Systems, New York, 2022.

[Fl22]   Fleischer, T. et al.: Das Virtual Reality Chemielabor ChemGerLab – Experimentieren in der virtuellen Realität. In (E. M.; Hoffmann, C., Hrsg.): Digitale NAWIgation von Inklusion. Springer Fachmedien, Wiesbaden, S. 115-122, 2022.

[Fr19]   Frohn, J. et al. (Hrsg.): Inklusives Lehren und Lernen - Allgemein- und fachdidaktische Grundlagen. Julius Klinkhart, Bad Heilbrunn, 2019.

[Le22]   Lewers, E.: Durch Raum und Zeit? Medienkritische Auseinandersetzungen mit Virtual Reality im Geschichtsunterricht. Medienimpulse 60/2, 2022.

[Sc23]   Schäfer, C. et al.: Virtual Reality in der Schule. Bedenken und Potenziale aus Sicht der Akteur:innen in interdisziplinären Ratingkonferenzen. MedienPädagogik 51, S. 1-24, 2023.

[SM21]   Smith, M.; McCurrach, D.: The Usage of Virtual Reality in Task-Based Language Teaching. In: Proceedings of the 28th Korea TESOL International Conference, S. 153-165, 2021.

Interaktionsmöglichkeiten und Potenziale digitaler Gamebooks unter Berücksichtigung der CELG-Taxonomie

Svenja Noichl [1] und Ulrik Schroeder [1]

Abstract: Digitale Gamebooks bieten durch das nicht-lineare und auf Interaktionen durch Nutzende basierende Grundprinzip großes Potential für einen Einsatz in der Lehre. Durch die Interaktion mit Gamebooks können sich individuelle Lernpfade ergeben und es können gezieltes Feedback und individuelle Zusatzmaterialien bereitgestellt werden. In diesem Beitrag werden Interaktionsmöglichkeiten wie z.B. Quiz, Memory, Lückentexte oder Sortieraufgaben aus existierenden Gamebook-Ansätzen zur Betrachtung der Potentiale von digitalen Gamebooks für einen Einsatz in der Lehre in die CELG-Taxonomietafel eingeordnet.

Keywords: Digitale Gamebooks, Interaktionsmöglichkeiten, CELG-Taxonomie

1 Digitale Gamebooks und ihre Interaktionsmöglichkeiten

Gamebooks werden nicht linear gelesen, da Lesende Entscheidungen treffen, die den Verlauf der Geschichte beeinflussen. Unter digitalen Gamebooks wird in diesem Beitrag jede Form von nicht-linearem, digitalen Material verstanden. Nicht-linear bedeutet hierbei, dass die Story, die durch Mulitmedia-Inhalte angereichert werden kann, bzw. die Reihenfolge der Inhalte nicht zwangsweise für alle Nutzenden gleich ist. Unterschiedliche Interaktions- und Entscheidungsmöglichkeiten, welche Einfluss auf den Ablauf des Gamebook haben können, können den Handlungsverlauf beeinflussen. Erste Ansätze zur Umsetzung von papierbasierten Gamebooks in digitalem Kontext traten in den 2010er Jahren in Form von eBook-Formaten auf (vgl. [BFN15], [Sa21]). Darüber hinaus gibt es webbasierte Gamebookeditoren wie Twine, Squiffy, Inklewriter sowie Inform7. In diesen Beispielen sind einfache Gamebooks ohne Programmierkenntnisse erstellbar. Dies beschränkt sich jedoch meist auf Entscheidungen und Multiple Choice Aufgaben. Einen ersten Ansatz diesem Problem mit bereitgestellten Templates für unterschiedliche Aufgabentypen entgegenzuwirken liefert die Software des Projekts MeinBerufBau [NKS21].

2 Potential von digitalen Gamebooks in der Lehre

Durch Multimedia-Inhalte und unterschiedliche Aufgabentypen können die Interaktions-

---

[1] RWTH Aachen, Lerntechnologien, Ahornstr. 55, Aachen, 52074, {noichl, schroeder}@informatik.rwth-aachen.de, https://orcid.org/{0000-0002-6374-7764, 0000-0002-5178-8497}

doi: 10.18420/delfi2023-67

möglichkeiten der Lernenden mit digitalen Gamebooks abwechslungsreich gestaltet und die Leistung in den Aufgaben genutzt werden, um die Story zu beeinflussen. So werden individuelle Lernpfade, die z.b. auf Kenntnisstände oder Interessen der Lernenden abgestimmt sind, ermöglicht. Lernziele und deren Umsetzung spielen eine bedeutende Rolle bei Gamebooks die in der Lehre eingesetzt werden sollen. Angelehnt an die erweiterte Bloomsche Taxonomie von Anderson und Krathwohl [Kr02] entwickelten Mayer et al. die CELG-Taxonomie (Computer Supported Evaluation of Learning Goals), ein Modell zur computergestützten Lernzielüberprüfung [MHW09]. Abb. 1 zeigt eine Zuordnung von interaktiven Gamebook Elementen in die kognitiven Prozessdimensionen und Wissensdimensionen der CELG-Taxonomie.

Wissens-dimensionen	Kognitive Prozessdimensionen			
	Reproduzieren	Verstehen/ Anwenden	Reflektieren/ Evaluieren	Erschaffen
Faktenwissen	Entscheidung/ Reihenfolge	Multiple Choice Quiz	Multiple Choice Quiz	
	Memory	Unterstreiche/ Markieren von Textstellen	Markieren von Textstellen	
	Multiple Choice Quiz	Drag-and-Drop (z.B. sortieren, zuordnen)	Sortieren	Freitext
Konzeptwissen	Unterstreiche/ Markieren von Textstellen	Puzzle	Zuordnen	Formeln
	Drag-and-Drop (z. B. sortieren, zuordnen)	Lückentext	Freitext	Feedback
	Puzzle	Formeln/ Berechnungen	Formeln/ Berechnungen	
Prozedurales Wissen	Lückentext	Feedback	Feedback	
			Vorherige ohne Multiple Choice Quiz	

Abb. 1: Interaktive Gamebook-Elemente aus [BFN15, Sa21, NKS21] in der CELG-Taxonomietafel

Um die aufwendige Integration von Lernressourcen unter Berücksichtigung von unterschiedlichen Pfaden und Feedback sowie die generelle Erstellung von Gamebooks zu erleichtern, sollte eine Plattform für Gamebooks leicht bedienbar sein und Schnittstellen zu bestehenden Lern-Management-Systemen (LMS) bieten. Auch eine Anbindung an Learning Analytics zur Auswertung der Nutzerinteraktion und der Lernpfade stellt eine sinnvolle Erweiterung dar. Insbesondere Informationen über die Lernpfade innerhalb der Gamebooks bieten hierbei wertvolle Einblicke, die insbesondere zur Verbesserung der Materialien genutzt werden können.

Literaturverzeichnis

[BFN15] Bidarra, J.; Figueiredo, M.; Natálio, C.: Interactive Design and Gamification of eBooks for Mobile and Contextual Learning. International Journal of Interactive Mobile Technologies (iJIM) 3/9, S. 24, 2015.

[Kr02] Krathwohl, D. R.: A Revision of Bloom's Taxonomy: An Overview. Theory Into Practice 4/41, S. 212–218, 2002.

[MHW09] Mayer, H. O.; Hertnagel, J.; Weber, H.: Lernzielüberprüfung im eLearning. OLDENBOURG WISSENSCHAFTSVERLAG, 2009.

[NKS21] Noichl, S.; Korth, S.; Schroeder, U.: Inklusives und handlungsorientiertes Lernen mithilfe Digitaler Gamebooks. 1617-5468, 2021.

[Sa21] Sarinho, V. T.: GEnEbook: A Game Engine to Provide Electronic Gamebooks for Adventure Games: 2021 20th Brazilian Symposium 10/2021, S. 59–68.

Virtual Reality im Grundschulkontext: Bienen-Lerninhalte im Sachunterricht

Caroline Schon[1], Olaf Ueberschär[2] und Johannes Tümler[3]

Abstract: Vergangene Studien haben die Fähigkeit von Virtual Reality herausgestellt, Lernende gezielt für Fachthemen zu begeistern und dadurch Lernerfolge zu unterstützen. wird eine Virtual-Reality-Anwendung präsentiert, die in einem partizipativen Entwicklungsprozess entstand und Grundwissen zum Thema Bienen vermittelt. Insbesondere soll dabei das Umweltbewusstsein der Kinder gefördert werden.

Keywords: Didaktik, Digitale Bildung und Bildungstechnologien in der Schule, Virtual Reality

1 Einleitung

In diesem Beitrag wird der aktuelle Stand und die Anwendungsentwicklung eines Grundschul-Lernprojektes zum Fachthema Bienen basierend auf Virtual Reality (VR) dargestellt, das zum gegenwärtigen Zeitpunkt noch in Umsetzung befindlich ist. Gerade für den Einsatz in der Grundschule ist es wichtig, dass immersive Anwendungen didaktisch hinreichend gut aufbereitet sind [EMB21]. Ziel ist es, die Entwicklung und Implementierung gemeinsam mit einschlägigen Lehrkräften durchzuführen, sodass ein didaktisch fundiertes Szenario im Unterricht genutzt werden kann.

2 VR in der Lehre

Der Einsatz von VR an Schulen steht noch am Anfang. Laut Eckes, Moormann und Büssing (2021) kann dabei eine Verknüpfung von Digitalisierung und Naturverbundenheit gelingen: „Während die Digitalisierung ein Grund für verringerte Naturkontakte sein kann, bieten neue Technologien ebenfalls Anlass, um über innovative Möglichkeiten von Naturerlebnissen nachzudenken" (EMB21, S. 361). Die Wirkung von Präsenz in VR auf den Kompetenzerwerb und Wissenszuwachs ist dabei jedoch noch nicht vollständig geklärt, insbesondere im Kontext eines Naturerlebnisses [EMB21]. Laut Möller (2021) hat die sich verändernde Umwelt auch Auswirkungen auf die Spezies der Biene, weshalb

---
[1] Hochschule Anhalt, Bernburger Str. 57, 06366 Köthen (Anhalt)
[2] Hochschule Magdeburg-Stendal, Breitscheidstraße 2, 39114 Magdeburg, Institut für Angewandte Trainingswissenschaft, Marschnerstraße 29, 04109 Leipzig
[3] Hochschule Anhalt, Bernburger Str. 57, 06366 Köthen (Anhalt)

durch sie Wissen zu Themen wie Artenschutz, gut vermittelt werden [Mö21].

3 Methodik

3.1 Beschreibung des Verfahrens

Als Ausgangspunkt wurde eine Bedarfsanalyse gewählt, welche sich Interviews mit freiwillig teilnehmenden Grundschullehrkräften bediente. Dabei wurden mögliche Themen diskutiert, um ein geeignetes Lehrthema zu finden und inhaltlich zu bearbeiten. Folgend hatten die Lehrkräfte die Möglichkeit, die umgesetzte Anwendung auszuprobieren und didaktisch zu evaluieren und zu kommentieren.

3.2 Beschreibung der Anwendung

.Die hier im Beitrag beschriebe Anwendung orientiert sich am Lebenszyklus der Biene. Um ein realistisches Bild zu vermitteln, wurden 360-Grad-Bilder mit Szenenwissen hinterlegt. Anschließend, haben die Kinder die Möglichkeit, das Gelernte zu vertiefen, indem sie die Aufgaben der Biene selbst ausführen. Die Anwendung wird mit Unity Version 2021.3.17f1, dem Interaction Toolkit 2.2.0 und der HP Reverb G2 erstellt.

3.3 Proband*innen

Für die Entwicklung der Anwendung wurden sechs Lehrkräfte einer öffentlichen Grundschule befragt, die weiblich und im Durchschnitt zwischen 51 und 55 Jahre alt sind. Die Lehrerinnen sind seit 31 bis 35 Jahren im Schuldienst und 3 haben Erfahrung mit VR.

4 Diskussion

Eine Herausforderung besteht darin, dass viele Lehrer im Bereich VR bislang wenig Erfahrung haben und die Technologie nicht als Werkzeug in der Lehre erleben konnten. Ihnen ist das Potenzial des Mediums im Kontext von Bildung oftmals nicht umfänglich bewusst. Umso wichtiger ist es, die Nutzung des Mediums aufzuzeigen und zu fördern.

Literaturverzeichnis

[EMB21]   Eckes, A.; Moormann, A.; Büssing, A. G.: Natur 2.0 – Erlebnisse in immersiver virtueller Realität als Möglichkeit für Naturerfahrungen?. In (Gebhard, U. et al., eds.): Naturerfahrung und Bildung, Springer, Berlin, S. 361-377, 2021.

[Mö21]   Möller, A.: Naturerfahrung mit Bienen, In (Gebhard, U. et al., eds.): Naturerfahrung und Bildung, Springer, Berlin, S. 283-307, 2021.

Navigationsgestaltung in Lernvideos

Janine Schledjewski[1], Alina Zumbruch[1], Sofia Schneider[1] und Claudia Schrader[1]

Abstract: Verschiedene Gestaltungsfaktoren, z. B. die Navigation, können die Wirksamkeit von Lernvideos auf kognitive und affektive Lernprozesse und die daraus resultierenden Lernleistungen beeinflussen. Im Beitrag werden erste Ergebnisse aus einer laufenden Studie (N=45) berichtet, bei der drei Gestaltungsvarianten von Navigation hinsichtlich ihrer Wirkungen auf die kognitive Belastung, die Lern- und Leistungsemotionen sowie die Lernleistungen verglichen werden: (1) Navigation über ein Inhaltsverzeichnis, (2) Navigation über eingebettete Entscheidungsfragen und (3) Kontrollgruppe ohne zusätzliche Navigationsmöglichkeiten.

Keywords: E-Learning, Lernvideos, Navigationsgestaltung

1 Navigationsgestaltung in Lernvideos und deren Effekte

Lernvideos sind von Lehrenden eigens produzierte Filme, die in formellen und informellen Lehr-/Lernsituationen in den letzten Jahren vermehrt für die Wissensvermittlung genutzt werden [Pe20]. Dabei haben sich Lernvideos als wirksam in Bezug auf die Förderung von kognitiven Prozessen, Affekt und die daraus resultierenden Lernleistungen erwiesen [KK12], wobei die Wirksamkeit von Videos beispielsweise von der Navigationsgestaltung beeinflusst wird [CJ17].

Hinsichtlich der Navigation bieten neuere Plug-ins wie H5P einerseits Inhaltsverzeichnisse an, um das Video in einzelne Abschnitte zu segmentieren und ein Zurücknavigieren zu einzelnen Stellen innerhalb des Videos zu ermöglichen. Andererseits können Entscheidungsfragen in Form von Crossroad-Elementen integriert werden. Während das Inhaltsverzeichnis aktiv durch die Lernenden aufgerufen werden muss, werden die Entscheidungsfragen systemgesteuert eingeblendet.

2 Methode und vorläufige Ergebnisse

Um die Frage zu klären, inwieweit sich verschiedene Navigationsgestaltungsmöglichkeiten hinsichtlich ihrer Wirkungen auf die kognitive Belastung, die Lern- und Leistungsemotionen sowie die Lernleistungen unterscheiden, werden in einer derzeit noch laufenden

---

[1] Bergische Universität Wuppertal, Institut für Bildungsforschung in der School of Education, Gaußstr. 20, 42119 Wuppertal, schledjewski@uni-wuppertal.de, zumbruch@uni-wuppertal.de, sofia.schneider@uni-wuppertal.de, cschrader@uni-wuppertal.de

Studie Teilnehmer*innen gebeten, sich mit einem Lernvideo (Länge: 22 Minuten; Thema: digital gestützte Feedbackgabe) zu befassen. Dafür werden die Teilnehmer*innen randomisiert auf drei Gruppen verteilt: 1) IV-Gruppe: Lernvideo mit eingebundenem Inhaltsverzeichnis, 2) EF-Gruppe: Lernvideo mit strukturellen Entscheidungsfragen in Form eines integrierten Crossroad-Elements, 3) Kontrollgruppe (KG): Lernvideo ohne zusätzliche Navigationsfunktionen. In einem Pretest wird u. a. das Vorwissen zum Inhalt und zur Erfahrung mit Lernvideos erfasst. Nach der Rezeption des Lernvideos werden die Teilnehmer*innen gebeten, den Posttest, u. a. mit Fragen zur kognitiven Belastung [KSS17], zum emotionalen Erleben [La16] und zur Lernleistung, durchzuführen.

Insgesamt liegen derzeit 45 auswertbare Datensätze vor (IV: 19, EF: 19, KG: 9). Hinsichtlich der kognitiven Belastung zeigt sich, dass die extrinsische Belastung bei der EF-Gruppe (M=2.07, SD=1.25) tendenziell niedriger ist als bei der IV-Gruppe (M=2.84, SD=1.33) und der KG-Gruppe (M=2.52, SD=0.43). Dies gilt auch für die intrinsische Belastung (IV: M=2.74, SD=1.52, EF: M=2.08, SD=1.17, KG: M=3.14, SD=1.33). Die Werte zu den Lern- und Leistungsemotionen unterscheiden sich primär hinsichtlich der empfundenen Langeweile, wobei die EF-Gruppe hier die niedrigsten Werte aufweist (IV: M=3.79, SD=1.51, EF: M=3.11, SD=1.37, KG: M=4.43, SD=1.4). In allen Gruppen zeigt sich ein Wissenszuwachs bezogen auf die Inhalte des Lernvideos in den Bereichen Behalten und Verstehen im Vergleich vom Pretest zum Posttest. Bezüglich der Verstehensleistung zeigt sich, dass die IV-Gruppe (M=8.18, SD=3.49) bessere Werte erzielt als die EF-Gruppe (M=6.94, SD=3.51) und die KG-Gruppe (M=5.14, SD=2.59). Die vorläufigen Ergebnisse der laufenden Studie zeigen, dass Entscheidungsfragen im Vergleich zu Inhaltverzeichnissen und zur Kontrollgruppe tendenziell mit einer niedrigeren extrinsischen sowie intrinsischen Belastung einhergehen und gleichzeitig tendenziell das Verstehen weniger unterstützen als Inhaltsverzeichnisse.

Literaturverzeichnis

[CJ17] Cojean, S.; Jamet, E.: Facilitating information-seeking activity in instructional videos: The combined effects of micro- and macroscaffolding. Computers in Human Behavior, 74, S. 294–302, 2017.

[KK12] Kay, R.; Kletskin, I.: Evaluating the use of problem-based video podcasts to teach mathematics in higher education. Computers & Education, 59, S. 619–627, 2012.

[KSS17] Klepsch, M.; Schmitz, F.; Seufert, T.: Development and Validation of Two Instruments Measuring Intrinsic, Extraneous, and Germane Cognitive Load. Frontiers in Psychology, 8, Article 1997, 2017.

[La16] Lallé, S. et al.: Impact of Individual Differences on Affective Reactions to Pedagogical Agents Scaffolding. In (Traum, D. et al., Hrsg.): Intelligent Virtual Agents. IVA 2016. Lecture Notes in Computer Science, 10011. Springer, Cham, S. 269–282, 2016.

[Pe20] Persike, M.: Videos in der Lehre: Wirkungen und Nebenwirkungen. In (Niegemann, H.; Weinberger, A., Hrsg.): Handbuch Bildungstechnologie. Konzeption und Einsatz digitaler Lernumgebungen. Springer, Berlin, S. 271–302, 2020.

Ein Konzept zur Evaluierung eines Ökosystems für die Integration von Learning Analytics in Virtual Reality

Sergej Görzen [1], Birte Heinemann [1] und Ulrik Schroeder [1]

Abstract: Das Interesse an Lernumgebungen für Virtual Reality hat in den letzten Jahren zugenommen. Eine Möglichkeit, die Effektivität dieser Lernumgebungen messbar zu machen, besteht im Einsatz von Learning Analytics. Allerdings erfordert die Einarbeitung von Programmier*innen umfangreiche Kenntnisse über Learning Analytics und ist häufig aufgrund von Zeitmangel nur oberflächlich. Um Hürden entgegenzuwirken, wurde OmiLAXR (ehemals EduXR) entwickelt, eine vielfältige Unterstützung für Entwickelnde von VR-Applikationen in Unity. Dieser Beitrag stellt kurz Prototypen und ein Evaluationskonzept von Entwicklungsprozessen mit vielfältigem Learning Analytics Ökosystem vor. Ziel ist eine anschließende systematische Anforderungsanalyse für die technische Perspektive auf Learning Analytics Infrastrukturen.

Keywords: OmiLAXR, EduXR, Learning Analytics Infrastruktur, Educational Virtual Reality, Programmierunterstützung, Automatisierung

Motivation und Vorstellung des Evaluationskonzepts

Ergebnisse aus Learning Analytics können zukünftige Entscheidungen beeinflussen oder Probleme identifizieren. Technologische Standards existieren bereits dafür, doch neben den vielfältigen Anforderungen im interdisziplinären und multimodalen Kontext [Eh20], gibt es auch diverse technische Hürden zu überwinden [Wö21]. Wegen unterschiedlicher Ziele ist eine Einarbeitung ins LA-Design sehr aufwendig. Unter anderem, deshalb bleibt die Datensammlung (aus unserer Erfahrung) häufig bei Neuimplementierungen auf einem einfachen Niveau. Ebenso müssen in interdisziplinären Projekten Wege gefunden werden, um die verschiedenen Stakeholder zu koordinieren und Technik, Fachdisziplin und Didaktik miteinander zu verbinden [HES22]. Eine hohe Qualität der Lerndatenerfassung zu erhalten ist eine Herausforderung, insbesondere wenn die Entwickler*innen sich nicht in der Lehre und dem Fachbereich des Projektes auskennen. Als Maßnahme haben wir ein Software-Ökosystem für eine (Teil-)Automatisierung der Dimensionen „Was?" und „Wie?" des LA-Referenzmodells [Ch12] entworfen. Dieses Ökosystem und ein Konzept dessen Evaluierung wird hier vorgestellt.

Im Sommersemester 2023 wird eine Fallstudie mit einer Master-Studierendengruppe von Informatiker*innen in Form einer Beobachtungsstudien mit sieben Schritten [Mo17] Schritten durchgeführt. Dabei soll die Produktivität [Li20] des OmiLAXR-Ökosystems

---

[1] RWTH Aachen, Lerntechnologien, {goerzen, heinemann, schroeder}@informatik.rwth-aachen.de, https://orcid.org/{0000-0003-3853-2435, 0000-0002-7568-0570, 0000-0002-5178-8457}

doi: 10.18420/delfi2023-70

(siehe Abb. 1), im Integrationsprozess der Lerndatenerfassung für Learning Analytics beobachtet werden und die Qualitätskriterien von Software-Architekturen nach ISO/IEC DIS 25010 identifiziert werden. Die übergeordnete Forschungsfrage dieser Forschung ist: *Wie können Entwickler*innen bei der Integration von Learning Analytics in VR-Lernszenarien mit Unity (teil-)automatisiert unterstützt werden?*

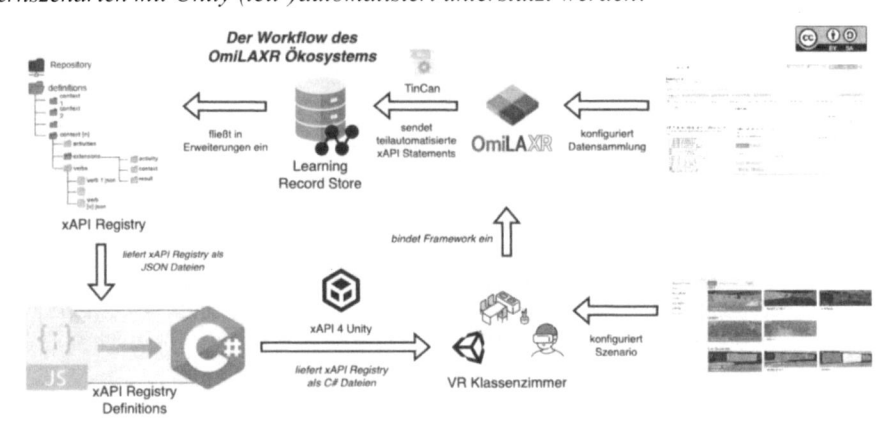

Abb. 1: Workflow des "Open and modular Learning Analytics in XR" (OmiLAXR) Ökosystems

Auf Basis der Analyse sollen weitere Entwicklungsprozesse optimiert werden und einen Beitrag in Richtung eines gemeinsamen Ansatzes zur Definition von Konventionen für xAPI [Eh20] geleistet werden. Die Übertragbarkeit auf abstrakter Ebene wird einbezogen, um weitere Anwendungsfälle zu ermöglichen. Ziel ist es unsere Vorerfahrungen mit den Studienergebnissen abzugleichen und erste Empfehlungen anhand von Anforderungen für die Integration von Learning Analytics in einer VR-Applikation auszuarbeiten.

Das Poster zum Beitrag ist online abrufbar: https://publications.rwth-aachen.de/record/959873 (zuletzt abgerufen am 16.06.2023).

Literaturverzeichnis

[Ch12]   Chatti, M. A. et al.: A Reference Model for Learning Analytics. International Journal of Technology Enhanced Learning, Vol. 4, Issue 5/6, S. 318-331, 2012.

[Eh20]   Ehlenz, M. et al.: Eine forschungspraktische Perspektive auf xAPI-Registries. In (Zender, R. et al., Hrsg.): 18. Fachtagung Bildungstechnologien (DELFI). Gesellschaft für Informatik e.V., Bonn, S. 331-336, 2020.

[HES22] Heinemann, B.; Ehlenz, M.; Schroeder, U.: Human-Centered Learning Analytics in Interdisciplinary Projects: Co-Designing Data Collection. In: Companion Proceedings of the 12th Learning Analytics and Knowledge Conference (LAK). S. 19-22, 2022.

[Li20]   Liao, Z. et al.: How to Evaluate the Productivity of Software Ecosystem: A Case Study in GitHub. Scientific Programming, Vol. 2020, Article ID 8814247, 2020.

[Wö21]   Wölfel, M. et al.: Entering a New Dimension in Virtual Reality Research: An Overview of Existing Toolkits, Their Features and Challenges. In: International Conference on Cyberworlds. IEEE, S. 180–187, 2021.

Task Definition in Big Sets of Heterogeneously Structured Moodle LMS Courses

Teodora Dogaru[1], Nora Götze[1], Daniela Rotelli[2], Yoel Berendsohn[1], Agathe Merceron[1] and Petra Sauer[1]

Abstract: Analysing Learning Management System (LMS) log data gives insight into student learning behaviour that can help to predict performance, and as a consequence to avoid drop-out. This contribution provides an application and an adaptation of Rotelli and Monreale's methodology [RM22] for defining tasks in a set of 10,532 online courses collected from seven universities. Unlike [RM22], we access the log data directly from the Moodle database. Even though our data set is much bigger and more heterogeneous than the one described in [RM22], we could adapt the data selection and filtering, as well as the components' redefinition and alignment and employ their methodology to define tasks. This work is a contribution to make log data preprocessing open, replicable and more transparent.

Keywords: LMS, Moodle log data analysis, Data preprocessing

1 Introduction

The DiSEA project is concerned with investigating factors leading to students' success or dropout in online degree programs. To provide students with feedback on their learning behaviours in the Learning Management System (LMS) and predict their performance, one aim of the DiSEA project is to analyse their interaction in the LMS. This is done by processing and analysing the log data that the LMS, in our case Moodle, stores. Unfortunately, there is little publication on how scientists preprocess log data, even though the decisions made in the preprocessing step influence the results. In this paper, we apply and adapt the methodology proposed in [RM22] to transform Moodle log data into tasks to better grasp students' learning behaviour, such as content or duration of their interaction with the LMS.

---

[1] Berliner Hochschule für Technik, Fachbereich VI, Luxemburger Straße 10, 133535 Berlin, Germany, {teodora.dogaru,nora.goetze,yoel.berendsohn,merceron,sauer}@bht-berlin.de, https://orcid.org/0000-0003-1015-5359

[2] University of Pisa, Department of Computer Science. Largo B. Pontecorvo 3, 56127, Pisa (Italy), daniela.rotelli@phd.unipi.it, https://orcid.org/0000-0002-0943-6922

2 From Data to Tasks

In the DiSEA project, we applied and adapted the methodology described in [RM22] to data collected via the Moodle platform that stores courses from seven universities that are part of a network of universities of applied sciences, Virtuelle Fachhochschule (VFH). Our data is vastly different with regard to data described in [RM22]. We have a high number of heterogeneous Moodle courses (>10,000) and we cannot use the log generation interface for log data extraction as done in [RM22], resulting in a more generic log that does not lend itself to easy readability. We only collect data from Moodle users that have explicitly stated their consent via a consent plugin that we specially developed. Each week, either new users consent to the use of their log data or existing participants withdraw their consent, resulting in a constantly changing data set. Because of the ever increasing, massive amount of log data, we must reduce our dataset to serve our purpose. Hence, we included only a) logs related to student activity, b) valuable Moodle components (at least 600 log records), and c) only courses with at least 75 records. After data filtering, our log contains 127 different events, categorised in 31 components. From the original 10,532 courses, only 982 are now left.

In the Moodle logging system every event is described by an *action* performed on a *component*, at a specific *time*, in a specific *course* or area of the platform. Components correspond to modules of the platform, like *dashboard*, *quiz*, *assignment* or *core*. Although they represent actions that the user performed on specific modules, some events are assigned the component *core*. To prevent information loss and a potential misunderstanding of users' behaviour, this component must be redefined. For every event assigned the *core* component that [RM22] describes and that we found in our data, we followed their example in redefining the component. Because the LMS Moodle is very flexible and feature-rich, allowing for several plugins and e-portfolios to be installed, we found events that are not described in [RM22] like (*mod_bigbluebuttonbn*, *activity*, *viewed*). These events can still be handled after the methodology described in [RM22].

Following [RM22], after component redefinition, each single record can now be grouped into so-called *tasks*. Roughly, a task is a sequence of log records with the same component for one user, that together can be construed as a singular, purposeful activity in one course or area of the platform. A task will have a number of actions, a course, a starting time and a duration. Once the list of components is established, the methodology of [RM22] to define tasks can be applied as is.

This work complements the study of [RM22], contributes to make log data preprocessing open, replicable and more transparent.

Bibliography

[RM22]   Rotelli, D.; Monreale, A.: Time-on-Task Estimation by data-driven Outlier Detection based on Learning Activities. In: LAK22, *doi:* 10.1145/3506860.3506913

Motivationen von Schülerinnen und Schülern bei der Nutzung digitaler Technologien am Lernort Berufsschule

Eine qualitative Befragung von Lehrkräften an Berufsschulen in Hamburg

Tim Komorowski[1], Meike Weiland [1], Daniel König[1], Lilli Heimes[1], Thomai Svenja Gruber[1] und Michael Heister[1]

Abstract: Die Digitalisierung der Arbeits- und Lebenswelt führt zu wachsenden Anforderungen an die digitalen Kompetenzen zukünftiger Fach- und Führungskräfte [He16]. Deshalb sollten die digitalen Kompetenzen bereits in der Berufsschule gefördert werden [KMK16]. Dies gelingt besser, wenn sich die Gestaltung des Unterrichts und der genutzten digitalen Technologien an den psychologischen Grundbedürfnissen der Selbstbestimmungstheorie [RD20] orientiert.

Keywords: Motivation, Selbstbestimmungstheorie, berufliche Bildung, Digitalisierung

Schülerinnen und Schüler benötigen als Fach- und Führungskräfte der Zukunft digitale Kompetenzen, um die Anforderungen der digitalisierten Arbeits- und Lebenswelt zu meistern [He16]. Ein wichtiger Ort für die Förderung digitaler Kompetenzen ist der Lernort Berufsschule [KMK16]. Wie aber steht es dort um die Motivationen von Schülerinnen und Schülern beim Erwerb digitaler Kompetenzen und der Nutzung von digitalen Technologien? Haben sie Interesse und Freude daran? Oder beschäftigen sie sich damit, weil Lehrkräfte oder Curricula dies vorschreiben?

Motivationen im Zusammenhang mit dem Erwerb digitaler Kompetenzen und der Nutzung von digitalen Technologien wurden in vorliegenden Studien zwar berücksichtigt [SLS20], jedoch sind nur wenige empirische Ergebnisse verfügbar, die sich auf die aktuelle Lage in der dualen Berufsausbildung und hier insbesondere den Berufsschulunterricht beziehen [Ge20]. Mit dem Projekt „Kompetenzen für die digitale Arbeitswelt (KoDiA) – Ertüchtigung zur Digitalisierung" (2021-2024) soll ein Beitrag zur Schließung dieser Lücke am Beispiel des Bundeslandes Hamburg geleistet werden [Ko23]. Das Projekt wird durch dtec.bw – Zentrum für Digitalisierungs- und Technologieforschung der Bundeswehr gefördert. dtec.bw wird von der Europäischen Union – NextGenerationEU finanziert.

Im Rahmen eines zweistufigen Forschungsdesigns mit Gruppendiskussionen [PW21] mit Berufsschullehrkräften und einer quantitativen Online-Befragung von Berufsschülerinnen

---

[1] Bundesinstitut für Berufsbildung, Abteilung 4 „Initiativen für die Berufsbildung", Robert-Schuman-Platz 3, 53175 Bonn, tim.komorowski@bibb.de, weiland@bibb.de, daniel.koenig@bibb.de, lilli.heimes@bibb.de, gruber@bibb.de, heister@bibb.de, https://orcid.org/0000-0002-6857-2289

doi: 10.18420/delfi2023-72

und Berufsschülern, das dem Prinzip der Methodentriangulation folgt, stehen folgende Forschungsfragen im Mittelpunkt: Wie schätzen die Lehrkräfte die digitalen Kompetenzen ihrer Schülerinnen und Schüler ein? Welche Motivationen, Interessen und Bedarfe haben die Schülerinnen und Schüler hinsichtlich der Nutzung digitaler Bildungsmedien und der Förderung der Partizipation in der digitalisierten Welt? Im 2. Quartal 2023 wurden vier Gruppendiskussionen durchgeführt, die mit Hilfe einer inhaltlich-strukturierenden qualitativen Inhaltsanalyse nach Kuckartz [KR22] ausgewertet werden. Die Online-Befragung ist für das 4. Quartal 2023 geplant.

Um Motivationen bei der Nutzung von digitalen Technologien zu untersuchen, greifen wir auf die Selbstbestimmungstheorie (Self-Determination Theory, SDT) zurück [RD20]. Die SDT unterscheidet zwischen intrinsischer Motivation und unterschiedlichen Formen von extrinsischer Motivation [RD20]. Die intrinsische Motivation zeichnet sich durch das Erleben von Interesse, Freude und einer inhärenten Befriedigung beim Ausführen einer Aktivität aus. Die extrinsische Motivation hingegen umfasst Verhaltensweisen, die nicht mit einer inhärenten Befriedigung verbunden sind [RD20]. Die SDT geht davon aus, dass sich solche instrumentellen Motivationen ihrem Inhalt und ihrem Charakter nach wesentlich unterscheiden und bietet einen begrifflichen Rahmen zu deren Beschreibung.

Unsere Untersuchung soll zu einem besseren Verständnis der Motivationen von Schülerinnen und Schülern an Hamburger Berufsschulen beim Erwerb digitaler Kompetenzen und im Umgang mit digitalen Technologien beitragen und eine selbständige und autonom-regulierte Lernmotivation fördern.

Literaturverzeichnis

[Ge20]   Gensicke, M. et al.: Digitale Medien in Betrieben – heute und morgen: Eine Folgeuntersuchung. Wissenschaftliche Diskussionspapiere: Bd. 220. Verlag B. Budrich, 2020.

[He16]   Helmrich, R. et al.: Digitalisierung der Arbeitslandschaften. Wissenschaftliche Diskussionspapiere: Heft 180. BIBB, 2016. https://doi.org/236147

[KMK16] Sekretariat der Kultusministerkonferenz: Bildung in der digitalen Welt: Strategie der Kultusministerkonferenz, 2016.

[Ko23]   Kodia, Projekt „Kompetenzen für die digitaler Arbeitswelt (KoDiA) – Ertüchtigung zur Digitalisierung", bibb.de/kodia, Stand: 16.06.2023.

[KR22]   Kuckartz, U.; Rädiker, S.: Qualitative Inhaltsanalyse. Methoden, Praxis, Computerunterstützung: Grundlagentexte Methoden (5. Aufl.). Beltz Juventa, Weinheim, 2022.

[PW21]   Przyborski, A.; Wohlrab-Sahr, M.: Qualitative Sozialforschung: Ein Arbeitsbuch. Lehr- und Handbücher der Soziologie. De Gruyter Verlag, Oldenburg, 2021.

[RD20]   Ryan, R.M.; Deci, E.L.: Intrinsic and extrinsic motivation from a self-determination theory perspective: Contemporary Educational Psychology, 2020.

[SLS20] Salikhova, N. R., Lynch, M. F.; Salikhova, A. B.: Psychological Aspects of Digital Learning: A Self-Determination Theory Perspective. Contemporary Educational Technology, 12(2), ep280, 2020. https://doi.org/10.30935/cedtech/8584

Erkenntnisse über die Entwicklung einer VR-Lernumgebung im Rahmen der Hochschullehre

Marc Dannemann[1], Pia Bothe[1], Simon Adler[1] und Sandy Grawe[1]

Abstract: Virtual Reality (VR) bietet viele Möglichkeiten für das immersive, interaktive Lehren und Lernen. Die Gestaltung und Nutzung virtueller Welten in der Hochschullehre ist jedoch immer noch herausfordernd und stellt daher eine Hürde für die breite Etablierung dar. Dieser Beitrag beschreibt, wie eine Kopplung virtueller Welten mit Fragebogensystemen wie in dem Lernmanagementsystem (LMS) ILIAS für eine strukturelle Verankerung von VR in der Hochschullehre im Rahmen des Projekts DigiLehR umgesetzt wird. Dazu wird das Mapping der Fragetypen aus dem LMS-Fragebogen auf immersiv-interaktive Handlungen in VR und die Übertragbarkeit dieses Mapping zwischen verschiedenen VR-Lernszenarien vorgestellt.

Keywords: Virtual Reality, Hochschullehre, Lernumgebung, Industrie, Mediengestaltung

1 Das Projekt

Der Einsatz von VR- Lernumgebungen stellt eine sinnvolle Ergänzung der digitalen Lehre dar [TO22]. Im Projekt „DigiLehR – Lehren und Lernen in erweiterten Realitäten" (FKZ: FBM2020-EA-630-08020[2]) werden Methoden entwickelt, um den Übergang theoretischen Handlungswissens in die praktische Arbeit durch VR zu unterstützen und diesen Prozess strukturell in der Hochschullehre zu verankern. Dazu wird von drei differenzierten Lernszenarien (Betrieb einer Industrieanlage, Durchführung einer Vergabevorbereitung, Verwendung von Medientechnik für Filmaufnahmen) als Test-Use-Cases ausgegangen, die sich in den Anteilen an deterministischen und kreativen Aufgabenstellungen voneinander unterscheiden. Bislang werden die Inhalte im Rahmen klassischer Laboreinweisungen bzw. Vorlesungen vermittelt, die praktische Unterweisung kommt oft zu kurz und ihr Erfolg ist nicht direkt messbar. Durch die praktische Einübung der Routinen in VR soll eine effizientere Praktikumsphase und eine Vermittlung der Lebensrealität ermöglicht werden, was für viele Hochschul-Lehrinhalte zutreffend ist. Ein für die Dozierenden leicht zugängliches Assessment des Erfolgs der eigenständigen Durchführung der VR-Übungen durch Studierende soll durch die Verknüpfung mit dem LMS ILIAS gewährleistet werden. Dies soll die Akzeptanz von VR in der Hochschullehre insgesamt steigern und so eine breitere Etablierung schaffen.

---

[1] Hochschule Harz, Hochschule für angewandte Wissenschaften, Fachbereich Automatisierung und Informatik, Friedrichstr. 57-59, 38855 Wernigerode, {mdannemann | pbothe | simonadler | sgrawe}@hs-harz.de
[2] Die hier dargestellten Arbeiten wurden von der Stiftung Innovation in der Hochschullehre gefördert.

2 Umsetzung und bisherige Ergebnisse

Um Fragebögen in VR abzubilden zu können, ist eine Kommunikation zwischen LMS und VR erforderlich, welche durch eine REST-API realisiert wird. Ziel ist es also, dass, während Nutzende Aufgaben in VR bearbeiten, ihre Entscheidungen automatisiert zur Beantwortung der zugehörigen Fragen im LMS ILIAS führen. Für das Projekt ist eine wesentliche Herausforderung, geeignete, allgemeinverständliche Interaktionen innerhalb der VR für die unterschiedlichen Szenarien zu finden, welche die im LMS definierten verschiedenen Fragetypen abbilden. Dabei muss die VR-Antwortinteraktionen eine klare Unterscheidung von der restlichen VR-Umgebung aufweisen (Tab. 1).

Fragentyp	UC „Automatisierung"	UC „Vergaberecht"	UC „Medientechnik"
Single Choice	Auswahl einer Komponente mittels zugehörigem Orb	Auswahl einer Antwort mittels zugehörigem Orb	Auswahl (Beurteilung) einer Kameraposition mittels zugehörigem Orb
Multiple Choice	Auswahl versch. Bauteile mittels zugehöriger Orbs	Auswahl von Antworten mittels zugehöriger Orbs	Beurteilung (gut/schlecht) von Kamerapositionen mittels Orbs
Zuordnung	Platzieren von Objekten in vorgegebenen Containern	Platzieren von Karten auf dem Tisch vor einer Person	Platzieren von Fotografien im vorgegebenen Raster

Tab. 1: Abbildung der LMS-Fragetypen auf Interaktionen im jeweiligen VR-Szenario

In der Softwareentwicklung werden Muster wie das MVC-Prinzip eingesetzt, um eine flexible und änderungsfreundliche Systemarchitektur zu gewährleisten. Dabei werden die Daten (Model) über eine Logik (Controller) mit einer datenadäquaten Visualisierung (View) gekoppelt [GR03]. Durch die beschriebene Vorgehensweise wird das MVC-Prinzip beim Einsatz in der VR-Umgebung um den Aspekt der Interaktion erweitert, womit die Interaktionen für die Verwendung in weiteren Lernszenarien verallgemeinert und die Komplexität der Entwicklung weiter reduziert werden können.

Die vorgeschlagenen VR-Interaktionen werden in den bisherigen Nutzertests mit VR-HMDs als leicht bedienbar und über die verschiedenen Szenarien hinweg wiedererkennbar beschrieben, sodass Testpersonen sich nach einmaliger Einweisung (auch nach mehreren Wochen Pause) in allen Szenarien selbstständig zurechtfinden. Aktuell beginnt die Erstevaluation der vorgestellten Use Cases, um die Ergebnisse der Tests im Rahmen größerer Stichproben zuverlässiger beurteilen zu können.

Literaturverzeichnis

[GR03]   Gamma, E.; Riehle, D.: Entwurfsmuster. Elemente wiederverwendbarer objektorientierter Software. Addison-Wesley, München, 2003.

[TO22]   Tugtekin, U.; Odabasi, H. F.: Do Interactive Learning Environments Have an Effect on Learning Outcomes, Cognitive Load and Metacognitive Judgments? Education and Information Technologies 5/27, S. 7019–7058, 2022.

A VR Classroom with Digital Media for Foreign Language Teacher Training

Stephen Tobin [1], Axel Wiepke [2] and Ulrike Lucke [3]

Abstract: We report extensions to a VR Classroom to provide trainee foreign language teachers with an opportunity to practice giving corrective feedback in the context of a digital media classroom. We propose further extensions to the classroom to give teachers feedback on speech clarity, which is critical for good communication and thus for effective learning in the classroom.

Keywords: Virtual Reality, Foreign Language Teaching, Phonetics, Clear Speech

1 Background and Motivation

The VR Classroom was built as a training platform for trainee teachers to gain experience in replicable scenarios in order to developing classroom management skills and learn to handle disruptions [Wi19]. The VR Classroom promotes teacher training without the administrative effort involved in organizing school placements. Trainee teachers also have the opportunity to correct and improve their technique, given that VR scenarios can be repeated identically, in contrast to real classroom scenarios. Various classroom seating plans are available, along with a chemistry laboratory and computer rooms. While the trainee teacher wears a HMD and interacts with the classroom via controllers, a coach initiates and adjusts virtual students' behaviour (see GitUP wiki[4]).

2 Extensions for Digital Media and Foreign Language Teaching

Further extensions to the VR Classroom, supported by the Stiftung Innovation in der Hochschullehre, are under way in the context of foreign language teaching and digital media. New scenes with an interactive smartboard have been developed to reflect modern schools. Thus presentations/videos can be played and a pen allows written input.

---

[1] Universität Potsdam, Institut für Informatik, An der Bahn 2, 14476 Potsdam-Golm, Germany, stephen.tobin@uni-potsdam.de, https://orcid.org/0000-0002-8229-289X
[2] Universität Potsdam, Institut für Informatik, An der Bahn 2, 14476 Potsdam-Golm, Germany, axel.wiepke@uni-potsdam.de, https://orcid.org/0000-0002-0555-4040
[3] Universität Potsdam, Institut für Informatik, An der Bahn 2, 14476 Potsdam-Golm, Germany, ulrike.lucke@uni-potsdam.de, https://orcid.org/0000-0003-4049-8088
[4] https://gitup.uni-potsdam.de/mm_vr/vr-klassenzimmer/-/wikis/home, last accessed 20.06.2023

doi: 10.18420/delfi2023-74

With regard to foreign languages, new lesson materials have been developed to provide trainee teachers of foreign languages a chance to practice giving feedback to students. The virtual students (VSs) are called on to given their answers to a listening comprehension task. The training session begins at a point in time immediately after completion of this task. On the basis of established findings on corrective feedback [LR97], the coach controls the VSs' uptake of or confusion with the feedback.

3 Planned extensions to measure clear speech

Oral feedback is of great importance for students as teachers are their primary language models, so their speech must be clear. Clear speech is an element of teacher language use, reflected by lower speed, higher volume and exaggerated articulation [SB09]. Clear speech reduces ambiguity, ensuring students have adequate input for learning.

We plan to extend the VR Classroom with additional components for the evaluation of clear speech. Speaking volume (sound intensity) can be extracted directly via the head-mounted display's built-in microphone. The sound-to-noise ratio in a given scenario can be obtained from the intensity of this signal and that of the schoolhouse background noise recordings of the VR Classroom. To measure speaking rate, an automatic speech recognition algorithm must first be applied to extract text. We propose to use OpenAI's open source Whisper model, which is reported to provide performance close to that of human transcribers [Ra22]. Word counts from the resulting transcript can then be extracted to provide users with an average speech rate in phonemes per second or words per minute. These metrics may be made available in real time on a floating panel in the immersants' field of view, depending on computational performance, thus providing trainee teachers with immediate feedback to adjust their speech.

The availability of the trainee teacher's speech signal and a transcript of their speech opens up many other options for measuring aspects of teacher talk at a higher level.

Bibliography

[LR97]   Lyster, R.; Ranta, L.: Corrective feedback and learner uptake: Negotiation of form in communicative classrooms. Studies in second language acquisition 19/1, S. 37–66, 1997.

[Ra22]   Radford, A.; Kim, J. W.; Xu, T.; Brockman, G.; McLeavey, C.; Sutskever, I.: Robust speech recognition via large-scale weak supervision. arXiv preprint arXiv:2212.04356, 2022.

[SB09]   Smiljanić, R.; Bradlow, A. R.: Speaking and hearing clearly: Talker and listener factors in speaking style changes. Language and linguistics compass 3/1, S. 236–264, 2009.

[Wi19]   Wiepke, A.; Richter, E.; Zender, R.; Richter, D.: Einsatz von VR zum Aufbau von Klassenmanagement-Kompetenzen im Lehramtsstudium. DELFI 2019, 2019.

Verzeichnis der Autorinnen und Autoren

Abke, Jörg 251
Adler, Simon 317
Akao, Kensuke 277
Augenstein, Dominik 181
Azendorf, Maximilian 225
Baberowski, David 193, 267
Bartel, Paula 251
Baucks, Frederik 41
Bechinie, Dominik 279
Beecks, Christian 281
Berendsohn, Yoel 313
Bergner, Nadine 193, 299
Berndt, Sarah 207
Bildstein, Andreas 175
Blanc, Berit 293
Bothe, Pia 317
Brandenberg, Tammy 129
Brenner, Ronald 143
Breuer, Martin 91
Brocker, Anke 269
Brocker, Annabell 103
Brzoska, Stefanie 295
Buchmann, Erik 79, 135
Buchner, Josef 299
Bültemann, Marlene 219, 289
Dannemann, Marc 317
Di Maria, Marco 239, 253, 297
Dietrich, André 255

Dogaru, Teodora 313
Dörr, Bernd 175
Dörringer, Antonia 251
Dürhager, Robin 123
Dux, Marcel 295
Ebbing, Stephanie 281
Ehlenz, Matthias 301
Elsebach, Jens 251
Erazo Sanchez, Juan Enrique 199
Fessel, Karl 255
Frochte, Jörg 247
Frohn, Julia 279
Fünfhaus, Annika 295
Gellrich, Mario 187
Glaab, Daniel 251
Goldammer, Marcel 123
Görzen, Sergej 249, 257, 311
Götze, Nora 313
Gotzen, Daniel 257
Grawe, Sandy 317
Gruber, Thomai Svenja 315
Hagel, Georg 251
Hahm, Nadine 97, 275
Hamann, Anne 265
Hänig, Christian 199
Hanze, Alexander 123
Hawlitschek, Anja 207
Heimes, Lilli 315

Heinemann, Birte 257, 211
Heinrich, Peter 53, 111, 187
Heister, Michael 315
Henrich, Andreas 291
Hirmer, Tobias 291
Hochstetter, Marvin 251
Hofmann-von Kap-Herr, Ulrich 285
Hollerer, Dagmar 187
Hossain, Imran 283
Hübsch, Thomas 161
Hupfer, Matthias 143
Jeuring, Johan 23
Judel, Sven 213, 225, 249, 269
Junger, Dennis 219
Jüttner, Victor 135
Kahl, Timo 129
Karthaus, Christoph 187
Khosrawi-Rad, Bijan 181
Kiesler, Natalie 271
Kimmig, Martin 175
Klopp, Marco 251
Knackstedt, Ralf 239, 253, 297
Komorowski, Tim 315
König, Daniel 315
Krishnaraja, Swathi 231
Lachmair, Martin 175
Langenbrink, Frank 123
Leikert-Boehm, Ninja 53, 111
Leonhardt, Thiemo ... 193, 265, 267, 299

Lilienthal, Lanea 193
Linxen, Andrea 281
Lucke, Ulrike 143, 319
Maquet, Frederic 301
Markgraf, Daniel 181
Martius, Joshua 249
Matter, Philipp 53, 111
Mejia, Paola 231
Melanou, Chrysanthi 175
Melkamu Jate, Wabi 167
Merceron, Agathe 313
Morawetz, Erik 97, 275
Müller, Hans-Georg 219, 289
Nell, Maximilian 259
Neugebauer, Malte 247
Nieder-Vahrenholz, Axel 271
Nitzke, Paul 261
Noichl, Svenja 305
Ochs, Michaela 291
Opel, Simone 281
Osinski, Meike 29
Otto, Joachim 123
Paaßen, Benjamin 293
Persike, Malte 91
Petersohn, Martin 85, 263
Pinkwart, Niels 65, 231, 289
Podeyn, Jens 265
Poquet, Oleksandra 21
Quakulinski, Lars 213

Radtke, Anna 29	Selmanagić, André 155
Reichow, Insa 293	Serova, Katja 29
Rinn, Heidi 181	Simbeck, Katharina 155, 219, 289
Ritzmann, Susanne 161	Sterck-Degueldre, Jean-Pierre 301
Robra-Bissantz, Susanne 181	Steuck, Paul-Ferdinand 239
Roepke, Rene 225, 269	Stirling, Veronika 123
Rörtgen, Steffen 143	Striewe, Michael 167, 173
Rossmann, Raphael 251	Thor, Andreas 79, 85, 97, 263, 275
Rotelli, Daniela 313	Tillmann, Alexander 283
Rüdian, Sylvio 65	Tobin, Stephen 319
Rudolf, Galina 207	Tümler, Johannes 199, 307
Rummel, Nikol 29	Ueberschär, Olaf 307
Rzepka, Nathalie 219, 289	Voelker, Simon 269
Sabah, Sam 283	Vogel-Adham, Elke 161
Sauer, Petra 313	Vogt, Andrea 295
Schaab, Lukas 251	Wagner, Miriam 213
Schaefer, Caterina 299	Walter, David 239, 253, 297
Scheffel, Maren 29	Walther, Johanna 265
Schiffner, Daniel 271	Wambsganss, Thiemo 231
Schledjewski, Janine 309	Wehrmann, Frank 279, 303
Schneider, Sofia 309	Weiland, Meike 315
Schöbel, Konrad 85, 263	Weiss, David 283
Schoch, Blanche 175	Wenzel, Karl 267
Schon, Caroline 307	Wiegard, Marwin 129
Schrader, Claudia 309	Wiepke, Axel 319
Schroeder, Ulrik 91, 103, 217, 225, 249, 257, 259, 261, 305, 311	Wiesche, David 299
	Wilhelm-Weidner, Arno 161, 295
Schürmann, Verena 129	Wiskott, Laurenz 41
Segieth, Fabian 253	Zender, Raphael 299, 303
Seidel, Niels 123	

Zimmermann, Holger 143
Zobel, Annett 143
Zug, Sebastian 207, 255
Zumbruch, Alina 309

GI-Edition Lecture Notes in Informatics

P-306 Arslan Brömme, Christoph Busch, Antitza Dantcheva, Kiran Raja, Christian Rathgeb, Andreas Uhl (Eds.)
BIOSIG 2020
Proceedings of the 19th International Conference of the Biometrics Special Interest Group
16.–18. September 2020
International Digital Conference

P-307 Ralf H. Reussner, Anne Koziolek, Robert Heinrich (Hrsg.)
INFORMATIK 2020
Back to the Future
28. September – 2. Oktober 2020, Karlsruhe

P-308 Raphael Zender, Dirk Ifenthaler, Thiemo Leonhardt, Clara Schumacher (Hrsg.)
DELFI 2020 –
Die 18. Fachtagung Bildungstechnologien der Gesellschaft für Informatik e.V.
14.–18. September 2020
Online

P-309 A. Meyer-Aurich, M. Gandorfer, C. Hoffmann, C. Weltzien, S. Bellingrath-Kimura, H. Floto (Hrsg.)
Informatik in der Land-, Forst- und Ernährungswirtschaft
Referate der 41. GIL-Jahrestagung
08.–09. März 2021, Leibniz-Institut für Agrartechnik und Bioökonomie e.V., Potsdam

P-310 Anne Koziolek, Ina Schaefer, Christoph Seidl (Hrsg.)
Software Engineering 2021
22.–26. Februar 2021,
Braunschweig/Virtuell

P-311 Kai-Uwe Sattler, Melanie Herschel, Wolfgang Lehner (Hrsg.)
Datenbanksysteme für Business, Technologie und Web (BTW 2021)
Tagungsband
13.–17. September 2021,
Dresden

P-312 Heiko Roßnagel, Christian H. Schunck, Sebastian Mödersheim (Hrsg.)
Open Identity Summit 2021
01.–02. Juni 2021, Copenhagen

P-313 Ludger Humbert (Hrsg.)
Informatik – Bildung von Lehrkräften in allen Phasen
19. GI-Fachtagung Informatik und Schule
8.–10. September 2021 Wuppertal

P-314 Gesellschaft für Informatik e.V. (GI) (Hrsg.)
INFORMATIK 2021Computer Science & Sustainability
27. September– 01. Oktober 2021, Berlin

P-315 Arslan Brömme, Christoph Busch, Naser Damer, Antitza Dantcheva, Marta Gomez-Barrero, Kiran Raja, Christian Rathgeb, Ana F. Sequeira, Andreas Uhl (Eds.)
BIOSIG 2021
Proceedings of the 20th International Conference of the Biometrics Special Interest Group
15.–17. September 2021
International Digital Conference

P-316 Andrea Kienle, Andreas Harrer, Jörg M. Haake, Andreas Lingnau (Hrsg.)
DELFI 2021
Die 19. Fachtagung Bildungstechnologien der Gesellschaft für Informatik e.V.
13.–15. September 2021
Online 8.–10. September 2021

P-317 M. Gandorfer, C. Hoffmann, N. El Benni, M. Cockburn, T. Anken, H. Floto (Hrsg.)
Informatik in der Land-, Forst- und Ernährungswirtschaft
Fokus: Künstliche Intelligenz in der Agrar- und Ernährungswirtschaft
Referate der 42. GIL-Jahrestagung
21.–22. Februar 2022 Agroscope, Tänikon, Ettenhausen, Schweiz

P-318 Andreas Helferich, Robert Henzel, Georg Herzwurm, Martın Mıkusz (Hrsg.)
FACHTAGUNG SOFTWARE MANAGEMENT 2021
Fachtagung des GI-Fachausschusses Management der Anwendungsentwicklung und -wartung im Fachbereich Wirtschafts-informatik (WI-MAW), Stuttgart, 2021

P-319 Zeynep Tuncer, Rüdiger Breitschwerdt, Helge Nuhn, Michael Fuchs, Vera Meister, Martin Wolf, Doris Weßels, Birte Malzahn (Hrsg.)
3. Wissenschaftsforum:
Digitale Transformation (WiFo21)
5. November 2021 Darmstadt, Germany

P-320 Lars Grunske, Janet Siegmund, Andreas Vogelsang (Hrsg.))
Software Engineering 2022
21.–25. Februar 2022, Berlin/Virtuell

P-321 Veronika Thurner, Barne Kleinen, Juliane Siegeris, Debora Weber-Wulff (Hrsg.)
Software Engineering im Unterricht der Hochschulen SEUH 2022
24.–25. Februar 2022, Berlin

P-322 Peter A. Henning, Michael Striewe, Matthias Wölfel (Hrsg.))
DELFI 2022 Die 20. Fachtagung Bildungstechnologien der Gesellschaft für Informatik e.V.
12.–14. September 2022, Karlsruhe

P-323 Christian Wressnegger, Delphine Reinhardt, Thomas Barber, Bernhard C. Witt, Daniel Arp, Zoltan Mann (Hrsg.)
Sicherheit 2022
Sicherheit, Schutz und Zuverlässigkeit
Beiträge der 11. Jahrestagung des Fachbereichs Sicherheit der Gesellschaft für Informatik e.V. (GI)
5.–8. April 2022, Karlsruhe

P-324 Matthias Riebisch, Marina Tropmann-Frick (Hrsg.)
Modellierung 2022
Fachtagung vom 27. Juni - 01. July 2022, Hamburg

P-325 Heiko Roßnagel, Christian H. Schunck, Sebastian Mödersheim (Hrsg.)
Open Identity Summit 2022
Fachtagung vom 07. - 08. July 2022, Copenhagen

P-326 Daniel Demmler, Daniel Krupka, Hannes Federrath (Hrsg.)
INFORMATIK 2022
26.–30. September 2022
Hamburg

P-327 Masud Fazal-Baqaie, Oliver Linssen, Alexander Volland, Enes Yigitbas, Martin Engstler, Martin Bertram, Axel Kalenborn (Hrsg.)
Projektmanagement und Vorgehensmodelle 2022
Trier 2022

P-328 Volker Wohlgemuth, Stefan Naumann, Hans-Knud Arndt, Grit Behrens, Maximilian Höb (Editors)
Environmental Informatics 2022
26.–28. September 2022, Hamburg, Germany

P-329 Arslan Brömme, Naser Damer, Marta Gomez-Barrero, Kiran Raja, Christian Rathgeb, Ana F. Sequeira, Massimiliano Todisco, Andreas Uhl (Eds.)
BIOSIG 2022
14. - 16. September 2022, International Conference

P-330 Informatik in der Land-, Forst- und Ernährungswirtschaft
Fokus: Resiliente Agri-Food-Systeme
Referate der 43. GIL-Jahrestagung
13.–14. Februar 2023 Osnabrück

P-331 Birgitta König-Ries, Stefanie Scherzinger, Wolfgang Lehner, Gottfried Vossen (Hrsg.)
Datenbanksysteme für Business, Technologie und Web (BTW 2023)
06.–10. März 2023, Dresden

P-332 Gregor Engels, Regina Hebig, Matthias Tichy (Hrsg.)
Software Engineering 2023
20.–24. Februar 2023, Paderborn

P-333 Steffen Becker & Christian Gerth (Hrsg.)
SEUH 2023
23.–24. Februar 2023, Paderborn

P-334 Andreas Helferich, Dimitri Petrik, Gero Strobel, Katharina Peine (Eds.)
1st International Conference on Software Product Management
Organized by „GI Fachgruppe Software Produktmanagement im Fachbereich Wirtschaftsinformatik (WI PrdM)",
Frankfurt, 2023

P-335 Heiko Roßnagel, Christian H. Schunck, Jochen Günther (Hrsg.)
Open Identity Summit 2023
15.–16. June 2023, Heilbronn

P-338 René Röpke und Ulrik Schroeder (Hrsg.)
21. Fachtagung
Bildungstechnologien (DELFI)
11.-13. September 2023, Aachen

All volumes of Lecture Notes in Informatics can be found at
https://dl.gi.de/handle/20.500.12116/21.

The titles can be purchased at:

Köllen Druck + Verlag GmbH
Ernst-Robert-Curtius-Str. 14 · D-53117 Bonn
Fax: +49 (0)228/9898222
E-Mail: druckverlag@koellen.de